H

Berliner. [...] [...] [...]bitious young actress. Hollywood starlet. International movie queen. Husky-voiced Ninotchka in Broadway's *Silk Stockings*. Wife. Mistress. Mother. Now she tells all —the successes, the failures, the scandals, the hard and twisting road that led from a hungering girlhood to fulfillment as a woman.

The Gift Horse

REPORT ON A LIFE

Hildegard Knef

Translated from the German by
DAVID ANTHONY PALASTANGA

A DELL BOOK

Life is a gift horse in my opinion.
—J. D. Salinger, *Teddy*

ONE

Declaration of Love for a Grandfather

Mine was called Karl; he was of medium height and was just as strong as he looked. He held his head straight, his spine too, and he had a large mouth with a lot of teeth; he still had all thirty-two when he committed suicide at the age of eighty-one. His violent temper was the best thing about him, mainly because it was never directed at me, and because it came just as ferociously and suddenly as it went, and when it was gone his face became as warm as a village pond in the summer sun, his movements embarrassed, like a bear fishing.

In winter we lived on Sedanstrasse in Schöneberg. Sedanstrasse was a treeless part of Berlin into which Grandfather didn't fit at all. He was always taking me for walks and buying me aniseed drops before lunch, and there was always a row about it when we got back.

My grandmother was delicate and diabetic, and the tragedy of her life was that she didn't love Karl and that he frightened her. He was of Polish-East Prussian descent; he rarely spoke about his family, and with difficulty I found out that his father had drunk and gambled away the family fortune, that his mother had had a nervous breakdown during a pregnancy, and that the resulting daughter went mad sixteen years later and regularly spent four to six months of the year in an asylum, about which she sunnily told the most awful stories when she was released. My grandfather became her guardian and I believe this caused him a great deal of misery; she sometimes took off all her clothes on a Berlin bridge (she had a thing about bridges) and my grandfather would have to go to the police station. He tried to conceal all this from me but of course I found out about it eventually, even though they all whispered and always looked to see if I was asleep.

In summer everything was different. We were in his little house near Zossen—it was really a glorified shack with four

rooms and a stove where we put the young chicks at night
to keep warm, and it had a large garden and fruit trees and
cabbage and asparagus and a small pond into which I fell
frequently, to be rescued either by my grandfather or by
our giant dog, who bore not the slightest resemblance to
any known breed. The aniseed drops I had eaten all winter
gave way to apples in the summer, only in far larger quan-
tities, my grandfather being of the obstinate opinion that,
even after regular bouts of vomiting, enough apple would
stay in my body to give me the requisite energy to face the
Sedanstrasse winter.

Our life became difficult on the two or three days of the
week that Grandmother visited our paradise. I wasn't allowed to run around half-naked and was wrapped up in
woolens, Karl shouldn't wear his undershirt "in public,"
apples were spurned as encouraging worms, I couldn't tie
my goat to the bedpost at night any more, and my favorite
rabbit had to lead a respectable rabbit-existence in his
hutch. Our summer life became organized and orderly in
the feminine manner.

Grandfather's first attack of temper occurred without
fail ten or fifteen minutes after the shy-hearty greetings,
following which he retired growling and muttering to his
furthest cabbage patch, returning after a little while to sit
on the sofa drinking Grandma's coffee and telling her of
my latest incredible, ingenious utterances. This was my favorite time; our mutual admiration bridged the sixty years
between us. Whether it was clumsiness or malice on my
part no one can say any more, but something always managed to get dropped and broken during these conversations,
putting an end to any understanding which might have
been growing between my grandparents.

My mother came on Sundays. She had to work; at that
time she was a secretary at Siemens Electrical Company.
(My father had died six months after my birth, and I
thought it important to be called a half-orphan.) Mother
came and I pretended each time that I didn't recognize her;
I curtsied respectfully and said, "How do you do, Aunt."
My grandmother started crying immediately and sniffled
something about it being an unnatural way of life for a
child of that age; my mother, with tears in her eyes, took
me in her arms and reprimanded my grandmother about
the woolen clothing in this scorching heat; before the ensuing row really got under way I extracted my Sunday pres-

ent from Mother and heard Grandfather say something
about emotional poppycock. On Monday, Mother and
Grandmother traveled back to Berlin and after heart-
breaking farewells and endless waving Grandfather and I
looked at each other like two conspirators who could now
go about their shady business without fear of interference.
On Mondays I could go through the garden stark naked,
make up for all the apples I had missed during the visit,
and more often than not have to vomit before lunch.

My grandmother grew thinner and more nervous and
her beautiful, very large light-gray eyes became agitated
and quite colorless. Sometimes she fainted, which made
Grandfather helpless and furious. She refused to go to the
hospital, explaining, "I will die in a hospital, I feel it." Nor
could she bear injections; they hurt too much in her thin
body. When she became too weak to resist any more, my
mother did take her to the hospital, and a little while later
she died. During this time I was taken every day to a kindergarten on Sedanstrasse which I hated with all my heart;
the eternally friendly sisters who dispensed their friendliness evenly on everybody made me unhappy; I would have
liked it better if they had shouted at me. I took no part in
the games, cried for hours on end to the sisters' and my own
despair, and longed for my grandfather, Zossen, and sunshine. One morning my mother told me that Grandma was
now in heaven, and cried. The only one who didn't cry at
the funeral was Grandfather and this seemed to me to be
correct; the combination of heaven and tears confused me.
He even laughed once on the way to the cemetery and my
mother said later that he had always been "coarse."

My mother gave up her job at Siemens so that she could
devote more time to me, as "one can't let the child grow up
with an old man," and bought a tobacco shop near Friedrichstrasse. She was very beautiful at that time and many
men came in and bought cigars, only to throw them in the
gutter a few yards further on. Mother caught one of her
best customers doing this one day and decided she was in
the wrong business, whereupon a candy shop was bought at
great expense; together we ate at least half of our stock. In
this period she met and married Herr Wulfestieg. He had
asthma and I copied his cough as I didn't like him and because of this the engagement was almost broken off.

On the wedding day I was overjoyed above all at seeing
Grandfather. I threw myself at him and screamed at the

top of my voice, "My mother's getting married today!" In the excitement I overlooked a small plump woman with a small head and small brown eyes whom he then introduced as Aunt Emma. The wedding lost its charm for me: my mother with a strange man, my grandfather with a strange lady. . . . My mother didn't seem terribly happy either and said, "A disgrace so soon after Mother's death!" I sat sulking under the table and he crawled in beside me, very sad, and explained to me that a grown man needs a woman, and this I understood.

Aunt Emma had been a cook in France, a fact which our relatives discussed only in undertones; France meant brothels and lewdness and a respectable German didn't even entertain the thought. . . . Emma had a difficult time with all of them except Grandfather; he blossomed, and her bustling attentiveness did him good. She even spoke openly about his somewhat deformed nose; it had been frostbitten in a severe East Prussian winter and went purple in cold weather and even broke open at times; it had always been taboo and became now a subject of sympathy, care, and attention. After much hesitation they married, lived in Zossen, and I saw Grandfather only seldom. Summer for me was now like winter and I was constantly ill, on one occasion so badly that I was taken to Grandfather and Aunt Emma, Grandfather insisted on it, fresh air would make a man of me again, not to mention the apples. Emma cooked me pigeons and always kissed me before and after the meal, which I found rather obnoxious as ours was not a great family for kissing—only at Christmas, birthdays, and New Year's, and since for me all these festivities fall in the same week, I had it over with comparatively quickly. But apart from the kissing I liked Emma very much, and was sad when she too was suddenly taken to the state hospital and died. She had had cancer of the stomach and my stepfather, whom I now called Papa, said that tasting the hot dishes had been the cause, so that for many years I was to regard cooking as a highly dangerous profession.

Grandfather was now alone again and I hoped our old summer life would resume. In vain; Grandfather had a fight with my "Papa," who then forbade me this "intimacy," as he called it. Once, as I was leaving school to walk home, I felt a tug on my satchel; I turned around and there he stood, old and thin with very white hair and tears in his eyes for the first time. We stayed together the whole after-

noon and he bought me a bicycle. When I got home there
was a row—my mother was for Grandfather, my stepfather against—and I tried to work out how long it would
take me to get to Zossen on my bicycle.

Grandfather finally got fed up with the lonely life in the
country and moved into an apartment at No. 13 Frobenstrasse with Great-aunt Hulda, one of my grandmother's
many sisters. Frobenstrasse was near Nollendorfplatz, no
trees, no park, only dark rooms and the roar of the elevated railway and buses. To this day I don't know why he
took this particular apartment; perhaps he wanted to put a
very definite end to his previous undershirt existence.

It was difficult to imagine that Aunt Hulda had ever
been young. She was extremely small and dried-up and had
endless patience; no one could listen like Aunt Hulda and
no one had such a soft voice, an almost inaudible voice that
compelled you to be quiet and tolerant, even when your
knee was badly grazed and you felt like screaming for sympathy. That was Aunt Hulda and actually Karl couldn't
stand her at any price, but, as he said, he was unable to
exist without a woman around him.

One good thing about the apartment was that I was able
to get there very quickly on the No. 8 bus, and after a
grudging, manly reconciliation finally took place between
Grandfather and Stepfather under the Christmas tree, I
was allowed to sleep there once a week. Aunt Hulda was
afraid of people and had insisted on two chains, a peephole
and a complicated series of locks on the door. After I had
gleefully fallen up the dark staircase and almost fractured
my finger pressing the old-fashioned doorbell, there would
follow two minutes of questioning, peeping, and unlocking
before I could finally race into the apartment with my
overnight bag. Grandfather wasn't as sunburnt any more,
but looked healthy and erect and seemed to have forgotten
the long, difficult months. His temper worked itself off in a
diluted form on Aunt Hulda, who did indeed complain and
closed each drama with a soft, long-drawn-out "Kaaarl,"
but who would not gladly have been without Grandfather's
rantings after the boring marriage she had endured years
before.

I slept on a wide sofa, with an enormous old clock hanging over it. At each quarter-hour the clock would gather its
forces and at the quarter give one, at the half two, and at
the three-quarter hour three thunderous strokes. The full

hour was announced with several furious explosions, which could only be compared to the gongs of the Korean opera. Almost invariably I would fall off the sofa, whereas Grandfather slept like a log in his half-occupied double bed. Before going to sleep, he always tapped six times on the end of the bed with his big toe; he swore that this was the only way to be sure of waking up promptly at six. Aunt Hulda didn't get up until seven, which Grandfather condemned as unhealthy. By that time he had always had a cold wash, done his exercises, got the stove going, fetched the rolls, and made coffee. Breakfast was a long and pleasant ritual which more often than not terminated with Grandfather reading us the daily serial in the morning paper. As I'd always missed the six previous installments, I usually dozed off or finished up the rolls and goose dripping. Then he'd take me to the bus stop and hold up the Berlin traffic while he explained the importance of my person to the feeble-minded (in his opinion) conductor, who, in exchange for a small sum of money, would finally agree to deliver me to the schoolhouse. The whole bus would stare at me with unconcealed, stupefied curiosity, and I was thankful when I could finally flee from them and the agitated conductor.

We were now living in Friedenau and had a shoe-repair shop very near the apartment, next to the Wilmersdorf railway station. My visits to Frobenstrasse became less frequent as I had to help in the shop, which I enjoyed, but I disliked having to deliver the repaired shoes; I was afraid of the cold dark passages, the dingy courtyards, and the people, who opened their doors sometimes indifferently, sometimes gruffly, and sometimes cheerfully, even giving me a tip.

My brother—or rather my half-brother, as he was confusingly called—was born. My days were full. I got to know a world in which my grandfather played no part. I forgot him for weeks on end, started to become "grown-up," became unfaithful. He didn't change, but he had expected the change in me, and didn't reproach me for it. We got over a crisis caused by his Christmas present, found the way back to each other for a few hours and parted again. I had wanted an accordion but got skis: "accordions are bad for the bosom," he said.

The war came and the ration cards and the freight trains full of soldiers; the neighbors' sons were called up and Grandfather said we would have to pay for the death of the

Jews. Then the air raids started, with the subsequent searching and hoping. . . . He was not bombed out, but we lost our home three times, at first only the furniture and finally everything, even the suitcases. After each air raid he would rush over with a bag of rolls and coffee, complaining about Aunt Hulda, who had prayed and cried in the cellar again.

One day he took me into a church. He sat there completely still and appeared to listen attentively, but as we left he was furious, with himself and with "the idiots who should have done something in thirty-three"—what they should have done he didn't tell me and I wouldn't have understood anyway. To please him I had once written "Hitler is nuts" in the sand with my finger, but he forbade me any further drawings of this sort, and so we didn't speak about it any more and by "it" I mean Hitler and the war and the SS and powdered milk. Only when I was due to join the BDM* did he and my mother put up a fierce resistance, citing all my various illnesses.

I never saw my grandfather having a "man to man" discussion; he didn't like men, didn't play cards, and hated familiarity. He was now alone. Aunt Hulda couldn't stand the nights of tears and prayers in the city any longer and had gone to her woebegone daughter in Zehlendorf. My mother and brother were evacuated on doctor's orders and I had a profession—or rather an apprenticeship which one hoped would become a profession—and lived in lodgings.

I visited him in the evenings or on Sundays, but now there was a feeling of duty about it and a longing for the soft warmth of forgotten summers which I didn't wish to admit to any more—now I was taken up with scholarship, ambition, forget the war, work, learn; I knew that the longing for our summers wouldn't help me to get away from shoe shops, the smell of leather, and stews without fat. I didn't race up the now totally dark stairway any more and the bell had long since been broken. I would knock and he would quickly open the door, cheerful and prepared; coffee on the table, home-made dripping and even rolls—rather watery, dark war rolls. We would sit at the big table, I on the old sofa under the alarming clock; the center light was bound with towels and looked like a wounded udder. First

* BDM: Bund Deutscher Mädchen, the girls' equivalent of the Hitler Youth.

I had to eat and while I chewed, he began to talk. . . . Many years earlier, before I could understand his words, he had told me of his youth and the Masurian lakes, which he had raced across in winter in a horsedrawn sleigh; he spoke of this time again now, of the school he had gone to after his father's downfall, of the other, still wealthy, relatives who had taken in the suddenly poor children only to set them to work in the fields and send them to the village school in wooden clogs . . . he had forgotten no detail and his hatred and sadness were still as fresh as on the day he had run away from these relatives to Berlin. Then he would sing a Polish song in a soft voice, a song I had often heard him sing but which he never translated for me. He was not fond of alcohol, but after the Polish song he would always drink a little red wine; this had always been so. Then the sirens would sound and we'd go down to the cellar—but not before he had cleared up, opened the windows so they wouldn't get blasted, and packed a few sandwiches and a thermos flask. The air-raid warden would be screaming in the corridor, the flak thundering and sometimes the first bombs would be falling; he didn't like to be hurried, either by Germans yelling at the door or by Americans droning in the sky.

When the Russians had already occupied the city, two Hitler Youths took it into their heads to defend No. 13 Frobenstrasse and threw hand grenades into the street, whereupon the house was demolished by tank fire. My grandfather lived through it and escaped from the burning, collapsing house with torn trousers and scorched slippers. It took him several hours to get to Zehlendorf, where I had been living. The people in the house told him they had not seen me since the fighting started. Then he went to Wilmersdorf and found my stepfather, who had developed TB and a disgust for the Russians, whose arrival he had always prayed for.

My grandfather and my stepfather lived in one room in a bombed-out house, hating each other and waiting weeks on end for a message from my mother, my brother, my uncle, and me. My mother was believed dead; the village where she had lived had been occupied by the English after savage fighting. My grandfather sat on a rickety chair by a glassless window, wearing torn trousers and a jacket that was too big for him, scorched slippers on his feet—that was how I found him when I got back from the Russian prison camp three months later. He raised his head quite calmly and said, "So there you are, my child," took my hand, and fell asleep. And an hour later he awoke and said that now he would like to wait for Mother.

Two weeks later I had my opening night at the Tribuene— it was the first theater to start playing again in Berlin— and before the performance a woman on a rusty bicycle brought me a letter; it was very thick and had no address. "My beloved child," it began, "I am too old to be able to forget the horrors, or to be of use to you any longer," and ended, "Perhaps you will one day understand and forgive me."

The handwriting was quite clear and not at all shaky.

He had then taken sleeping pills, bound up his chin with a handkerchief, and drawn the sheet over his head.

TWO

Fräulein Weise (Wise) didn't live up to her name; she was malicious and that was what she should have been called, as a warning to her pupils. She wore pink, pink for every season, and out of this pink popped a greasy white fishhead like the white meat of a cooked lobster. Her flat watery eyes were quick and piercing and her stupid sarcasm killed any interest one might have shown in the twaddle she talked. She wore a party badge on each pink garment. She was our form mistress and hated us all heartily.

There was a great deal of talk about the war and defending the Fatherland and when one day I ventured to ask whom we should defend ourselves against since we hadn't been attacked, I was sent home for three days to my delight and my mother's despair; the block warden had harsh words with my stepfather and I had to apologize.

Fräulein Weise entered the classroom every morning without giving us so much as a glance. The desks were too small for us and we almost broke our legs so as to stand with the required stiffness while screaming HEIL HITLER, and we had to remain standing until she screamed back SIT DOWN. Only then did she take a look around her and at us, seeming surprised to find something living and breathing among the desks. Her attention was usually directed first at me; she addressed me only by my surname and in a voice which suddenly became soft and disconcertingly gentle, she sighed KNEF. It wafted through the classroom and she would ask me a question, which, since I was always startled and hypnotized afresh by this fishhead, I could hardly ever answer; she then spent about five minutes describing my inferiority, and the older I got during these stupefying years the more convinced I became that she must have passed her teaching exams at Gestapo headquarters. She taught us German, geography, French, and of course history—history she kept a secret from us altogether and spent the allotted time revealing the splendors of the reigning government. The Dinaric race, the Nordic race, the Wends, the Slavs (inferior), the Nordic Woman, wide pelvis broad shoulders blond hair blue eyes, it slid past us like posters in a subway station, races races everywhere races . . . we had to describe our racial characteristics: "I am Nordic because . . ."

But what about Margot Wiener? We had shared a desk at Wilmersdorf People's School; she lived in Bayerischerplatz in an overpoweringly large apartment with one toilet in the passage and one in the bathroom; this was something new for me and she explained that the one in the passage was for guests. Margot was small and dark and had large light-brown eyes, could laugh like a hyena and had the good nature of a well-fed Saint Bernard—where was she? She had disappeared one day and Fräulein Koch, a teacher who was as sweet, kind, and considerate as Fräulein Weise was nauseating, told us in her small, clean voice that Margot had suddenly moved with her parents.

I am Nordic because . . .

Biology period and Fräulein Lerche (Lark), a thin shriveled-up lark who told us daily of the importance of a toothbrush which had been dried in the fresh air, and who constantly chewed her upper lip with her long yellow teeth. Her father must have been a horse—not just because of the teeth, she also galloped; we tore through the Grünewald forest together and she would point out various trees and birds; sometimes of course there was a lark among them and she pretended not to notice our silly sniggering, chewing resignedly on her upper lip. She was not malicious and we even liked her in our own sadistic way, but I can still tell a conifer from a deciduous tree only with the utmost concentration, which has nothing to do with my nearsightedness, and so her influence on me was tragically unsuccessful.

With Fräulein Müller it was another story—she has a special place in my memory, alongside Fräulein Weise. She was our gymnastics teacher. The only attractive thing about our school was the gymnasium; it had large airy windows and a highly polished parquet floor, a setting for a gay sport rather than gymnastics. This impression proved false, however, with the appearance of Fräulein Müller; she was an overdone omelet that had been left lying in a warm pantry for several weeks. Her face was yellow and huge, her

hair, damp with sweat, hung darkly around a head too
large for its body, the shiny gym shorts too long, the legs
flabby yet muscular—she reminded me of a Turkish wrest-
ler. When we had formed lines or "sections," as she called
them, we were obliged to scream HEIL HITLER again and
raise our hands; she would raise hers back. Then she usually made a short speech in a hoarse voice like a barking
dog's, rendered unintelligible by the echo; scraps of "Soldierly" and "Emulate" and "Show the Führer" (but what?)
came through, then on to the parallel bars. As I had weak
wrists I could perform neither handstands nor any other
stands on the bar without falling off, but one day she encouraged me with a cane; I did a handstand or at least the
beginnings of one, but before it had taken on any real form
I fell and dislocated a vertebra; it still looks like a camel's
hump in my evening dresses. She wasn't at all distressed,
spoke only of Soldierly and Emulate and Steeling-the-Body
and Healthy Spirit and Healthy Body. I was a thorn in her
flabby side. I wasn't in the BDM, my mother and grandfather had seen to that, helped by the infantile paralysis I had
had at the age of seven. She wanted to steel me, to show
me what it meant to be German. She tried for a long time
until one day I hurled a medicine ball at her stomach with
such force that she went hopping around the dusty play-
ground in circles. . . . I apologized, she boxed my ears, but
that was surely not as painful as her ovaries after the medicine ball.

Herr Rabe (Crow) loved Weber, Karl Maria von, and I
shall loathe *Oberon* till the day I die. He played the piano
like a car driver in peril, honking with all his fortissimo,
darkly singing nebulous verses. Before the war several English teachers had visited our school to observe our teaching
methods; we were made to dance rounds to the tune of *Ro-
senstock, holder, blüh'* and he clapped his hands the whole
time, which he had never done before, to give the impression of national happiness, even among the youngest.

He was big with a lot of dark crinkly hair and would
have been a miserable failure at Fräulein Weise's racial lessons. But he believed in Victory and Strength-Through-Joy
and Weber and wore his party badge on a shabby gray suit
with leather elbows. On top of the music lessons he taught
art one hour a week; he always put the same withered gera-
nium on his desk for us to draw, we were to reproduce it in
perfect orderly detail while he ran from desk to desk with a

pair of dividers, like a bridge engineer going about his measuring. Though my proportions were never correct he gave me top marks for drawing, which endeared him to me as I wanted to be a painter. I drew Grandfather Karl and Mother when she had the time to sit still and Aunt Hulda. Aunt Hulda had lovely lines and wrinkles and was the easiest to draw but she inspected my work with such unspeakable mourning for her beauty that I finally abandoned her as a model out of pity. I took my drawings to school hoping to be able to show them to Rabe and earn a word of praise, but was usually waylaid by Fräulein Weise, who viewed my sketches and advised me to think more about the history course and her French lessons rather than waste my time with such "rubbish." Off again with Wotan or Odin and Thor, the Nordic thunder-dispenser, Siegfried and Krimhilde, those endlessly expiring heroes of the Nordic saga.

Afternoons were devoted to handwork. We knitted socks for the soldiers at the front and before we got busy with the scraps of wool a speech would be delivered on the necessity of war and how the German people needed more Lebensraum, which I could never quite grasp as I had only seen a real honest-to-goodness crowd at Christmas on Potsdamerplatz and perhaps at Wannsee beach in July. I declined to make further inquiries, however, since the only thing I had really learned at this institution was that Questions meant Trouble; only once did I make an exception to my rule, in the school hall on VDA* Day after our white-haired chemistry teacher had made a speech describing the suffering and homesickness of the Germans living in the Carpathians, on the Volga, in the Sudetenland, and even in South America, who longed only for the day when they would be able to squeeze themselves back into our densely populated Lebensraum—I then asked wouldn't it be better if they stayed where they were, where they had enough room; the question was out before I could realize how deep I'd put my foot in it. . . .

Most of them in the class wanted to be teachers or nurses at the front line—they must have been hoping for a Thirty Years' War—very few deviated from these professions, which were highest in our teachers' esteem. There

* Verein der Auslandsdeutchen, the Legion of Germans in Foreign Lands.

was Vera Ress, a pretty girl with a snub nose and laughing freckles; she wanted to be a dancer and was sniffed at. Nanette also wanted to paint, which was almost the basis for a friendship, and one girl wanted to go to China with her engineer father—how she was going to get there and what she was actually going to do when she got there she didn't say, but the mere idea of China was pretty good and one shouldn't be petty. One girl came to class every day in the same threadbare, stained taffeta dress; she was in love with Johannes Heesters and went every night to see *The Count of Luxembourg,* the operetta in which he was appearing. She treated us all like village idiots because we went to the theater so seldom; I had been only once and had seen *Fidelio,* which had acted on me like a sleeping pill—the fat lady disguised as a man filled me with sorrow. Our addict in the taffeta dress had a crisis after seeing a film in which Heesters played a love scene with Marika Rökk. Her essays looked as if they had been written in shaky senility, tears flowed over the taffeta and exercise books, and we had to prevent her from taking more serious steps—she wanted to throw herself from the balcony onto the stage, aiming to land right at Heesters' feet. I held it to be an undoubtedly effective entrance into his life but not one guaranteed to provoke undying passion on his part.

It was at about this time that we started to read the classics under Fräulein Weise's watchful eye. "The classics" were Schiller and more often than not *William Tell.* I was given the part of poor Armgard, so I stood in front of the class and as I began with "Here he cannot escape me, he must hear me," I suddenly noticed a warm friendly feeling in the region of the stomach, like a soft hot-water bottle in a cold bed, and when I got to "Mercy, lord governor! Oh, pardon, pardon," I was already on my knees, tears streaming from my eyes and nose, and sobbing to such an extent that I could only finish the passage "My wretched orphans cry for bread" with supreme difficulty. The fishhead was in favor of a more restrained performance and her cutting voice drove me to the back of the classroom with words of Un-German Hysterical Conduct. It was a nightmare, I almost died of shame and prayed for an earthquake or an air raid to deliver me from the derision and shock . . . apart from the nagging voice all was still, the others stared at me as though they had unwittingly harbored a serpent in their midst. The rest of my days with Weise were torture. I was afraid of the others and of myself for I could never be certain that I wouldn't again throw myself down in tears because of the orphans. I thought of my great-aunt who had undressed on bridges and was depressed.

There was an air-riad warning every night and we would all be tired, slumped at our desks, and if we came late there was trouble: "The soldiers at the front can't afford to be tired either!" Hardly any bombs fell; one sat in the cellar, heard fretting children, the murmur of flak, sometimes had toothache, sometimes not, smelled the dank cellar, contemplated the water pipes, fell asleep over unfinished homework, woke up with the all-clear, dragged the suitcases upstairs, fell asleep again, was awakened by a second siren or the alarm clock, drank thin warmed-up coffee, twice a week ate powdered egg diluted and stirred, scrambled, fried, tasting of glue, ersatz marmalade on water rolls, sometimes margarine, wore home-made pullovers of prickly wartime wool—ill-cared-for sheep get bristles—old, turned cloth coat, satchel under the arm and off to the happy seat of learning, to the informative refreshing Fräulein Weise.

Early Sunday mornings I was given the coupons to fetch my little brother's liter of skimmed milk, and one Sunday I met Martin Witt; he went to the Treitschke School, had a bicycle and wore a turtle-neck pullover. Swinging the milk can, he invited me for a bicycle ride on Monday. Rapture; even Fräulein Weise seemed attractive on Monday morning, we met at four in the town park and giggled and pedaled until five, then he had homework and I had to collect my brother from the kindergarten. Tuesday came the reckoning: I sat at my desk cow-eyed with happiness and lost in reverie—he'd said I rode like a boy and had nice hair—suddenly Fräulein Weise's soprano seared through my dreams: "While our soldiers are dying for us at the front certain girls here have nothing better to do than to fritter away their afternoons with youths on wheels" . . . youths on wheels . . . it conjured up a vision of youths who had wheels with rubber tires instead of legs and at this I started to grin. There came a thundering KNEEEF . . . the lobster was on the boil again, the shame registered in the black book, warning letter sent to parents, blissful cow-happiness cowed, end of the affair.

Some afternoons were devoted to cookery, presided over by the frantic gymnast Müller. There was not a great deal

one could cook in the dingy cellar referred to as the kitch-
en: spoons were stirred under the incentive "How to make
an inviting meal for five people with water and pearl barley."

I was fifteen and the question was, shall I stay and take a
scholarship or not? I didn't and had to go to the Labor Exchange; compulsory Labor Duty hung over me like a yellow thundercloud and then came the examination; Fräulein
Weise asked demoralizing questions but the rector was
there; I got through the oral examination and we could
choose our own subject for the written test. I wanted to be
a painter and at the same time do threadbare Rabe a favor,
so I wrote a long treatise on Dürer, I had been impressed
by the drawings of his slant-eyed mother. I handed in my
beautiful copperplate and slept in the firm belief that I was
a genius, and on this, my last day at school, our pink Weise
struck her last blow, maintained I had copied everything
from an authority on Dürer, which was the final proof of
my bad character. To her last question, what I thought
would become of me, I promptly replied a painter, drawing
from her the memorable phrase, "Well, I suppose there
have to be some of those too," with which I was dismissed.

THREE

Bernhardstrasse was a horseshoe without a curve, a square with three sides, one street that was actually three, that went in three directions (south, east, and west). The northern side of the unfinished square was formed by Wexstrasse, a loud, big-city street which ran from Kaiserplatz to Innsbruckerplatz. Bernhardstrasse was football field and race track, a village of eighteen four-story houses with front and backyards.

We lived first at No. 5 in two rooms, a few years later at No. 6 in four. No. 5 was gemütlicher. Both were on the south side, and our shop was on the southwest corner. It had two large windows and a large sign which bore the legend "Soling Establishment," my stepfather had something against the word "shoemaker." The lathes and polishing machines stood on one side of the entrance to the Soling Establishment and they were deafeningly loud; a piano teacher lived next door and Stepfather had made an arrangement with her that he would work the machines only in the afternoons; she had to have her piano tuned every two weeks and several porcelain figures had fallen victim to the machines, even the teacups would dance from her table when he switched on. She was a benevolent, sensible woman and taught in the mornings; from eight till one one heard *The Virgin's Prayer, The Volga Song,* and sometimes excerpts from *The Bird Fancier,* then Stepfather would tap tentatively on the thin wall, she tapped back and he took over the afternoon noises.

Wilmersdorf station was situated on the south side; one of the entrances was opposite the shop and this brought us a lot of passing trade, people who wanted a seam stitched in a hurry or a new heel, often merely a pair of laces. The steady customers all lived on Bernhardstrasse. There was the baker Sehmisch and his family; he had his big clean shop on the west side and Herr Sehmisch looked as crisp as his rolls. The Neumanns lived over the Sehmisches' shop; their balcony overlooked our establishment and part of the station. They had a daughter called Edith who took tennis lessons; twice a week she went with a tennis racket, white blouse, and short white skirt to Kaiserplatz, where there was a tennis court on which one could skate in winter. I wasn't very good at skating since I always got cold feet and I couldn't play tennis at all; Tuesdays and Fridays I got livid as I watched Edith strutting past the shop window. Next door to the Sehmisches was a grocery, then came a candy store, a fish shop, and Wexstrasse; on the other side was a dairy run by an old frostbitten couple whose faces stayed blue even in summer; further on was a lending library.

Apart from a spare-part store there were no shops at all on our side. The owner of the spare-part store lived exclusively for his red-haired wife and spare parts, we hardly ever saw him. Mother told me once that they said he wore a silver corset, and from that moment on he filled me with awe. Right beside the station entrance was the tobacco shop, run by the Gorczellanceks; they had to give it up later though —after '35—and the Toedt family took it over; they were nice people and the whole business with the Gorczellanceks upset them greatly. The G's lived on for some years in their apartment on Cosimaplatz in Friedenau, and some of the Bernhardstrasse residents went to see them at night, taking provisions and magazines—the G's were proud people and wouldn't accept gifts, so we were gradually obliged to buy part of their crockery and linen and cutlery, half the street had things of theirs in the end.

One evening Mother and I were on our way to Cosimaplatz when a woman stopped us at the corner and told us not to go up, they had been picked up or rather were due to be picked up, for when the Gestapo rang the doorbell at four or five in the morning they didn't answer and poisoned themselves and their children.

There was another Jewish shop at the corner of Wexstrasse and Bernhardstrasse, a haberdashery; they were called Kaufmann; the wife had dyed her hair bright blond and always told my mother nothing would happen to her. One morning they collected her husband; she escaped to the roof and fell. Everyone was very upset about the Kaufmanns; they had been in Berlin a long time and even hung the swastika from their window on Hitler's birthday, they thought it would help.

Frau Block was our caretaker at No. 5; she had no husband but made up for it with two daughters, Marianne and Lorchen. Frau Block was big-bosomed and comfortable and spent the better part of the day brewing coffee, the whole house smelled of hot inviting coffee. One summer Sunday morning we were sitting on our balcony in silence —not because we had had a fight but because the elevated railway prevented conversation on the balcony. When a train was standing at the platform one had just enough time to yell for the sugar or the milk before the train from the other direction arrived and the stationmaster bellowed "Wilmersdorf," as though the passengers were all deaf illiterates; then someone shrieked "Aaall aboard, dooors closed keeep well back," and the train panted squeaked groaned whistled hummed and shot off toward Schmargendorf and the whole performance was repeated on the other side. Then came a one-minute silence, sometimes three, and we all expressed simultaneously the thoughts which had been suppressed until then by the state railway. At such a moment on that Sunday there was a desperate hammering at the door; my stepfather went, then called Mother, and she stayed away so long I finally went to see what the matter was. Frau Block was sitting on the stairs by the front door crying bitterly. Lorchen had had a baby on the way to fetch the milk that morning—she had wondered for a long time at delicate Lorchen's appetite, had put it down to puberty, and now this . . . Lorchen had worn a corset and poured red ink over her underclothes every four weeks, the crafty slut, but now the bastard was there and a brat into the bargain and did Mother still have half-brother's baby clothes?? My stepfather said, "Who would have thought it of Lorchen?" and when I bought my first lipstick, wore it secretly to the movies, was seen and reported by one of my stepfather's card-playing friends, he said simply: "Think of Lorchen," but Lorchen got married and order and faith in good breeding and justice were restored.

Frau Block, whom we all called Mother Blocken, was one of the bravest and most resourceful later during the air raids; she and her family came to the shelter with saucepans on their heads, on top of the saucepans a cushion, and the whole structure held together with a strap. During the first heavy raid on Wilmersdorf, when for hours the bombs howled, the walls wobbled, and the lights went out, she said repeatedly, "As long as you can hear them you're all right." The next day she had a nice case of shingles; the doctor said she should scream during the next raid, it would be better for the nerves; she didn't scream and kept the shingles.

As my mother, my brother in her arms, and I waded through broken glass and upturned buckets after the first big raid, we saw that our roof was burning and that the barber's house behind the station had collapsed. I realized then that it was war and that it would go on for a long time and I started to cry. By the light of the fire we noticed also that my brother wasn't sleeping as peacefully as we had thought, he had turned blue and was breathing strangely, gasping; we ran through splinters, torn-off window shutters, and excited crowds, and after hours of searching found a doctor who said that my brother had had a heart attack and wouldn't live through a second raid, my mother had to go away. I wanted and I had to stay in Berlin and on Bern-hardstrasse; it was a bad farewell, for my mother, for my stepfather, and for me.

I stayed in the apartment until it was bombed out. It was New Year's Eve '43-'44, the rooms were ice-cold, the windows long since blasted, stuffed with cardboard, the house hadn't smelled of Mother Blocken's coffee for years, and Werner and Klaus, my cycling friends, were at the front, and two from our street had fallen already. That evening I came home, one could have conversed on the balcony for hours on end, trains were infrequent and irregular, in the freight depot at the back there was a flak unit which bleated occasionally in emergencies—black-out, the stationmaster's WIIILMERSDORF was valid for the first time. On this evening I came home, felt my way up the stairs, and said to my stepfather that I would go to bed, it was too cold to wait for midnight and we had nothing to toast with anyway, cups and glasses were long since broken, we ate in canteens and bars, and nobody really felt like celebrating. I pulled on my air-raid things—the trousers of a track suit, two sweaters, and socks—and went to bed. Stepfather had an idea, we still had an electric blanket and if the current was working I could have it for a while. I fell asleep and woke up again because the bed was on fire; at the same time I heard that gentle whine we all knew so well and then another and then another and I screamed AIR RAID and screamed and screamed—our sirens had been silenced in the last raid and nobody had noticed it, and as we scrambled through the cellar door our house suffered a direct hit and we were buried. They dug us out and we thanked the electric blanket.

There was an apartment vacant at No. 6; we moved, that is to say we took our hand baggage, a table, and two bowls we had rescued by way of the undamaged back staircase. Our piano still perched on a ledge which had been part of the living-room floor, but we couldn't get to it; we sat in No. 6, looked at our piano on the fourth floor of No. 5, and waited for it to fall; on the third story there was a picture still hanging on the wall, a mountain landscape with snow and chalets.

Mother arrived from Uelzen and we collected our "Bombed Out" certificates. When I saw her standing at the shop entrance I said "Happy New Year," not trying to be funny, but I couldn't think of anything else, and I felt so sorry for her standing there in the cold winter sunshine, crumpled from the long night journey, staring at the ruined houses which looked like hollowed wisdom teeth. A new air raid started almost immediately and, rumbling angrily, our piano sailed down to join the other pianos, sideboards, tables, toilet seats, and bedroom cupboards which had been transformed into charred heaps of matchwood.

It was a time of prewarning, warning, all-clear, new warning; radios spluttered out their air-information oracles; bomber formation destination uncertain, new wave destination southeast, wide formation approaching Berlin—that meant they wanted to distribute their bombs fairly and evenly, not just favoring Wilmersdorf or Ostkreuz or Gesundbrunnen—fighter squadron direction Brandenburg, bomber formation over Neuruppin. And there sat Goering, who had said they could call him Meier if an enemy aircraft should ever dare to venture over the Sovereign German Realm, as he had turbulently called it—they had been calling him Meier for some little time now, and they had their revenge in the cellars, timidly swapping quiet jokes about Meier.

It was a time when the postman was awaited as anxiously as one awaits the first words of a gypsy fortuneteller. The first green letters arrived with the black letters POW stamped on them, and on the back "Do not write here,"

"Hier nicht schreiben," "Non scrivete qui," or something in Japanese—they had part of the war behind them and were picking cotton. But months of waiting and no letter at all meant wounded, Russian prison camp, or death, and forgotten dancing-lesson friends became unforgotten because they had written two hesitant letters and then no more, because soldiers at the front are loyal and write, even when they have nothing to say and their fingers are cold and there's no light in the foxhole.

There were letters from the still-alive to the still-alive, or, when they finally arrived, letters from the dead to the still-alive or vice versa; but with their newly arrived letters they were still there and not frozen, bleeding, blown up, crippled, starving, burned, drowned or crashed. . . .

When the next big night raid started we didn't feel like sitting in No. 6's shaky cellar any more so we set off with our bags and coupons and Bombed Out passes for the Bahnhof Zoo, the main railway station, where the only big bunker was situated. We joined a long queue and waited as one does at a bus stop. When the forewarning sounded the big door was opened and we all rushed inside. We sat on our bags the whole night, dim lights flickering on and off, children screaming, an old man showing us countless photographs of his wife, who had died in the last air raid, flak soldiers sliding the whole length of the bunker on their hobnailed boots, like children on a frozen pond. We were then forbidden to speak as the ventilators had to be closed, it was burning outside, and always the pointless chattering of the flak on the bunker roof—that stopped then too: a land mine fell on the station and blew flak and soldiers from the roof. All-clear, no trains, walk through the burning streets, warning again, strange cellars, and then finally home and No. 6 is standing, without doors or windows, but still standing. Not for long. The next evening a bomb came in vertically over the railway station and sliced off the upper stories. Mother and I were standing under the railway bridge and the blast pressed us gently, almost lovingly to the ground. Father was still in the hallway and a wall hit him; we pulled him out, he coughed and swore and then began to cry. Herr Keilbach, our dentist on Wexstrasse, had gone back into his burning apartment and rescued all his used and unused razor blades, he'd actually wanted to get his gold watch; Mother Blocken brewed real coffee beans in her provisional home at No. 3 and said, "Main thing is we're still alive," and scratched her shingles.

In the morning we waited around at the town hall for our "Totally Demolished" cards. When, after many hours, we finally stood in front of the emaciated Nazi lady's desk, she made the mistake of asking my mother: "Can you prove that you are totally demolished?" whereupon my patient mother lost control, started shouting so that her voice doubled back on her, screamed that the Plutocratic Warmongers had forgotten to drop cameras with their bombs and that all witnesses who might have been called upon were either dead or too busy with themselves and that she'd had enough of the whole goddamned business anyway—the emaciated lady didn't scream at all, smiled like a benevolent nun and I thought, "That's it, now she'll be arrested, she's bound to get her revenge," but judgment of character is a matter of luck, especially when one's tired, living under a dictatorship, and all women over forty look like Fräulein Weise. Mother's residence permit for Berlin was not renewed and she had to go back to the half-brother, the loveless half-relatives, and Uelzen.

FOUR

I, Hildegard Frieda Albertina, had given my mother, Frieda Auguste, very little joy. There were the constant, endless, countless, family-disrupting illnesses, streams of drops and medicines. "Hilde is always ill," they said. There was my fear when she was out, my fear when she was there, fear that she might go out again. There was the waiting around hallway doors, fear of darkness, fear of being alone, of forgetfulness. There were swollen eyes and sties, wobbly polio legs, a broken collarbone that wouldn't mend, rheumatism that kept me and her awake all night. One nose, broken; one jaw, operated on; one foot, cut open with a razor blade because Mother was at the movies and still not home at eleven. There was anemia and there were blood tests, ghostly pale face, shadows under the eyes, and there was jolly sympathy from the neighbors. And if the flood of horror was once stemmed for a short while and I was allowed to visit her, perhaps, one afternoon at Siemens in the big room where she typed, where forty typewriters all chattered simultaneously, where she typed until the chain of chocolate, tobacco, shoemaker shops began—then I promptly fell down. Fell on the stairs, got bumps on my forehead and other places, brought disgrace, snot, and pain where proud presentation had been wished for, expected.

"It really is a trial with that child," she would sometimes say, when all hope forsook her. And the grand ball, the only one—I spoiled that for her too. Ruined it. It was at the Imperial Ballroom in Lichterfelde. Mother and Stepfather's first ball together—Mother in long gown, Stepfather in navy blue, scrubbed and eager, already in the taxi. And the torchlight procession for the children. Chinese lanterns in the twilight, orchestra plays something by Lincke, parents clap, beam, are proud, puffed up. I stand there, look at torches, the procession does a sudden turn, I lose sight of Mother—panic. A man comes, lifts me onto the stage, light, fanfare.

"We have found a stray child. Now what's your name?" Chuckles and sniggers from below. "What's your name?" Louder, sharper. Don't know. Panic. "Now, now," he says beside me, above me, "it's not as bad as all that."

Mother pulls me down. "Dear God," she says, "dear God, can't you take care of yourself for two minutes?"

The children poke each other in the ribs, laugh. The adults exchange glances, smile. Stepfather drinks a quick beer, too quick, starts coughing, goes his asthma color, lilac at its most lilac. We go. No one says a word. Go home on the train, in long festive black.

And I wasn't pretty either, God knows, nobody but Grandfather thought I was pretty. The saleswoman in the bookshop next door once said: "You get more like your Aunt Hulda every day," and although I loved Aunt Hulda dearly, I didn't want to look like her. And Mother said to Stepfather, one night as it was getting dark: "A pity Hilde isn't prettier." And Stepfather, cranky, wanting to sleep, murmured: "Yes, but she looks quite interesting."

That was a blow. A worse one fell the day Lieselotte wanted to go to the movies with her friend. She took me along because her mother had said, "You're not to go alone." Her friend brought his friend, pimply, damp hands, rubbing his cheeks and rolling his eyes, sighing: "This shaving drives me crazy." When the film was over, the three of them said: "Auf Wiederseh'n." Left me standing at the cinema in the black-out, said Wiederseh'n and went.

And Mother was beautiful, very beautiful. She had the longest, loveliest legs in Schöneberg, the greenest eyes, was healthy, slender, tough, powerful, fearless. A little disappointed perhaps, disappointed because she had such a lovely clear high voice, but had not, after all, become a singer. There wasn't enough money for the training, and to go around begging for a scholarship—no, one was too proud for that, if it came to that, one would rather not fulfill one's most cherished dreams. She had been brought up on Prussian discipline and when she was twenty-three my grandmother asked her whether she still had a right to wear that white summer dress. She didn't. She had met my father. It was love at first sight and I believe my mother still loved him when she died thirty-five years after him.

His name was Hans Theodor, he was big, wild, restless, red-haired, he charged through life and professions like an express train through stations, won races swimming against the current in the Rhine, football trophies, amateur boxing contests.

He was desperate.

I would like to have known him.

At seventeen he was awarded the Iron Cross second class, at seventeen and a half the Iron Cross first class. He had volunteered, was at the Somme, at Verdun, and was once in a brothel. And when the war was over, the revolutionaries tore off his ribbons and epaulettes at the railway station in Berlin. What remained was the illness. "Cured," the doctor said a year later, "got away with it this time."

He had trouble adjusting himself to a Germany reeking of cabbages and turnips, sought war, sought a fight—until he found his Frieda Auguste. They got married. Packed, unpacked, moved, moved again; it was a marriage on the move. He had success and a chauffeur-driven car, lost both, landed in Ulm. Then came the biggest, once-in-a-lifetime, puts-everything-else-in-the-shade chance: Turkey, own factory, independence. I put an end to that. I made my entrance in December. My father ran through the apartment shouting: "Is her blood all right, Doctor, is her blood in order too?" It was.

A month later Mother found the syringe. In the hall was a high cupboard, in the high cupboard a carton, in the carton the syringe. What's the syringe for? she asked.

The illness I had once has come back. I'm having treatment, giving myself the injections, they say it will go away again.

It didn't. He got fever, he got angina. Whether the one had anything to do with the other the doctors didn't know. He was taken to the hospital. Mother too—she had appendicitis. He lay on the second floor, she on the first. Ten days later he screamed for his Auguste, the priest came. Taking him gently by the hand, he spoke: My son, he said, we all have to die one day, it is God's will. We have to find the way to *Him, He* is good, *He* is great. *He*, in his mercy, will take care of you, let us pray.

Hans Theodor stood up, took the comforting priest by the throat and throttled him until he turned purple, screamed and screamed: I am twenty-eight I have a wife and a child of six months it's not true it isn't *His* will can't be *His* will you're lying. . . . Then he fell over the unconscious priest and died.

My mother was informed four hours later; they had simply forgotten about her.

She took the urn and a hammock, strung me up between two luggage racks, and traveled back to Berlin and her parents. There was no money left, she had to work in offices again, as she had done before she was married. Grandmother and I went regularly to the Schöneberg cemetery and she said, "If we water the grave well enough, perhaps Father will grow again, we must be patient and wait until spring," but in the spring the cemetery and the grave looked the same as ever, Father had not grown again and I was disappointed and cried all the way home.

When in thirty-three the Nazis took over Berlin with parades and uproar and children waving little flags and squealing Heil Hitler, my mother said: "A blessing that he's not alive, a blessing that he's not alive." He had been a Social Democrat, and despite his many professions, had even spoken in the Reichstag once; but she wasn't thinking of this so much as of his inability to avoid a row, to take anything lying down; stupidity and fanaticism threw him into a rage, besides which he'd never been averse to a good fight.

My stepfather went about things in a more prudent manner. He had a shop together with a Herr Gold, and when the Nazis advised him to join the party and get rid of Herr Gold, he asked simply and quietly how much it might cost not to become a party member as he had asthma and would not be able to take part in the sporting activities of the community. They said uncertainly that they would leave this up to him, so he pulled out his wallet and cordially placed a one-mark piece on the table. He was looking for a new shop the next day.

He didn't like hanging out the flag either and was constantly being warned by the Blockleiter. Finally he bought one, about the size of a child's handkerchief, and was warned again. The Blockleiter said severely that the flag must be relative in size to the shop window. So Stepfather bought one relative in size to the shop window, but it hung down onto the pavement and people got tangled up in it; with a really good gust of wind it would envelope whole families. The Blockleiter came again and demanded something shorter, so Stepfather rolled it up around the pole so that the black swastika in the white circle disappeared and we now had a flag of exactly the requisite dimensions, but red—which at that time was not at all fashionable. Several inquisitive people, who probably thought that they'd misunderstood the latest news bulletins, gathered in front of the shop and asked excitedly what the new flag meant. The purple-faced Blockleiter steamed up and put an end to the disorder with a threatening: "If one more incident comes to my notice . . ." and then left Stepfather's haven of quiet mirth without reporting him.

I always carried with me a small photo of my father; he looked sad and angry with his deep-set, somewhat slanting eyes, his square chin and soft mouth. I always looked at him when I had troubles, or when I was especially happy about something. My stepfather was jealous of my quiet photo love affair, Mother pacified him with: "But she's only a child." As I got bigger, she often looked at me in astonishment and said: "You laugh just like your father—he always bellowed like that too and laughed till the tears rolled down his face." I tried to tame my wild laughter, but sometimes I forgot and then Mother looked startled, grew pale, went out.

FIVE

During the last weeks with Weise I went to the Friedenau Labor Exchange. I had my sketches under my arm: Aunt Hulda, worried and creased in pencil, Grandfather four times in pencil and charcoal, Mother in pencil, self-portrait in charcoal and crayon, sketches of the Wilmersdorf railway station, view from the balcony, pen and ink. I waited two, three hours in a linoleum-laid hallway and was afraid. My mother had registered me at a business school in a month's time to escape Labor Duty (fields, plows, cattle dung, drive tractors, sing songs, wear brown), at least for the time being. But I wanted to paint, so I entered the lion's den.

A gentle, gray-haired lady examined the studies, and, red as a tomato, I asked whether, where, if it were possible, could be possible, to really learn to paint without having any money.

She gave me a contemplative-surprised look and admitted hesitantly that she too liked to draw, and that the framed watercolor tree hanging behind her desk was from her own hand—I knew I had carried the day, she was going to help me. She didn't say that painting was "nonsense," that it was disgraceful even to think of pictures and colors while those brave, unflagging soldiers . . . I didn't have to say that my ambition was to erect a monument to the Führer in oils or design posters saying "Save Coal Dust" and "The Enemy Is Listening." In a Labor Exchange reeking of disinfectant, a gray-haired ration-book user Class II had understood that somebody simply wanted to paint. She wrote first a letter, then an address on notepaper adorned with a swastika and advised me to go there—they were looking for two or three gifted artists to be trained. The address read UFA, Ltd., Dönhoffplatz, Trick Film Department.

I went. Was directed to Herr Klemke, who regarded my

folder of portraits and views of the railway station carefully and inscrutably through rimless spectacles balanced on a pointed nose over a small mouth. He marked me down for a nine-o'clock drawing test in three days' time. I played truant from school and in my best wool dress and with a pounding heart took the punctual, eager train to Potsdamerplatz, ran over to the subway, traveled on to Hausvogteiplatz, crossed Leipzigerstrasse and Dönhoffplatz, and stood before the squeaking black gates of the UFA lift at 8:30. The studio was on the fifth floor, and to reach it I had to go through a big room full of people bending over lighted desks, who contemplated the stumbling intruder with dazzled, half-closed eyes, like lazy lions watching a lolloping rabbit. The model for the drawing test, an old woman, sat on a stool, dipping rolls into coffee and munching.

Ten girls and three boys stood around looking at each other suspiciously. Then Klemke came in and they all gleamed at him, as though they could bribe him with humility. He looked past us through his rimless glasses. The old woman stopped munching. She was eighty, or perhaps even ninety, and had creases and furrows like chewed-up asphalt—Aunt Hulda had a child's face in comparison—and after looking at her twice I could have drawn her in my sleep. In the afternoon the drawing-sheets are collected, all neatly and legibly signed, new ones are pinned on the boards, the old woman departs, leaving behind an empty chair—now we are to draw that. In the slanting afternoon sun it has four shadow-legs, the real ones are giving me enough trouble, perspective's not right, the wool dress gets hot and scratches, fingers are sticky, arms covered with charcoal and pencil shavings, new sheet of paper—at last, a chair; a little puny perhaps and the back's still not right, but nevertheless a chair.

At six I cross Leipzigerstrasse, depressed and ready for business school, walk along to Potsdamerplatz, cursing chairs in general. At 8:30 next morning past the squinting, lighted-desk lions and on to rimless Klemke, not confident at all any more—if only an old woman or man would come, even a fifty-year-old would be all right, only please God no chairs and benches, crates or spheres. Klemke says absently, "Today you have six hours to draw something from your imagination." I blossom and rush to my board but in front of the empty sheet I become empty, lame, the

feverish scratching around me makes me panic. Thank
God, the pencil timidly draws a horse, but it becomes a
dog, horse's head with dog's body, black-haired woman
with drooping fan, lace handkerchief wafting in invisible
wind like a sharp-edged page of a magazine, girl under fir
trees stretching up to the sky like toothbrushes—plates are
clattering in the square UFA courtyard, people calling out
incoherently, sun shining, I have visions of adding machines and dictation pads. "You will be informed within
three or four weeks," says Klemke and we all file out.

Three weeks mark time. Liszt's *Préludes* drones from the
Volksradio, sets the stage for a special announcement from
the Supreme Command . . . so many gross tons are scut-
tled, Hitler is volubly pleased, nights in the cellar, days
with Weise and no letter from UFA. Nightmares of business school and Labor Duty: a travel agency, later perhaps,
but who travels in wartime, except soldiers and they don't
need a travel agency; graphic artists wanted, but my chairs
being the way they are; or the interpreters' school—the examination's supposed to be grueling, but perhaps I'd get
through after all, after years of cramming, then to be permitted to say word for word what someone else has already
said. . . . The classroom buzzes and hums with blissful
plans for the future, clear-cut ambitions, unshakable decisions are being made, they're going to be teachers, nurses,
dancers, explorers in the jungle which the Führer will make
German and habitable, nuns, post-office officials, secretaries, third flute players in the Eichwalde Labor Duty
band; domestic school, preparation for marriage and moth-
erhood—I alone despair because of a chair with a straight
back.

Twenty-two days later Mother stands at the door waving
a white piece of paper. I fall over chairs, squash my
fingers, spring about, hop up and down, send a telegram
"I've been accepted Hurray" to my dancing-lesson friend at
the maneuver camp in Gardelegen. Off with Mother to
Dönhoffplatz, radiant, thankful, UFA-loving. Three-year
apprenticeship contract signed by Klemke and Mother.

Pots, pans, jugs from 7:30 A.M. until 6:30 P.M., in lead
and charcoal, height in relation to breadth, breadth in relation to height, measure, erase—unnerved, shaky line.
Klemke says: Again.

Later: Cloth and folds, drapery. I wake up thinking
drapery, I go to sleep thinking drapery.

Much later: Nude study. The model between seventy-five and eighty, male. The others in this line have all been called up along with others in other lines. Ours froze pitifully, disclosed under protest his shivering frame, demanded heating, demanded soup, received neither one nor the other. Drops ran from nose over toothless mouth. His sniffling, the scratching charcoal, Klemke's irritated: Again. It was the morning I saw a naked man for the first time. Pots, pans, and jugs again in the afternoon, this time in tempera.

No Nolde, no Kokoschka, no Modigliani, Chagall, Utrillo, or Van Gogh enjoyed the scrutiny of this German drawing regiment. No "Degenerate." Taborch and his drapery were the unattainable goal of the class.

Stalingrad fell. The imprisoned, forced-labor artists of the Newsreel and Trick Film Department in the UFA building, Dönhoffplatz, fifth floor, showed their delight as inconspicuously as possible. In his Soling Establishment at Wilmersdorf station my stepfather was of two minds. There were boys being slaughtered like cattle, he said, and here was hope for the end. The beginning of the end. But there was General Paulus too. He'd had Stepfather repair his shoes for some time now, as he lived nearby in the Detmolderstrasse. He'd had them done shortly before he left for Russia. He had come to the shop and said: "Nobody repairs my shoes the way you do, Herr Wulfestieg!" The General had said that. And my stepfather, who didn't like generals, had been pleased. He'd been so pleased that he drank too much cold beer and had an attack of asthma.

The Pole, in our drawing class, who fought a continual battle with the language, a breaking voice, and obstinate, yellow, matchlike hair, interpreted the battle as a signal to get out, and went. They caught him near the Pyrenees. Before they executed him, he sent us a card. Wilfried, the Dutchman, disappeared together with the carrots he always wore in his buttonhole on Orange holidays. Three weeks later a letter arrived from Basel.

We stayed. The pots stayed. And Klemke's ice-cold rimless gaze stayed.

It was evening, ten minutes before the dismissal bell barked. We jostled around the toilets, packed bags, packed lead and charcoal, dusted drawing desks. Helga dawdled, as always. She was sly, solid, gifted, more learned than the rest of us, but a slowpoke. We missed the train regularly at Hausvogteiplatz and I my connecting train from Potsdamerplatz. She went on to Breitenbacherplatz; better district, newer houses. She lived with Mother among countless pictures of Father. He had been an actor until one day he had gone to the Mediterranean to entertain the troops, slipped from a cliff, and drowned. She gave me well-thumbed plays, held lengthy dissertations on the contents, said: "Let me be your Leporello."

Eva sat combing, painting, squeezing a pimple. She was the prettiest, blond and tall, with a bosom and legs and a constant cold. She was in love with a director who had told her on the subway between Nollendorf and Wittenbergplatz that she had eyes like Garbo. She had never seen Garbo, was nevertheless thankful, and became his slave from then on. On Saturdays she went to his apartment and cleaned. It was then that he said not only did she have the Swedish lady's eyes but she also possessed the qualities of a true German. We were envious, pressed her for details, she declined.

Reni sat on the window ledge and chewed. She had baby fat and black hair and was always hungry, which in those days was a cruel stroke of fate. She dreamed of ham rolls, which weren't to be had, and of "black kisses," a sticky cake which wasn't available either. She was in love with two soldiers who were continually not on leave in Berlin. She had a lot of pictures, Reni with soldier A, Reni with soldier B. Then they both came on leave at the same time and she went through a crisis which left her looking thinner.

Nefertiti had already gone, her train went at 6:15. Our Nefertiti bore not the slightest resemblance to the other one. She spent most of her unnoticed youth at railway stations and on suburban and metropolitan trains. She lived in Rangsdorf and had to leave home at five in the morning to be at Dönhoffplatz at 7:30. She painted as though she were the daughter of all the impressionists, but her talent waned under Klemke's mild drapery-mania.

The bell pealed, barked, groaned, and died away. Halfpast. The door was torn open. In it stood somebody in a never-before-seen yellow leather coat, thick-soled shoes, a scarf with ends that wagged idly around the long hair at the neck. He looked at us one after another, seemed to lose interest, marched up to Klemke's closed door, knocked, went in. Interval. Came out again, followed by the Grim One who announced: "Fräulein Knef, would you come in please." I stood in front of Klemke's desk, looked at the UFA courtyard, the windows of the newsreel department, saw charwomen, and thought to myself: that's the end of that. Of what exactly I didn't know; just that's the end of that. Leather-coat sagged against the door and smoked, which was strictly forbidden. Then Klemke said: "You are to be at the advertising film studios at eight tomorrow morning." Leather-coat said softly, "Bring a bathing suit." One of them said Heil Hitler and I was dismissed.

I put on my frayed maroon bathing suit and the make-up woman said, "Well, we'll just have to try and do something about you, won't we?" She smeared a lot of brown onto my face. Next to me sat an excited girl. "I'm from Mannheim," she rattled away, "I'm bound to get through, lots of great actors come from Mannheim."

The one from yesterday came in, without the leather this time, grinned and leaned against the door, saying: "All right, let's get on with it." With what I had no idea.

A man came out from behind the camera and in my excitement I curtsied. Then I was told to stand on a crate and make believe it was a diving board, give a squeal of joy and jump into the nonexistent water. I did so and gashed my knee open. They all looked at me and one murmured, "Was this the best you could get?" We shot it again. I kept peering at the cameraman, whom I took to be the director, and never heard what Leather-coat, who *was* the director, had to say. And so I jumped up and down in my maroon frayed one-piece and pretended to be a joyous German maid in the summer wind.

When we were finished, the director, whom I had still not recognized as such, asked me whether he might walk with me to the subway. When we got there, however, he decided the weather was too nice, and so I pressed on along behind him. He spoke of films which had never been made and said that I would be perfect for a script he was thinking of doing next. I was very photogenic, he said, one could make something of me.

When I got home, thirty minutes late, Mother was standing at the door: "Now we're not going to start those games," she said.

Summertime. Leipzigerstrasse dusty, warm, smell of

things burning. It's windy on the corner where the Air
Force building is. Skirts fly, guards peep. Photogenic, he'd
said. We walk as far as Potsdamer, save the fare. The
wooden soles clatter. New skirt on coupon F, down to the
country on Sundays, organize some strawberries. Short
nights in non-icy cellars. Lunch-break on the sooty UFA
roof, sunburn in the afternoon and still pots, pans, and
jugs.

Somebody had been standing there in the subway watching me, six stops long, every evening except Sunday. Then
he plucks up courage: "May I see you home?" It's a short
walk, I live opposite the station. Next evening: "I'm flying
to Augsburg tomorrow, would you have coffee with me or
go to the theater, opera, concert, movies?" We go to the
movies—they're showing *Die Goldene Stadt*. I cry until I
can't see any more. He, the smooth type from the city, puts
her, the peasant girl, in the family way. She is beside herself, he laughs, she implores him, he doesn't give a damn.
She runs over the big bridge in Prague, hammers on her
forehead with her fists, screams. Behind it all, Smetana's
Moldau. I've forgotten my neighbor.

His name is Emmert, he's an airman, an engineer, Air
Ministry. A cheerful, gentle Swabian. "You cry beautifully," he chuckles as the lights go up and reveal my swollen
eyes.

"Rubbish," I say, "it was silly," I say, think of classics-
hour Armgard and her poor orphans, think of nothing at
all, am confused.

SIX

"Let me see your profile," said the red-haired Eskimo lady named Else Bongers. We are in the Berlin Film offices, Unter den Linden. "Can you give an audition?"

"No," I whispered.

"Why do you want to be an actress?"

"Because I'm talented."

"How do you know?"

"I just know."

She looked at me, stood up, went out. The sun made patterns on the desk, the windows were clean. People were drifting along toward Friedrichstrasse station, others just drifting, it was a Saturday. A Volksradio crowed traditional airs. The linden trees on Unter den Linden were yellow-green, it smelled of perfume in the office.

When she returned, I wanted to fling myself to the floor, throw my arms around her knees, beg indulgence and belief in my unproven talents. I remained seated, staring at her suit jacket. She gave me two slim scripts, said, "Learn the marked speeches."

Again my emotions urged me to the floor, to kiss her hand, moisten her hem, shout thank you. I stood up, whispered, "When?"

"A week from Monday, Althoff Studios in Nowawes at nine o'clock."

"How comes that lovely casket here to me?" I call out delightedly as I spy the cigar box lying on the studio floor; it's Gretchen finding the jewelry Mephisto has cunningly planted in her room.

Bongers looks like a Cheshire cat: so does the director. They like me, I think to myself, and go blubbering into "Incline, O maiden . . ." Then Viola's "I left no ring with her: what means this lady?" Where so much grace is desirable, I grow bulkier by the second; a tractor in the living room, sandbag legs, penguin arms. The Eskimo-angel says, "Enough of that." She strides into the studio next door with the pensive director type, I follow. Someone thrusts a piece of paper into my hand: scene in a hotel lobby, conversation with concierge. They light, make up, one of them nails a strip of wood to the floor and says: "When you hit the mark, say the first line!" Then they sit me on a chair, I have to turn my head this way and that, look serious, smile, serious again, once more to the left, now to the right, not so fast. Clapper-board. We'll let you know. I want to tell Bongers that I'd had a toothache, that I'm a half-orphan, that I am being persecuted, that I urgently need help, that I am most certainly talented. I take off my make-up and walk to the station.

Fourteen months ago it was chairs, now it's Viola's stupid ring.

I stumbled on the subway stairs, a young man in uniform caught me, looked at me and said, "You have beautiful eyes." "Yes, thank you," I said. Thought: that's a fat lot of help. Eight weeks had dragged by and no letter, no call. Perhaps something has happened to Bongers or the film caught fire. I telephone, ask for her, she's at UFA now, somebody says, I hang up. The uniform said: "May I introduce myself, my name is Manfred. I'm on leave and have to go back tomorrow, would you have coffee with me?" Nobody was waiting for me particularly. Mother was in Uelzen, sometimes she came back for a few days, on the last occasion she had said, "From now on you're responsible for yourself."

He had a handsome, good face. I went with him to his tiny studio on Grolmannstrasse. We sat on two stools and he explained to me that the wooden head hanging on the wall was a mummy case. "I'm an architect," he said. I had to laugh. "Yes, I know that sounds a little incongruous at the moment, but we'll be needed after the war." He pulled out a record player, took an age winding it up, played something American called *Harlem*. We sat there swinging our legs, and then he took me home. At the door he gave me his food coupons since, as he said, he wouldn't need them at the front. He wrote from Brückenkopf, south of Vitebsk: "One dares not forget the immortal things—music, nature, the creative force—during this melting process

which is swallowing the world. We have been ordered not
to retreat, Berlin had many raids, I heard, I thought of
you."

"Listen, Liebeneiner's sitting in the canteen," Helga said
breathlessly. "He's the head of UFA at Babelsberg." "So
what," I said and ran like a bat out of hell. I stood behind
the lavatory door for half an hour, then they came, at least
twelve men all talking at the same time. Liebeneiner was
the last. I hung on to him, grabbed his jacket, hung onto it.
Astonished at the desperate attack, he did his best to turn
around, said, "Hello, yes . . . ?"

"Herr Liebeneiner"—I forgot that he was a professor—
"Herr Liebeneiner, six months ago Frau Bongers, the one
who's now at UFA. Frau Bongers did a test of me and I've
never heard anything, please have a look at it, my name is
Hilde Knef I want to be an actress here's my telephone
number only nobody here must know about it or they'll
send me to the Labor Exchange." I couldn't think of anything else.

He stood on the stairs, looked at me, wrote my name
down on a cigarette pack, said, "You'll hear from us."

"That's what they said six months ago," I shouted after
him. Then I went into the lavatory and cried.

When I came back Klemke asked, "Where have you
been all this time?"

"I've had a toothache."

"Then go to the dentist and not the lavatory."

Bombs fell on Bernhardstrasse. Mother came to Berlin
for a few days. We were standing in the windowless bedroom, glass splinters on the bed, on the floor, deep in the
walls. Suddenly the telephone rang. It was about the only
thing that still worked. Bongers was on the line: "We
would like to put your daughter under contract, a three-
year student contract with options. Your daughter is a
minor, we need your permission." Perplexed, my mother
murmured, "Yes, but she's not talented . . ." I heard the
cutting voice: "Please allow us to be the best judges of that,
Frau Wulfestieg." My mother said yes. She didn't know
why; perhaps she looked on the contract as a way of bridg-
ing the war, as a refuge from the sword called Labor Duty.
That my enthusiasm for art school had cooled somewhat
had become apparent to her when she got a letter from

Klemke monosyllabically deploring my lack of interest in pots and drapery.

The State Film School, Babelsberg, had been evacuated to Woltersdorf. My mother and I tied up a blanket and packed my three pullovers, two skirts, and a washed-out track suit in a carton. When we were finished, she started throwing the glass splinters into a bucket, one by one. She said nothing, didn't look at me, she seemed completely occupied with the splinters. She had had no idea of my dream, of the test, of the endless months wasted in waiting, of a longing so great that I couldn't have mentioned it without betraying it.

I had to be in Woltersdorf in two days. UFA Films saw to it that my art contract was dropped; they were one and the same firm, after all, they belonged to the State and the State gave the orders. Mother's train went at 7:30 P.M. from Lehrter station via Stendal and Salzwedel to Uelzen. She went downstairs to the shop, spoke with Stepfather. I sat on the bed with the lilac cover. For the first time I had the feeling that I should be happy but I wasn't. A feeling I was to get to know well. Guilt-feeling. No man's land.

Mother came back, didn't need to ring the bell or unlock the door, it was a heap of splinters in the hallway. "It's time," she said. We picked up her bundles and two cardboard suitcases and went down to Stepfather. Above the din of the machines they shouted " 'Bye" and "Keep smiling." When the train came in she gave me a kiss, called out before the automatic doors slammed shut: "Perhaps you can come down at Christ——" The "mas" was drowned out by the stationmaster's "Keeep baaack."

Two days later I was at Ostkreuz station changing trains. The sirens howled and I lost my blanket in the pushing and shoving. After the all-clear a fat, dead rat lay on the tracks. I looked at it until I felt sick. The train came, ran over it. The compartments were full, the windows gone. I squeezed and squirmed, scraped and scratched, got on. In the darkness somebody said, "I'm savoring life at its fullest." End of the line, all change, suburban streetcar—one of those senile, due-for-a-pension ones, but the man standing under the sign "Conversation with the driver is strictly forbidden" hadn't realized it. He hurtled along the village street, the car groaned and shuddered until finally, with a crash, the trailer derailed. I walked the rest of the way, arrived in

Woltersdorf at midnight, found the desolate restaurant in which I was now to live and learn, found the room next to the former beer bar with ten neat campbeds, found the voice teacher, Frau Kaminsky. She was sitting beneath a dimmed lamp, reading. I apologized, since I was late, still clutching my remaining carton. She looked at me, friendly-cool, and said quietly and beautifully, "My child, do you *have* to have that Berlin accent?"

In the morning I was introduced: this was Maria, softly sighing and unmistakably from Saxony; this was Elinor, black and big and superior; Annerose, all symmetry from forehead to chin and married already; Chiquy, pretty in a sporty way; Heidi, dreamily wandering on endless legs; and, above all, this was Karl Meixner, the teacher, our dramatics teacher. He needed only one match a day, from then on he lit the fresh cigarette from the fag-end of the old. His black eyes squinted through clouds of smoke, his skin had the enlarged pores of actors who remove their make-up quickly and lovelessly, for whom mirrors hold no mystery except when they're sticking on a beard.

They all wanted him to like them—they dressed and changed, combed and straightened seams, hung transported on his lips. Not me. I wanted to learn, quickly, constantly, impatiently. He could have been a robot, Rasputin, Himmler, Hitler, or all of them rolled into one; I wanted only one thing of him: knowledge. The wild ambition didn't go unnoticed—the one without vanity, whose only vanity it was to be the best. He drove me, he demanded, he shouted, he bored, overlooked me, left me hanging, led and drove and spat. There were no bombs, no hunger, no priority vouchers for goods that didn't exist; there was Gretchen, Luise, Ophelia, the classics from top to bottom, and all this in front of a bar that still stank of beer. In the afternoon he dashed off in a swirling trench coat, clutching cigarettes, always late, always just catching or just miserably missing the train—to play at the Schiller Theater with Heinrich George. Whether he was a great actor or not I never knew; he was a great teacher, the best a beginner could wish for. He created—like no other director I have ever worked with—a world out of two chairs; he let the hesitant, giggling, stuttering greenhorns wallow in feeling, much too much, uncontrolled feeling, didn't dissect, didn't analyze, didn't prattle, didn't drown us in a cesspool of theory, didn't expound science where none existed. He encouraged courage—courage to make mistakes, to be loud, to be big: "You can reduce whenever you want," he said sarcastically, "restraint needs control, and that's something you haven't a clue about." And when, with the afternoon sunlight pouring through the windows, we couldn't believe in the poison that Ferdinand had slipped into poor Luise's lemonade, wanted to discuss it a bit, gain a little time, he said coolly, "Lie down, for Christ's sake, get down—you're dying, do you understand, dying—'poison, Ferdinand, poison' "—the way this rattled in his throat made one feel quite faint. Courage returned, the rays of sunlight on the bar were forgotten.

When he dashed off I went to Kaminsky; she would look at me, worried, and invariably say, "We must work on your lisp and your end syllables, they are appalling." "Abraham sass nah am Abhang, sprach gar sangbar zaghaft langsam"—I never got that far in *Der Kleine Hey*, the actor's elocution bible, for already at the word "sass" her face would disintegrate. I tried hard but my *s* opposed me and it still does.

I awaited the new day like a jilted lover awaiting a sign; if he worked with others my day was ruined, wasted, time lost, never to be regained. I learned all the roles, even the ones I knew I'd never get. Else Bongers visited us. She brought her poodle; it surreptitiously polished off our crate of provisions and then licked our hands, the bastard. She played audience in our bar-theater, kept reactions carefully to herself. "If you speak of anything but theater, she gets that vacant look," she said to Meixner, meaning me. She had tried, my Eskimo-lady—I had secretly named her that because she looked Eskimo, Mongolian, foreign, a peculiar head on slender German shoulders—she had tried for months to get me a job, to get someone excited or at least interested in her find. But Jonen, head of Berlin Films, had laughed, laughed until the tears came. And it wasn't funny, the scene we'd done in Nowawes, it wasn't funny at all. She stood in the projection room, observed the tears and said: "She'll be laughing when you've long since stopped." She then gathered up coat, handbag, film, and left. Went to UFA; but it was the same story—until Liebeneiner came, engaged her, engaged me.

Three months later the school was deevacuated back to the UFA studios in Babelsberg. Woltersdorf had proved to be too far and too dangerous; there were munitions factories in the neighborhood and we were less protected in our glass bar than in the city cellars. Those who had no home, or none any more, were allowed to continue to use the Woltersdorf Studio—I didn't care, I commuted between Babelsberg, Wilmersdorf, Woltersdorf with my carton, slept on floors, sofas, at a student's home, in dressing-rooms, and most of the time in cellars anyway.

I wolf a month's meat coupons in a week, loaf along the road between the stages in the lunch-hour chewing a water-roll, thinking all the time: I'm at home here, this is my home. At 7:30 the day begins: an hour of ballet; fencing with Frau Gerresheim—they say she was in the Olympics; singing with Frau Röseler: "Oh my child, you're so delicate and the voice is not—we must try to get it higher." I twittered and cheeped; after an hour we were both hoarse. Eleven thirty to Kaminsky, she shuddered the moment she saw me and didn't stop until the hour was up. She wouldn't give in, I wouldn't give in, we fought, syllable by syllable, but they never got to be fine sentences. Then on to the chanson hour with Inge Bartsch and the Dutch pianist, bony as a starved mastiff with a horse's face. He played the same tune thirty times over as though his life depended on it.

Meixner came at one o'clock: the overture was at an end. After seven, I hover around Bongers' office, perhaps I'll see her, I can tell her that he didn't get to me yesterday *or* today, that Meixner's concentrating on others. Resentful, muttering curses, I hover, she sees me, knocks on the window—I'm to come in. Standing in front of her desk I say nothing, don't dare to any more, anger gone, thankful student again. She coaxes it out of me and next afternoon she's sitting there saying: "What's Hilde Knef studying at the moment? I should like to see something, Herr Meixner." He looks at me, grins, can't fool him. Not blushing too much, I innocently inspect the portrait of Goebbels; profile, slanting fox-ears, jutting back of the head—innocently, I inspect our patron.

Sundays are despised: no Babelsberg, no school, no Bongers, no Meixner. I go to Wilmersdorf, to Stepfather, nail up cardboard where there used to be glass, collect letters from Mother and Manfred; we sit silently in the cellar, have nothing much to say to each other any more. "Recite something from one of those plays—that's what you're doing, isn't it?" He wants to take part, I won't let him.

It is December 1943. Mother writes that it's cold in the

garage she's living in, that the relatives keep the illegal butter for themselves, that she has to break the ice with a hammer in the mornings, that the school's open only two days a week, that she's applied for a nightgown at the Uelzen town hall, that a mouse ran into the trap, got out again, and then cried and died by her bedside. "And the bombers —day and night they fly over on their way to Berlin. One of them crashed in the next village and the farmers went for the pilot and beat him to death. I am sending you some sugarbeet, hope it arrives. Tried to telephone you after the last big raid, wanted to know if you'd lived through it— after trying for twelve hours I was put through to a funeral parlor in Tegel. I pray to HIM every night to protect you. P.S.: Have you been to see Grandfather?"

Manfred is wounded, in the stomach; he is lying in a military hospital on the Black Sea. "It happened as we were trying to take the Orscha runway," he writes. "I'm recovering but you have to watch that you don't get sent to a different battalion on release, later on. It's strange here, at the southeastern tip of Europe; the Greeks were here, the Romans, the Goths, and the Venetians, and now us. A white bed, a bathtub, the whistle of a railway engine have become the supreme achievements of a whole civilization. Where are the operas of Mozart, Gluck, and Flotow? I think back on evenings in the Oden forest with my parents, the mountain road, the timbered cottages of my youth. . . . P.S.: There's a boathouse on Wannsee, the manager's name is Kupke—go there and take my canoe when it gets warm."

Shortly after six on Monday morning, the train marked "Potsdam" would roll into Westkreuz station and I would feel much better. It was a short walk through a wood from Babelsberg station to the studio. To the right, in a clearing, there was a prisoner-of-war camp: Englishmen, who looked at us, who were looked at by us.

Right after New Year's came the raid when the bomb, the decisive one, fell on Bernhardstrasse and the Wilmersdorf station. One Sunday morning I wound up at Wilfried Frass's in Zehlendorf. He was an assistant director at UFA, a cheerful Viennese who loved Berlin unconditionally, with or without houses. I couldn't have called Bongers, didn't want to—everyone was bombed out sooner or later and it was taboo to expect help, an unwritten law that everyone adhered to. This didn't apply, however, to strangers or new-found friends—why, I don't know. The Berlin-addict had hot water, I could bathe; to eat there was nothing. He took me up to a studio apartment two floors above, with "Dippert" on the name plate. She was small and round, moved quickly, spoke quickly—a rubber ball, solid rubber. And her name was Alike. Wilfried told of the New Year tragedy; she hugged me emotionally and said, "Oh my poor child, they're cheating you of your youth." I wasn't used to so much feeling, it overpowered me, bowled me over. She pulled me into another room. In it there was a huge drawing table with countless bottles of ink, colors, pens, brushes, cups, tins, very neat, exact, I felt I was back with Klemke. Behind it all sat a lean man who got up bleakly and with difficulty; this was Fritz from Munich. He waved his long arm about until he finally encountered my hand, shook it silently, commiseratingly. Alike said breathlessly, "We have to help people, the same could happen to us tomorrow, isn't that so? We've got a room that we hardly ever use." Fritz shot her a glinting glance which she chose to overlook. She sloshed water into the midday stew and exclaimed: "Now there's enough for everyone!" Fritz hadn't said anything, just looked desolate. Alike made up a bed; cupboard space was no problem since I didn't have any clothes; she showed me the toilet, the bath, talked incessantly: "You'll feel at home with us all right, there's a shelter in the yard, and the cellar, of course, but we don't go down because of the hot-water pipes—oh yes, there is some sometimes—I've always wanted a daughter and now I've got you, don't listen to Fritz"—he still hadn't opened his mouth—"he's a bit slow on the uptake, well there you are, he's just not a Berliner that's all, but deep down he's good really and he'd like to help but he doesn't know how to go about it."

That night in the shelter, during a lull, I was introduced to the community. Our next-door neighbor worked in the box office of a movie theater in Wilmersdorf. After the all-clear she took Alike aside and said, "I wouldn't take in an actress if I were you, after all I'm in the business, I know all about them—they're unreliable, goings-on with men and that sort of thing." Alike repeated it jubilantly as we rubbed our frozen feet.

Every three months we gave a public performance of scenes from the classics. Flushed with stage fright, we jerked around Meixner like chicks around a hen. He smoked, subdued all anxieties with a "Yes yes," sat down and yelled, "When you're ready!"

And there they sat, the heads of UFA, Tobis, Terra, Berlin Films, Prague Films, and sometimes a theater manager. They sat there with friendly-jovial or bored-arrogant, with soon-be-over expressions; behind them sat the teachers, in front of them Bongers. I was fifth. A blond, snub-nosed boy was Ferdinand, I his Luise. We did the poison-in-the-lemonade scene from *Kabale*. And then it happened—the same friendly feeling blossomed in my stomach as with Armgard in Weise's classroom. I heard sniffling, and throats being cleared; then I fell down dead, noticed that my dress was up high, felt a draft on my thighs and elsewhere, the deceased discreetly adjusted her apparel. But they still hadn't laughed, indeed they were clapping. Only Liebeneiner said later, "Just because one's dead, it doesn't mean the play's over, my dear."

Kaminsky had aged. She circled around me and said, "My dear child: it was lovely and very moving, only you'll never play the classics, unthinkable with the dreadful *s* and those end-syllables"—she stopped, looked at the wall, looked at me, dabbed her nose, dabbed her eyes, gathered strength. "We shall have to work, work very hard." Gave hope where hope was in vain.

Röseler embraced me firmly with both arms, hummed, sang, "My dear child, it was touching, yes I have to admit, I was moved—but the voice, dear God, the voice . . . it's too deep, wrongly placed, and hoarse. We have to work on that voice, work, work, and work again."

Meixner smoked, grinned, said nothing.

Bongers pierced me with her blue rays ("My eyes may be small but nothing escapes them," she often said), observed me through her detectors: "Liebeneiner cried, Jahn and Jonen cried, and I did too. That's enough to start with. And the Deutsche Theater's interested, by the way." For the second time, I felt I should be happy.

It was a Wednesday; it was cold, the sun shone, lighting ruins and railway tracks that stuck up from their beds like raised index fingers. It took hours before I finally arrived at Friedrichstrasse station. I ran into the Deutsche Theater and asked for Herr Karchow, who was to audition me. I was hungry, as always, and afraid, as always. All the charwomen of the neighborhood were at work in the rehearsal room, clanking pails, blowing their noses furiously; they were against newcomers. Karchow said: "You may begin now, please." I looked at the chairs, he said they wouldn't disturb me. *Joan of Arc* performed on a freight-loading platform couldn't have been worse. I dried up, started again from the beginning only to hear the same pail-handle rattle at the same place as before, vacant stare, dry throat— dry again. Gretchen's prison scene was a silent-film performance—that Karchow engaged me despite it all made me wander around in a mystified daze until the day I was handed the part assigned to me in the next production. I was to walk on about six times without saying anything, then once with a revolver, whispering a frightened "Hands up." Bongers came to the first night; I bellowed my line, doing neither myself nor the play any good. Karlheinz Schroth played the lead; every night on the stairs he looked at me in surprise and said, "Well, little girl?" smiled and forgot me till the next time. He never noticed me on the stage—I wore a mask in the only scene I had with him, the once-daily, much-longed-for "Hands up."

I rush to the station after the performance. At the Friedrichstrasse bunker they're lined up in front of closed doors, burdened with bags and bottles, everything but the kitchen sink, awaiting bombs and sirens. I rush in the hope of reaching the train and Zehlendorf before the inevitable raid, barge into a not very young, not very big, rather inconspicuous, rather gruff-looking man, untidy-tidy hair, tidy appearance. Murmur, "Sorry," gallop on.

Hilde Jansen, with whom I share dressing room and make-up table, giggles next evening, says, "You knocked Demandowsky for a loop last night." "Who?" "Demandowsky, the head of Tobis Films." Hilde was married, husband in Russia, and he was a friend of my victim's. "Do you want to come? He's showing a film on Saturday night, a new one, he's picking us up after the show."

The Tobis offices were on the other side of Friedrichstrasse station, near the Admiral's Palace Theater. The studios were out in Grunewald. That was all I knew or wanted to know—I was with UFA after all, the big one; looked down on Tobis, the little one.

The car is waiting at the stage door. Make: charcoal burner; fuel: coke. Standing next to it there's a thin chimneysweep. Hilde and I get in, he follows suit. I'm excited— haven't been in a car since the Grand Ball fiasco in Lichterfelde. He switches on the ignition, gets out, stokes the oven which is sticking out of the trunk, gets in, switches, gets out again, stokes. Thirty minutes later, our stoker-driver says: "Won't go." The film was being shown at Demandowsky's house and that was in Dahlem, ten miles away; we take an underground train, then an elevated one, walk through parks and finally come to Gelfertstrasse; the film is already running, the master of the house displeased. On the screen Hans Albers is playing the trumpet and singing a song about Paloma, Ilse Werner comes on, she's wearing my dress—UFA had got sick of my track-suit trousers and had presented me with a dress from the studio wardrobe; she's up there, I'm down here, same dress. Then comes Hilde Hildebrandt, sings "Beim erstenmal, da tut's noch weh," followed closely by the siren. He has a shelter in the garden, a reinforced one with wooden beams and electric light and two benches. The flak bleats in the distance, then there's a gurgle and a buzzing noise, the beams grind, slant, straighten up again, the light flickers, goes dim, goes out. A flashlight inspects the beams: sand and mortar trickling, gushing down. Again the gurgle, again the buzzing but different this time, long, drawn-out, like a child's whistle; the beams grind again, slant again, stay slanted, someone shouts: "Out!" We squat on the stairs with our mouths open. Shrapnel chirrups through the trees, grrr-grrr—cheep-cheep, severing branches. This goes on for an hour, two hours. What are they looking for in Dahlem? I ask myself; there's nothing but villas, fir trees, and duck ponds. Then it gets hot. I know that feeling, don't like it, and holler, "Incendiaries—it might be phosphorus"; at night the English dropped phosphorus, every child knew that. Head down in the regulation-sized bucket of water, then the blanket, wrap it around, watch your step, out. The lawn's on fire, the house opposite too, and it's daylight over the city, pink-smoky. Doodoo doodah of the fire-engines. All-clear—first wave's gone. Warning—second's on its way.

At dawn we're clearing away the shrapnel when the chimney-sweep-stoker-driver appears and grumpily reports that the car's a write-off. Demandowsky sits there in his windowless living room and suddenly bursts out laughing—oh, I say to myself, he can laugh too. "He's making the same face he made at the première," he says. There'd been a film première: Grumpy is supposed to pick him up, doesn't arrive. Hours later he comes home: beer fumes, shaky hands. "Where's the car? Where were you?" He stands there swaying, takes a deep breath, lets it out again, says: "Well, it happened at the corner—he comes tearing across, doesn't see a thing, being drunk, and then, well, crash bang wallop and all that sort of thing, must have been a simple sort of fellow, no relatives or nothing."

Telephone rings, Tobis in the Friedrichstrasse is still there. I call out what about Nollendorfplatz, Wilmersdorf?— I'm suddenly afraid for Grandfather, Stepfather—no, it was the railway junction and the Tiergarten and Kurfürstendamm and the Zoo and Potsdamer. I say thank you, have to go now, say it as though the visiting hour were up.

Where do you live?

In Zehlendorf.

I'll take you on the bicycle.

He pedals away with me on the carrier. At No. 5 Teltowerdamm he gets off, helps me off, keeps my hand, raises and kisses it, says: "It's sad that I have to go to Prague tomorrow." Alike and Fritz are awake and worried, ask questions. Alike makes ersatz coffee lovingly called *muckefuck*, sits down on the bed, says dismally: Fair maiden, fair maiden, that's no way to carry on.

They trusted me. They spoke of Brecht, of Mann, of Wedekind and Schnitzler, told me about writers whose books were no longer available, initiated me into the mysteries of forbidden astrology, numerology, spoke of Elisabeth Bergner, Walbrook, Pallenberg, and Reinhardt. At night they listened to the BBC. It crackled and squeaked and was mostly incoherent but it gave them hope, a sense of freedom, of protest in a time without protest. They trusted me implicitly. Stepfather related that Hannelore from Varzinerstrasse had reported her mother. Her father was in a prison camp in Russia; her mother was picked up and put in a prison camp in Germany; Hannelore was in a Nazi youth hostel, cherished and revered. And Stepfather said, "Do you remember '36?" Our class had been taken to the Olympics stadium, out of Westend, and Hitler had made a speech. It was hot—"Hitler weather," they called it, the sun shone on his every public appearance—we drank cocoa through straws, sticky hands, stains, cocoa-brown on Führer-brown. I saw flags and backs of heads, was miles away. At dinner I said, "It was a wonderful day, I saw the Führer." My mother stared at me, snapped: "Have you taken leave of your senses?" Stepfather shot her a warning glance and said gently, "But that's a grand thing for the child, isn't it?"

He looked sick now, was thin, shaky, longed for wife and child, lived in one room at a butcher's and went every day to the police station in the hope of getting a travel permit to Uelzen, even if only for three days. When I visited him briefly, he stayed behind his counter and whispered, "Don't come too near, I cough up blood in the night."

Bongers rushed into rehearsal, said: "You're to stay here tonight, child—for tests." For what or for whom, you didn't ask. You stayed. They shot until midnight; I slept in a dressing room and didn't rack my brains over why they had shot silent profiles and that stupid scene over and over again. Goebbels, patron of the film industry, had invited me to dinner, privately, in order to "get to know me personally." Bongers had intercepted the invitation; for her this meant action-stations, danger on all sides; clairvoyant, knowing, suspecting—avoid catastrophes in a world full of catastrophes, the small ones in any event. She informed the Ministry that the favored Fräulein was unfortunately not available—tests, new film of great importance to the war-effort after all, impossible to present the students except on the screen, sorry. I learned this much later. That night I slept in my dressing room.

The next evening on the train I'm squashed in between crumpled passengers and the man next to me babbles, "I'm a production manager at UFA, seen you at the school and the canteen, we're planning a new film, wonderful part in it for you, could we meet tomorrow night to discuss it?" When I told Bongers she started sparking and said that he was a third or fourth assistant, one of the ones who yell "On your marks" to the extras. She sent for him and said the following: "I am informed that you are unfit for military service. I am also informed that not many men of your age are fortunate enough to be in this position. We are not training the girls at this school to be whores. Bear this in mind and pass it on!"

To me: "You are in a profession, or rather you soon will be, which men and those who would like to be known as such misunderstand. Learn one thing: you choose the men, not the other way around. And something else: never say yes from exhaustion." I went red, redder, was afraid I'd burst.

On Sunday Alike and Fritz accompany me to the lakes. We drift around in circles until I learn to handle Manfred's canoe, then glide on to Griebnitz and Stölpchensee, and squat under the weeping willows, Fritz in a hat and a waistcoat, Alike in her suit with the gray, frayed blouse, the only one she has left.

I stay on the water alone one night; tied up to a buoy on Griebnitzsee, I lie in the gently rocking canoe and look up at the stars. Frogs croak, sirens wail, white fingers feel around the sky, grope the stars away. A plane enters the searchlight-cross, tries to escape, falls apart, burning. There's a noise like an organ crescendo, a whistling, and suddenly I'm in the water, gasping, looking for the canoe; it's upside down. One, two, three bombs hit the lake, I scream help, fountains shoot up, the water quakes, the canoe leaps up, slaps down again, I turn it over, hang on, wail, climb in. The next formation's flying over; they hum, rumble, sound friendly. I reach the boathouse at dawn, tottering, midsummernight spirit of adventure cured once and for all.

The play at the Deutsche Theater dragged wearily to an end. We rarely got as far as intermission anyway; more often than not the sirens went off before I could deliver my "Hands up." The stage manager received a telephone call in advance; he could work out roughly when he would have to drop the curtain and the audience silently file off to the nearest cellar.

The play's supposed to come off at the end of July. On the twentieth, I am sitting in a surprisingly empty train. At Friedrichstrasse station there are SS, tanks, military police—known as leash-dogs—roughly demanding identity papers, destination, why, address, and the like. They say I should go to the theater. I thread my way through the tanks and the glowering SS. The wardrobe mistress is standing at the stage door, trembling. I ask what's wrong, she doesn't answer, goes on trembling. "Where are the others?" "Not here," she rattles. A policeman comes up and says, "Go down to the cellar." We sit in the cellar and don't know why. Three hours later I look out at the street. The SS have gone, one tank is creeping by. I walk down to the station, no trains to be seen, no stationmaster, no one pushing and shoving—moonland scape. An SS man runs up to me and shouts: "Go down to the cellar!" Thinking it must be poison gas or something similar, I look for the nearest cellar. They are all sitting there silently, eyes lowered, just sitting there. "Was there a warning?" I whisper into the gloom. No answer. Hours pass, then the door is flung open and somebody roars: "Papers!" I show mine, hope for a word, an explanation. The man says, "Stay here," the door slams, silence again. In the morning I arrive at Babelsberg—there hadn't been time to go home—and here too they're all dumbstruck, not prepared to discuss it. Meixner grins: "Have you heard the latest? The telephone's been renamed Selb, the Führer's decreed that all foreign words be eliminated, erased—just like the towns," he adds suicidally. Only when I get home to BBC-educated Alike do I learn of the generals and the assassination which never took place.

"What'll happen to the school when the war's over?" I ask. Meixner looks at Bongers, Bongers looks at Meixner. "Over" has no meaning for me. "Hinkel wants to see us all at nine in the morning," she says. We sit in rows, teachers, students, Bongers, in the projection room of the Reichsfilmkammer on the corner of Kurfürstendamm and Uhlandstrasse. Goebbel's lackey stands there in braid and ribbons; I catch scraps of Final Victory, Need Every Man Woman and Child, War Effort, Total War, The Hour Has Come, We'll Show the Imperialist Warmongers, One for All, All for One, Nation Arise Storm Break Loose, Heil Hitler.

"May I visit you, Frau Bongers?" She doesn't answer, doesn't hear.

SEVEN

We are now "factory workers," painting luminous numbers for night-fighter instrument panels. Meixner has been called up. On Sundays we are sent to the barracks at Gardelegen or Ratenow. We sing the songs Bartsch taught us, sing them pitifully, don't do her justice. A star turns up, too, one Sunday, but refuses to go on after hearing us; the soldiers are thankful-deaf, clap, are happy not to be out there at the front. Mondays back to the luminous dials.

A "Fräulein Knef, telephone," interrupts our daubing. It's Bongers, she says, "Engel wants you, I showed him your tests, you start shooting tomorrow, six o'clock make-up, Babelsberg."

Erich Engel is sitting in his director's chair gnawing a ham roll, the ham's hanging over the edge. Käthe Dorsch is standing beside him, Rudolf Forster behind him. They look me over. I see a vanishing roll, see ham and butter, swallow saliva. Engel chews absently, gazes absently. He finishes the roll, takes a cigarette, the assistant gives him a light, he sips coffee, strokes his slender bald head, says, "Please." The studio hooter goes qwark qwark qwark, the clapper-boy yells, "Two hundred and thirty take one," Dorsch gives the cue, Forster gives the cue, I say my line—"Mama," I say to Dorsch. "Print," Engel says, gets up, goes out. I become a question mark—was it good? the question mark asks . . . but they're already on the next scene. An assistant comes and says, "You won't be needed before lunch." I have a dressing room with a sofa, and I have a script. *Fahrt ins Glück* (Journey to Happiness) is the printed title; underneath, in handwriting, "Daughter's Part." Six weeks' schedule, four in Babelsberg, two in Austria. I'm skeptical. A year ago I'd had one day's shooting on a film called *Träumerei*, directed by Harald Braun. Hilde Krahl had played the piano, as Clara Schumann, and I, as a Swedish princess at court, had had to listen; Braun had thrown his arms

around me and exclaimed, "Delightful, simply delightful."
Three months later we met at Babelsberg station: "Oh
there you are, my child"—he looked depressed—"yes, well
we had to cut the Swedish sequence, film much too long,
now don't get sad about it, your life's just beginning."

As usual I had neither meat, bread, nor any other sort of
coupons, walked around the studios during the lunch-hour,
past the deserted school, felt deserted, bombed-out in the
company of the well-housed. Meixner's classics had been
home, the first since Zossen and Grandfather, since the
apple diet. Friendship, fellowship, brotherhood, sisterhood,
unity, community—I didn't need them, didn't want them.
Childhood pains childhood fear dead buried forgotten
since Meixner, Bongers, Gretchen Luise Ophelia Viola and
Hero. I didn't take part, didn't communicate, was a lone
wolf, unfaithful, independent—except in the afternoons,
the afternoons when I had become a "juvenile lead with
character possibilities," as my contract with UFA read.

I sensed, tasted, wanted beauty.

I hated the smell of burning, the sweet fatty smell of the
buried, not yet dug out, hated familiarity, customer's familiarity behind Stepfather's counter, beery smell, glue pot;
the one with gold teeth who screeched, "You can see it's a
girl now, look at her jersey, a couple of lemons"; hated the
back yard, rats at the garbage pails, lavatory on the stairs,
hated fear-for-life fear-of-death faces in the cellars, trembling chins folded hands, the "what have I done to deserve
this" moaners who only yesterday had had such big
mouths—"That'll be the day"—and then trampled over
their wives because it was burning and the ceiling was cav-
ing in together with the twelve apartments above it; loud
envy, gloating over other people's misfortunes, the loudmouths, the greed, the joviality, the "uncles" with hairy
hands who felt under your skirt and hissed "Woe betide
you if you tell your mother, you busted my glasses and she
can't pay, not with her shoeshop"—they'd trodden on
them, the nickel granny specs, thought you were dumb,
made you frightened, threatened, the slobberers with wife
and six grandchildren. Hated the hospitals, the wards, the
groans in the night, the Lord Professor, the swine who
operates on your jaw forgets anesthetic yells "Hold your
tongue, pull yourself together, stupid wretch!"—you're
lying in the vomit, the nurse grins and slaps an ice bag on
the sound, grins as the blood runs from nose to vomit. I

hate the bugs in summer, peeling wallpaper and greasy doors, lighted twists of newspaper to smoke the bugs out. I hate that look, the leery smeary one on smug faces so indispensable to the home front, with fire bucket and helmet; they look you up and down—"Try her later on, they're soft after the raid, the girls"—shit their pants at the first landmine, foul up the cellar, call on God for most personal protection, want their smug existence extended, want to go on swilling it back, tucking it away, easing the bowels, looking leery, smeary.

I hate, hated, hate.
I sensed, tasted, wanted beauty.

I'm standing in the corridor holding the suitcase with my dresses for the film. The train is full, couldn't be fuller: soldiers, policemen, officers, and a few civilians. No glass in the windows, drafty, soot gets in your eyes. The engine crawls into a wood and stops, a dragon seeking camouflage; it buries its head in the sand, can't see so can't be seen. There are fighters overhead. Two of them come down, pretend they're hawks, peek through the branches, go brr brrr and hurry off; are back again with friends. The man next to me says bugger this and climbs through the window; he drops to the tracks, jerks his legs forward, his arms backwards, shouts, red gruel wells from his coat. They all struggle to the door and jump down, crawl under. I'm under the bumpers and think to myself: if it moves off now I'll be mincemeat. It doesn't move, the engine's on fire, hawk family flown. Groans and moans all around me, doodoo doodah—fire engines on their way. I walk over and sit down on the embankment, look the other way. I start to walk along the tracks and come to a station several hours later, ask where I am. North of Nüremberg. Twenty hours on the train and still north of Nüremberg. A special train chugs in at four in the morning, chugs on and finally takes a breather in Salzburg. I look at the houses, houses with roofs, houses with windows and balconies full of flowers and say isn't Austria beautiful. Standing there on platform 2 I say isn't Austria beautiful. A man with a red cap and red flag turns and stares at me, goes flag-red, petunia-lilac and shouts: "You mean Ostmark,* don't you?"

---

* After the Nazi takeover in 1938 the name of Austria (Osterreich) was changed to Ostmark.

The village street in Schörfling smells of stable, cow, and milk, thick yellow milk, not blue, decreamed, demilked milk. Lake Atter is lapping, has nothing to do with war, lives and laps with its frogs and fish. We start shooting: the mother's (Dorsch's) past has a bad influence on the child (me)—she used to sing in a murky bar, that was her past. But toward the end, many a true word is spoken, one sees the light, conciliatory insights are exchanged and breakfast is served on the sunny terrace in a civilized manner, crafty Grandmother warmly dropping pearls of jolly wisdom. I had a temperature but didn't know why, my back hurt but I kept it to myself—the Berlin factory threw a long shadow.

Alike writes in Alike-language: Fitti (Fritz) is crunched (unhappy) because of an eye infection, she's lost the door-opener (key), is cooking marma (marmalade) between raids, E.v.D. (Demandowsky) called twice and asked for Martl (me), requested address. I see him standing beside his bicycle in front of the door in the moonlight: cool deep-set eyes, straight nose, fine soft uncontrolled petulant mouth, light flat hair; he stood there smiling and said, "You are sylphlike, yes, sylphlike." I didn't understand, didn't dare to ask, had learned not to, afraid of ridicule, had learned that knowledge, general knowledge, was a guarantee seal, membership badge; gaps were not admitted, should have been filled by the time you were fifteen, you concede something by asking so don't, never ask what when who why. I see him before me, unfunny beside a funny bicycle, a gentleman, one with authority, who doesn't need effects to be a gentleman, who controls panic, smiles away anxieties, who thinks where others are thoughtless. A mentor whom I can perhaps ask what sylphlike means.

After three weeks the location work is finished, the floor manager distributes travel permits, letters of confirmation, UFA passes, tickets, identity cards, registration and departure forms.

Berlin has grown older, deranged, destroyed. Another fourteen days' shooting in Babelsberg, another fourteen days' grace from the factory. Erich Engel smokes, drinks coffee, is reticent, indifferent, inaccessible, strokes forehead, pate, gives directions courteously, softly. I'm not allowed to see rushes, the theater's out of bounds. The war is not discussed; not in the canteen, not in the make-up room, not in the studio.

Alike stares at astrological hieroglyphs every night, adds and reckons, murmurs crunchedly, "We'll be separated, Martlchen, you've got a Mars square, it's awful, we're entering a horrorful period, my poor child." She gives me a "what a shame about you" look. "Isn't that right, Fitti, horrorful times." Fritz wore a broad black band around his eyes, saw nothing, said nothing, a silent Cassandra. The infection had gotten worse, he couldn't take the bandage off at all any more, we led him to the cellar, sat him down, guided him up again, laid him on the bed, he said neither thank you nor please, was deaf and blind and wanted to be.

My temperature rose again, the doctor said kidney inflammation, septic tonsils, you need fats, fruit, and that sort of thing; he didn't say malnutrition, that would have been defeatist.

Manfred came with a big shapeless package under his arm; he'd brought me his mummy case, the one from Grolmannstrasse. "He's to protect you," he said. "May he protect you against the things to come, the things that surely must come. I have great faith in you. I have to report back tomorrow, I'm being sent back to my old regiment, or at least what's left of it." He was thin, the rough, gray uniform flapped around him, he was young and old at the same time. "Does your wound still trouble you?" "No, not much, I'm thankful it wasn't my eyes." He caught his breath, looked at Fritz in dismay. In the hall he said, "It's good to see you again, you're so positive, so full of plans, you give me hope again, at least a little."

"What shall I do with the mummy?" I asked Alike. "Is it worth anything?" She said it was. I lugged it down to the cellar every night, annoyed. One day I unpacked it; a smiling, peaceful face looked at me, looked away, seemed to grow serious, seemed to smile again.

Trains are limited to those for whom travel is a professional necessity; inspectors check papers at the ticket office, on the train, on the platform—and yet, one evening, Grandfather is standing at the door, he's walked from Nollendorfplatz to Zehlendorf, some nine or ten miles, stands there smiling, dusty-white, upright, with a paper bag in his hand, and says, "Good morning, my child." He goes up the stairs in his squeaky shoes, shakes Alike's hand at length, sits down on a kitchen chair, opens his paper bag and says, "First you must eat." He has brought rolls and dripping, doesn't say where he got them, only, "Now eat." He wants to leave right away, doesn't want to be a burden. Alike persuades him to stay, he refuses to take Alike's or Fritz's or my bed, sleeps on two chairs, taps three times on the back of the chair with his toe, wants to get up at three, to avoid inconveniencing us. "Have you heard from Mother?" he asks. "Yes." I show him her last letter: "There was a loud knock at the garage door toward morning, I went out and called into the darkness, nobody answered, and I thought something must have happened to you"—he looks up at me as if to say: flights of fantasy, thinks better of it, sighs and goes on reading—"the bombers fly over us toward Berlin almost every hour. A hedgehopper shot at Heinz on his way to school. They'd learned to zigzag at school and that saved him—that's all they're taught now, to live through it. Make yourself scarce before the Russians come. They're fighting in East Prussia. Hamburg and Münster and have been wiped out. Aunt Hertha gave me some bay leaves—if only I had something to cook with them."

"I'm making a film," I tell him.

"Yes, my child."

"With Dorsch and Forster."

"Of course."

He'd known from the beginning, is irritated that fame and recognition are denied me, that I'm being held up by the war. We sit together in the cellar at night; he holds my hand, is calm, sits reverently as if at a concert at the seashore, shoots scornful glances at those crouching against the wall. "Stay at Alike's—you can't walk all the way back." "Oh yes I can, besides I sleep better in my own bed." In the morning, before leaving for the studio, I kiss him, embrace him suddenly, feeling that I've betrayed him, deserted him, that I must protect him. I embrace him, kiss him, and say Grampa. He holds me at arm's length, studies me for a moment, and says: "God be with you, my child," goes off calmly in his squeaking shoes, with his erect, steady stance.

I'm at the drugstore on Teltowerdamm that evening to buy Fritz's eyedrops. The woman's not listening. I say, "The eyedrops for Dippert, please." She goes into the back room, I hear sniffling and blowing, she comes back with a red nose, still sniffling a little. "Oh yes, the eyedrops." I make no comment, somebody's always crying, the son has been killed at the front, the daughter in a raid, son—husband—grandchild; daughter—mother—sister. She gives me the drops, I open the door, the bell above me does a stupid dingadingding, she calls after me: "The Russians entered Warsaw this morning." Is she crazy to tell me that? I think to myself, she listens to the BBC, she's so frightened of the Russians that she forgets to be frightened of the Germans.

Stars are waiting at Babelsberg station, the not-so-big ones: the big ones: Marika Rökk, Ilse Werner, Hilde Krahl, waiting patiently. The train's not full, people don't rush, jostle, push, any more. Swinging in front of me there's a man with spiky hair standing on end, blown high by an invisible dryer, held there, caught up like crumpled antennae; melodramatically he rolls his eyes, big comic eyes, and brandishes a long wooden spoon. "I'm bombed out and what do the damn fools give me? They give me a wooden spoon, how do you like that?" He turns, expecting a reaction, has spoken in general, addressing the driver, the passengers, has launched a general appeal. "It's a fact— they gave me a wooden spoon." He holds it up, as though at an auction. "What am I supposed to do with a wooden spoon, stir up the shit?" Those present turn to stone, gaze fixedly at the floor or the horizon, are absent, couldn't possibly have heard since they're miles away. He laughs a merry goat-laugh and nails me to the door with his index finger. "What's your name?" he asks loudly. At every *s* he produces a sound like a bottle of lemonade being opened in the hot sun. "Hilde Knef," I whisper. "You an actress? I need a girl like you, yes"—the bottle fizzes again—"a girl just like you, my name's Barlog, Boleslaw, I'm making a picture for Terra Films—*The Green Salon, Green Salon* —lovely, harmless little film but enormously important for the war effort, oh you'd be amazed how important." He'll talk himself to the gallows, I think to myself; I think of Bongers, but he doesn't look like one of the could-we-meet-to-discuss-it-tonight directors. I stutter something about being at the UFA school. "Ah well, I'll have a chat with Bongers. . . . Do you always take this train? Then I'll see you tomorrow night—when the bloody war, this whole goddamn nonsense"—this was a siphon exploding—"is over, I'm going to start a theater and if you're any use you can come and play—you simply come along and we'll put on decent theater again at last."

At Westkreuz we got out to change trains. "You'll be hearing from me," he yelled. If you're still alive and kicking, I thought to myself, with that lip it'll be a wonder if anyone hears from you much longer.

We shot the last scenes for *Fahrt ins Glück* the next day. The sirens wailed at Zehlendorf station, I ran along to the Teltowerdamm and found Alike and Fritz in the garden shelter. "E.v.D. telephoned, he's showing a film tonight and wants to pick you up," said Alike disapprovingly.

"What have you got against him? You don't even know him."

"He's a Nazi."

"How do you know?"

"He wouldn't be head of Tobis otherwise."

"Liebeneiner's head of UFA and he's not a Nazi."

"He's an exception."

"Who told you that?"

"One gets to hear things," she said grandly.

The movie cashier was sitting opposite us staring offended at her suitcases, sitting there neatly in her head-scarf and gloves looking offended. "From her, I suppose," I muttered. An argument flared up but was interrupted by flak, bombs, the lights going out. On the stairs Fritz suddenly said: "Alike's right." We stopped and stared at him, Alike from the right, I from the left. It was a weighty speech; it hit the bull's-eye, took on meaning, being the first in weeks. There was a ring at the door; he was standing there saying, "I hope you got my message." I said yes. Went along. They're beginning to behave like parents—have to put a stop to that. I went along, defiant-gay. Duwe, the driver, was downstairs with his charcoal-burner, we drove along the streets to Dahlem.

I woke up, saw swaying branches, light-gray sky, it was Sunday morning, he said, "I wonder what time it is."

"Ten to nine." It splurted out of me.

He turned over and awkwardly fished his wrist watch from the bedside table: "So it is."

"I've got a built-in clock," I said and grinned proudly.

"You're a child." He pulls at my middle finger and says, "You're a child and you have beautiful hands, but your nails—like a boy's." He smiles understandingly, gets up, doors slam, water gushes.

I look at cupboards, built-in, orderly ones, the whole length of the wall; one of them is open, on the inside a neat, typewritten card held at the top and bottom by neat drawing pins: 16 dresses (summer), 10 blouses (white). Underneath, in handwriting: one blouse (blue), one blouse (green). Must belong to Lena, his wife. She'd been in a film I'd seen, she was beautiful, famous, had children, was evacuated. I didn't care one way or the other. Marriage was equal to bankruptcy. I had asked Alike: Will I have a career or do I have to marry? She had stared strenuously at my horoscope wheel and said cautiously: You won't have to marry if you don't want to. Thank God, I'd said. Funny that I'd known the time, I thought. He stood in the doorway and said, "Will you roll me a cigarette? The ends are in that jug there." I rolled but it fell apart, tobacco crumbs on the pillow and carpet; he looked at me reproachfully. I went red, slut in an orderly household; went to the bathroom, looked at the bidet, had no idea that it was one, turned the tap on, got drenched from head to foot, walls and ceiling dripping. "What are you doing all this time?' he calls from downstairs. "I washed my hair." "Good God," he murmurs.

He was sitting at the table stirring his tea, stood up as he heard me coming down the stairs, stared at my hair in dismay, stared at Duwe who was clinking glasses in the background, held the chair for me, sat down, and said, "Good God, why did you wash your hair?" I'll have to say something, I thought to myself, but nothing occurred to me. There was butter and marmalade. He ate quickly, pleasantly, looked about him rather shyly, busily, looked over me, through me, already occupied with his day, uncertain, unclear how to fit me into it. Slate-gray eyes and that lovely petulant, sarcastic mouth.

I drop my spoon and ask, "Where are the spoons?" I pull the drawer open—too far; knives, forks, big and small, tongs, carving knife, poultry shears, thump jump clatter around my feet. There's a ring at the door, Duwe goes out, returns and announces: "Madame." And there she is, a Russian grand duchess with black, slanting eyes, wearing a muff and a hat with a veil; she extracts a ringed hand from the muff, stretches it out in front of her, and says, "Good morning, my son." He wipes his mouth with his napkin, kisses the outstretched hand. Says, "Mamma, I should like to present to you Fräulein Knef." I stand up, don't know whether to take shake or kiss the hand, cautiously decide to do nothing, stand there sandwiched between chair and table. "Don't let me disturb you," she says. "Lord, the

trains are unpunctual—exasperating, and full to boot. I
can't understand it, no one can get a travel permit and yet
the trains are overflowing and on a Sunday at that. Unbelievable. Sister Amalia became quite ill." Sister Amalia
emerges behind her; white cap, white hair, timid smile
prays forgiveness, Red Cross badge under her chin, white
collar, white cuffs. The Grand Duchess notices the heap of
cutlery and says, "What's all this?" He squints and says, "I
pulled the drawer out a little too far." She claps her hands:
"Oh Duwe, do clear that up and set two more places,
please."

"I have to go now," I say. I was wearing my silk stockings, with runs, darned, the only pair I had. How do I get
out without her seeing them, I think to myself, and fold my
feet under the table. "You can't do that, my dear child,
you'll catch your death with that wet hair, won't she,
Ewald?" He winces at "Ewald."

I take his bicycle and ride off, pedal around the Grunewald lake, up and down the Argentinischeallee, on to
Krumme Lanke. I don't want to share, don't want to let
anyone share with me, don't want the mother, the Red
Cross auntie, don't want butter for breakfast, life together;
want to be alone, have house butter breakfast marmalade
alone, want to be host, not guest.

In the evening I ride on to the Teltowerdamm. Alike's
moody. I've got a temperature, sore throat, go to bed, factory tomorrow. I take out Father's picture, the yellowing
one with the donkey ears. I look at him. What's wrong? I
ask. Nothing, the picture answers. You're proud, and right
you are. I'll look after you, it says. He has the same mouth,
yes exactly the same and the eyes are similar—deep-set.
Yes, there's a similarity.

He calls again two days later. "Come along with me," he
says, "I looked at your tests, you're sublimely talented."
Sublimely, must remember that, lovely word: sublimely.
"We're about to start a new film and we haven't cast the
lead yet—a pleasant girl, very young, turn-of-the-century
story. You're to make a test tomorrow."

They all jump up as he enters the studio, click their
heels, bow, and say, "Herr von Demandowsky, allow me,"
pull up chairs, make streaks on the floor. He beckons to the
make-up man: "Why is she made up?" The make-up man
stutters, panic in his eyes.

"Do you know him?" they ask afterwards. "No," I say.

In the evening he winds up the gramophone, plays Bach, is uncommunicative. After the all-clear: "I went to the Ministry, the film has been canceled. The war's coming closer."

Dr. Rode, the throat specialist, lives at Lehninerplatz. People are running about excitedly at the Zoo railway station. A man stands on tiptoe, stretches up above the others, and calls out hoarsely: "Air raid." There's a raid more often than not, what's he getting excited about? Three thousand are said to be on their way to Berlin, 3000 Americans. The sirens screech, I shove and jostle my way to the bunker, the door is shut, full right up. They're droning through the bright blue autumn sky, perfect triangle on perfect triangle, clear-cut patterns, very high, unattainable; smudges appear beside them, little black smudges which blossom get bigger Someone kicks me from behind and I'm knocked flat, bashing my chin and grazing my ear on the gravel. "Under there!" a man in uniform shouts— under the ambulance, he means. I roll under, he follows. The earth heaves arches its back. the blast grabs my lungs, sears my hands, whips rips tears, the man beside me leans up and knocks his head against the wheel, raises his fist and hits me on the shoulder, looks at me amazed, stays amazed, is dead. It's scorching, spitting, I can taste blood and sand in my mouth. up my nose. I claw the earth with burning fingers, drown, come up for air. The incendiary storm gets under way—hurricane. whirlwind—I crawl out from under the truck, the wind gathers me and throws me against the wall of the bunker, above me the triangles are making fresh smudges, smudging the blue. I hammer on the bunker door, crawl into a niche, make myself part of the stones, the wall. the bunker. The storm screams. blinds. deafens, deadens all feeling at last. "She's dead," someone calls out. I turn over, see my bloody arms, the sky no longer blue, feel the heat, cutting heat, try to speak, taste blood, throw up, choke. Stand up fall down stand up.

They're wailing on the Kurfürstendamm; people are digging, burrowing in the smoking rubble, a woman's voice is singing, "My eyes, my eyes." Kneeling behind her there's a man taking bricks one by one from a burning heap. He sees me: "Have you seen my little girl, she's six, have you seen my little girl, she's six."

Dr. Rode sits there looking gloomy, his niece holds my

arms. He picks up a pair of tweezers and says in his thick Russian accent: "It hurts now, a little bit." He coaxes something from my lip: "Here we have shrapnel, now show me hand." He picks and dabs, gropes around my mouth collecting the tiny American splinters, looks me over like a Saint Bernard, like a mother chimpanzee with her young, discovers something in my knee, then my shin: dabs, cleans, bandages. "I have to operate, tonsils bad, very bad." There's a bed free in his clinic, next to a dyed-blond old woman who moans, "My bowels, my bowels." The nurse throws her a threatening glance: "Take that lipstick off at once! I keep thinking you're bleeding." She doesn't hear, goes on moaning. It feels as though I've eaten fire, my throat flares, the sirens whine, the nurse says, "Come on," takes me down to the ground-floor corridor, props me up against the wall and says "Don't fall down!" I'm picked up and hurled against the other wall. Now I get angry, now I've had enough of being thrown around; my head crashes against the floor, I stay down, the ceiling starts spitting lime at me, spits in my mouth, in my lately operated throat. They tug at my legs, pull me out of the darkness, debris, and lime. One wing of the clinic is on fire, the emergency bay badly damaged, the maternity ward gone completely. Dr. Rode says, "It hurts now, a little bit," and furtively gives me an injection under the blankets: morphine is rare, needed for worse situations. Next to me they're amputating an arm, the boy bellows: "Mother, mother." Rode sews up my throat. I look at the ceiling, splashes of blood have formed a map; river, lake, straight road, I feel warm, warm from the blood, from the morphine, want to sleep sleep in the warmth of the blood. I see an arm, small hand, blond hairs. Silly, I think, an arm all by itself, just an arm.

There's a tap on my hand and a voice whispers, "Visitor." I see a badge on a lapel—gray lapel, party badge; fingers slide over the lapel; take the golden badge, slip it into the pocket; the lapel edges downward, his face appears: "How are you?" You're a member of the party, I try to say, but nothing comes out. Dumb, swollen, speechless. I see slate-gray eyes, a mouth like Father's, think to myself: You've got the party badge, why have you got it? He says, "I was at the Ministry, I'll come again tomorrow." The dyed-blonde screeches, "Lovely man that was, fine head, you ought to marry him, you should, got to think of the future, take what you can get. Jewels, lots of jewels." I long to sleep, to get away from the whorehouse prattle, the party badge.

Ewald von Demandowsky is not a comfortable man, not one to run with the hounds. He is ambitious, competent, agile-minded, in need of roots. And he finds them. Ewald von Demandowsky believes. He believes in the master race, in the mission; believes in those called upon to govern, to dictate; believes in Germany's vocation in a bored, comfortable world, a world of the small-minded, the greedy, who call themselves democrats and communists. He's no firebrand, no street-corner barker. He reveals, explains, convinces, is confident; a confident victor, for whom victory is a matter of course, almost uninteresting. He cites Marx, Lenin, Kant, Nietzsche, Jaspers, contradicts them, agrees. Money doesn't interest him, and death only vaguely. He is accessible on three planes of irritation: he is small, his ambition has been to be a great actor, he can't stand actors. Since he's obliged to spend a great deal of time with actors he suffers from ulcers. He is thirty-six years old. He plans and influences, forms opinions, leads. He has no superiors except Goebbels. He admires Goebbels, has a student-tutor relationship with him. He overlooks overhears, the loudmouths, the sycophants, the masses, the Sieg-Heil screamers. Victors don't need to get excited.

I cannot argue with him.

These are the words I have heard at school, from Weise, in history class, on the radio, in newsreels, from the block warder. I cannot argue with him since the dissenters are reticent, talk only in riddles, a secret language, because they're careful with us, the youngsters who have no idea what it was like before.

Only the faithful can afford to be articulate.

Wenck's army will repulse the Russians, Wlassow is only waiting for the word to join up with the Waffen-SS and the other elite troops. The master plan will be announced shortly, defeat is unthinkable. The Führer won't let us down.

Says he.

EIGHT

Alike and Fritz have rented a room to a Finnish woman who speaks Russian. Emmert, the gentle Swabian, comes by one evening and tries to persuade me to leave; the Russians are only sixty miles from Berlin, he says. Stepfather says the same. He gets out his last big piece of leather and starts to make me a pair of boots. "Head west toward Uelzen. The Americans will meet up with the Russians here in Berlin, you've got to get out."

"I haven't got a travel permit, no chance of getting one."

"Go by night, on your bicycle."

"Perhaps Wenck will arrive, or Wlassow."

"If such people existed they'd be here already."

In February the radio announces three hundred victims in Uelzen. No mail, no telephone, no way of finding out whether Mother's one of them. The Tobis Film offices burned down during the last raid. He's at home now; he listens to the news, goes down in the cellar and listens to the news. Duwe has been called up. I try to get through to Bongers but it's impossible. We are bombed continuously now, by the Americans, the English, and sometimes the Russians—they send old rickety crows over, fat lazy crows that sag through the treetops.

They say you can get marmalade in Dahlem. I join the queue; we shuffle forward, take cover in the doorways, peep out, line up again. Trucks full of women and children rattle past, refugees from Frankfurt on the Oder, from Strausberg, from Spindlersfeld. They shout, "Clear out, the Russians'll rape you, beat your brains out!" One of the women rants, "They crucified my husband, nailed him to the door, and cut off my sister's breasts; clear out!" A Russian plane hovers in slowly, bored, drops two bombs; they explode beside the truck, tear it to pieces.

"Is it true what they say about the Russians?"

"Yes, it's true." There's a rifle lying on his desk. "I've been called up," he says.

Liszt's *Préludes* ripples from the radio, Goebbels screams of providence, justice, final victory, the turning point, the great turning point, Roosevelt dead, Russian cannibals, inferior Bolsheviks—now we will beat them, now we will drive them from the land.

"I can't take it any more, why doesn't he shut up," I say and start to cry.

"It will be all right, believe me."

"Let's try to escape, we might get as far as Uelzen," I say.

"That would be desertion, they'd shoot me."

"If we stay here the Russians'll shoot you, or the Americans, or God knows what." I am desperate, afraid, the old panic has come back. He's been ordered to rifle practice, he says, and goes off down the drive, his ski boots crunching on the gravel; the garden gate slams to and I sit there alone, thinking to myself if only a bomb would fall on the bloody house, why don't they hit it. I won't go down in the cellar any more.

There's a murmuring in the distance, a strange murmuring I've never heard before, like a lone dog barking, like thunder, or trucks or trains—I don't know. A knock at the door. A man in uniform addresses me as Frau von Demandowsky and tells me to keep calm, stay in the cellar. I ask him what the murmuring is. "It's artillery," he says, "Russian artillery."

On April 18 English troops capture Uelzen; the radio announces that after a long and heroic battle the town finally surrendered.

"I'm to report to Schmargendorf Headquarters tomorrow."

"Take me with you," I say.

"That's out of the question," he says.

"Then shoot me. I'm not going to wait until they come and rape me or beat me to death."

"That's out of the question."

We'll see about that, I say, and fill his two canteens with slivovitz. Then I dig a hole near the fence and lower the mummy case into it, put on a beret, tin helmet, turtleneck sweater, training-suit trousers, and Stepfather's new boots. We get on our bicycles and ride to Schmargendorf.

The streets are quiet, empty, dead; people are sitting in their cellars, waiting. The murmuring is clearer, nearer. The bombers have gone, they're leaving it to the artillery, the infantry, the tanks. No sound but the murmuring. My stomach aches, the bike bucks and shudders, the handlebars jam, worse than a mule; I can't think, can't feel—only the bellyache.

We arrive at Headquarters. They give me a tunic, a battered Italian cap, helmet, belt, machine gun, ammunition, hand grenades, pistol. A bloated beery soldier yells at me Name, age; I say nineteen; he starts and looks at me with screwed-up eyes that say what are you doing here, why aren't you at the front, you sod: take that thing off, he bellows. I take off the helmet, then the beret, his face stretches, dissolves, he slaps his thigh, howls with glee: A gal, he howls, wanna join us? Yes, I answer. How about that for guts, he whinnies Several lieutenants are standing around, they smile at me weakly as if to say welcome to the club, one of us now, could have been classmates, don't let him worry you. E.v.D. comes to attention and says: My fiancée.

They drape the ammunition belts over me, show me how to work the safety catch and then say, Take a shot at that tin over there I hit it They shout bravo, get excited, beam at me proudly He and I, two soldiers, and two old reserves are detailed to a ground-floor flat in Schmargendorf; no windowpanes, closed shutters, cupboard on the floor, bed with no mattress They lean their rifles against the wall, stretch out on the floor and say, Who's on watch? They sleep, snore, gaze into space Someone hammers at the door, two soldiers came in lugging a big pot full of potatoes. One of them says, He's been assigned to the bunch of you. Behind them there's a little pimply kid covered with ammunition, hand grenades, knives, and guns He's fifteen at the most Our snorer wakes up, looks stupefied, sits up, belches, bellows: Now I know why they let me live through Stalingrad— to have the honor of fighting with infants and virgins Words fail him, he struggles up and goes for a pee. The kid looks mean, vengeful.

They give me a jackknife and I start in on the potatoes; they're slippery, hard to hold. Something bangs against the shutters, the boy pulls out his pistol, click goes the safety catch, the Stalingrader chops at his wrist and shouts: That's all we need, for you to start taking potshots. Ourside someone bleats: Change positions, bunker opposite. The kid says in a small voice: Well it might have been the enemy you know. Aw shut your face, says our front-line warrior, picks his teeth, looks disgusted.

We run across the street; it's dead, still, empty, our boots make an echo like fifty horses. The murmuring has stopped. We stand there in front of the bunker and listen intently—yes, the murmuring has stopped. We look at each other: perhaps they've gone, retreated, gone back to Moscow, changed their minds, funny bunch. The Stalingrader puts an end to the warm soft secret hope: They're like that, that's the way they are, it's the calm before the storm.

The cellar's bursting; privates, young-old, very young reserves, SS. Uniforms have been crossed with each other, it looks like a carnival. There's a smell of sweat, cabbage, unwashed bodies. No one speaks. They point their thumbs at a bench, we sit down and peel potatoes. I nudge him, his knife clatters to the floor and he spits, Can't you be careful. I bite hard on my lip, can't start crying here in front of them. I keep biting till it wears off, say to myself, That's something you'll have to learn to do without, and pretty quick. There's a young lieutenant leaning against the wall studying his hands. Shut up, he mutters, E.v.D. looks up sharply, goes crimson, champs on his lips, goes white, is not used to being told to shut up—general manager to shut-up soldier in one easy lesson. He swallows, sniffs, goes on peeling.

The bunker door groans and in comes an SS officer: helmet, high boots. He blinks squints shouts: Detail the watch! The lieutenant says: Hey, you there, beckons to E.v.D. He gets up and goes out with three others. I sit on the bench and listen, listen to the breathing, the helmets and ammunition belts squeaking, listen to the snores, listen beyond the walls: it's still quiet.

Two hours later he's back. He lays his head on the table and falls asleep. At four the door's torn open: Alarm, fall in outside with your guns, lights out. I pick up the machine gun and the hand grenades and run after him. Fifty yards on there's a bombed out cellar, two rats are sitting on the steps, they squeal, shoot us vicious glances, scurry past. The cellar's full of water, we squat on the steps, put the guns on top of the wall, and wait. I arrange my hand grenades neatly, carefully, they lie there like pigeon eggs. He whispers, Don't forget—pull, wait, throw. Silence. Two hours later one of them crawls up and hisses: Follow me. We crawl after him, back to the bunker. They're standing in the corridor, in the alcoves, an oil lamp is smoking, making rings, flickering, they're standing there helpless cool tired brave frightened indifferent depressed resigned angry surprised, looking at the door, looking at us, expecting release to come in from the silence. At ten the watch is detailed again, he's among them. I want to go too, the lieutenant says You stay here. At noon the murmuring starts, steady murmuring; suddenly a machine gun goes ratatat, then silence, four hours' silence. At six I run past the lieutenant, streak through the door before he can grab me. I look for him in the ruins, up and down the street, hear ratatat, gasp my way back and lie down flat in front of the bunker. The trembling starts in the feet, the shivering the shaking creeps up my body takes hold of my teeth till they chatter, till my face bangs on the stones, I cry, sob, don't want to live any more don't want to wait for him for something I don't know can't name—they drag me inside and set me down on the bench, are gentle, understand, know all about it; I sniffle and cry and shake, they say all right, it'll be all right, we all know what it's like, all been through it. They hold out handkerchiefs, black sticky snotrags, look the other way, wait till its over. A belch, a giant one blossoms from my belly, forces my mouth open and echoes through the cellar. He comes back, nobody tells him, he'll never know.

The artillery opens fire at five in the morning. They shout and scream, their necks swell, veins stand out on their temples but they're inaudible, drowned swallowed by Ahh Soomm Ahh Soomm Ahh Soomm. Worse than bombs, land mines, phosphorus, worse than anything the Ahh Soomm Ahh Soomm, they don't fly off when they've emptied their bellies, they stay, come closer, are physically near, reach out and touch you. I pick up the jackknife and tuck it into my boot, thinking, You'll decide when it's time, cut upwards not crosswise, upwards from the wrist. The iron door is lifted from its frame, pushes two old men across the room, and squashes them against the wall. We run out, fall into smoking holes, scramble across to the ruins, stumble over rubble trip on the machine gun—the hand grenades, dear God don't let them explode—I fall, they're hanging on my belt, please don't let them go off. We lie in the water on the stone floor, can't breathe, hold each other tight, a blast whips across the water, waves slap around us. Two hours later it's over. We struggle up, stumble on the slippery steps, fall back again, lie there gasping, pull at our belts and helmets, lie there in the water.

The bunker's gone. Three Russian hedgehoppers come weaving in laboriously, don't shoot, don't drop bombs, just bumble over the craters: vultures, death-watch birds, seeming to say that's the way to do it.

There's a rustle up above: Hey you. I see a helmet and a pair of eyes, black face. Come on up, he shouts. Now I see the SS uniform.

Where are the others?

They bought it, he says. We plod along after him, come to a doorway, the Stalingrader's lying in the corner asleep. I unbuckle my canteen, slivovitz runs down my chin into the neck of my tunic, I drink like a chicken, splutter, it's gone up my nose, drink half the bottle, fall asleep. I wake up and scream; I've screamed myself awake. He's lying beside me. He takes hold of my face and says: It's all right, everything's all right It's dark, it's cold, the cold has eaten into my bones, my legs, my head. A match flares, illuminates an arm, a wrist watch, a pair of dice, trousers, tin hats, goes out.

Get her, she sleeps like a log, I hear, slept through a Stalin organ.*

There's something smooth and light-colored lying across my legs. What's that?

It's a trench coat. The Stalingrader found it in one of the rooms.

What time is it?

Around eleven.

At five it starts again. On the dot as usual, one of them crows, then we stretch out flat, stay that way for one, two hours, then up and along the wall, duck into nooks and doorways and craters. Suddenly ratatat. That one of ours? I cry. No such luck, they answer I clamber out of the crater and one of them bellows, Take that coat off, you nuts with that coat? Gets het up, blows out his cheeks, and strikes his forehead: Christ Almighty, off she goes in a white coat just like she was He searches for the comparison, presses a finger against his left nostril, blows what's in the right one to the ground, takes off his helmet, drapes it over the muzzle of his rifle and raises it—bsss. He lowers the gun slowly

---

* A multibarreled artillery piece for continuous fire.

and says shit. The four of us in the crater exchange glances. Damn good shots, the Russians, he says appreciatively, as though at a shooting match, Saturday afternoon on the range. He tries it again. Bsss. It's coming from an allotment garden. We push our machine guns up to the edge, take off the ammunition belts, stow our pistols in our pockets. I forget about the safety catch, it goes click click and they all turn on me; chains are rattling squeaking whistling. I can't stand it and jump up, bsss past my head—there they are, at the corner.

What do they look like? our marksman asks.

One of them's got a charcoal-burner and they've all got crosses.

Jesus Christ, they're ours! He shouts, laughs, is ecstatic. We wait until dark and then jump out of the crater one at a time. The tanks are still there, their barrels leveled at the allotment.

At Headquarters there's a new commander: he barks at us, keeps us at attention; I pull the helmet down over my eyes, don't want him to notice, he might say this is no place for women, send me back to a cellar without him, without pistol and hand grenades, to wait until they come. Crowded together we stand there, aged fourteen to seventy, the puny lamp throwing enormous shadows. Two lieutenants push their way through and look us over, check our weapons and ammunition, detail new squads: Schmargendorf freight yard ten men, we're among them. They tell us how to get there, we come to attention, about face, off. Two of them have been through Russia, two are Hitler Youths, the rest SS and reserves. We space out, twenty yards apart, run, jump, crawl until we get to the freight yard. It's a wide-open space, several abandoned freight trains are standing there. Bsss; the snipers have spotted us. We hop over the rails like kangaroos, dive under the trucks, wait until the one in front's across. Bsss, bsss, bsss. One of the boys stumbles over the ties, crouches, gets up again and shouts, screams Mother, twists his legs, twitches and stares up at the sky, endlessly. Three privates are lying under one of the railway cars, smoking, watching, sizing up the game. I fall on one of them and my helmet flies off, he gazes at me, mouth open, fag-end sticking to his lower lip, says, Hey, what are you doing here? I have the feeling that I'm at a croquet game. I push my hair back under the helmet and say: I like the climate. They grin, give me a cigarette, and squint across to the next train. It's an oil tanker. Jesus, one of them says. Our destination is still two hundred yards away, behind the tanker. I look at it and suddenly see that E.v.D. is lying under one of the great drums, trying to get out. I return the cigarette. crouch down, tense myself, and spring away, reach the embankment; our objective is behind the embankment near the tennis courts. Twenty foxholes, to the left a lean-to full of spades, watering cans, rakes, and hoes, to the right a shed. A young lieutenant is sitting in the doorway on an overturned bucket; he's wound twigs and foliage around his helmet and shoulders for camouflage, looks as if he's waiting for his cue to go on in *A Midsummer Night's Dream*. He raises a pair of binoculars and stares over at the tennis courts. E.v.D. beckons me into the shed. It's cold, raining heavily, the ground is soggy, the holes full of water; I crawl past the holes and the usual collection: SS reserves Hitler Youths soldiers. A first lieutenant is squatting in the shed with a rabbit between his knees. He digs a knife in behind its ear. I come to attention, eyes straight ahead—there's a towel hanging neatly in front of me, and embroidered in red across the corner is "A rolling stone gathers no moss." The lieutenant looks up at me with light bright colorless eyes and smiles. Something sharp hits me on the neck, clicks against my helmet. I duck down, don't want them to see I'm afraid, try a grin. Ordeal by fire, the first lieutenant says, throws the rabbit in the corner and goes out.

The rain's drumming on the roof, seeping through, making puddles. E.v.D. looks at the packet of cigarettes lying on the table. There are brown spots on them, they're damp, falling apart. Take one, I say. He'll never notice. He shakes his head, looks away. There's a bang on the wall and the first lieutenant shouts, Out here, come on out. There's an SS man lying in front of the door, eyes open, black-red spot on his forehead. The first lieutenant closes the lids and motions to the other lieutenant; he crawls up with a shovel. We bend down and tug at his arms and legs, start digging, lower him in, into the bog, cover him up, slide down into a crater. Orrraaaay! It's coming from behind us, behind the tennis courts. The lieutenant looks up: They screech like monkeys, he says, when they attack they always screech like monkeys. He raises his fist and slams it down in the mud, twenty machine guns start rattling and chattering, we pull ours up and stick an ammunition belt into it. It starts heaving and bucking, wants to go it alone, resents our meddling, starts throwing itself from side to side, gets hot, jams, dies. E.v.D. picks it up, crawls out and runs for the shed. The houses behind us are on fire. The water gurgles around my knees, the lieutenant jumps down beside me, bends and lights a cigarette, shields the glow with his hands and offers me a puff. We're standing close together, facing each other, waiting for the music to start for the next dance. He jerks his head toward the tanker and says, We've had it if they're full.

It gets dark. It's still raining, heavily, constantly, threads of rain, ropes of rain. There's a commotion a long way off, behind the burning houses, the bsss bsss has stopped. Our machine guns are lousy, he says, if only we had one of Ivan's, they don't mind the rain. I show him my hand grenades, he says: Better not, they might hit the fence and bounce back.

I must pee, immediately. It's excruciating, worse than the bellyache, can't think of anything else, I must pee, simply got to. The lieutenant is smoking, mumbling to himself, is here for the day. I squat down lower, down in the water, hold my pistol up high, squat and lean against the side as though I'm too tired to stand any longer. It gushes down my leg into the water—can he feel the warmth? Too late now. Warm, gorgeously warm, cozy, content, hungry, tired. E.v.D. comes back with the machine gun and a tin of cheese. The lieutenant crawls out and disappears into the rain and darkness. Our last rations, says E.v.D., the first lieutenant's gone off to organize some more, he'll be back tomorrow. We eat the cheese. I'm tired, he says, by God I'm tired. I'll stay on watch, you go back to the shed, I say. All right, he says, I'll relieve you later on. He hands me the lieutenant's binoculars and creeps off. I stand there in my hole, in the water, keep a firm hold on the machine gun and the pistol, peer through the glasses over the yard, see shadows, chew the rest of the cheese, hear something crack and rustle, hear screams, dreadful heartrending screams, high thin shrill. I call out softly to the next hole: Are you there?

Yes.

What's that screaming?

Russians are in that house over there started on the women shitshitohshitohshit.

It starts again at five. Reds in the morning! someone
crows. They pound the yard, slam the freight train, my
crater stretches dances shakes disintegrates, buries my feet
and legs. It rains it pours, hails stones, shrapnel, big pieces
little pieces thud in the mud bore their way through worms,
cut the cheese tin to shreds. Two hours later it suddenly
stops. I start with my face; feel it, feel my neck, my chest,
my belly, pull my legs out, they've gone to sleep, rub them,
feel again: everything intact. I crawl up—bsss. My neighbor hollers, They're wiping out their own Ivans with that
Stalin organ, they don't give a damn. Out on the rails someone shouts Help help, there's a soldier lying there with his
belly split open, entrails spilling over the tracks. He shouts
Help, softer now, hoarser. I sit there staring, forget the
sniper—Can't you help him? Two are on their way, trying
to reach him. My ear's warm, bss and then clack, I fall
back into the water, hold my head down, take off my helmet put it on the machine gun hold it up—clack. He's got
his eye peeled, I say to myself, and he's pretty close, where
the hell is the bastard—bsss clack. The lieutenant's dead,
one of them shouts. They start again, Stalin organ, mortars,
but it doesn't stop this time, won't ever stop again.

Face in the mud, mud in my mouth, I wake up: What's
going on? You alive, you all right? He's lying beside me
crying, sobbing, holding my shoulders, wiping my face. It's
dark again, still raining, it must have lasted hours, I must
have fallen asleep, fainted. It's completely quiet. We grovel
through the mud, roll over to the shed. Twelve are dead, he
whispers. I lie down on the floor, my hand on my pistol.
My belt hurts, the helmet's crushing my head, my skin is
burning with fatigue, lips swollen from the mud, from
thirst. A man staggers in with a bottle of water, E.v.D.
finds a bag of coffee beans and says. We'll make a fire as
soon as it's light. There's a brown fat-bellied teapot on one
of the shelves, a real old allotment garden-teapot without a
lid and half its spout gone. I fill it and crawl out toward the
others in the foxholes; I hold it up in front of me, careful
not to spill any—clack, I'm left with the handle. Back to
the shed. The one who brought the water squats there and
says Jesus Christ. A while later he says, We won't be seeing
the first lieutenant any more, I know him, he's off his rock-
er, got wounded in France, hasn't been right since. He gets
up and heaves a sigh, rubs his back and seems perfectly
contented; allotment gardener on a Sunday, weeding in an

open shirt, picking gooseberries—green sour ones, dark red
ones that burst when you bite them—tying up the runners;
deck chair and Sunday paper, off home at seven, rolling
down his sleeves and fastening the padlock, rolling up the
beans in the paper and tucking them under his arm, striding off contentedly.

Let's get married, says E.v.D. He looks down at me and
says, Hm, let's get married.

Are you crazy? You're married already.

Nobody knows that here, I want to marry you, I want
you to be my wife before . . .

Before what?

Maybe before it's too late.

The shed starts to shudder and sway, the shelves collapse, there's a rumbling coming from the tennis courts,
rumbling, tinkling, squeaking, high steady clanking. A tank
is weaving through the craters, flattening bushes fences
sheds: it stops, nods its barrel to the right, to the left, stops
again, thinks it over. A small fellow in a Hitler Youth jacket jumps out of a hole behind the shed and goes hopping
off toward the tennis courts carrying a length of pipe.

That's the relief force, E.v.D. is shouting. I knew it I
knew it, I always told you they wouldn't let us down.

The roof is lifted from the shed, the walls cave in, it's
hot, bright yellow, red, white. The first lieutenant is
sprawled out beside me covered with blood. He snorts,
That prick, that godforsaken prick, he's blown up the tank,
he's got an antitank gun, he's blown up one of ours. Gets
up, straightens his jacket and bellows: Retreat! E.v.D. rolls
over, sits up—bsss—flattens down again and says, We'd
like you to marry us.

The first lieutenant's bloody face peers down at us: What
would you like?

We'd like you to marry us, we want to get married.

He stands stock-still, doesn't hear the bss, stands in the
glare of the burning tank and says curtly: I'm not authorized, says Retreat! says Ahhh, starts spinning rolling, falls
down stays down, face gone, red meat under the helmet.

There were thirty of us three days ago, three nights ago,
now we are five.

Back across the rails—crouch tense spring, crouch tense
spring. It's stopped raining. Behind the embankment: ruins,
poking out of the ruins: muzzles, trained at us, following
us. A helmet bobs up, bobs down again.

Comrades! the man next to me shouts, Comrades!

They're scared, they think we're Ivans.

For Christ's sake, can't they see our uniforms?

That doesn't matter, they put ours on sometimes, plenty lying around.

A hand comes up over the wall and motions us to wait; they're going to give us cover.

They blaze away over our heads and we run for our lives. Hands reach up and grab us, pull us over the wall. Got away with it that time, they say. There are fifteen or twenty of them, all soldiers, no reserves, SS or Hitler Youths. Old ones, young ones, they all know their business, were at it long before Berlin. We lie down in the corner and E.v.D. says: Don't fall asleep, we don't dare fall asleep.

Who knocked the tank off? one of them asks.

Hitler Youth.

They give antitanks to those bleeders? Must be off their rockers.

E.v.D. asks Was it one of Wenck's or Wlassow's tanks? They look at him suspiciously, with the who-the-hell-let-you-in-look and say, That'll be the day.

One of them with binoculars keeps a lookout, the others lie behind their machine guns. The tanker's still there, perhaps it was empty after all. Two of the freight cars have been overturned, one of them looks like a sieve, one corner is still intact, ULM ON THE DANUBE painted on it. That's an omen, a good omen—I get excited, dig him in the ribs, whisper, and point to the freight car. Quiet, one of them barks.

Christ Almighty, here they come, the lookout gasps. Orrraaaay—the screeching starts behind the sheds over the rails, Orrraaaaay, a hoarse long-drawn-out howl. I'm holding the ammunition belt, he has the machine gun.

Hold it, hold it, one of them whispers. Let 'em come, let 'em come—now! he bawls. Meeeeeh-eeh meeeeh-eeh meeeeh-eeeh. One of them stretches back, pauses, throws a hand grenade, Ahh Voomm—then it's still. Tak tak, tak tak far off . . . then still. They reach for their bottles, raise them and stick them into their beards, hold them neatly in their hulking, split, and calloused hands, cut off hunks of bread with their jackknives, distribute the hunks and crusts and say: We'll have to get out of here, we'll sneak off in the dark. The Stalin organ starts pounding away, pounds on for hours.

That night we come to a cellar. They're sitting there in rows, stiff, silent, around a candle stub amid bundles, buckets, crates, sitting there reverently on garden chairs, kitchen chairs. Go away, they shout, we don't want any military here, they'll murder us if they find you here, clear out.

We need water, says one of the soldiers.

Have a heart, a fat woman says, we've got children here, have a heart.

A toothless old woman creeps out from a corner and hands us a bottle: God have mercy on us, she mumbles. They're mad, I think to myself, sitting here waiting for the end like sheep in a slaughterhouse, mad.

It's burning outside, a heap of uniforms are huddled in the next doorway, a lieutenant steps out: Where have you come from?

Schmargendorf freight yard.

Officers?

Dead.

Follow me. We run after him and come to the Hohenzollerndamm cemetery. It gets light, opaque, glassy, like coming up from the bottom of the pool in the town-hall baths after jumping from the ten-foot board. We start hacking at the hard stubborn earth. Two Hitler Youths run up crying and blubbering, Can we stay here with you? We've got guns.

Go home to Mother.

We're from Johannistal, the Russians have taken it, the smaller one whimpers.

Dig in and no shooting—that's an order! They come to attention, the big one says Ow ow, as though he's barked his shins or squashed his finger, falls down in front of me and stares at me with surprised wondering saucer-eyes. The other one howls Helmut, oh Helmut.

Get down, they shout, get down and shut up. Bsss clack bsss clack. E.v.D. bangs and jabs at the ground, we squeeze in and stand pressed against each other, holding the machine gun, the pistols, and hand grenades.

Perhaps it's better on the other side, he says, looking at the staring eyes.

Are you frightened? I ask him.

A chicken goes clucking past; it flaps, gargles, runs back and forth, head out head back, ruffles its feathers and stalks haughtily over to the dead boy—Oh God, the eyes, if that sod goes for the eyes—I pick up a stone and hit it on the

tail, it squeals, sheds a few feathers, and stomps off
squawking. Where there's a chicken there's an egg, I say,
and am on my way. Come back, he yells. I crawl through
the gravestones and benches, along a hedge, there's a shed
behind the hedge, beside the shed three chickens, beside the
chickens two eggs. Bss clack bsss clack, a branch falls and
hits me on the left hand, the eggs are in the right. I crawl
back on my elbows, eggs held high, slide in beside him
proudly. We pierce holes and drink them. A yell from the
next hole: Any more where they came from? There ain't
no justice. We start work on our hole again, hack and bur-
row like moles.

Help -from behind us—heelllp. He's old and thin and
yellow, in uniform; he sways toward us like a drunkard and
lets himself fall, drags himself on jabbering Help. Blood is
running down his back, we pull him in and I cut his jacket
open; I'm calm, and my hands are steady. It's flowing,
pulsing from his back, I tear off his shirt, tear it into strips
and tie them around his thin chest. He groans, screams,
collapses but there's no room to fall, he hangs there between us. Orraaaay—there they are, for the first time I can
see them, running toward us, machine guns at their hips,
bayonets glinting flashing in the sun; gun and bayonet coming toward me coming closer arm's length; earth spurts up
into my eyes, ratatat, it's the gun beside me, I remember
the hand grenade—pull throw duck—AhhVoomm,
splinters clatter on my helmet, I fall across the old man—
where's the bayonet? I wait for it, my back tenses, here it
comes, must come—the bayonet . . .

Complete silence. We look at each other over the old
man's bleeding back and wait, don't dare to look up. His
eyes are bright, desperate, sweat is pouring over his eyebrows, dripping from his eyelids to his cheeks. He crashes
his fist down on the gun, hurls it over the edge and sobs Oh
God, my God. There's a whinnying noise and then a bark,
the dry bark of a tank gun. An arm floats past us, an arm
without its hand, cemetery arm; we follow its flight, the old
man moans, straightens up, splutters, rattles, is dead, can't
fall down, leans against us with his head on my shoulder.

Move on, the lieutenant cries. The Russians are lying in
the roadway in heaps with twisted legs and heads. The soldiers run over and pick up the machine guns, unbuckle the
ammunition belts, the Hitler Youth claws at our jackets
and gabbles Take me with you please take me with you.

There were more than forty of us when we arrived, six hours later there are seventeen. We crawl across the cemetery and see a house in front of us, crawl toward it. E.v.D. stutters, Why, that's Bobby's house, Bobby Lüdtke's house . . . he stops, realizes that this is his home town, his Berlin, city of friends and acquaintances, not an anonymous battlefield. He's a close friend, he says reproachfully, as though Bobby were responsible for the uproar and the slaughter.

There are holes where there once were doors and windows. Bobby, he calls out, Bobby. The ceiling is sagging, the chandelier swinging, mortar spilling steadily, quietly, an egg timer building dunes on the bookshelves, on the carved black elephants with hanging trunks. He picks up the smallest and hands it to me saying, Take it, as a mascot.

A tank coughs, the ceiling creaks and breaks loose bringing down the wall and the elephants. I open my mouth to scream in the darkness, dust lime darkness rush at my throat and my lungs, I hear the grinding hear my name, he's shouting at me, pulling my arms, shaking my shoulders, hitting me in the face and screaming Are you still there answer me answer me. I want to say yes, try to breathe can only splutter, bite my tongue, full of lime, want to breathe must breathe again, live again.

There's a horse lying outside with its mouth and belly wide open, beams and timber are burning, falling on bodies and heads, they're screaming, jabbering, growing silent. The tank's still barking, it's standing at the corner barking at the dead street. We've lost the others, the ones from the cemetery.

If I'm wounded don't leave me lying there, I say, don't just leave me there, promise—

If one of us is wounded the other must use the pistol, let's swear to it.

How do you do it? I ask. If you put it to your forehead it might just blind you.

He shows me the spot in the neck, the hollow at the base of the skull, picks up the pistol and fastens the safety catch. I hold it against his neck and he says, Yes, that's the spot. We sit there waiting for the darkness, our tongues sticking to our palates with thirst. If we can get as far as Kurfürstendamm we might get some water, I have a friend who lives near Halensee, he says.

As we're crossing the Fehrbellinerplatz at the corner of

Hohenzollerndamm I feel a tug at my trousers. I'm snared in the barbed wire. It winds its way around my legs and ankles, nails me firmly to the middle of the burning square, there's a bsss clack bsss bsss from one of the windows, I rip my hands, legs and trousers, drag the wire along behind me, trip run trip again, reach the other side. Two men are running toward us with machine guns at their hips, machine guns with big round ammunition drums. Russians! I yell, they're Russians! I tear at my holster, they shout: Comrade! and hurtle past. Sweat tumbles down my neck and chest.

We get there at dawn and squat down in the doorway. Stay there, he says, she's probably down in the cellar. Three tanks with charcoal stoves go choking by. One of the hatches opens gingerly and a helmet appears, then a face, young and grimy. He looks up and his head jolts backwards, the tank goes lumbering on with him dangling from the turret, disappears.

A woman's voice: Come along, my dear. She has white hair and is wearing a dress with a jacket, frilled collar, gloves, silver-topped cane—she must have been in the stables, not the cellar, was inspecting the meadows and horses, consulting the bailiff, time for coffee now, mocha in tiny fragile cups. She pushes the front door gently and steps into the long hall, smiles and says, Ewald, my dear fellow, you do look a sight. What do you need? How can I be of service?

We need water, he says, and sleep, if we could just sleep for a few hours.

The house is rolling like a ship, like a trawler in the Baltic. For the first time I smell my sweat, my dirt. I look down at my torn hands, the dried blood, look up into a mirror, see a face I don't know.

We're sitting on Regency chairs; there's the street, the corner, the Kurfürstendamm, a shop sign opposite saying SICKROOM NEEDS, it's lopsided.

There's a cabinet full of broken glasses in the corner. My mother gave them to her on her birthday, he says sadly and falls asleep. Tanks grind past, on their way to Halensee Bridge, clouds of yellow-gray smoke billow up and seep through the holes in the wall. I've still got a little coffee, she says, and places a tray on the floor. You really ought to come down to the cellar, you know. She smiles, nods her head, and goes out again.

Doesn't she know what's going on?

She's eighty-two.

I must write to my mother, perhaps I can leave the letter here, she might get it one day, perhaps she's still alive. I write that it's all over, that there's no way out, that she shouldn't take it too hard, that I'm grateful for everything. Tears fall on the paper and blotch the ink, I tear it up and start again, fall asleep, wake up again. The Russians are here—she's standing there swaying, gasping—the Russians are next door in the cellar. We don't move, look at each other, can't believe it. You'll have to leave, the other tenants insist on it, I'm terribly sorry, the Russians will demolish the house if they find soldiers, I'm sorry, she says, trembling a little. She kneels down in front of a chest and takes out an envelope, hands it to E.v.D.: Here are some cigarettes.

We stand on the steps with our pistols in our hands, have no idea where to go. They shout up through the grating: Clear out, we don't want any soldiers here, the Russians are next door, get going.

Up at the corner tanks are creaking, coming back, heading for the Gedächtniskirche. They're ours, they've come back, they're ours, I scream, and we skip across the road, run on past the tanks.

Legs are dangling in front of me, swinging to and fro; a boy in uniform with a blue face and his tongue sticking out is hanging from a tree. There's a cardboard placard on his chest: I AM A COWARD I WAS TOO AFRAID TO FIGHT FOR MY FATHERLAND. We thread our way through soldiers and tanks, an officer with clusters on his collar stops us: Where have you come from?

Schmargendorf, we lost the others.

When?

Yesterday, yesterday morning.

Follow me. Headquarters are in Albrecht Achillesstrasse; they're standing in line in the big parquet-floored hall, gawking at a captain. Someone shoves us over to a desk in the corner, the officer sitting behind it looks up and says: You deserted your company. He points to the others and says: Stand in line.

An old private's next to me, he whispers: They're gonna hang us.

Shut up. A soldier with a rifle goes up and down the line saying Shut up. The big door cracks and bursts open, splinters and shrapnel plow into walls ceiling floor, those near the door are writhing and screaming, I throw myself down next to the Shut up soldier and say, I'm a girl, turn to E.v.D., and rip the envelope of cigarettes from his pocket: Here, take these and let us go, he's my husband. The Shut up soldier looks at me and doesn't answer. I shake him: Please let us go. He stares at me, doesn't hear, he's dead. The wall grates and bends over, I see it toppling toward us, I start to roll, jump up tread on hands and legs, see the wall sagging on the writhing screaming heap. Outside an old reserve's kneeling with his head between his knees spitting out teeth and crying, My wife, oh my God my wife, she's in that house, in the cellar. He points to a pile of rubble, a courtyard, a burning house collapsing tumbling falling apart. E.v.D. pulls me to my feet: Come on, we can't stay here.

Halt! Don't move! A lieutenant's standing in an alleyway pointing a pistol at us: Where are you off to?

I pull off the helmet and tug my hair loose: Let us go.

He grins, digs in his pocket, and throws us a bar of chocolate, motions with his pistol and looks away. We start to run and come to three soldiers lying in a crater. Put your lid on, they scream. I'm carrying the helmet in my hand, only notice now how light my head feels, neck and shoulders free of pressure, no sweaty leather cutting at my forehead. Put it on, they bawl, Bsss clack. They're over there in that house, one of them says, E.v.D. passes the cigarettes. They want to string you up? they ask.

Yes, I say.

Yeah, yeah, they got their problems, that's a fact.

Night falls and they take lengths of rope from their pouches, tie the ends to their belts, link up like mountaineers. Two tanks have collided at the corner, there are soldiers sitting on them, others standing around. Hitler's dead, they shout, Hitler's dead, the war's over. Someone down the street repeats it, it echoes through the ruins, over the bridge, up and down the canals. They crawl out of their holes and doorways, surge together into a trampling, stamping, swelling herd. The rope between us breaks, we shout our names, clutch each other, and are swept forward by the endless torrent. By morning we have reached Spandau; we sit jammed together on the stairs of an apartment house and stare through a lonely leftover stained-glass window with lilac-green motifs. They smoke their fag-ends, chew the last of the rations, are baffled and stunned. Rumors flurry up and down the staircase: A tank division general is going to surrender the army to the Americans but where are the Americans? Nobody knows, they should have been here long ago, not going to go and leave Berlin to the Russians, are they? They're angry, sore, feel they've been left in the lurch: Yeah they played it big as long as they were up in the air . . . and as for Hitler—suicide, that's a fine way to get out of it, maybe we'll be able to get home at last. They're from Pomerania and Silesia, from Berlin from the Rhine from Mecklenburg and Hanover, they hope, mutter, and sleep. E.v.D. gazes through the window at the tanks, at the bridge, gazes at Spandau quietly burning and says, We must find the Americans; if we can cross the bridge and get through Spandau we should manage it.

Here we go, they shout from below. We jump up and clatter down to the street. We're detailed off, fifty men to a tank; we fall in beside them, behind them, wait for them to start. Not a word is spoken, no sound but the rattling chains, the tramping feet. The first tank is across the bridge, we're second. It lurches forward, we follow it over the bridge keeping our distance, suddenly the windows and roofs explode, the tank catches fire, blows up, I'm lifted and whisked through the air, smashed against something hard as iron and left there. It's creeping, oozing down my face, my hand comes up, I see the fingers touching my nose, holding themselves up again, full of blood, sinking away. I'm dead . . . so that's what it's like . . . no point in getting up. . . . His face is bleeding too, is close, coming closer, lips are moving. . . . Pistol, give me pistol, no use . . . they're falling down beside me, falling over each other, mound of bodies, getting higher and higher; I grip the pistol and scream No, start running dragging him over the bodies past the burning tanks.

The shop smells like Stepfather's: leather, glue, chalk. The big lathe has been knocked over, the sewing machine with the three-edged needle is standing in the corner, the shelves have been ripped from the wall, shoes gone, yellow number cards drift through the air like feathers. We sit on a pile of bricks and planks, the Russians are on the first second third floors, in the loft, the flames from their flame throwers gush past the window, we listen to their mortars, machine guns, voices, shuffling of boots. Our pistols are like a present, a promise, a pardon. Blood trickles through my hair line, runs steadily down my face, drips on my jacket, the left sleeve is ripped, is heavy and scratchy from dried blood. His chin is gashed open, the edges waggle when he talks. I look at his mouth and see my father's face, sad face with donkey ears on yellowing paper. No, I say, no. One more try, one last try.

The dead are piled up to the ground-floor sills; I follow the face, the face in the photo, see it in front of me, see and hear nothing else, only the face, run after it, don't stumble don't trip, run run, lie down on the soft earth, plowed field, red spots approach me, move away, come back go black envelop me, swallow me up. It's dark, the earth is cold and damp. He holds my head and says, We must have a guardian angel. We are lying in the roots of a huge tree, there's a rustling noise, I jump up and want to run, he holds me and whispers, There are fifty or sixty of us, keep down.

The march begins, march of the fugitives. We march at night, roped together, tread softly, steadily, don't talk, for two weeks no one says a word. We share our last crusts of bread, chew them carefully, then grass and barks of trees; file through woods, see castles palaces lights chandeliers, hallucinations from the hunger, the fatigue; panic at the snap of a twig, the creak of a branch. At daybreak we bind ourselves to the tree trunks and sleep standing up, hidden by the branches. The hedgehoppers search patiently, chattering like sewing machines, searching the woods for the likes of us. A fourteen-year-old with a shoulder wound loses his nerve, frees himself from his tree, and runs out into the field. They fly off in a hurry. Two nights later we see them: tanks, gun carriers, columns of soldiers. They shout out to one another, sing, howl, are sure of themselves. We lie behind the trees, their legs and boots are within touching distance as they march into the field and set up camp.

In the morning they bombard the wood, knock it flat; trees crash float stumble over each other, into each other, sag down, hold each other up. The man in front of me starts to run, his leg flies off, flies up high, he doesn't notice and goes on running, does a hop and a jump and then falls, falls with the trees. They pull off their jackets and shirts, raise their shirts over their heads, and walk out toward the light, sway onto the field, fall forwards fall backwards, are cut down. We crawl flat on the moss, stay under the trees, hardly breathe, ants scurry across my hands and face, up and down my legs; we lie and wait. To my left there's a corporal, a veteran, a "swine from the front," he whispers. They're clearing out.

The noise of the tanks grows softer, shouts echo singly— a bayonet stabs the ground. They leap up; the one in front of me and the private leap up and knock the bayonets from their hands, drive their butts into their stomachs, hold the bayonets to their throats, shove their fists into their mouths and hiss, How many, how many are there? Where are the rest of the tanks?

They are flaxen-haired, light-eyed Ukrainian peasant lads. Ten, one of them says.

Where?

They point: Over there, to the right of the road.

We run back into the wood, deeper and deeper. Don't shoot, they whisper, pass it on, don't shoot. We lose our way in the dark, come back to the same clearing three times. They stare up at the black sky, search for stars, can't find them, detail the watch, roll into a hollow, sleep rolled up in leaves and moss, sprawling, sleep the sleep of the dead. It's getting light as I wake up, awakened by gun-fire; I clamber over a tree trunk, stretched across it on my belly I look up and see the Russian, he's standing there looking at me raising his pistol, I see the muzzle see the hole as it tilts up, his hand and arm sweep in a circle, now his body, he's somersaulting, collapsing like a burnt match, hand arm body knees. My trousers are wet, from the ground, the moss, the urine, water runs down my thigh into my boot, Stepfather's boot. Someone tugs at my arm and says: Come on now.

Are there any more of them?

Don't think so, must have been about ten all told.

White beard, nanny-goat beard sprouting from his cheeks and neck, pine needles, leaves, and moss dangling from the whiskers, tongue nestling beside a single tooth; he clicks his fingers and slaps the butt of his gun. I want to say Thank you, but it won't come out, I want to say Thanks for being quicker, for saving my life, but nothing comes out. I run along beside him trying to say Thank you. E.v.D. is lying behind the hollow staring straight ahead, has panicked, broken down, doesn't understand any more.

Hunger is driving us crazy; we talk, forget caution, think only of food; see farmhouses but don't dare to go near, walk on past Nauen, on to Friesack. Cows with swollen udders are bellowing in the fields, we lie in the woods and look at them, don't dare to go near. They must be here somewhere, the Americans—on the Elbe perhaps, can't be much further, one or two nights at the most. There are some twenty of us now, twenty babbling, stumbling lunatics, insane with hunger.

NINE

They woke us by nudging us with their rifle barrels. I felt it in my back, between my ribs, then at my neck. I tried to turn over but the barrel pinned me down. I felt them taking my pistol, my machine gun and ammunition belts. "You up," they shouted.

A tall man with epaulettes and a row of gay ribbons on his tunic stood looking at us intently. There must have been eighty or a hundred of them, wearing uniforms I had never seen before. Clean-shaven, clean clothes, fresh, behind them two horses and carts.

"The jackknife," said E.v.D., "give it to them, they'll kill you if they find it."

I doubled up and let myself fall, tried to faint but couldn't, lay there feigning unconsciousness.

"What you say?" the tall one asked.

"She's"—he sucked in his breath—"He's sick."

I got up and dusted my trousers thinking to myself they're bound to notice, what then? They lined up on either side and marched us across the field, coming to a stop in front of a barn. They lit cigarettes and began talking among themselves. "They're Poles," the one with the white beard said, "they don't know what to do with us."

"They'll shoot us," said E.v.D.

Toward nightfall they locked us in the barn. Rats ran over us, we hardly noticed, kicked out now and then, fell asleep. In the morning they hammered on the wooden walls, opened the door, ordered us to fall in, counted us, quick march. We marched along country roads and through villages, deserted villages. A long column of men and women came toward us, pushing prams, carrying bundles and haversacks, going westward. As we drew level they held up Dutch and French flags sewn together from rags, waved them over their heads, laughed and sang and spat at us and shouted: "Swine, German swine."

We were hungry, thirsty, our feet blistered, talking was forbidden, unnecessarily. The Poles formed a circle and made signs that we should urinate. I squeezed in between two privates and went through the motions. That evening they put us in an empty cowshed. Two of the men had dysentery and lay there with their knees drawn up, groaning.

"Where the hell are they taking us, the war's over, they should just have taken our guns and turned us loose."

They brought soup in the morning. A few still had their messtins, the others took off their helmets and held them out but the Poles said, "No helmets," and pushed them aside. We waited until the others had finished with their tins, then lined up again. "Eat slowly, you'll get the shits otherwise," one of the old ones said. We sipped the warm water with the dab of margarine swimming in it, sipped thankfully, slowly became human again, regained hope.

One of them took off his boots and examined his blisters, a Pole shouted "Out!" and he struggled to get them back on again but couldn't, started marching in his ragged socks, then barefoot. His feet started to bleed, he stumbled and fell down, couldn't get up again. The Poles stood around fingering their pistols, two of the soldiers lifted him up and dragged him along between them, others relieved them, when my turn came E.v.D. pushed forward and carried him for the second time.

The tall man with the epaulettes walked along beside me and kept looking at my chin. E.v.D. called out, "He's young, he's sick." The Pole went on ahead, looked back again, was clearly worried.

Three days later we came to a church. Five Russians with machine guns were standing at the door licking sugar out of the palms of their hands and sucking their teeth. An officer came out of the neighboring farmhouse, put on his cap, and buttoned up his collar as he talked to the Poles.

The church is full. Soldiers are lying on the pews, on the floor, on the gallery. One or two of them sit up: "Where did they get you? Got anything to eat? There's room upstairs." There's a candle stub flickering beside the altar. We clamber up the narrow stairs and lie down under the choir stall. E.v.D. gropes for my arm, grips it tightly and says, "They've turned us over to the Russians, we've got to escape."

Someone creeps up beside us, a match flares, lights up our hands and faces, goes out. "You haven't any water left, have you? I thought you might have some water." He gasps and swallows, his breathing is shallow and feverish. "You've managed to keep your watch, I see, they'll take it in the morning." Outside the Russians are laughing and whooping, firing off bursts. "Let's hope they don't get drunk again.

The great church windows shatter, stained glass rains down on the men below, they grunt and swear, drag themselves over to the wall; machine guns explode downstairs, echoes ricochet through the rafters, someone at the door shouts excitedly in Russian, and then it's still again except for the groans, a high thin scream that ends in a rattle. They throw the doors open at dawn: fall in. Several remain lying there, dead. The others gather their boots and messtins, dig in their pockets. The man who spoke to us in the night reaches for the balustrade and pulls himself up, leans there shaking his head, and whispers, "I don't think I can go any farther." He's my age, black hair, one eye bloodshot, the gash running from his cheekbone to his chin is forming a scab. We take his arms and stagger down the stairs. The Russians scurry around us like dogs around a herd, pushing and shouting, digging us with their butts. In rows of six we start to walk. One of them rushes up to E.v.D. and screams: "You—watch!" takes it and straps it to his forearm next to five others, grins, slaps E.v.D. on the back, and howls, "Hitler kaputt, Germanski kaputt, you for Sibir!" The black-haired boy leans on my shoulder and looks at me closely, turns to E.v.D. and whispers, "Do the Russians know?"

"No, keep quiet."

"We'll have to get her away before they notice."

They lock us in a chickenhouse that night. Two of our lieutenants squat on the floor and ask, "Where did they capture you?" The boy falls over on his face and lies there motionless. They turn him over, a blond soldier folds his jacket, puts it under his head, and starts to examine him methodically. A few minutes later he straightens up and asks, "Have you been together long?"

"Since yesterday."

"He's got diphtheria, if we could get to a camp we might be able to save him."

"Why are they keeping us prisoner?" one of them bleats. "I thought the war was over."

"We did the same with them," the blond soldier says. He

stands by the papered window staring at the filthy floor.
The other kicks out at a crate and bawls: "That was war,
for Christ's sake! Is it going to go on like that?"

"We put them in camps before the war ever started."

The boy moans and murmurs, "Water, please water."

"Is it going to be like that forever now?"

A little man with his arm in a sling and a dirty bandage
around his head says, "Perhaps they're taking us to a camp
to check us in and then they'll let us go. Could be that."

The number of prisoners has grown. The procession
straggles along the hot dusty country road, Mongolians gallop up and down clubbing heads and shoulders with their
gun butts and roaring *davai*, searching for watches, demanding boots. Those left barefoot gradually lag behind,
can't make up the lost ground, and are shot. In the night I
take my jackknife and cut holes in Stepfather's boots to
make them less desirable, push the knife up into the toecap,
under my toes.

Tanks are rolling by, overtaking us; the last one swerves
suddenly, I see the treads coming at me and throw myself
down in the ditch, look up and see a horse standing over
me, see the Mongolian face, feel the blow on my jaw, teeth
on my tongue, look at them in the palm of my hand, look
at the blood on the road, hear *davai*. The first ten rows are
gone, clods of blood on the road, *davai*, they roar and herd
us forward over the bloody clumps. The blond soldier's no
longer in front of me, the black-haired boy's lying in the
ditch with his head split open, we pick him up and drag
him along between us but he's dead by evening.

The sun burned our faces, eyelids, and lips, some threw
their helmets away, tore open their jackets. It rained in the
night and next morning they threw themselves down in the
puddles and sucked up the muddy water; on the road they
doubled over, brown stains soaked through their trousers,
seeped down their boots into the sand, they stumbled and
fell, couldn't get up again. E.v.D. had fever, sweat sprang
from his hair and poured down his swollen cheeks, he doubled up with cramp, put his hand over his mouth to stifle
the screams, his trousers turned bloody-brown and stank.
They died during the night and we carried them out in the
morning, laid them down beside us for the roll call. Sometimes there was soup; we stood in line holding each other
up; one of them stumbled against the pot, the Mongolian

laughed, tipped the boiling brew over him and giggled, "No soup."

A young Russian dug me in the ribs and pointing at my helmet, said, "What vou?" E.v.D. tapped his forehead and said, "He sick." The Russian went away whinnying, delighted that he'd understood.

Several days later we came to the camp: a cluster of huts in a field surrounded by barbed wire, soldiers lying propped up against the huts, observing our entry. There weren't many of us left. They pushed us into an empty room and locked the door. In the morning an officer came in and shouted: "Haircut!" The two soldiers behind him clicked their scissors, I groaned and doubled over, E.v.D. said, "He sick," and I shot past them through the door as though heading for the latrines. I ran to the last hut, squatted down between the prisoners and blurted, "I'm a girl." They stared at me, some of them left in a hurry, the others pulled me into the middle and huddled around me.

In the evening they ordered us to line up in rows of four and two officers went up and down the line slowly, followed by several Poles carrying machine guns. The officers stopped and examined the newcomers closely, discussed their findings, and walked on again.

"What are the Poles doing here?"

"They're looking for Nazi officials who were stationed in Poland," said one of the privates, "Gestapo and big ones like that." We were back in the hut; it was too full to lie down, we sat and squatted, slid over each other, dozed and snored. Two of them started fighting over a mess tin, the elder of the two said, "He stole it from me, honest, you're not safe from your own side any more." The younger one hit him in the face and said, "You're lying, you shit!" They soon got exhausted and dozed off again. "We've got to get out," E.v.D. whispered. "They'll betray you one day in hopes of saving their own skins."

At dawn they unlocked the door and two young Russians came in and shouted: "Up!" As we pushed past them the smaller one—he must have been sixteen or seventeen—took hold of my arm and pointed at my confirmation ring. I tried to slide it off but it wouldn't budge; I worked it around and pulled as hard as I could but my hand was too swollen, the skin broke but the ring stayed put. The boy felt in his pocket, brought out his knife, and I realized he was going to cut my finger off. For a moment I

couldn't believe it, I looked at him, saw his pimply child's
face as he bent over my hand, saw red, and took him by
the throat, squashed his Adam's apple, heard the knife tinkle to the floor, saw his eyes, his white-blond lashes—then
they pulled me away and the boy tore out of the hut and
down the path to the gate with his machine gun and pistol
and ammunition belts. E.v.D. was lying in the doorway,
the boy had knocked him over. We sat down and waited,
but he didn't come back; we sat there waiting for the rest
of the day and through the night, but we never saw him
again.

We'd been standing at attention in the pouring rain for
hours. "Maybe I can cut my hair with the knife," I whispered to E.v.D. "Be quiet," he hissed. A Russian officer
emerged from the barrracks and went swiftly down the
line. The two Poles behind him came to a halt and said
"You." The old reserve in the brown jacket and the Italian
cap straightened up, keeping a firm hold on his dirty gray
trousers. "Where you come from?"

"Berlin," he said, shaking, "Berlin, Neukölln."

"Where were you?"

"Berlin, called up right at the end."

Next to me somebody muttered, "They think he's one of
the specials because he's wearing the jacket."

"You in Poland!"

"Never," he shouted, "no I wasn't . . ." They knocked
him down, he struggled up again, they beat him until he
was dead. Then they marched us away calling out, "You
pigs, you all pigs." My jaw ached, the stumps of my teeth
flared with pain; rage and fury kept me awake.

"They'll sort us out and then release the ones who
weren't politically active, that's what one of the lieutenants
told me."

"Bullshit, they'll send us to Siberia."

"No, no, they'll be glad to get rid of us, they're only
after the political ones." They debated, hoped, resigned
themselves.

Typhus spread through the camp, dysentery, and, above
all, everywhere one looked, lice. We squashed them day
and night but they seemed to multiply, an army of lice with
endless companies of reserves.

One afternoon a Polish officer came and ordered all sick
and wounded to step forward. E.v.D. held back and whispered, "They'll murder them and take the rest with

them." The Pole asked questions, made notes, took his time. Then he looked at me—fixedly, interminably. They started to get restless behind me, coughed, and scratched, but he just stood there, looking at me. Finally he said, "Come." I stepped forward and he removed my helmet and my beret. "What you do here?" I made no answer, looked at him, and thought, Go ahead, hit me, beat me to death. The fury flickered, spilled over and flooded me. "What you do here?" I made no answer, waited for the first blow. "Come with me," he said. The Russians gaped as we went past them through the gate and into the farmhouse. We entered a dark room on the first floor, he struck a match and lit a candle, sat down behind a table, pointed to a linen chest and said, "Sit down." He chewed a cigarette, pulled out a wallet, extracted a small photograph, and held it out over the table: "Do you know her?" Picture of a girl sitting on a bench with her legs crossed. Looked like me. It was quite still in the room except for the soft sucking noise he made as he puffed on his cigarette. We looked at each other, then, after a while, "Where are you from?"

"Berlin, Wilmersdorf."

"Who are your parents?"

I told him.,

"Your grandparents?"

I told him. His German had improved since we'd been alone.

He pointed to the photo: "That's my daughter. She was killed in an air raid on Warsaw."

I thought of the old reserve and said, "Will I be killed now?"

"Perhaps we're related," he said. He went on questioning me, asked me where the family had lived, when my grandfather had come to Berlin, why I couldn't speak Polish.

"Will I be killed now?" I asked.

"I am a doctor," he said angrily, got up, and went out.

Two Russians were standing in the doorway, grinning at me. The doctor came back into the room and said, "They want to cross-examine you. Tell them everything you know."

They took me downstairs, opened a door, and came to attention. Through clouds of smoke I saw flushed faces. There were five of them, sitting behind a big rough-hewn table in front of a map; three wore officer's uniforms, the other two had on olive-green jackets I'd never seen before.

They pointed to a three-legged stool; I sat down, the legs spread-eagled, and I sprawled on the floor. The fury flared again, made me glow, made the lice start dancing. I stood up, shaking with anger, with thirst, hunger, fear. They were surprised, hadn't realized that the stool was wobbly, had a little laugh about it. I told myself, They're going to kill you but you won't crawl. An officer with slanting gray eyes said, "Hitler kaputt, Germanski kaputt." I stared at him and thought, Not too original, are you, even the *muzhiks* managed that one. He read my thoughts, measured my fury with his fury, jumped up, and bellowed: "What you do here? What you do in German army? You spy!" They'll ask a lot of questions, answer them themselves and then kill you, what the hell, I thought to myself.

"What you do in German army?"

"I didn't want to be raped," I said. His hand was open and it didn't hurt very much, just made a lot of noise. I let myself fall, stayed down, and thought, Picked the wrong one this time Ivan, if you're going to start boxing I'll stay unconscious till your teeth fall out. They threw cold water over me, patted and pummeled, more water, and then: "What you do in German army?"

I got up and said, "I didn't want to be raped."

He slapped me again and bawled, "Russian soldiers not rape!"

Just like being back at school, I thought, just like Weise, they don't like the truth. I'd lost my fear, there was no way out, and I wanted to cut it short, get it over with. "I saw them—the women jumped from the windows on Heerstrasse, it was night and I saw them by the light of the fire, Russians were standing behind them."

They looked at me and then pointed to the stool again, forgetting that it was broken. Gray-eyes bellowed once more: "Russian soldiers not rape! German swine rape!" sat down and apparently translated what I'd said. One of the olive-green jackets came to life and started talking excitedly. Gray-eyes pulled me over to the map and asked, "Where did German army go?"

I put my finger on Spandau, then Nauen, the Friesack and said, "The Poles caught us here, just behind Friesack."

"Where you going?"

"To the Americans."

"Why?"

"I didn't want to be raped."

He chose not to hear this time. He stubbed his boot againt the wall, pawed the floor like a horse, chewed his papyrossi cigarette with the long cardboard tip. "What name of general?"

"I've no idea."

"What name of general?"

"No idea, the soldiers said he was a tank commander."

"What his name?"

"I don't know, I never saw him."

"What your name?"

"Martina Wulf," I said. It came automatically: they'd called me Martina at school sometimes, Martina-Albertina, and the UFA film people had wanted to rename me Wulf —an abbreviation of Wulfesteig. I'd never become a film star with a name like Knef, they said, just think how it'll look on the posters.

"We found out who your husband, your name is Demandowsky, you married before end of war."

Someone's squealed, I thought, how can he know the name, nobody knew it. "I forgot about that," I said lamely.

He translated, they laughed and slapped each other on the back, laughed and gave me a glass of vodka. "Forgot," he chortled. The vodka burned my empty stomach. "Drink, drink vodka," they said.

I woke up. It was pitch dark; I felt around, felt a wall, then a bedpost. There was a queer sweet smell in the room. I pulled myself up by the bedpost. There was something soft lying on the bed, something clammy, sticky. I screamed "Help help!" The door opened and a Russian soldier came in with a candle: an old woman was lying on the bed with her stomach ripped open. He opened the window, looked out, picked up the body and tossed it through the window, said, "Good," beamed at me, and went out again, locking the door behind him. I lay down on the floor, brought up the vodka and fell asleep.

In the morning they took me downstairs and lifted me onto a horse-drawn cart. The Russian holding the reins turned around and said, "Come," pulled me up beside him, and groped in his pocket. He brought out a handful of loose sugar and said "You," held out his enormous hand, I opened my mouth carefully and he tipped it in. Then he clapped me on the shoulder and exclaimed, "You woman, you good."

The village street was full of women in Polish and Russian uniforms. They ran after the cart and shouted at the soldier. One of them caught hold of my foot and screeched, "Kill her, kill the German." The soldier leant over and spat on the ground, cracked his whip at the two thin nags, and said, "You good." The women shrieked in outrage, lunged at me again, but he was faster.

We pulled up at the gate of the camp. They were lined up in rows of six. E.v.D. bent down and patted his boot, telling me to get rid of the knife. The cart moved off and they marched along behind until, toward evening, we came to a field with barbed wire. They filed through the gap in the wire; sentries were posted and the cart drove on, finally stopping at a farmhouse. The three officers and one olive-green jacket questioned me again, asked the same questions, gave me vodka, and locked me up. Hours later the door was opened and I heard someone being pushed in. It was E.v.D.

He spoke quickly: "They might let you go, if they do go to Viktor de Kowa, he's a friend, we never saw eye to eye about the war but he's a good person, he'll help you, tell him everything. I was mixed up in politics, much more than you realized, if they find out who I am they'll shoot me. You have to get away. Remember they can't stand sick women, they never touch them so limp or something like that and for God's sake throw that knife away. Hide during the day."

He must be mad, why should they let me go?

He continued, "The Nazis betrayed us, perhaps the Russians can use me, I'll become a Communist, they betrayed us all."

Three Russians are standing in the door looking at me. They move in and form a semicircle, look down at me and grin drunkenly. "Frau come," one of them says. I hit him in the stomach, he laughs and grabs my wrist, I bring my knee up, the others throw their arms around me. "Don't struggle, you can't do anything, they'll club you to death," E.v.D. says. They start pulling me about, I scream in the darkness, lash out with my feet, and they suddenly let me go. A candle flickers and the doctor's face appears. One of the Russians is stretched out on the floor, the other two have disappeared. The doctor pulls me into another room, a room with a bed; at least he's a doctor, I say to myself, at least he won't have a disease. He sits down on the bed and says, "You must go, you can't stay here in the camp." He goes out, turns the key in the lock, comes back with bread and bacon and water. In the evening they question me, the same questions over and over. Gray-eyes coos through clouds of smoke, "I marry you, you come to Moscow."

"I'm married already."

"You not married, you come to Moscow."

They locked me up again. In the night the doctor came and took me down to the cellar. It was full of German soldiers, Stalingraders, the Russians had set them to work repairing their trucks and gun carriers. I stayed with them for two days and nights. There were no sentries since, as they said themselves, escape was pointless, there were Russians everywhere, they'd rather stay and hope for a formal release—they'll give us a certificate when they've settled the issue, they said. "Did the green-jackets question you?"

"Yes, two of them wore green jackets."

"They're from the MVD."

They shook me in the night: "You shout in your sleep, you can't stay here, you've got to get away." They gave me poppy seeds to combat dysentery, smuggled a note to E.v.D. in the camp, brought me a skirt and a head scarf and said, "There are two Germans in the village, an old couple. Their daughter was in Bernau, the last they heard —they want to try and get through to her."

Russian soldiers entered the cellar. I crawled under the sofa, the springs pressed against my face, I was sure they'd find me. Some time later I heard them in the yard, heard the horses gallop away. The Stalingraders came back with a scrap of paper: *Go to Viktor.*

The next morning, before sunrise, I was limping down the village street. I'd folded the scarf over my forehead and knotted it under my chin like a Russian peasant woman, tied the skirt with a piece of string, put on a louse-ridden sweater and Stepfather's boots—knife still under my toes— and squashed poppy seeds over my cheeks. An old couple with a wheelbarrow was standing at the end of the street behind a shed. We set off. "You must go to the office," they said, "you can't go without papers." They were frightened, didn't know where I came from, went on and on about the papers. We came to another village and I wanted to skirt around it, avoid the main street, but they insisted on the office and the papers. A Russian officer stepped out from a barn and shouted, "*Stoi!*" I ran into a field zigzagging like a rabbit, he chased me, bullets zipped around my feet. I stopped and raised my hands, remembered I was no longer in uniform and lowered them again. He came up and stared at me, stared at the poppy seeds and said "Ugh," fired a few rounds into the air and went away again. I was terrified, terrified of the night, of being alone. I stood there for a long time wondering whether I shouldn't go back, back to the camp, to E.v.D.

Two days later I found a farmhouse. I waited until it grew dark, hoping there were no Russians inside. Then a woman came out carrying a pail. I ran up to her and asked for water, she fetched a cup and said, "Go away, I've nothing to eat, the Russians come at night."

Five nights later I was seeing castles palaces lights chandeliers; I stared at the sky, followed the stars, lost my way, tried to remember how we had reached Friesack. Then I gave up caring. I went up to a house and knocked at the door; an old man opened it and I tried to speak but couldn't. He beckoned me into the kitchen and gave me water and a piece of bread with rock salt on it. A woman came in and said, "Are you mad?" My tongue was swollen, my lips cracked and flaking, I babbled, "Please let me stay, just for one night." She took me down to the cellar and I lay down on a potato sack among coal briquettes and heaps of wood shavings, squashed lice, heard rustling and squeaking, wanted to cry, couldn't any more.

TEN

The man in the filthy once-white smock reaching down to his ankles skipped along beside me, pumping my hand heartily and gazing up at the pale-blue early-summer sky, exclaiming, "My aunt, my aunt, I'm going to visit her, she's got the papers, she's expecting me." I must be in Wittenau, I said to myself: there's an asylum in Wittenau, not much further to Berlin. The lunatic stopped and stretched his neck, smacked his forehead against mine, and whispered confidentially, "My aunt's got all the papers." He galloped along behind me stumbling over his billowing smock, fell down and cried: "My aunt, she's got the papers!"

Two Russians were repairing a telephone pole at the corner. I limped across the road, they put down their tools, came over to me, and said, "Frau come." I'd eaten my poppy seeds so I squinted at them and drooled a bit but they didn't seem at all put off, just said, "Frau come," stubbornly. I turned and ran, they fired over my head and shouted "*Stoi!*" I kept on running until I came to the first house stumps: Berlin, I said to myself, I've made it. I sat down on the curb and watched women with head-scarves and buckets, old men with flapping trousers rummaging through the rubble, watched them knock stones into shape; a wave of warmth went through me, embraced me, held me close. I felt safe, secure, I was back in Grandfather's shack in Zossen, great feather bed with the dip in the middle in front of the glowing stove, wind slamming the door of the goat's stall, apple-tree branches stroking the roof.

I reached Wilmersdorf before nightfall. Stepfather was standing behind his bench hammering crooked nails straight. He stared at me, his chin trembled, his mouth puckered, his calloused hands groped through frayed pockets. He sat down beside the old sewing machine and said, "Hildekind, my God, Hildekind," over and over again. He cried and I stood there under the painting of Hans Sachs wondering desperately how I could comfort him. "Have you heard from Mother?" He shook his head, wiped his face with a dirty rag, and said, "Grandfather's waiting at number 8."

That evening we sat on the stairs near the hall door and listened to Grandfather snoring. Stepfather said, "My hands saved me. I held them out and said 'raboti' (workers), they felt them and said 'Yes, you raboti.' They shot some of the men in the cellar, and the Bartsch family—you know, they had a daughter—they took the mother and daughter away together with Mother Blocken and the rest of the family committed suicide." He stood up and felt his way down the stairs, bent forward, and had a dreadful fit of dry coughing, came back, and sat down again. He seemed to reflect, put his index and middle fingers inside his frayed collar and stroked his scrawny neck, cleared his throat, and said, "They say the SS treated them the same way, but if they hadn't behaved like that—I mean if the Russians hadn't collected an eye for an eye and a tooth for a tooth—believe me, child, the whole of Berlin would have gone over to them, we'd all be Communists now. I was one already, only waited for the day when they'd march in and liberate us, but now . . ." He rubbed his nose and his bald, bony head. "Now I'm not anything any more." He coughed again and then went on, "You know, old Bismarck always said that Germany and Russia belonged together—ah well." He stood up and pushed the bullet-riddled front door shut, lay down on the floor, and said, "Oh yes, your friend, the tall one from Wexstrasse who was in your class, she threw herself out the window. They still turn up at night when they're drunk—you can't stay here, there's no water, we have to fetch it from Prinzregentenstrasse, but I've still got a little bread, I can give you some. The people who lived here escaped, that's how we came by the extra room." He sighed and turned over on his side, murmuring as he dropped off to sleep. "Wish I knew where to send you."

Grandfather got up in the morning, placed his chair by the window so that he could see the street, and said, "All is well, now I'll just wait for Mother."

I walked to Dahlem. Russians were living on Gelfertstrasse. I found E.v.D.'s mother and Sister Amalia in a cellar and showed them the scrap of paper with *Go to Viktor* written on it. His mother said, "Yes, that's Ewald's handwriting," folded the paper carefully, and added, "We were raped."

Sister Amalia tugged at her bonnet and whispered, "Oh please, not in front of the child."

"They are like animals," his mother said undaunted. "The first ones to arrive were quite acceptable, they must have been the elite, but after that . . ." She sighed and looked up at the ceiling. "Animals, there's no other way of describing them. They shot the young woman next door through the hand. They had some potatoes they wanted to wash and put them in the toilet, one of them pulled the chain and of course they were flushed away. 'Sabotage!' they screamed and fired off their weapons. The irony of it was that we hadn't seen any water for weeks, never thought of looking in the cistern. 'Sabotage!!' It's quite unbelievable to think that they don't know what a toilet is—never stop going on about *Kultura* and are really completely uncivilized." She lay down on the mattress, Sister Amalia drew up a blanket and whispered, "You mustn't excite yourself." His mother held up the slip of paper again and said, "I often felt that Ewald went too far in his opinions, but good Lord, how right he was."

By noon the next day I was at Branitzerplatz shouting, "Bongi!" A French window on the first floor opened and I heard "Child," saw red hair, black poodle, blue eyes flashing through tears that spilled over sunken cheeks. She opened the front door, embraced me; I said, "What now?" She started to laugh, tears flowing down her cheeks again. A door slammed in the house and she said abruptly, "Russian officers live on the ground floor, you can't risk staying here."

That evening I was standing in front of Viktor de Kowa's house. A Japanese flag fluttered on the roof and a gray-haired woman in an apron was busy weeding the garden. She came up the gravel drive to the gate and asked, "May I help you?" "I'd like to speak to Herr de Kowa," I said hesitantly. She weighed me up with bright canary eyes, blinked inquisitively, and piped, "One moment, please." I sat down on the ground, looked hopefully at the spiky octangular house, and squashed lice. Footsteps softly crunched the gravel and a gentle voice cooed a long-drawn-out Yeees?" I stood up and looked at the beautiful laughing impenetrable Asiatic face. "Ewald von Demandowsky said

I should come to you," I said. "I've got lice and dysentery
but no papers." The fine eyebrows went up and stayed up. I
stood in the hall; silk-covered walls, fragile chairs on elegant rugs. She brought me a kimono, took my things and
threw them into the courtyard, ordered water to be
brought, heated and poured into the bathtub; it was my
first bath in three months.

We sat in the library. Viktor inspected his graceful
hands, freed a candlewick with a matchstick, let his tongue
glide back and forth behind his closed lips, bowed his
splendid head, and listened reverently as I told my story.
When I had finished he stood up and stretched himself,
buttoned his jacket, said, "Potz Blitz!" with immaculate
enunciation, walked over to the door, turned around, gazed
at me with his large earnest gray eyes, and added, "I shall
call you Mechthild; I feel you are a Mechthild." Michi de
Kowa smiled and scrutinized me with her black eyes, didn't
believe a word. Twenty years later we were sitting together
in a Berlin night club; she looked at me over the flickering
candle, sipped her Louis Roederer, and called out above
the deafening rock music, "I thought you were a werewolf,
I was too afraid to send you away."

Sitting in the oval dining room with the oval dining table
were the two well-known actors Günther Lüders and Karl
Schönböck, together with a Luthuanian actor named
Dohnberg. Frau Müller squawked "Frau Müller" from a
dark corner. "The parrot wishes to be introduced," said
Viktor. We ate vegetable soup and bread, they drew me
into the conversation and behaved as though I'd been
with them for years.

I lay between the white, ironed, sun-scented sheets and
tried to keep myself awake, the longer to breathe the fra-
grance, the cleanness, the quiet community of the big sleeping house. How far everything is when one has to walk, I
thought to myself, a thought that has stayed with me ever
since.

On my way to breakfast the next morning I heard dreadful tortured sounds coming from the dining room. I opened
the door carefully and saw Frau Müller riding on a cocker
spaniel. Claws hooked into its collar and screaming obscenely into the popeyed animal's ear, she urged it to go hurtling around the oval table at breakneck speed. After ten
laps Frau Müller hopped into her cage, winked an indolent

evil eye at me, and grated, "Good morning, Mechthild."
Karl Schönbröck, whom everyone called Schampi, came in
sneezing, looked at the terrified dog, and sniffled, "Aha,
morning exercises completed, I see." Michi tripped in and
chirruped, "Good morning, my dears," and, "Yes, yes, the
pets." Günther Lüders drifted toward the table smoothing
his hair, found my astonishment at Frau Müller's behavior
highly amusing, and uttered a great rolling Ho Ho Ho
which Frau Müller promptly echoed with deadly accuracy.
Günther broke off immediately and sat down indignantly,
shooting peeved glances toward the cage.

Michi inhibited me. Women inhibit me. Men had become friends. My relationship to men had been formed on
the run, in the prison camp, by Grandfather; the implicit
honesty and trust which had arisen out of mutual fear, exhaustion, helplessness, and communal life led to untold difficulties and misunderstandings later on. Especially in
America, where a man was never a woman's friend nor
ever will be, where the man-woman conflict has been retained and nurtured from the pioneer era and has led to an
insurmountable rift, a setting-up of limits of which the
women are the more implacable wardens. If, in my conversations with American men, I went beyond the accepted
giggling stage, they became suspicious and frightened and
took me for a dangerous bluestocking who didn't observe
the rules, a busybody who might ask about politics or even
money. The trust had been strengthened by my work in
film studios where the crews are ninety percent male, but
above all it had been the prison camp, where human being
sought human being, not man woman or vice versa. Man's
pursuit of woman was left to the victors for the time being.

"Good morning Viktor, good morning Viktor!" Frau
Müller shrieked delightfully, banging her beak with her
claw. Viktor strode to his place at the head of the table,
said, "Ei der daus, what a splendid morning," and sat down
to examine his egg. "How are our beloved chickens?" he
asked, each syllable pronounced with painful precision.
"Good, good," cheeped Michi, "the dog makes them nervous sometimes." He tapped and peeled and then swiveled
around toward the door, calling out in a voice just loud
enough to be intelligible in the kitchen, "The fact that we
are occupied doesn't oblige us to cook eggs in the Russian
fashion." Schampi sniffled and patted his bunged-up nostril

saying, "I slept marvelously; and how's our Mechthild today?" I bubbled thank you for asking and thank you for everything and wonderful and had forgotten what it was like to sleep in a real bed and eat breakfast and once again thank you. My cascade was acknowledged by thoughtful nods and Viktor broke the ensuing silence with, "Mechthild should not go into the garden; it would be inadvisable for her to be seen by the Russians, besides which we must procure her some papers." Dohnberg, also known as Donschi, burst in on the solemnly munching gathering begging forgiveness. Günther and Schampi stood up and said in unison, "We'll fetch the water." Donschi stared into his teacup, his face creased with sleep and life. "The Russians are a race of rustic nature boys, only interested in women, completely overlook such delightful morsels as myself, primitive clods," he mumbled. Viktor leant across to Michi and said, "Heart of my heart, the chill emptiness of our walls depresses me. What do you say we fetch the Monet from the cellar?" He unpacked it lovingly, hung it over the sideboard, and stood there marveling. "May I speak to you for a moment?" I whispered, breaking the spell. I followed him into the library and said, "If you could get me some papers I'd like to go back to Biesenthal, I know the way, and I might get through. I want to persuade Ewald von Demandowsky to escape before it's too late, before they send him to Siberia—the Stalingraders will help me."

Viktor stood up, put the tips of his fingers together, crossed to the desk with measured, abrupt steps, turned shortly, went to the fireplace, from there to the window, retraced his route, seemed to have forgotten my presence, finally sat down again, and stroked his eyebrows. "Dear Mechthild, your proposal does you credit; under no circumstances will I support it, much as I treasure Ewald von Demandowsky as a friend. You are young and you will forget Ewald much sooner than you can realize at present. Go and write down your experiences, it will reconcile you and keep you busy. And don't try to steal away unnoticed."

Schampi and Günther came puffing up the hill with buckets full of water. I saw them speak with Viktor and then Schampi came toward me sniffling contentedly. They didn't let me out of their sight again, always stayed close, guarding me unobtrusively, or so they thought. In the afternoon I offered my services as water carrier. Schampi surveyed the terrain and said, "Can't see any Russians, we'll chance it." We crossed the wide street and entered an allotment, filled our buckets from the pump and started back. Viktor was on the terrace. "Mechthild must go down to the cellar at once," he shouted. They pushed a cupboard in front of the door and I heard Donschi shouting excitedly, heavy footsteps, cries and gunshots, then a long silence. At long last there was a scraping and scuffling and Michi came through the door saying, "Come, let's have tea." Schampi was sitting in the hall. "They must have seen us, they were drunk as lords, wanted blond woman, started shooting at Viktor, too drunk to hit him, thank God," he whispered excitedly, ending with a tremendous sneeze. The wall behind him was full of holes, the frame of the Monet hanging in shreds. Viktor plucked at his cuffs and drank his tea, leaned forward and took Michi's hand. "Heart of my heart, I think a gentle nap would do my delectable person no harm whatsoever." Viktor exalted everything except his own heroism, goodness, and helpfulness.

Our provisions were at an end; Günther and Schampi patched up inner tubes, straightened spokes, and rode off to the Brandenburger Tor bristling with documents and identity cards in the hope of finding people willing to swap: shoes for flour, a frying pan for a rucksack, powdered eggs for a bicycle pump, a teapot for dried peas, pearl barley for a Persian rug. . . . Schampi came back with a poor haul; he was alone, Günther had disappeared. We sat on the moonlit terrace, long after the curfew hour, and had visions of him being dragged off to a camp on his way to Siberia. "I shall go to the Kommandatur in the morning," Viktor said. "Moo," said a deep voice right behind us. A black-and-white speckled cow was standing in the shadows chewing absently; hanging on to the frayed rope around its neck was Günther. "I've brought a new tenant," he said. He'd run into a group of Russians with a bellowing cow; they'd displayed such keen interest in his bicycle that he'd felt obliged to offer it in exchange for the cow. The beast's udders were at bursting point and Günther, lacking (a) the necessary experience and (b) a bucket, had been forced to surrender the milk to a quickly gathering crowd of people armed with pots and pans. We felt it to be an act of providence and saw ourselves churning butter, making milk soups, nibbling cheese. Two Russian officers accompanied by three soldiers appeared the next morning and maintained that the cow had been stolen. After an endless discussion, led by Viktor and translated by Donschi, they decided to waive their right to military court proceedings and went off dragging the cherished animal behind them.

Michi's battery-powered radio was our link with the outside world; we treated it like an only child, turning it on for five minutes at a time. One afternoon in mid-July we heard unmistakable American swing instead of the usual Russian marches and we all stared at the radio thunderstruck. Two hours later a jeep pulled up in the drive and a man in a uniform I had seen in the newsreels climbed down and asked to speak to Frau de Kowa. I watched Michi fall down the stairs, throw her arms around his neck and burst into tears. "Percy, how wonderful, how absolutely wonderful," she cried. Michi came from a famous Japanese family and had lived in Europe for many years, making a wealth of friends in many countries who had not forgotten her during the war; one of them was General Montgomery. He had sent their mutual friend Percy, a correspondent for *Life,* to ask whether he could be of any assistance.

Shortly after this reunion the English, French, and American forces arrived to sit down with the Russians and split the city up into sectors rather as a child shares out his birthday cake. Viktor was appointed Civilian Director of Army Welfare "Berlin Showboat," and received a license enabling him to reopen the Tribune am Knie, the first theater to start production again. The Russians had now left our sector and returned only as visitors, as in the case of our première. We had hammered and sawed, removed Russian excreta from the rickety Bechstein grand, made evening dresses out of curtains and sheets, and learned verses by Wilhelm Busch which Viktor had adapted for the occasion. I was allowed to be the announcer: "Eins, zwei, drei im Sauseschritt läuft die Zeit, wir laufen mit . . ."* was my opening line, heralding a succession of lean and hungry stars who recited poems, played the piano, sang songs, and danced by candlelight.

Michi had consulted an astrologer and his forecast was rosy: "Your mother is alive," he told me. "You'll be hearing from her soon."

A woman on a rusty bicycle came to the theater bringing me a letter from Grandfather.

Englishmen were now living in Else Bongers' house.

---

* One, two, three, time runs at a gallop, and we run with it . . .

They were polite and distant, left their cigarettes lying around. and then indignantly accused the landlady of theft; they behaved like testy governesses whose wards were not responding correctly to discipline. The contempt shown at military offices and on the streets left us unmoved; their mere presence had meant liberation for us.

Actors, students, writers, and directors started visiting Else Bongers again. among them a journalist named Edith Hamann who greeted everybody with "Who's dead?" which surprised no one. the survivors being in the minority. We had almost given up hope by the time the Allies finally did arrive and their coming didn't transform the ruins into houses, bring the dead back to life, the missing marching home again. didn't still our fears or prompt the millions of rats to take to their heels. But for me and the meager remains of my generation their coming meant access to the book with seven seals: stories were told, secrets disclosed, fates and destinies traced and unraveled. A vast multitude of questions arose: Who's who, Who was who, When was who what. and Is he or was he who he says he was?

I busied myself with a fresh outbreak of dysentery and concentrated on the only thing I had ever really learned: survival, which now offered itself in the form of theater. Karlheinz Martin had seen me at the Tribuene and offered me two parts in his coming productions. "You will accept the offer," Viktor said, "I can replace you, two parts are better than one Chorus." Again I had the feeling that I should be happy but wasn't, for good reason as it turned out, for I was suddenly banned by the military authorites: grounds, friendship with E.v.D. and the honeymoon we'd spent between Friesack and Biesenthal. A few days later the ban was lifted, this time without explanation, but it couldn't surprise me any more for I had long since realized that my never-ending succession of overlords all had one thing in common —capriciousness. Four years later I was relieved of an American film contract for the same reason— a film in which my costar was to have been an actor for whom I had the greatest respect, Montgomery Clift—and in the course of my inquiries I learned that another actress with designs on the part had succeeded in bringing the old file to light, and that Viktor de Kowa and Else Bongers had gone to the authorities and persuaded them to drop the charges against me. I also learned that Else Bongers had been married to a man actively engaged in politics who had been forced to flee to Shanghai in 1933, that she had been forbidden to leave the country until 1945 and had been held as a guarantee against further political activity on his part, that her father-in-law had been a pre-Hitler government official, and that he had been knocked half-blind by the Nazis and kept in a concentration camp for twelve years.

I left the de Kowa residence when the new rehearsals began. They had deloused me, fattened me up, protected and saved me, and it was time to show my gratitude by relinquishing my bed and board in favor of some more needy applicant. The house on Gelfertstrasse was vacant so accommodations were no problem; what to live on was the question—my salary had no buying power, there being officially nothing to buy. On my last evening I squeezed through the English, French, and American officers thronged around Viktor, stepped out onto the terrace and took my leave, whispered a Dankeschön up to the dark sky. "Vous êtes très belle," a voice said. My school French felt overtaxed so I remained silent. I recognized a Russian uniform, medals and ribbons, general's pips and stars, a friendly face with dark eyes. "Merci," I managed after considerable thought and dashed inside. Michi took my arm and whispered, "Make us a few sandwiches. I wanted to keep the food for tomorrow but they've brought alcohol and on an empty stomach—you know what I mean." I picked up a candle, went to the kitchen, sat down and cut paper-thin slices.

There's someone here, I tell myself, and turn around, can't see anyone, hear heavy breathing, stand up, bread knife in the right hand—there's my Vous-êtes-très-belle Russian. He's standing at the door, says nothing this time, just looks—that international United Nations common-to-*muzhiks*-and-generals look. I slam the knife into the table, the wooden handle quivers, slowly he advances, stops at the table, we gaze at each other over the knife. Shouting's no good, I tell myself, murder's exaggerated, rape I don't relish, talking won't help much, and Merci not at all. He comes around the table, I tug at the knife, it's stuck. He grins lazily and grabs my neck and other things. "I think that's low down, vile, and absolutely beastly of you," says a tearful voice behind me, "to steal that gorgeous Russian stallion from me, I'd never have thought it of you." Donschi's standing at the door dabbing his eyes, badly in need of

support. My general stalks from the kitchen and the house,
I run over to Donschi, wanting to thank him for coming to
my rescue, he knocks aside my outstretched hand, says
"Bitch," and sweeps out too.

I dug up my mummy case. It had forfeited part of its
headdress but smiled, forgiving and mysterious, no offense.
"What you doing?" an apparently very long-legged, chewing individual called over the fence. The garden gate opened
and two Americans came through it, took the case
from me, and studied it dubiously. "I live here," I said. The
second one was small and dark-haired; he ground a cigarette-end morosely into the earth with his toe and said in
surprisingly accent-free German, "This house has been requisitioned, Fräulein, you can take along a suitcase, be out
in two hours." "I've got an uncle in Chicago," I said hopefully but he wasn't listening. "It's curfew, I'm not allowed
on the streets," I said. He shrugged his shoulders and went
through the living room into the kitchen. E.v.D.'s mother
and Sister Amalia picked up their bundles and moved back
to the bombed-out cellar.

We played *Raub der Sabinerinnen* in the Renaissance
Theater in the evenings and rehearsed *Kammersänger* with
Hubert von Mayerinck during the day. One day between
the rehearsal and the performance a messenger boy arrived
and said, "Herr Barlog's looking for you, please go and see
him, he's living at this address in Lichterfelde."

He was standing in the garden; he bit into a tomato and a
fountain of juice shot into the air and settled on his hair-
antennae. "There you are!" he yelled. "Well well, want a
tomato? All we've got is tomatoes." He pointed to his vegetable patch and introduced me to his wife Herta. "Well, we
licked the shit, didn't we?" he said, handing me a tomato.
Herta smiled gently and blinked her big cat's eyes. "Now
then. I'm opening a theater, they're giving me a license"—
the fizzing was well under way—"Schlosspark Theater in
Steglitz; we start in November. Got thousands of actors but
no nails—Christ, we need nails for the sets and everything.
My idea is that you recite a prologue by Goethe and then
we'll play *Hocus Pocus* by Curt Goetz. What do you say?"
I nodded enthusiastically. "Where you living?" "I'm not, I
thought perhaps I could spend the night . . .?" He gave me
the address of the actress Hilde Körber, saying, "She's in
good with the Yanks, got a big place and no fear of requisi-

tioning." I went to her and said, "Barlog sent me." I might
have said "Open Sesame"; I was ushered in, given bread,
soup, and a bed for a fortnight, made to feel at home.

Mother had given several letters to refugees heading for
Berlin and one day one of them came through. "I stand at
the crossroads," she wrote, "asking what happened in Wilmersdorf and Zehlendorf, they say a great many were
killed or raped, I have little hope of seeing you again. I'm
trying to procure papers so that I can return to Berlin—
they all say I'm mad since there's nothing to eat in Berlin
and typhus and dysentery have broken out, but I don't
care, I have to find you. We got through unscathed, the
fighting was terrible of course, but we lived through it."

Hubert von Mayerinck, lovingly known as "Hubsi,"
came into our long narrow dressing room and yelped,
"God I'm in a tizzy, first nights send me stark raving, the
whole orchestra's full of Americans and English and
French and they don't understand a word, poor lambs. By
the way, a new batch of Americans arrived today, saw
them standing at Roseneck playing with their guns, they
stood on one side of the street, we on the other. They
looked over and spun their pistols—they're children, absolute infants, but my dear, the way they're built—faaabulous; shoulders like this"—he stretched his arms to their
full extent—"and hips like this"—brought his hands to
within an inch of each other—"faaabulous, especially the
blond one." The stage manager yelled, "Five minutes," and
Hubsi went out rolling his eyes. My part required me to
speak with an American accent so I slurred and drawled
my way through as rehearsed. After the performance I was
ordered to play without an accent in future, it would look
as if we were making fun of the troops. I practiced my
lines without an accent the whole next day, went hopefully
to the theater, and ran into a completely crushed Hubsi.
"What do you say to this," he squealed, arms raised on
high, "what do you say to this: I come home last night and
that lovely blond one from Roseneck is standing there in
front of my door chewing gum—which I personally don't
find too exciting—and says to me 'Your house is requisitioned!'" He stared at us, horrified. "What do you say to
that?"

The curtains parted and in came Herr Raeck, the manager. His nose was white, the surroundings green. "I have
to inform you that the theater has just been requisitioned.

We can't play any more," he said. All I possessed was the mummy case and a bicycle which Hilde Körber's son had given me. My gums and jaw were festering with infection and my dysentery had decided it was time to pay me another visit. I set out for Dr. Rode's office and found a heap of rubble with a note bearing the new address fluttering between the stones. He said, "It hurts now, a little bit." A young man in civilian clothes—a rare sight, the youngsters were either dead or in camps—stood in the corner with a cigarette holder between his teeth, talking to Dr. Rode in Russian. "Aha," I started to think but a shooting pain interrupted further conjecture. The youth's name was Mischa Schewatowsky, he gave me a chunk of bread and three cigarettes and asked, "Do you have somewhere to live?" My cheek was all puffed, I looked at Dr. Rode, who laughed and said, "No, no, he is friend, he been in Berlin for years." "They say there's a pension at the corner of Kurfürstendamm and Leibnizstrasse where one can still get a room for a few cigarettes," Mischa Schewatowsky said.

I fainted on the way there and when I came to it was dark and a lean boy with soft gray eyes and protruding ears was sitting beside me holding a cup of tea under my nose. "Have a sip first," he said. His name was Ricci Blum and he possessed, apart from the cup and the sofa on which I was lying, a camera and a gift for playing the piano in C major. During the day he photographed Americans and Englishmen for their family albums and at night he played in a little bar which called itself "Don Juan" and "Club." His repertoire included "It's a Long Way to Tipperary" and "In the Mood," and in fact anything that sounded all right in C major and warmed the hearts of the occupying forces. In exchange he received coffee, soup, and sometimes cigarettes. The bar was off limits, which meant no Krauts except for the frantically scurrying bartenders, the female rest-room attendants, the one-man show Ricci and a Viennese queen who sang *The Merry Widow* in full drag and called himself Marcel André. Ricci took me along, saying, "I'll be getting a bowl of soup at eleven, you can have some." He informed the English sergeant at the entrance that I was his sister and indispensable to him as a page-turner; the fact that he couldn't read a note he kept to himself. At ten the place was packed and by midnight they were all jammed around the piano singing and waving their glasses. The Americans called out "Hello Fräulein" and

seemed to have great difficulty in doing so: cowlike chewing motions and strangled mumblings in the back of the
throat. The Englishmen lolled serenely against the bar and
the walls, displaying India-trained sahib masks.

In the morning, as soon as the curfew was over, I went
to the Elton pension, the one Mischa had recommended;
the four-story house had been reduced to two by fire and
the rooms were hardly wider than the weak-springed sofa
that each contained. There were no windowpanes, no blankets, no sheets, no water, no light, but there was a kitchen
with a senile stove around which dozens of whores from
Augsburgerstrasse gathered in the mornings to warm their
curling tongs, bread, and cans of corned beef. As soon as it
was established that our professional interests didn't clash
they became very friendly and invited me to share their
nocturnal swag with them. A rotund redhead filed her nails
and announced to the weary congregation: "I struck a penicillin mine last night." Moth-eaten feathers fluttered on red
green violet negligees, voices rose shrilly, tongs and cans
clattered to the floor, the ampules were passed from hand
to hand and the initial excitement gave way to a blissful
thanksgiving. The milky liquid, which had been bought
with hard, honorably slept-for-cash, turned out to be a
mixture of flour and water; united around the gas stove,
they solemnly swore revenge.

I now had the choice between Ricci's soup plus a sleepless night on the piano bench and the Elton's lumpy sofa
minus soup. One morning I ran into the actress Sonja Zie-
mann, who'd been at the UFA school; she told me that she
was going into a production with the contemporary title
Love at First Sight, and that the female lead was still un-
cast. I went along, got the job, and we started to rehearse in
a living room with a pathetic old dysentery-plagued director who divided his time between the rehearsal and the lavatory. The play was to run at a movie house in the north of
Berlin; on the first night Russian officers and soldiers filled
the first ten rows; behind them sat a few frightened Berliners. When the final curtain came down two Russian soldiers jumped up on the stage; the director, emerging from
the toilet, yelled "Watch out!" and we sprang through the
dressing-room window, grabbed our bikes, and pedaled for
our lives.

The play soon came to an end and my career continued
with poetry readings on Sunday mornings for the Russian-

controlled radio station; since the electricity was more
often switched off than on, only the sound engineer and a
few hardened listeners were able to enjoy my tussle with
consonants and final syllables. Ricci regularly nodded off to
sleep over his Variations on a Sentimental Journey in C
Major, since his days were spent cycling from Kurfürstendamm to Lübars (some fifteen miles) and back, "swapping" with the farmers. One evening he brought a liver sausage; we put it between us on the piano bench and waited
for our pickled pals to go home. A dead-drunk Teddy bear
fell in love with the scratch on my nose, which had been
with me since the fateful first night, pulled me up off the
bench and cried, "Now you just tell me what happened to
your little nose." Uncertain with the language and disin-
clined to go into details anyway, I shot a forlorn glance at
Ricci; our young Goliath lost his composure and yelled
"You goddamn German," which didn't upset anyone particularly, and then grabbed me with a hand the size of an
umbrella. Gaunt little Ricci interrupted his performance,
got up, and knocked him flat with one dapper punch and
the ensuing free-for-all was eventually terminated by the
arrival of English military police armed with truncheons.
Ricci and I escaped through the lavatory window and shot
across the fields of rubble, avoided arrest, sacrificed a liver
sausage.

ELEVEN

Soldiers with swelling rumps and glittering rifles stood stiffly at attention outside the American Headquarters—OMGUS—in the residential suburb of Dahlem. Feeling feebler than ever in the face of this resolute virility, I slid through the rows of jeeps and august limousines and went up the steps to the entrance. German secretaries in the service of illustrious conquerors responded monosyllabically to my inquiries as though German had been relegated to the dead languages. It was here that the Americans de-Nazified, Nazified, testified, deduced, examined, pondered mysteries, judged, witnessed signatures, made declarations, comprehended the incomprehensible.

In the corridors stood rows of benches; on the benches sat the threadbare disheveled starving Germans with strained I-was-forced-to or indignant I-had-nothing-to-do-with-it expressions casting sidelong glances at the fag-ends lying in the corners like sparrows squinting at worms. Your name was called out and you entered a uniformed American secretary's outer office. Mine was telephoning: "Just a moment," she said, wagging her hand to dry the bright red nails. I looked around but found nowhere to sit so I stood and looked at the coffee cups, sugar bowls, and filing cabinets, keeping a respectful distance. An officer came in: he was faultlessly turned out but seemed harrassed, aghast at the weight of his responsibilities. The girl put down the receiver and allowed a sweet smile to blossom, moistened her lips with the tip of her rosy tongue, plucked at her seams and the hem of her skirt, crossed and recrossed her legs, patted and nudged her perfectly ordered hair, gave him a lazy wink that said: I'm game, or I know your tastes, or I felt we made an adjustment last night, or we don't know each other well enough yet, we should stick together so far from home, or thirty Krauts are waiting outside. The agitated officer flapped my questionnaire at me and I followed him into his office.

I needed permits, licenses, health certificates; the Schloss-park Theater was situated in the American sector and was therefore subject to American and not English control; authorities being what they are, I was obliged to go through the whole procedure of being checked once more. As was so often the case in my dealings with the occupying forces, my officer had language difficulties to begin with, became more and more fluent in the course of the lengthy examination, and finally forgot his accent altogether. He gave my questionnaire the full benefit of his loving attention to detail. The fact that I had answered "No" to the question "Were you a member of the BDM?" cast a pall over the proceedings. He leaned back in his chair, tapped the edge of his desk with his pencil, and honored me with a stare; the stare and the pose were designed to make clear to me that he was informed, in the picture, not to be fooled under any circumstances. My training in Biesenthal stood me in good stead and I parried his stare coolly, although palpitations made it none too easy. The "No" irritated him, and this new irritation trickled down and mingled with the old which had been provoked by the fact that I'd neglected to emigrate at the age of seven, had failed to grasp the situation, organize a revolution, form resistance movements, had wantonly ignored the developments around me and squandered myself on the trite business of growing up. I couldn't argue with him.

This was to be only the beginning of a series of visits to the authorities which continued for twenty years. Five and a half years after this disheartening interview I was finally granted American citizenship and the judge in the Los Angeles courthouse told me to raise my right hand and swear that I wasn't, never had been nor ever would be, a member of the Communist Party. I was loath to bind myself so conclusively but after five and a half years of being stateless I felt it advisable to keep my doubts to myself. A stateless person is subjected to treatment comparable only to what I imagine smallpox or cholera victims have to suffer: at airports one is locked into rooms usually used for air freight and medically examined in a manner which is otherwise practiced only in the Orient when the police raid the red-light district (so I'm told); tax payments are exacted with an eye to creating total chaos and invariably succeed. At the end of the proceedings the judge offered me his hand and my papers, and dismissed me in the knowledge that I was now a tolerated member of an eminent State. I plodded back down the long courtroom but, as I finally got to the door, was pulled up by his "By the way, were you a member of the Nazi Party?" My "No" was free of any binding oath this time but he nodded happily just the same and let me go.

During the fifties I made a number of European films and was often absent from the American continent for longer periods than were allowed for naturalized citizens. As a result I spent a lot of time dashing from one consulate to another, meeting friendly consuls who said friendly "No's" to my request for an extension and thus obliged me to board the next plane for Washington, or unfriendly ones who did the same in an unfriendly fashion, or small-town consuls who seemed to welcome a change and, after much beseeching, renewed my permit for a further three months, making it possible for me to cross the border between Salzburg and Berchtesgaden. In a town in southern Germany a sharp-profiled lady consul sat there just waiting for distraught extension-seekers like a tarantula waiting for its prey. "As an American you should be happy to work and live there—get a job as a waitress if you don't like the films they offer you. You have a duty to your country." I knew her speeches by heart but still hoped with each visit that I might hear a variation on the theme—in vain. In 1962 I married an Englishman and automatically received a British passport; since American law decrees that one can love only one country, I was required to forfeit the slim little booklet that had given me such joy. I hurried to the glass-domed consulate and was brought before the tarantula (who looked better nourished from year to year): "No more extensions for you, dearie!" she screeched delightedly. I placed the passport on her table, held up my new one, turned on my heel, and left with the gorgeous picture of her horror-struck face stamped indelibly on my memory.

In mecca-OMGUS, anno 1945, desk drawers were locked up, ashtrays emptied, my questionnaire carefully filed, points not covered put off till the morrow. On my way out through the main door I heard heels being clicked together: a general was puffing up the steps. The recent past crowded in on me and only in the nick of time was I able to prevent myself from saying Heil Hitler.

TWELVE

Boleslaw Barlog jumped onto the feebly lit stage. It was the size of a pocket handkerchief and the auditorium was long and thin like a village movie house, totally unsuited, it seemed, to the demands of live theater. The actors stood around in a half-circle, their frail bodies bowed forward as though incapable of bearing the weight of their bones. Barlog explained and demonstrated, explanation and action becoming one. He was a dreadful actor; unhampered by vanity, he made his points and illustrated his demands by preposterously overplaying and so evoked from his audience a warm cocky feeling of being able to do better. He spread confidence and enthusiasm, made us forget the hunger and the illnesses, celebrated improvement with spontaneous cries and wild gestures, heart-rendingly mourned our slowness on the uptake or lack of talent. He underplayed his brilliant observations and directions, he didn't need intellectual dissertations as awe-inspiring fill-ins to help him find the clue to a difficult passage; he would take a sticky speech or a bad scene which couldn't be cut and breathe life into it, make it bloom with apparent ease; dictated without becoming a dictator, prodded and stabbed without the sadism which so many of his less gifted colleagues love to employ—a demanding creator who reveled in the glory of his gifts. With Barlog I took up again the life which had already seemed ended when Meixner was called up. Creating discipline in the midst of chaos, unmelodramatic earnestness in the face of general cynicism, he was the initiator of the most glorious epoch of theater that an actor, experienced or greenhorn, could wish for.

To begin with I sat behind Herta, his wife and assistant, waiting for my tiny entrance in *Hocus Pocus* and the Goethe prologue. She sorted and ordered the tattered pages of the script, wrote down his directions between the lines and in the margin, raised her index finger at the end of re-

hearsals to lend import to her timid "Ten o'clock tomorrow
and word-perfect." We came to rehearsal either on foot or
on rickety bicycles whose tires tended to deflate every few
yards, or, taking the risk of coming late, on the irregular
metropolitan railway. From Hans Söhnker, Biegel, Leibelt,
Matthes, Bluhm, Marie Luise Ludwig, and Winnie Markus
down to the ancient Ernst Stein, everyone was there
promptly at ten o'clock. Söhnker, who lived in a garage in
Zehlendorf and whose tires looked like a patchwork quilt,
once had the misfortune to board a train which came to a
stop miles from anywhere and remained there for over an
hour. He stumbled onto the stage puffing his apologies and
was greeted by icy silence. So he peered into the murky auditorium and tried a charming, persuasive "Now look,
Bolli, you know that . . ." A thunderous blast from the siz-
zling organ drove him back to the wall: "You needn't bother to show up here any more—even if you are a star, get
me?" After ten minutes the crisis subsided and work went
on.

A few days before the opening I was crossing Rheinstrasse in the pouring rain when a jeep pulled up beside me.
"Hello, Fräulein," a voice called. One didn't react to this
sort of thing; I raised my dripping nose high and walked
on. The jeep crawled along beside me. "I'll drop you somewhere if you like," he said, gargling his *l*'s and *r*'s. A short
while later, "Now get in, for God's sake," in perfect German. I peered through the rain and made out a grinning
youth. "You'll catch your death," he said, pretending concern. I got in, thanked him coolly. "May I pick you up
tonight?" "No." "Tomorrow?" "No." "Next week then?"
"No." He stamped on the brakes and I was thrown back
and forth like a yo-yo between the seat and the windshield.
Not wanting to wear out my welcome, I jumped down and
ran off.

It was cold on the first night. The audience had responded to the posters in the foyer and handed in buckets full of
nails, and now sat muffled in horse blankets and army
greatcoats waiting for the curtain to go up. It was a great
success—for Barlog, for the actors, and for the tunnellike
hall which had become a theater. Each evening I went in
front of the curtain and spoke the prologue, changed, and
then played the part of the housemaid. An usherette giggled, "A Yank comes in every night, buys a ticket, listens
to the prologue, and then goes out again." It was the tem-

peramental boy with the jeep. His name was Kurt Hirsch; sometime later he became Erich Pommer's assistant in Berlin, later still a husband of mine, and, much later, an exhusband of mine.

We rehearsed Rolland's *The Game of Love and Death* during the day, played *Hocus Pocus* in the evenings, and spent the time between rehearsal and performance rubbing our growling bellies in the communal dressing room. At five Schulz would arrive; she was a plump dresser, loved heartily by one and all, who developed bloodhound instincts on first nights; she planted herself in front of the door, sniffed out the uninvited guests without ever having to ask, and sent them packing down the stairs again regardless of age, rank, or nationality. One night "Snow White," who, thanks to her attentiveness and unbounded love for the spoken word, had been born for the prompter's box, entered the dressing room tragically and said, "Winnie Markus is ill." Barlog was close behind her. He said, "Now show us what you can do, you're taking over." I knew the part but had never rehearsed it. There was just enough time for a hasty conference and then I was on. I played the part until Winnie came back on New Year's Eve, thoroughly ruining my enjoyment of that holiday.

It grew colder, our hunger increased; the Morgenthau Plan was still a well-kept secret, but its effects were very tangible. The intervals between my stomach cramps grew shorter and our theater doctor, Dr. Schaake, risked imprisonment to procure vitamin injections for us, helping us over the worst. An actor gave me half a cigarette and said, "Here, take a drag, the cramps'll go away." I started to smoke, cigarettes cost fourteen marks each but were at least obtainable, as opposed to bread or butter.

The American Kommandant invited Barlog and his ensemble to a reception at his house on the Wannsee. Each of us put on his treasured best suit or dress and we filed into the luxuriously heated hall looking like a bunch of starving refugees, hoping not to be attacked by sudden cramps. Our eyes flickered and flamed as they lighted on the long tables full of sandwiches and our feet slowly lost the numbness which had become a permanent condition since the beginning of winter. The General and his officers were standing in a long line like tin soldiers. He stretched out his hand to each of us with a jovial smile. Just as he was turning to me,

I felt a terrific blow in the back; my legs gave way and I sprawled forward on the polished parquet. Something moist and spluttering burrowed in my ear and neck, sat on me, made my joints and bones creak and my senses reel. I was eventually relieved of the load, hauled to my feet and found myself looking eyeball-to-eyeball at a grinning animal the size of a donkey; its head was as big as a baby carriage and its body seemed to be swathed in a heap of furs. It was led away; I was beaten and brushed until the black of my dress slowly became visible again and then brought before the general for a second attempt at a handshake. "That was our Leonhardiner hound, he seemed to take to you," the General's translator said. The door behind him opened and in came a waitress carrying a large tray, followed closely by the dog, who let out a moan of delight, stood up and planted his paws on my shoulders, this time sending me flying backwards, sat on my stomach, and proceeded to lick my face with a tongue as long as a bath towel. After a short scrap with five members of the occupying forces he was overpowered and dragged to the door again. He craned his neck and gazed back at me with damp eyes, let out a couple of woof-woofs and wagged his bargepole tail, which, as he came into line with the long tables, swept plates, sandwiches, cups, and coffeepots effortlessly to the floor, shortening in his ardor the chances of survival for our shaky ensemble.

Although fraternizing was strictly forbidden, Kurt Hirsch stood at the stage door, groped into one of his bulging pockets, and brought out a hamburger dripping fat. "I got them at the officer's mess," he said, "I thought you might . . ." My pride had a sharp tussle with my hunger and hunger triumphed. I wolfed it down, he groped in a second pocket, a strange fluttering coursed from my stomach to my neck, and I threw up over his beautifully creased trousers. He held my head carefully like a trained nurse and said "Jesus Christ."

He was a Czechoslovakian Jew, born in Teplitz-Schönau and raised in Prague. At fourteen he escaped to New York with his parents, became an American citizen, parachuted into France, and fought his way through to Germany and Berlin. He had a benevolent Teddy bear's face, liked to laugh, lost his temper readily, was young and uncomplicated. A few days later he invited me to a black-market restaurant. We ate "Chinese"—chopped-up horse meat—and he settled the bill with a tin of cocoa. He wrote an exuberant letter to his parents who replied with ten devastating pages in which they accused him of the most unbelievable lack of gratitude and loyalty and an unpardonable incapacity to hate. His dismay didn't stop him from smuggling me drops and creams against bleeding gums and other manifestations of malnutrition. The authorities had enforced typhus vaccinations and the actors at the Schlosspark Theater went on each night shaking with fever. Barlog was rehearsing Pagnol's *Marius,* my heart had bled as I heard that he'd given the lead to Gertie Soltau.

"The Russians are showing a film in Pankow tomorrow; they've only invited the Allied military but I know the Russian film officer and he said I could bring you along—what do you say?" Kurt Hirsch and I sat in the second row of the tiny cinema looking up at the stained screen; the English, American, French, and Russian officers fidgeted on their rickety chairs, smoked and chatted, the lights went out and Russian credits appeared, the film broke almost immediately, the lights went up again to general laughter, and we settled down to wait. A Russian officer got up and went out, we heard him swearing and banging doors, the credits came on again and then a watchtower, barbed wire, a tractor shoving a huge heap of bones into a hole in the earth, a shed full of plain wooden bunks bearing skeletons with death's heads and wide staring eyes. "That's the concentration camp at Auschwitz," whispered Kurt Hirsch. Hours later the lights went up, they turned around and looked at me. On the way home Kurt Hirsch said, "I lost sixteen relatives."

He dropped me in front of the pension and drove on to American Supreme Headquarters in Heidelberg. I lay on my sofa and wanted to talk, to Bongers or Meixner, wanted to talk the pictures away, wanted to hear that it wasn't true, thought of the old Volksturm reserve being beaten to death, the soldiers being run over by the tank. High heels pattered down the corridor and the redhead came in saying, "I've cracked some ice, want a hot-water bottle? I've got a cold, gonna take it easy for a bit."

"Did you know about Auschwitz?"

She was silent for a moment and then she said, "I knew one of the SS and he told about the Jewish camps—'do 'em no harm to work a bit,' he said."

Two days after the première of *Marius* one of the theater
secretaries came to see me at the pension and said, "Miss
Soltau has caught diphtheria, you're to take over the part."
She was young and unattractive with a tight old maid's
mouth. In the train on our way to the theater she said, "I've
seen you with that American—he's a Jew! Well really, I'd
have my pride, I wouldn't have anything to do with them."
We got out at Steglitz; I was extremely nervous since, as always, I knew my lines but had had no opportunity to rehearse. The secretary started again: "I can't understand it,
we're not being forced to go with them, I'd rather starve."

"Hold your tongue, you stupid cow!" I shrieked, then
felt even worse for letting her provoke me.

"I'll tell Barlog about this," she spluttered.

"Tell him and anyone else who cares to know, I don't
give a shit." Blackness welled up around me and in falling I
remembered that I hadn't eaten for two days. The show
was canceled, but I felt better the next day and played my
first performance. Barlog ran from the wings with outstretched arms and shouted, "You did us proud, a couple
more rehearsals and you'll be really good." He ducked behind a tall man with a pear-shaped head and cried, "Look
who I've brought you—he wants to say hello."

"You were excellent, I'm certain we'll be hearing a great
deal about you." Wilhelm Furtwängler shook my hand and
presented me with a rose, the first I had ever received and
the origin of which, in a bloomless Berlin, has remained a
mystery to this day. He smiled at me, left me standing
there speechless. I had seen him conducting Beethoven's
Fifth at the Philharmonic; the sirens had wailed and the
flak chattered, he had gone on conducting and the audience
had stayed in their seats.

Schultz, whose girth remained undented by the famine,
gazed at me in awe and then sniffled, "That's a grand start
and don't let anybody tell you different."

A rehearsal was called for the next afternoon and in the
morning I went to see Hans Söhnker, who was playing
Marius, to discuss our scenes. Teltowerdamm was on my
way, so I called on the Dipperts. Fritz's eyes were better
but he'd lost even more weight, seemed hardly present, and
Alike's solid rubber had shrunk; her skirt, which formerly
had always been in danger of splitting at the seams, now
hung around her like a sari. We embraced each other,
Alike cried a little, the war and the capitulation were not

mentioned, neither here nor at the theater; that one had survived was enough. "Do you want your room back?" she asked. I was earning and they'd have time to go to the black market, so I accepted gratefully.

"Are you pregnant?" Söhnker asked as he opened the door of his garage. "Soup," I said. Malnutrition caused my belly to swell for days on end, but it would then deflate back to its normal proportions for no apparent reason. During the swollen days I was often asked if I was expecting.

A man of medium height wearing a faded turtleneck sweater and a battered hat on the back of his head leaned around the door of the dressing room after the show and, slipping his words in quickly between wild bursts of coughing, said, "My name's Staudte—like you to do a test—preparing a film for DEFA." He tugged an old trench coat from his shoulder, went through at least three pockets before he finally found a bundle of folded pages. He placed them on my table and said, "Learn that by the day after tomorrow," and went out again. Schulz, who had been standing in the background, came over and said, "I know an old make-up man who works for DEFA—they're licensed by the Russians, so he's bound to be a Communist if he's with them."

He picked me up at seven in the morning and we wedged ourselves into his tiny car, which was rather like a mongrel dog, several makes having gone into the final composition. I was astonished that he had one at all, with gasoline to boot, and, after he'd switched on the deafening engine and brought the car up to a lively gallop, I shouted, "Are you a Communist?" He blinked his little blue eyes and went into a fit of laughter. I had no idea what a Communist was and his mirth didn't enlighten me any. Russian sentries were standing at the border between Berlin and Nowawes, the beginning of the Soviet sector. They shouted "*Stoi!*" and settled down to study our passports. I noticed that my knees were quivering and sweat was starting to pour from my forehead. They went into a hut and had a discussion, Staudte called out "Artista" and "Film," the magic word was spoken, and we were allowed to proceed. We shot two short scenes; he was gentle, patient, passed his hand thoughtfully over his eyes and furrowed cheeks, scratched his brow, pulled on his ear lobes, and said, "I'll let you know." Ten days later Herbert Uhlich said, "I'm the production manager—you've got the part." I had the feeling I should be pleased and was. I threw my arms around his neck and shook him like a cherry tree in my excitement. "How am I gonna do plays if they're all off filming?" Barlog said testily.

The remains of the Stettiner railway station loomed up out of the desert of rubble like a prehistoric skeleton; it formed both foreground and background to our first day of shooting on the first postwar German film: *The Murderers Among Us*. It was from this station that the trains to Swinemünde, Stettin, and Danzig had started; the only thing it had retained was the name; everything else in this region—squares, avenues, cul-de-sacs—had been renamed, each passing Kommandant setting up a monument to his nation in the form of a name plate, which was often the only visible indication of the previous existence of a thoroughfare.

The extras hung like bunches of grapes around the furiously snorting locomotive, intent only on protecting their places on the crowded footplates and handles; their job was simply to portray their recent experiences. For the leads, Wilhelm Borchert and myself, it was no different. In this respect there was in fact little difference between our methods of filming then and the contemporary methods employed by most of the German "Young Filmers," if one disregards the fact that Wolfgang Staudte was not an aging amateur and that his scenario was first-class, that he was capable of directing actors and of delivering a message, a message one could name as such with good conscience.

Friedl Behn-Grund, our cameraman, limped across the plowed-up platform spreading sweetness and light, squeezed in behind the antique camera wiping away the tears which rolled down his rosy cherub's cheeks and furtively massaged his stump, which was not yet healed and still caused him great pain under the crude wooden peg attached to it. "He was fetching water on the last day of the war when it happened," the floor manager whispered; Staudte's vitriolic glance brought his attention back to the job in hand.

For the next few months I commuted between the American-licensed theater and the Russian-licensed film. The *Murderers Among Us* crew received Russian "food packages" containing bacon and flour now and again, and the Americans gave a weekly "soup evening" for the

members of the Schlosspark Theater. We acknowledged
these Samaritan gestures with due respect and noted blissfully that our stomach cramps were occurring less and less
frequently. We received invitations and started going to the
gatherings they called "parties" (it was our first confrontation with either the word or the institution), listened to the
AFN,* learned to jitterbug, enjoyed the whisky-drenched
and vodka-besotted fights between White Russians in
American uniforms and Red Russians in Russian uniforms;
were kept in a constant state of amazement by the habits
and customs of our tenants as they slowly began to feel at
home. Kurt Hirsch had received his discharge papers together with a ticket to New York in eight weeks' time. He
seemed despondent; Berlin's wasteland with its busy
breathless hopefully planning inhabitants had become
home to him, in spite of all resolutions to the contrary. He
picked me up in the evenings, drove me to flattened Alexan-
derplatz, where we were shooting locations, and tried out
his Russian on the officers who discreetly stood around
watching the filming. We spent most of the shooting time
either beating off hordes of rats or repairing spluttering arc
lights, failing cameras, dead microphones, and flimsy film
which broke every few meters. There were no distributors
to harass us, no reporters to hold us up, no concerns about
money or star-images; we waited patiently, thankful to be
able to shoot the first film.

Apart from a few hours at night, I saw very little of my
room at Alike and Fritz's; we bumped into each other sleepily as I rushed out on my way to the studio, and all was
harmonious and friendly until, one fateful evening, Fritz
didn't return from a visit to the black market. He'd found a
new potato dealer and left in the early morning, saying he'd
be back by the afternoon. By nightfall he had still not
shown up and Alike went running up and down Teltowerdamm desperately crying out "Fitti!" At this tense moment,
Kurt Hirsch drove up in his jeep cheerfully blowing the
horn. We told him what had happened and just as we had
decided to go to the military police, Fritz staggered through
the door covered with blood and crumpled to the floor
whispering, "Two drunken Yanks beat me up." We carried
him upstairs and laid him on the bed, Alike sobbed and
fetched compresses to put on his blue-black eye, he opened

* The Armed Forces Network.

the other undamaged one, saw Hirsch's uniform, let out a dreadful wail, and fainted again; he revived after a few minutes and started screaming in a Munich dialect he used only in moments of extreme stress. This understandable outburst was greeted with cries of "Poor old thing" and "Don't get excited now." His inflexibility, often a cause of irritation for Alike, made it impossible for him to forget the incident and our relationship suffered accordingly.

I found an apartment on the Schlachtensee and paid the rent with cigarettes. The film was almost finished, and we started rehearsals for *As You Like It*. I had a lot of trouble with the sparkling Celia, traipsed leaden-footed through the papier-Mâché forest, and delivered my speech on Gargantua's mouth with the eloquence of a yokel. Else Bongers laughed till she cried and said she'd never seen such a devastating approach to Shakespeare. Luft and Karsch, the much-feared critics, hampered by the fact that they'd credited me with talent on the strength of my earlier performances, were not uncharitable. After the première, Barlog sat on the dressing-room sofa rummaging in his antennae, let well-wishers embrace him and congratulate him on his success, sat there looking depressed. After a while he nudged me with his elbow and said, "Well listen, I've got another play, *Three Men on a Horse*. There's a Ziegfeld girl in it, she has to dance and, the main thing, she's got a speech defect—ought to be right up your alley."

Walter Bluhm played the tip-happy bookkeeper, Erwin Biegel, Otto Matthes and Axel Monje the crooks, and I the dumb broad of the last-named. The rehearsals lasted five weeks and this period was to be the happiest and most fruitful I would ever experience in my whole career, with the exception perhaps of *Film Without a Name;* Barlog's brilliant production became a milestone in the history of postwar Berlin theater. For some inexplicable reason, the prescribed speech defect gave rise to unexpected difficulties: stuttering took too long, slurring tended to become ances, were not uncharitable. After the première, Barlog lapsed into a breathtaking rage and his lisp took on the proportions of a waterfall; we stood there transfixed by the force of the torrent; it ceased abruptly and, with enlightenment shining in his eyes, he shouted, "That's it!"

The dress rehearsal was attended by a commission of Allied officers appointed to assess the quality of the work. A Russian chauffeur lost his way, stumbled onto the stage, and thrust his head through the curtain: Barlog, whose sense of danger had never been his strong point, grabbed him by the scruff of the neck and the seat of his pants and yelled, "Would you kindly take your Russian arse off my German stage." Awed silence and paralyzed horror descended on the company; Herta wrung her hands and grinned desperately; Barlog, noticing none of this, merely spat, "House lights—curtain!" leaving the astonished chauffeur no opportunity to take action. The performance began and almost immediately sniggers and snorts became audible, the officers enjoyed themselves and applauded heartily, preparing us for the glorious first night which the discharged Hirsch was obliged to miss since he was on a packed steamer bound for New York.

Whenever Barlog galloped back and forth in the foyer during a successful first night, fizzing over with infectious enthusiasm, there were those who sourly called him a ham; incapable of relating to his great artistry, of popping it into one of their neat pottery-class pigeonholes, they sought to group deportment and talent under the same heading, to cut his success down to size; the same ever-present, ever-recurring, overlooked disciples of the Muses, who spent eight terms studying Theater Science,* who carry the confrontation with the written word heavily upon their shoulders as though digestion be equal to creation, for whom the gravity of art is its sole raison d'être, for whom mirth has not value, for whom the most fleeting acquaintance with the greats develops into megalomania—I always feel like yelling at them: Genius isn't catching.

"That's Erich Pommer," Erwin Biegel said as we took our bows, indicating a white-haired gentleman sitting in the first row and applauding generously. "Christ, Pommer's back in town!" the stage manager cried excitedly, and Barlog, dashing up and down like a sheep dog deciding who should take his curtain call when, said, "Pommer arrived today," between cries of, "Now you—on you go—get going—curtain up—good, hold it—down—I said *down* you idiot!"

Erich Pommer, the almighty UFA boss of an UFA before my time, leans against the iron stage door and says,

* *Theaterwissenschaft:* One can take a degree in this subject in German-speaking universities.

"Can you be at OMGUS at eleven tomorrow?" Heavy lids over clever, alert eyes, mocking smile, speech slow, hesitant, with a precise Hanover accent; impatiently he seeks to disguise his impatience, his hands hold, crumple, smooth a pack of cigarettes, take one out, tap imaginary ash into an overflowing ashtray, neglect the drooping ash on the half-smoked cigarette, irritatedly brush it aside as it falls. Someone comes in, says, "Hi Erich," is not aware that one can't call him Erich. Peering disinterestedly out the window, watching saluting soldiers and parked jeeps with raised eyebrows, he says, "You will make a career. I would like to advise you until I can start production again; it would be a pity if you were to make false decisions now."

He became friend, marriage witness, divorce adviser, motivator, comforter, and, above all, my producer, whose monosyllabic criticism was more instructive than all the harangues of well-meaning friends and colleagues, and whom I addressed in my letters as Mr. Pommer until his death twenty years later, and still think of as Mr. Pommer and not Erich Pommer.

THIRTEEN

Mother opened the makeshift front door, the windows rattled, the door slammed against the wall, we stood and looked at each other. "Hilde," she said at last with a query in her voice, as though she'd expected someone else. A stringy, pale youth pushed past her. "We crossed the border secretly!" he piped proudly. We sat down at the window where Grandfather had sat. Her hair was streaky, gray, cheeks hollow, she wiped the flaking surface of the table with the palm of her hand, it wobbled, a leg detached itself and clattered to the floor, she rubbed her forehead with thumb and forefinger, her shoulders twitched, I saw her thin neck, the veins on the backs of her hands. My half-brother came in and asked, "Can I go out?"

"You're alive," she said softly. She cleaned her spectacles on the hem of her skirt, put them on; one of the lenses was missing, she tapped the rim and said, "I'm getting old," took them off again. "Three times I tried to get through but had to turn back after a few hours, I couldn't find anyone to help us cross the border, and then, three days ago, we finally managed it. I had some flour and sugar when we started out but it got lost."

"I won't be living with you any more," I said.

She stared at me, smiled, and I was sorry that it had come out that way; I'd meant to imply that she needn't worry on my account; now it was too late. "Do you want to tell me about it?" she asked.

I tried but it sounded wrong, I left a lot of things out, enlarged others.

There was a knock at the door. Stepfather stood at the head of the stairs breathing heavily; he was wearing his brown smock and had a loaf of bread under his arm. He put it down on the slanting table, stroked Mother's back, and said, "One of the customers brought it in." He looked at her shyly, as though not yet certain how to speak to her.

"I should have stayed in Berlin," Mother said suddenly.

"The boy would never have come through," said Stepfather, "none of us would have. You can take the knocks better on your own, isn't that right?" He blinked at me.

"Father's right," I said.

Mother looked at the bread: "They were all so arrogant, always shook their heads as though I'd gone mad when I tried to telephone you or stood at the crossroads; but then when the fighting started all they could do was pray and shiver, and there were hundreds of refugees from East Prussia and Pomerania, they sent them on their way—might have wanted some of their food. Two of the people there were decent but the rest . . ." She got up and went into the kitchen. "I should have persuaded Grandfather to come with us."

"No one ever persuaded Grandfather," I said.

She smiled faintly and murmured, "Yes, you're right, he wasn't one to be talked into anything."

"Will you come to the theater?" I asked.

"I've got nothing to wear, only this." She pointed at her gray jacket and the baggy skirt.

"The others don't look any different," said Stepfather.

Frau Schulz embraced her, fat tears rolled down fat cheeks. "Dear God, it's as though I've always known you, your daughter told me lots about you, if only I could see my boy again, two years he's been missing." She blew her nose, straightened her bun, and said, "There'll be a turn in the weather, my legs ache."

Mother smiled self-consciously as Barlog greeted her: "Tell at a glance whose mother you are," he bubbled. He put a chair in the aisle of the full auditorium and whispered, "Don't get a shock—your daughter runs around half-naked at one point."

During the intermission she looked her old self and said, "I still can't grasp it—you on the stage, that there's theater at all—I feel like a stranger, I don't recognize anything in Berlin any more either."

A letter from Kurt Hirsch arrived from New York; he wrote that he'd enlisted for another two years and would return in the autumn. I wrote, I know I should share the collective feeling of guilt for being German but I can't. His father intercepted my letter and sent it back; in pencil in the margin he had written that this was an outrage and typical of a German.

The première of *The Murderers Among Us* was held at the Admiral's Palace, next to the former Tobis Film building, on October 15, 1946. The English had refused to attend; their reason: one of the cast had been a Party member. The other Allies were either not informed or had dismissed the fact as uninteresting. I sat between Erich Pommer and Wolfgang Staudte and wished for one and a half hours that there were room for me under the threadbare carpet, received my first lesson on the subject of film premières and the infinite variety of tortures they hold in store. At one point the sound track broke down, at another the film decelerated, the picture faded, the voices grew sadder and sadder and finally sank into the cellar as the film broke altogether; scenes which I'd treasured in my memory as bearable had been cut, others, which I'd forced myself to forget, seemed to run twice; the balcony had been taken over by a company of influenza victims who settled down to an orgy of sneezing and coughing; one man got up in the middle and went out slamming the door behind him, another fell audibly asleep, and a woman in the first row dropped her handbag and it was a long time before she found it between the feet of the spectators sitting behind her. They applauded as the lights went up and a photographer said, "I'm Walter Sanders from *Life* magazine." He leaped around me, clicking tirelessly. Erich Pommer drove me to the Schlosspark Theater and I was thankful when the curtain went up at 7:30 and I could lollop about the stage lisping outrageously.

I was standing on the lavatory seat as the American military train, the Berliner Two, pulled into the main railway station of Munich. The production manager was leaning on the barrier sleepily, watching it arrive, when he was jolted wide awake by a suitcase slamming onto the platform and a cry of "Help me out of here!" I squeezed through the tiny window and ran for the exit pulling him along behind me. We careered through the ruins of Munich in a veteran production car with very smooth tires; crossing the Isar bridge it went on strike, gave a last cough, and sighed to a halt. This was the auspicious beginning of my work on the first American-licensed postwar film in Munich. Barlog had released me for eight weeks to play one of the many parts in

Zwischen Gestern und Morgen, starring Viktor de Kowa. The Berliner Two left Wannsee station in Berlin and traveled to Salzburg via Frankfurtam-Main and Munich, crossing the Russian border with sealed doors. The train consisted of several first-class luxury cars, a dining car, and, at the back, one freight car which had been fitted out with wooden benches along the walls and which was reserved for the few Germans who, having filled out numerous forms and questionnaires, presented confirmation of employment by American-licensed firms, and convincingly stood the tests and interviews, had received permission to board the train for the purpose of traveling within Germany. These chosen few were forbidden to enter the dining car or any of the first-class carriages. Sitting alone in the pitch-dark car, I had heard the marked footsteps of a military gentleman, been dazzled by a brilliant flashlight beam, and then thankfully accepted an offer to spend the rest of the journey in an empty sleeping car. Two hours later my host, the commander of the train, opened the door, staggered in under a cloud of alcohol, and breathed, "It's a long night." After a short skirmish I took my leave, ran back to the German car, locked myself in the lavatory, and sat down to await the inevitable act of vengeance. Shortly before we reached Munich I heard soldiers tramping down the corridor and the commander's voice bellowing, "All Germans are to be searched, three cartons of cigarettes have been stolen!" I ignored the impatient hammering, the threats to break in the door, and the insistence that I'd have to come out sometime, and by employing my wartime experience in leaving crowded trains when conditions became uncomfortable, foiled his plan to keep me there until Salzburg and then arrest me for illegal entry.

Filming started in the afternoon. We shot in the ruins of the Regina Hotel. "I'm so glad you've achieved your ambition," a voice said softly. Manfred was standing behind me leaning on a stick; checked sports coat instead of field gray, white streaks in the dark hair, skin stretched over cheekbones and the bridge of the nose, the face seemed smaller, the shoulders bonier. He clumsily got out of the way of a stagehand tugging a cable: "I got one in the hip, right at the end," he said with a nervous chuckle, as though ashamed of mentioning it. "I'm trying to start work again, I'd like to make furniture, simple things, not too expensive."

"I've got your mummy case."

He stared at me in surprise. "Please keep it," he said quickly.

"I don't want it."

"It brought you luck, so please keep it."

An American clambered over a mound of debris and came up to us. "I'm Percy Knauth, we met at Viktor de Kowa's; *Life* magazine wants to do a story on you, German girl makes career in the ruins of Berlin, that sort of thing." He grinned and filled his pipe from a tobacco pouch.

I was playing a refugee who had managed to survive with her younger brother by dealing on the black market. The gentle director looked worried, leaned over to me, and whispered, "You mustn't be so earnest—younger, jollier."

Erich Pommer arrived and visited us in our broom-closet-sized dressing rooms, contended himself with casual comments after seeing the rushes, and said as he left, "The English have finally issued a film license, Helmut Käutner's written the script, *Film Without a Name* it's called, they'll be getting in touch with you." He slapped the hood of the car with his army cap, tightened his belt, shuffled his feet. "Kurt Hirsch is now my assistant, has been for three weeks," he said discreetly, knowing that I knew. He opened the car door, closed it again, took me by the arm, and moved away a few steps, stopped, looked intently at the Stage A drainpipe, offered me a cigarette, lighted it awkwardly, and said suddenly, "He wants to marry you. That's madness, you would have to leave Germany within thirty days, you'd lose your passport, your nationality, your profession . . ." He unwrapped a piece of chewing gum from its silver paper, slid it into his mouth, and chewed angrily. "Hollywood doesn't need Germans," he said, pulling at his belt again, looking for a further hole, and not finding one. He turned up his dollar and said, "You don't look well, you need a holiday and some decent food." I tried to remember what that meant; he read my thoughts, grinned a crooked grin. "I was thinking of Switzerland but I don't think you'd get a permit from the Americans. We might try the French." He got in beside the chauffeur, turned off the radio, and muttered, "Let's go."

Five weeks later the French film officer in Berlin poured champagne into one of my well-worn sandals, cried ecstatically, "Let me drink from your slipper!" and watched in dismay as it trickled through the cracked uppers. At the end of the drunken evening he presented me with a sealed, signed, and approved travel permit.

Red-and-white awnings flap over quiet balconies, light-colored curtains sway through sparkling French windows, freshly washed water slaps against glistening boats, gleaming motor cars purr, people glide along on crepe and leather, swinging their gloves, handbags, scarves, displaying rings, rosy skin, shining hair, wearing hats, ribbons, Alice bands; they look plump, well rested, just bathed, highly polished, like the town, like the Zürich Bahnhofstrasse, like the sky over the dull red, dove-gray roofs, like the shimmering gold fingers of the clock on the church tower, the glittering tram rails. The shop windows gloat, taunt, reflect, defy choice between bars of chocolate, cherry jam, mattresses, blankets, carpets, beds, pillows, clocks for the table, for the wall, for the bedside table, banks, stock exchange, cake, sausage, ham, egg-liqueur, cigars, cookbooks; odor of the well-nourished, smell of hot bread, buns, breeze of perfume. In a shop someone says, "The war was dreadful, we couldn't get rice or cocoa." She drops brightly wrapped candy into a bag, weighs, writes, says, "Merci vielmal." There's a woman sitting in a café on the Limmatquai; I see her back, her arm; her smooth, well-kept hand raises the fork to her mouth, puts it back carefully on the plate, raises the cup of coffee, puts it down again, picks in a handbag, takes out a purse, and places money on the table. The woman gets up, moves between the banks of flowers, the ice-cream cups and cake trolleys, drapes a light coat around her shoulders, plucks at her veil, coaxes it over the rim of her hat, walks out securely on long legs, wrinkles up her eyes as the sun strikes her, looks as Mother might look if she weren't so thin.

"What's wrong?" Kurt Hirsch asks. "I want to leave." He looks at me, doesn't understand, is a stranger. I want to go back to a town without houses, without windowpanes, without roofs; holes in the asphalt, rubble, rubbish, rats; want to be poor among the poor. It was a world war, they'd said.

I stand in a doorway and see contented, unwondering faces, relaxed, smiling, safe apartment dwellers, unaccustomed to cellars; feel it slipping away, the clean solid ground, feel ridiculed by the mirth, the repose; "Paradise was just around the corner," they seem to say; "They had lice in the Middle Ages"; "Dysentery? What's that?" The concierge looks at me curiously. Our room's on the fourth floor; I stand at the window and look down thinking if I were to jump there'd be a bloody mess on those clean stones, they would stop, look at each other, and ask, "What's that red there?" Pity for Mother, Grandfather, Stepfather wells up, self-pity floods and shakes me, makes me cry for the first time since the bunker that no longer exists, in Schmargendorf.

I didn't know that the Palace Hotel in St. Moritz was famous, with a reputation for being the best, most splendid, most impeccably run of all. The difference, the nuances between good, better, and best were unknown to me. An unknown continent with bathtubs into which hot water flowed day and night, with tables set, menus, fussy generals who fussily supervised your meals, guardian mountains that cradled the valley, the lake, the corridors, rooms, balconies, and turrets, with white lace behind dark drapes and endless carpets that swallowed the ping of a teaspoon on a saucer, the whispering of the waiters, the click as the elevator came to rest. Movements as in a dream, a ballet, silent motion before the snow-capped sentinels. A stranded ship that had flown from the sea, that had retired, was resting, dispensing rest.

When we left two weeks later I had gained five pounds and felt healthy for the first time. Driving down the Julier Pass I wished to myself to come back, sometime, to return just once to the sleepy rawness, the unexcited beauty, the indifferent peace.

An old train with four carriages, a dining car, and no engine was standing on an unused siding on Lüneburg Heath. The first member of the crew of *Film Without a Name* I saw as I walked along the tracks was a tethered sheep; I stroked it, it gazed at me and said "Meeh." Hans Söhnker poked his head through a carriage window and yelled, "Stop that, you're stroking our dinner." He jumped down, threw his arms around me, and said, "Thank God you're here at last, we start shooting in the morning." He stepped back a pace, examined my newly gained pounds, and said ungrudgingly, "Get you, trips to Switzerland . . ." Igor Oberberg, the cameraman, Rudolf Jugert, the director, the electricians and sound engineers gathered around and assessed me like a prize cow. I stood there feeling like a traitor, like someone who has hoarded his rations and is unwilling to share. I moved into a third-class carriage, slept on the wooden bench, woke up covered with bug bites, drank my *muckefuck,* and ran across the fields to the location.

Igor Oberberg furiously dismantled worn-out spotlights, inspected bent camera tracks and scratched lenses, peered dubiously up at the sky through his boxer's eyes. Rudolf Jugert, who was shooting his first film after having gone through the assistant-director mill for years, stood there scratching a sparse beard and leafing through the script. Hans Söhnker squatted against a silver birch and devoted his attention to several dark red bug-bites on his left calf. The stagehands, chewing grass, ran back and forth between the camera and a lopsided truck dragging cables, lights, and planks of wood. The script girl sat in the middle of the lane sharpening a pencil which broke each time she applied it to the page. Twenty or so villagers had been engaged as extras; they stood around watching the activity with expressions of open distaste.

Jugert, Söhnker, and I sat down on a box and discussed the first scene, forgot the babble about us. Jugert's patience and the fact that Söhnker and I were old friends helped us over the horror of the first day of shooting. There are no set rules that can be applied in learning and practicing the acting profession; you stumble into each new part, each new film as you might stumble into a mountain lake at Christmas time. You have only a vague memory of things learned, of past experience, and you can exercise knowledge gathered in previous roles only to the disadvantage of the present one. Without the benefit of the weeks of rehearsals necessary for a stage production you are obliged to project a finished performance onto each foot of film which rolls through the camera. The first day becomes a monster, a nightmare, a head-on collision of strangers for whom it is imperative that they forget their strangeness as quickly as possible. I can recall some films because of the good or bad result, others because of the happy or unhappy working conditions, still others not at all. *Film Without a Name* was a harmonious whole from the word go; it created a community in which everyone understood, liked, and tolerated everyone else: it became the often sought after but never again attained example of unity in the chaos of film-making.

After several weeks of nocturnal bug-battles and daily shooting the location work was finished. We had a month's break, in which I played a new O'Neill and the indestructible lisping Mabel with Barlog until the studio work started in Munich. We pulled our suitcases down from the luggage racks, took our leave of the smoking and no-smoking compartments, sat down for the last time on the precarious garden chairs in the buffet car, and listened with bated breath as Willi Fritsch went into a detailed description of meals partaken of long ago. He had reached the crepes suzettes when we saw headlights moving across the meadows, watched them turn and approach us, heard the snorting of an automobile obviously unsuited for heavy duty. It pulled up beside the train, the engine fading with a heart-rending groan. Kurt Hirsch got out waving a magazine with one hand and helping my sleepy mother from her seat with the other. She looked down the crowded corridor in dismay and said, "I must speak to you alone." Kurt was still waving the thick magazine and, shining a flashlight at it, he said, "You've got a six-page story in *Life,* I'll translate it later."

"You can't go back to Berlin," Mother said. "The Russians came at four in the morning—simply came into the American sector in an army car, I thought that wasn't allowed. They had a telegram and they said, 'How your daughter in Switzerland, who give permission, passport, who she work for, what she do in Switzerland, your daughter spy.' They waved the telegram around and said that I must sign a form, a Russian form. 'What does it say?' I asked. 'You not ask you sign,' they said. I thought they'd arrested you or something had happened in the zone." She looked out the window. "I made a mistake, I shouldn't have signed; they gave me the telegram, it was the one you sent from Zurich saying 'Arrived safely.' They'd intercepted it. It would be madness to come home." I could hear from her irregular breathing that she was crying; she blew her nose and said, "Kurt's a nice boy, but he wants you to put on an American uniform and—" The carriage door was pulled open, Kurt Hirsch came in, put a cup down on the folding table, and said, "Drink some coffee." He sat down chewing his thumb. "I've brought you an American uniform and Söhnker's willing to come with us; perhaps he can distract them with the *artista* bit. We'll give it a try.

Momma stays in Uelzen for two days, I'll pick her up day after tomorrow."

We started out at five in the morning. We dropped Mother in Uelzen; she stood there stiffly on cramped legs, her arms dangling hopelessly, surrounded by sourly smiling relatives who weighed the Yank car and uniform, Hirsch's age, Söhnker's looks, my behavior, weight, and hair style with shifty glances. The AFN was playing Glenn Miller; we whistled, forgot our anxiety. A hundred yards from the Russian border our whistling grew thin and then stopped altogether. Söhnker looked at his watch, Kurt Hirsch watched the road, I watched the three soldiers standing in front of the lowered pole. It was drizzling, the windshield wipers droned, Kurt Hirsch applied the brakes and said, "Shit," grabbed at the handbrake—too late, we slammed against the pole, splinters flew up, and we came to a stop. The three soldiers came running up bellowing in Russian, Hirsch bellowed in Czech, got out and slammed the door, disappeared into the gray hut. They stood with their mouths open; bellowing balked, assault thwarted, they circled the car gingerly, fingered the emblem and tires, pressed their noses to the window, met Söhnker's steady gaze, blinked like cats when the jump doesn't come off as well as expected. An officer came out of the hut followed by the steaming Hirsch. "Come," said the officer. Söhnker got out. "You"—he pointed at me. I smiled lazily, closed my eyes, and leaned back. He opened the door and jerked his thumb in the direction of the hut. I stretched myself, swung my feet slowly to the ground, followed him, tripped over the step and staggered into a stovepipe which detached itself from its moorings and clattered to the floor. A fat man with rows of ribbons was sitting at a garden table smoking, Stalin behind him, hanging on a long nail. Kurt Hirsch placed his feet as far apart as possible, leaned back against the doorpost, and unbuttoned his jacket, disclosing the pistol in his belt. "Papers," said the one at the table. Söhnker cried, "We theater, we *artista*, theater tonight." "Papers," the Russian repeated patiently. Söhnker pointed at his identity card: "There they are." The Russian picked it up, examined it, took a thick book from a drawer, riffled through greasy pages, inspected the card again, handed it back. "Good," he said. He picked up his cigarette and put it in his mouth, gazing at me expectantly. "I don't need a——" I said in English but couldn't think of the word for passport; I turned to Hirsch, he said something in Czech, the Russian shook his head.

"Show him your card," muttered Hirsch. The fat man picked up my papers and exclaimed, "You German!" "That's what I keep telling you," puffed Söhnker, "we artists, we theater." The Russian leaned forward, placed his heavy arms on the table, and let his eyes travel from the hem to the collar of my army greatcoat. "Amerikanski uniform." "I was cold and the coat was in the car." He settled back with my identity card in his hands, reached again for the thick book, his fingers slid down the list, turned pages, turned them back again. "Verboten!" he roared suddenly, pointing at my coat. They changed the guard outside, a pencil rolled across the table and fell to the floor. "Verboten," he repeated and slapped the book with the flat of his hand. I took the coat off and removed the cap. "I was cold," I tried to say but no sound came. Kurt Hirsch looked at his watch, said something loudly in Czech, the Russian laughed, coughed, cigarette ash fell on the table. "Let's go," said Hirsch and strolled to the car. A soldier raised the splintered pole, Söhnker doubled up and turned green, gasping, "You'll have to stop, my dysentery's started up again." "Try to hold out until we're round the next bend," said Hirsch; he thumped the steering wheel and spat, "Goddamned brakes, now we'll have to crawl to Berlin." He stopped and Söhnker shot into the woods; I wanted to smoke but my chin wobbled and the cigarette fell to the floor. "Well, you're not on the list, that's one thing," said Hirsch.

The stage manager bawled "Fifteen minutes!" Otto Matthes, who played the bookie with a hoarse voice as though someone had stepped on his vocal cords, came in and wheezed, "Got any coffee? I feel awful." Schulz poured boiling water on a heap of Nescafé; he sipped it hurriedly and went off rubbing his stomach. I scrambled up the iron ladder, waited for my cue, jumped down the three steps onto the tiny stage. Applause broke out, prevented me from delivering my first line, applause that said, We've accepted you, say yes to you, expect things from you; let's forget the cellars, the cold, the illness. It healed, warmed, compensated for the wounds, intimidated, pampered, threatened, lifted me up on a cushion of hot air.

Rehearsals on a dim bare stage, fear, dread of failing,

learning lines, first-night nightmare, the uproar under the ribs, there on the left at five in the afternoon; last yell at the prompter: "Jump in if I dry on that line." "You've never dried yet." "I will tonight." "Hold the curtain, I can't go on; got to go to the john"—too late. The applause says, You've made it, for the moment you've made it, we like you, love you, you're out of the woods, you're not "I suppose there have to be some of those too," "Knef, we won't be able to move you up a class if you go on like this," or "Painting is nonsense," any more. Fame without cover photos, public relations, interviews, place and year of birth, favorite color, favorite dish, sport, hobby, vacations when and where. Crouching at the starting line, the first steps, naive faith that the time has come to feel securely happy, thankful, in love with everyone in general and in particular; the gift of success, of having lived through it, of survival in a city pronounced dead, a city now on the mend and making steady progress. The world becomes tangible, available, is waiting to be conquered. Success without agents, percentages, thirty-page contracts; ambition, in its positive connotation without the sneer coined by those who lack the tension, the excitement, who mistrust passion and Dämonen, gave them a dirty name in order to excuse their own incapacity, to canonize things left undone, to conceal their own unscaled peaks behind assumed selflessness and sacrifice. We were ambitious in the best sense of the suspect word: I was ambitious, am ambitious, and will remain ambitious; ambition accompanies me like a love affair which has good and bad days.

Applause broke out as the stage manager put on the scratched Benny Goodman record of "Sing, Sing, Sing"; the actors started to dance, I threw myself onto the swaying brass bed, and Matthes, Biegel, and Bluhm launched into their whiplash dialogue. Matthes boggled at me, missed a line, went spinach-green and doubled over like a jackknife; I jumped up to try and cover him but the curtain was already falling. Barlog's cry of "Jesus Christ, he's puked" carried to the last row of the balcony; he grabbed Matthes as he sagged into the wings and thrust his head into a fire bucket. Bubbles rose and Biegel yelled, "You're drowning him!" Barlog pulled him up and inspected him, he was now lilac in color and gasped, "All right now." From the stage we heard the stage manager announcing, "Ladies and gentlemen, we beg you to excuse the short delay and kindly re-

quest you to remain seated." We picked up the scene with
my "What's up, Patsy?"—a panicky squeak since the rag-
ing gangster boss was bearing down on me. It got a bigger
laugh than usual and I sensed a draft around my belly and
bosom; the straps of my dress had broken, the flimsy wartime silk fluttered to the ground. They roared with laughter, screamed, and hooted—it had nothing to do with us or
the play any more, but remnants of war, membership
badge, sign of the times: the skinny girl and the retching
man. The curtain fell again. "I'm gonna close," Barlog
sobbed, "one of them pukes and the other's naked, I'm
gonna close."

"Selznick is interested in you," said Erich Pommer.
"William Dieterle was in Berlin looking at old UFA tests
and saw *Murderers Among Us;* he must have told Selznick
and the *Life* article did the rest."

"Who's Selznick and who's Dieterle?" I asked excitedly
but he didn't hear, was looking across the crowded living
room, nodding absently. He got up and I followed him into
the hall; he pulled out a crumpled cigarette and poked it
more by luck than judgment into his mouth; it hung there
like a soggy comma as he spoke. "Hollywood won't run
away, it's too early"; and as an afterthought, "Don't let
Kurt Hirsch talk you into it."

Why not really, I thought to myself, it would be marvelous to be the first . . . "What's Hollywood like?" I asked the
dyed-blond American secretary, born in Berlin, who was
pouring whiskey and who reminded me a little of Alike.
"Oh fabulous, palm trees and studios and men who make
world careers, Selznick brought Ingrid Bergman over to
America." She said "Ummurica," as though afraid one
might think she didn't belong. "He produced *Gone with the
Wind* too, fabulous."

Karl John sat at the piano singing songs from the *Three-
penny Opera.* Erich Pommer shook hands with a medium-
sized gentleman in civilian clothes, waited until he'd hung
up his coat, and said, "This is Carl Zuckmayer." Big dark-
blue eyes twinkle gently gaily in a broad generous face,
ruddy skin, more befitting a farmer than a writer. I thought
of *The Captain from Köpenick* and *The Happy Vineyard.*
Where do they all come from? I asked myself; where have
they been until now, the names that are suddenly coming to
life? "She'd be a wonderful Pützchen in *The Devil's Gener-*

al, what do you say, Barlog?" Barlog nodded and muttered
derogatively, "She's always making films, gone over to Bio-
scope." Wolfgang Staudte and another director, Karlheinz
Stroux, were talking at each other simultaneously, made a
momentary truce in order to greet Zuckmayer; a spindly
film producer, whose chief occupation was waiting for a
film license, ate the last of the salted crackers and, thus re-
vitalized, set about peeling a German girl away from an
American officer from Pomerania. Karl John had got to
"Oh, the shark has pearly teeth, dear," and, transported,
cried, "Oh Hilde, to think that you missed it all!"

Erich Pommer looked at his watch and growled, "It's
two o'clock!" hovered for a moment between indulgence
and severity, then pushed me toward the door: "Concen-
trate on your film and forget Hollywood; and don't paint
your face, it's not becoming to you." I went red, felt
stripped and X-rayed, felt ashamed of my delight in camouflage after the German-woman-doesn't-make-up epoch,
said "Auf Wiederseh'n" and "Thanks very much": obedient
child as Father catches her creeping up the stairs at half-
past midnight.

"Are you quite sure they don't search the train?" I asked.
"Sure," said Kurt Hirsch. "Well, you don't need to worry,
you're a DEFA star," chortled the American-employed
Berlin driver on the way to Wannsee. "I get faint every
time I see that station," he groaned as we pulled up at the
shunting yard where the Berliner Two was standing. "They
put us on a freight train here in forty-three and off we went
to Russia—Jesus!—the journey alone would've been
enough but when we got there—Merry Christmas." He
wiped fingerprints from the radiator, called out, "All the
best," and stood there shriveled up beside Kurt Hirsch,
who raised his hand and waved rather unconvincingly.

Söhnker unpacked our provisions, shared them out,
made a plan; more than half had gone by the time we
reached the Elbe. "He's a fine boy, Kurt," he said, breaking
the guilty silence.

"He's got to go back."

"When?"

"January."

"Oh Lord, oh Lord," he sighed. He rolled his threadbare
coat into a pillow, lay down on the bench, and addressed
the emergency chain: "Jugert wants to make another film

with you next year. If only one knew how it'll work out
here—no one can really advise you." He rolled over, grunt-
ed a parting "Fine boy," sat up again, and asked, "Can you
cook?"

"When and with what do you suppose I might have
learned? Why do you ask, anyway?"

"Because we've got to cook for ourselves in Munich,
that's why."

It was hot in Frankfurt; the platforms were full of
Americans with kit bags, children begging, women with ei-
derdowns and rucksacks, shifty black marketeers and
whores in taken-in men's jackets with padded shoulders;
smell of burning, toilets, and cellars, of mothballs and stale
water.

We moved into our dressing rooms in Geiselgasteig the
next evening, organized a hot plate, pooled our remaining
reichsmarks, sent the dresser off on a reconnaissance tour
of the black market, and divided the household chores between Jugert, Söhnker, and myself. We shot at night in
order to avoid the daytime power cuts and stopped in the
middle of scenes because the director had to put the split
peas on, the leading man's potatoes were burning, the leading lady had poured soup over her foot, or the prop man
needed the saucepan for the take. We sat around on camp
beds and wobbly sofas during the nocturnal lunch breaks,
eating and laughing, savoring every minute. Each evening
Colonel Rogers, the American studio warden, left his requisitioned villa at the entrance to the lot to pay us a brief
visit; he stood there peering down from his great height,
bewildered at the hilarity which invariably confronted him.
"Watch out, the Chattanooga Choo-Choo's coming!" the
electricians would yell from the bridges as he stomped
through the iron door; we'd found out he was a railway engineer in civilian life. The nickname stuck until one day a
fire broke out in the archives and he ran around swinging a
bucket and shouting incoherently as he directed the fire
fighting. The script girl doubled up with laughter and gurgled, "They're all the same, give them a uniform and whiff
of danger and they become field marshals or firemen."
From then on he was known as the fireman.

On Sundays we saw American films whose opulence and
abundance, Technicolor and super-stars, perfection and
slickness, either impressed or bored us, or we boarded the
antique tram and went to the opera, sat there reverently

until the point where Othello chokes the life out of Desdemona but can't stop her singing; or walked in the pale later-summer sun along the banks of the Isar to Grünwald and back, shared cigarettes, talked until daybreak, looked forward to the next night's shooting. When over half the film was finished, Jugert showed us a rough cut. They all embraced me and paid compliments; Irene von Meyendorff said, "I've got an idea for a film for Hilde, listen." Erich Ponto blinked inscrutably and commented "Very gifted," Minna the make-up girl whispered, "I'd go to Hollywood if I were you, who knows when we'll be able to make another film here."

Two days later Kurt Hirsch arrived. "You can sign the contract in London. Germany's still enemy territory officially and they're not allowed to make contracts with Germans."

"It's sheer madness," said Jugert.

"Why? What can happen? At least I can give it a try." I became refractory and immoderate, saw myself doing big things in a big world and took their opposition to be fright and bourgeois interference, thought they'd lost their courage.

Else Bongers sat on the edge of her worn armchair. She stared angrily at the bare tree in front of her window, drew deeply on her cigarette, flicked the tiny fag-end into a dish filled with water. Her poodle lay wedged between her back and the back of the chair and growled each time it unsuccessfully tried to change position. She dipped into a half-empty packet of Player's and flicked back the lid of the gold lighter she'd been holding in her hand ever since I arrived. She stood up and went around the low coffee table several times, the poodle stretched itself and yawned, she stopped in front of it, turned around and retraced her steps. One could tell that she had been a dancer, her movements were controlled, coordinated, had great beauty. She clicked her index and middle fingers together and the dry sharp report, which other people can only make with thumb and middle finger, startled me. "Child," she said, "several people have asked me to persuade you to stay here. You're at the beginning of a great career. There's lots of time." She enunciated her words even more precisely than usual, as though by speaking clearly and unmistakably she would create clarity. "You can't go to America with a boy who

went straight into the army upon leaving school and who
has not the slightest idea of our profession. Was Kurt
Hirsch ever in Hollywood?"

"No, only in New York and then in Fort Worth at a
training camp."

"So I thought." Sparks flew at me, she pushed her red
hair back from her forehead and turned away.

She loved success as my grandfather had loved it. She
had no time for the untalented, the uncertain, the unsuccessful. Her long strong hands stretched out purposefully
and took hold of things, they didn't feel their way. Nothing
about her was dreamy or fey. She had reconciled herself to
her fate, held no one responsible for it, hated pity and self-
pity, didn't say "if" or "might," was demanding of others,
overtaxed everyone. To win her interest and her friendship
was an honor.

I said, "I met the blond army secretary in Munich, I
think her name's Zuckerberg, she said she'd go to London
with me and that I could sign the contract there and that
Selznick's the best producer."

"How does she know?"

"She was at UFA and in Hollywood before."

"So were many others."

"Yes, but she wants to become an agent and manage
things for me."

"And that's a reason for going to America? Child!" Her
voice became clear and cutting, it was the voice I'd heard
on the telephone as she'd told my mother, "Please allow us
to be the best judges of that, Frau Wulfestieg." She clicked
the switch of a crooked standard lamp with a paper shade,
forgetting the power cut.

"Everyone says it's uncertain what will happen with
films and theater here, what'll happen in general."

"No, that no one knows, we are a beaten and disrupted
land and we have nothing to offer, nothing at all. Frau
Zuckerberg was here, by the way; she wanted to tell me
how talented she thinks you are. Whom is she telling? After
three smash films and numerous stage successes she displays remarkable critical ability. 'Fräulein Knef has already
been discovered,' I answered her, 'she's the first postwar
star we have.'" The poodle got up, stretched itself and
barked at me, as though it had only now noticed my presence. Else Bongers snapped, "Don't make a fool of yourself, Püti." It scratched its ear and lay down under the

table. "You will be 'discovered' time and again and these people will make you promises they can't keep. I mistrust their arguments. And as for Kurt Hirsch, of course you shouldn't marry him, neither him nor anyone else. It's too early, America, marriage, everything."

My witness, Erich Pommer, was standing in front of the registry office. He said, "Take your passport and get into my car, the chauffeur will drive you to Munich. I'll take care of Kurt Hirsch."

My mother looked at him aghast and whispered, "We can't do that."

"Get in the car," he said impatiently.

Kurt Hirsch called out from the top of the stairs, "What's holding things up?"

"Get in the car," he repeated.

"No," I said.

Erich Pommer threw his cigarette-end at a mound of dirty snow and said, "As you please."

FOURTEEN

I wanted to jump out of the plane as it took off from the English military airport in Gatow, to run back to the shed where they had stood around in a semicircle: Mother, Stepfather, Else Bongers, Erich Pommer. I wanted to say I don't know the man beside me, it's all a mistake, no we're not together; then I'd go to the station and wait for the train, get on and ride to Steglitz, get off and walk over the cobblestones, turn the corner at the house with the brown-red tiles, turn first left and then right into the Wrangel-strasse, left again, on past the black iron railings, down the three steps to the stage door; the doorkeeper will say "Evenin'" and "Brass monkey weather again"; Schulz will be doing up her bun, sticking pins in the top and the bottom, she'll tie up her apron strings, rub her legs, and put the kettle on.

Else Bongers had cried, looked old, her red hair had looked wrong against the frozen face, like a wig or a hat rented for the occasion. "You'll always know where your handbag is," she said, "come back if you're unhappy." I can't come back, I thought to myself, I'm a war bride, married to the war, the war's wife. Erich Pommer had sat on the windowsill like an eagle, malicious, feathers ruffled, had twitched the dog-eared cigarette to the corner of his mouth and said "Good Luck," looking as he did so at the ice-framed puddles, had stretched out his hand and scarcely brushed the palm of mine, shrank back at the contact as though I had skin disease or something. And Stepfather had said "Hildekind" with a wobbling chin and Mother had put her arms around me just as I'd always wished she would do when I was a child, my head between her chin and the curve of her bosom. She hadn't said anything, just held me like that.

Kurt Hirsch nudged me and held up a photo of a stained apartment house with a fire escape going from floor to floor, with windows with only one pane and no balconies, with a tent on thin poles leading from the entrance to the road. "That's where my parents live," he said, "only the good houses have awnings."

The shadow of the plane slid across the gray-white fields and fir smudges, a lake, two flat houses standing at a distance from each other as though estranged, having nothing to do with each other; houses in which one would be frightened at night. I won't see the Baltic, that's further north and the part I know is somewhere quite different again, to the north of Berlin and then over toward Danzig. It has the whitest sand and the whitest dunes and what it's like in winter I don't know; I only know it when it's hot and dry and the basket chairs are spongy from wet bathing suits and suntan oil and sand and the fir-tree forests behind the dunes are full of blackberries and Mother says, "You're not to go barefoot, there are lots of vipers," and when the island of Rügen is just a strip of lilac there where the water and the sky meet and the island of Oi is a spot no bigger than a mussel, it's got a lighthouse, that's all, not even a tree and when one stands in the middle one can see the water on all sides. You go over on a fishing boat and if you lean over the side you can see the white sand on the bottom. Mother went into the village one day and I stood on the part of the beach where the sand gets darker and grittier, where it's always wet and easier to make sand castles. The sea was smooth like a clean sheet on an unslept-in bed, I couldn't understand why it had been so wild yesterday, you couldn't go more than a few steps without falling into one of the deep holes between the sandbanks, and why it looks so limp and done-for today, perhaps it's tired, I said to myself, must have slept badly. I turned around to go back over the dunes but they were gone, lost in the mist; I looked at the water and then back again at the pale thick mist and thought, that's what it must be like for Father since he's dead. And I ran until I found Mother in the fish market next to the church and ran up so fast that I knocked the bag of herrings out of her hand. "I've seen Father," I said and her nose went white and she looked funny with a white nose and a brown face. Two summers later she sent me to a holiday camp in Zinnowitz; she took me to the Stettiner railway station, tied a label around my neck with my name and address on it, rubbed my hands because they'd got black and grubby, and helped me up the steps to the carriage. "Now don't start crying," she said, "all the other children are happy and you start crying." I'd had to wear sandals I hated, the ones with the thick soles and the sharp catch—I always tripped over in them to show how uncomfortable they were—and drawers that flapped around my legs like a skirt and were too tight at the waist and squashed my stomach. Her belly was big and her face fat and strange. "When you come home in six weeks you'll have a baby brother or sister," she called after me. In Stettin a pale girl with corkscrew hair got her finger caught in the sliding door and screamed like a pig and the governess hunted around in her case and dropped the bottle of iodine. When it rained we sat in the big hall and wrote home or were made to sing and once they brought a record player; they cleaned the needle and wiped the felt turntable and played "Glowworm glowworm." The one with the squashed finger was allowed to dance on tiptoe in a short white frock and pink ballet shoes, but afterwards as we were having supper we heard it dripping under her seat and she put her hands in front of her face and the governess said, "There's nothing to laugh about, she's sick." I would have loved to be able to dance the way she could even if it meant having a squashed finger and a weak bladder.

"What a shame we can't see the white cliffs of Dover," Kurt Hirsch said, "the English are so proud of them." Why are they proud of them? I thought, people are always proud of a river or a mountain or the weather or something or other, proud of things they have no influence on. The sky was like flour and the plane bored its way through the flour like a worm, went up, went down, dropped still further, caught itself, bounded on, splitting the flour, stirring it up like Grandmother making dumplings. "Dumplings are unhealthy," Grandfather always said and went out slamming the kitchen door. I should have visited his grave, just once, I never went to the cemetery at all, didn't see the point of praying and watering, but I should have gone once—I'd always pulled back his eyelids in the mornings in bed, wanted to see his eyes, was afraid of them closed, afraid they'd slid up like that horrible doll Hansi which I'd hidden at the bottom of the cupboard behind the mirrored door which always creaked and wouldn't close and sometimes swung open and banged against the drawers knocking off bits of glass; the cupboard smelled of mothballs and newspapers and my maroon winter coat hung on the right side; I was always cold in it and it had been too tight from the word go, the good thing was I was only allowed to wear it on Sundays when Grandfather took me to the park to feed the ducks. Grandfather had shown me my first airplane, in Tempelhof, I was so excited that I got a cramp in my left calf but he didn't laugh, he'd never made fun of me the way Grandmother did when she hid in the alley beside the butcher shop in Sedanstrasse and I tried to find her but couldn't and got frightened among all those people's legs.

The ceremony had had little to do with a wedding. After the breakfast they all went back to their offices and I sat in the bathroom looking at the flowers the frost had printed on the windows. The "Yes" was like a verdict—guilty. After New Year's he had packed crates and organized and shopped and sold things and shipped the Airedale bitch, which someone had given him in front of OMGUS ("I can't feed her any more," the man had said and walked away), off to New York. I had been X-rayed, screened, examined, questioned, sent backwards and forwards from the victors to the vanquished, out of the warmth into the cold, from no man's land back to Headquarters, from the known to the unknown. I had stood in the middle of the room as it grew emptier and emptier, and had felt dismissed, expelled, and imprisoned at the same time, had watched my courage grow threadbare, my elation sag to a whimper.

"Welcome to England," Frau Zuckerberg said, "you must always speak English now," and, "You need a new coat."

"What did she say?" I asked.

"You can't possibly go to Ummurica in that summer coat," she said.

I looked everywhere for rubble and burnt-out houses in the hope that they would remind me of Berlin, make me feel less strange among cars driving on the left and incomprehensible cries. On the radio they'd boasted that they'd razed it to the ground, but London was like Zürich, only darker, grubbier, surlier. "This is Hyde Park and there's Marble Arch," said Frau Zuckerberg and sat up quite straight as though she had a contract with it, a pact of allegiance. "There's a bombed house." She pointed to a roof with no tiles. In Berlin one had displayed the same warm interest at finding a building still intact.

Two photographers and a reporter with pad, pencil, and

thick glasses were waiting at the hotel. "Were you a
member of the Party?" he asked brightly and looked past
me, his mind made up. One of the photographers danced
about, wanted to know what they thought of Christian
Dior's New Look in Germany. When they had left Frau
Zuckerberg said, "Well, the Lacey agency will negotiate the
contract in New York; as soon as you get there Hilde can
sign." They went on to speak about options and clauses and
money and then took me to an apartment in which a family
was sitting around a large dining table. The younger ones
spoke English, the older ones German; they spoke of Churchill and the weather, food and Roosevelt, petrol and cigarettes, of all manner of things but never Germany. "They
left in '33," Frau Zuckerberg said, "it was an awful blow
for them when their son was called up and came back with
a German bride."

The rain gushed as though hoses had been trained at us,
it scythed and shoved, propelled the passengers backwards
and forwards, they leaned into the deluge as though thrust-
ing a raft upriver. In the shed they shook themselves like
Saint Bernards, smiled a little smugly as if they'd stood
some sort of test. We were in Shannon in Ireland; Ireland
had been out on the left on the school atlas and gray
threads had hung from its coast from the constant rolling
up and down; Fräulein Weise had tapped it with her cane
and said, "Exploited by the English." The plane stood there
with hoses in its belly and wings; in the shed they drank
coffee mixed with whiskey; at the crackling of the loudspeakers they jumped up with air-raid wardens' "once more
into the breach" expressions, hiding their "now for the
ocean" dread.

The engine beside my window spat fire at the darkness,
glowed like an overheated shell chamber, illuminated wisps
of cloud, fountains of rain, the circle made by the rotating
propellor blades. The storm seemed to brush us aside, blow
us back, leave us standing. After seven hours we were over
the middle of the ocean between Ireland and Newfound-
land; at the same time a thin stagehand was winding down
the curtain at the Marmorhaus cinema on Kurfürstendamm, the première of *Film Without a Name* was over,
Hans Söhnker walked onto the stage carrying a chair; he
put it down, bowed and gestured to the director, Rudolf Jugert, who tugged at his beard and peered shyly at the audi-

ence. "The chair," said Hans Söhnker, "is meant to symbolize the empty place that Hilde Knef has left behind her. At this moment she is flying over the Atlantic and our thoughts and best wishes go with her." The film was a success; a year later I found the following paragraph under the heading "Film" in a two-week-old German newspaper: "Hildegard Knef was awarded the film prize for her performance in *Film Without a Name*. She is the first postwar German actress to receive this honor." I called my agent and said, "I've won a prize at the festival in Locarno." "Where's Locarno?" he asked. "In Switzerland." "Oh well," he cooed benevolently, as though speaking to a child that has just passed its swimming test, "that doesn't interest anyone here."

"You're about to set foot on American soil," said Kurt Hirsch as the plane banged down and shuddered over the icy landing strip in Gander. The cold rushed in as the door opened, bit at our hands and lungs, we slid our way across to a shed smelling of disinfectant where a sour, frostbitten-looking man in a lumberjacket was selling lukewarm coffee, soggy doughnuts, picture postcards and stamps. The disheveled passengers crowded to the washroom, a fat boy threw rolls of toilet paper, held his thumb under the tap and sprayed the people entering, then kicked his mother in the shins to which she merely said, "Darling, please." Six hours later our plane took off again and landed in Boston "in the worst snowstorm the East Coast ever had," as one much-traveled passenger delightedly established. The immigration and customs officers steeled themselves and awakened memories of OMGUS and home with an avalanche of questions, pushed their faithful pens across printed forms filling yeses and noes, wrinkled their brows and took on a more earnest mien at Article 21c which required one to swear that one was not part of a conspiracy to murder the President. They dug around in cases and bags, wanted to know where we had hidden the gold, narcotics, and oranges, thrust the bulging heaps of clothing up the bench to the next one. Suspicion and mistrust reached their zenith in the middle of the table, the questions grew more threatening, the scorn more open; shaking as if senile, ready to admit to anything, convinced of being a sooty smudge on the sparkling white waistcoat of the United States of America, one eventually ended up next to the Coca-Cola machine at the end of the table. A photographer was standing beside it: before he could raise his camera I held out my papers, he waved them aside, thrust an ice-cold bottle with a straw in it into my hand and said, "Take a drink and smile." I did both, he seemed unhappy, said, "Say cheese."

"What should I say?"

"Cheese."

"Why should I say cheese?"

"Because you smile when you say cheese."

"I never smile when I say cheese." He lost interest and moved away.

A round gentleman clapped his hands and shouted. "All flights have been canceled, folks bound for New York'll have to take the train." A bus drove us through dark streets and we finally reached an underground railway station; newspapers scurried up and down the platform, posters flapped from the walls, two or three heavily muffled people tramped back and forth. The train was wide with wide aisles and wide windows and shot along at a suicidal pace and apparently of its own volition, swaying violently. It was after midnight when we reached Grand Central Station in New York. We changed trains, again nothing but rails, posters, and shivering people, got out of the chewing-gum-bespattered compartment at Astoria, a part of the city cut off by a river from the skyscraper island of Manhattan and which had nothing in common with the New York I knew from films, newsreels, postcards, and magazines. Had there not been a snowstorm I still wouldn't have recognized the house in the dismal street; although the flaking paintwork had been visible, the photo had otherwise conveyed no impression of the misery of the four- and five-story flat-roofed houses as identical as boxes, forbidding as bunkers, lovelessly thrown up, forlornly to be entered, listlessly to be left. They stood there as if expecting an earthquake or an air raid, siege or evacuation.

In front of a narrow door on the fourth floor a bald man of medium height and a thick-set blond woman embraced their son in a flood of tears and Czech.

I'm swimming to and fro between muddy mists of flu and sticky sleep, try to wake up in the dry overheated air, recognize the living room, the couch, hear the radio whistling, plates clattering, scraps of dialogue, toilet being flushed. His mother is sitting in the kitchen reading a newspaper as big as an eiderdown; she looks up and says, "My but you're thin," and, "Do you often catch cold?" I sit

down on a chair between the humming icebox and the
loaded kitchen table, don't know how to proceed against
tension, condemnation, rejection; mother-in-law—
daughter-in-law dissonance, Jewish mistrust of the Christian, Czech of the German, emigrant of the one who
stayed, persecuted of the persecutor. She folds the paper
clumsily and goes into the bedroom, shakes pillows, opens
windows, busies herself with vacuum cleaner and saucepans. A neighbor with hair curlers and a dazzling apron arrives and wants to see her boy but he's gone already, down
to the docks to see about the crates and the dog. She stares
at me glumly and goes out. Another woman with a thick
face and beads around her arms and neck comes in tinkling
like a doorbell, then an aunt with wild gray hair and lots of
bags. She embraces me, squeezes and shakes and says,
"Welcome, herzele, now my boy's got his heart's desire."
She flaps out to the hall, gathers up her bags and runs off
again; the mother says, "She's meshuge, ever since her husband left her she's been completely meshuge." I can't see
her face, she's standing at the kitchen window with her
arms folded; I feel she expects me to say something. I try a
weak joke, a Berlin one, go on to theater stories, back-stage
gossip, build them up, make them nice and sunny. She goes
to the sink and turns on the tap. I speak of the contract
that I'm supposed to sign. "Do you know California?" I
ask. "No," she says shrugging her shoulders as though she
didn't want to know either. "Dietrich made good, and Jannings . . . perhaps I'll be lucky." She unties her apron
strings, puts on a coat and goes out. I shouldn't have mentioned Jannings, he might have been a Nazi; I shouldn't
have mentioned Germans at all, the comparison was stupid.

The father comes home, stamps his feet on the door mat,
rubs his coat, wipes the rim of his hat with his sleeve and
says, "All hell loose in the hotel again today." He lights a
cigarette, tilts his head back and says proudly, "I work at
the Waldorf-Astoria on Park Avenue."

We go to Manhattan the next morning. The train is full
of gray-faced girls who all want to look like the wantonly
laughing or sultrily glowering beauties on the crinkled posters adorning the sooty station walls; the women are wearing nests full of flowers, pink veils, lilac circles of rouge,
and livid red mouths, the men are swathed in billowing
trousers, staring dispassionately at female legs and breasts.
Soldiers, sailors, girls are pushing through Times Square, a

huge mouth is blowing clouds of smoke out of a wall, a mammoth fist brandishes a pack of Camels, signs blink and white words slide across buildings, yellow taxis swoosh past toes and curbstones; news vendors shout, gramophones howl, drunks are lying on the steps of the subway, red prices have been crossed out and replaced by lower ones on greasy windows, high up above there's an oblong of sky, skyscraper tips poking into it, lights already on in some of the windows small as fingernails, winking like Christmas trees. Two hairy giants in chef's hats and open shirts throw hamburgers into gaping mouths of bread, slither them down the counter; next door a camera shop with cardboard figures: big-game hunter, proud boot planted on the slain beast, captain on the high seas, redskin with bow and arrow, Mexican with donkey, sombrero, guitar. The faces under the hats are open holes; two soldiers poke their heads through, are now Mexican and captain; flashbulbs explode. Fairground in the morning, fairground at night, with stalls of stone.

The packed movie house is a cross between the public baths and a set of an operetta, between a temple and a railway station; in the balcony they're making love, smoking, and chewing brown-white balloons of absorbent cotton from cardboard cartons; they run in and out during the film, during the stage show, whistle like crazy when the chorus girls kick their legs, jitterbug in the aisles; girls with mottled frozen legs sticking out of tennis shoes and white ankle socks squeak and faint, crawl about among the flower boxes on the front of the stage, cry with the crooner who's singing something in Spanish. Now there's a preview: a bulldog face bursting out of a German officer's uniform barks orders in English; behind him there's a swastika hanging the wrong way round; on comes a soldier in an SS jacket and an SA cap, clicks his heels and yells "Donner and Blitzen," "Jawoll!" and "Heil die Führer!" The reclining couples break apart and join the stalls in a chorus of boos.

Further up, in Central Park, they're skating; at the edge of the pond nurses in white caps and women in minks and little white gloves—we are suddenly in another city, a rich city with clean windows, discreet displays with no price tags, towering doormen with gold braid. On Park Avenue liveried lackeys are walking greyhounds, Pekineses and impeccable poodles on delicate chains, the girls are beautiful and composed, nonchalantly they settle into cars a block long. On the other side I see the sign WALDORF-AS-TORIA. "We could visit your father," I say. We find the side entrance and he's sitting on the flap-seat of the luggage elevator, hands between his knees. He jumps up buttoning his waistcoat and yelps, "What are you doing here?" A man pushes a trolley full of suitcases into the lift and growls, "Sixteenth, what are we waitin' for." His father closes the iron gates, purses his lips, floats up out of sight.

The New York representative of the Arthur Lacey agency is standing behind a desk laden with three telephones, full ashtrays, stacks of letters and photos. She chain-smokes, speaks rapidly, Kurt Kirsch translates for me. After asking, "How do you like New York?" and "Have a good flight?" she says, "Selznick'll be in town tomorrow, he wants to meet you, be at Hampshire House at five o'clock. We've got a problem—he doesn't want to pay the salary we agreed on in London. Fox has sent me a scene they want to test you on, one of the scouts will hear you read tomorrow morning—maybe we ditch Selznick altogether." She pushes her glasses up into her hair, rubs her chin like a man testing his beard, perches on the corner of the desk, lights a fresh cigarette, follows the flight of a smoke ring and says, "Who needs Selznick? Everything's going to be fine. Can you speak any English? Don't give it a thought, you're the new Garbo." She pushes letters and photos around the desk, lets them fall onto the floor, shouts at the closed door and a girl comes in with an envelope. "Here's the scene, go home and learn it and don't forget, everything'll be fine." I start to say thank you but she's telephoning already, looks up at me in surprise as though I'd just walked in without knocking.

On the train home he translates for me:

> IRENE *is sitting with a book in her hands, but her attention is elsewhere. She looks up at the clock, then at the door. There's a knock. Full of excitement she leaps up.*

> IRENE: Come in.
> [HARRY *enters.*]
> IRENE: Harry darling, how sweet of you to come, how are you?
> HARRY: Fine.

IRENE: (*tenderly*): I waited for you.

HARRY: Yeah?

IRENE: (*joyfully*): But now everything's fine. I cooked your favorite dish.

HARRY: I can only stay a minute, got some business.

IRENE: (*dismayed*): Oh Harry. (*pulling herself together*) I do understand.

HARRY: Yeah, I gotta go now.

IRENE: (*sexy*): In the old days you used to take me along, remember the old days, Harry? Remember the Sunday under the oak tree? You sang to me, oh so softly, then we went and had ice cream.

HARRY: (*lighting a cigarette*): Yeah.

IRENE: (*panic in her eyes*): You do still love me, don't you, Harry? Say you still love me.

HARRY: I gotta go.

IRENE: (*warmly*): I love you, Harry.

HARRY: Sorry, Irene, but Mary's waiting for me.

IRENE: (*screams*): Mary!

HARRY: Sorry, Irene—Mary needs me.

IRENE: (*tearfully*): Harry!

[HARRY *goes out.*]

IRENE: (*in a small voice*): Oh Harry—why Mary? Why couldn't it be me? (*She falls to the floor in anguish.*)

THE END

"I won't do it," I say, "that's even more asinine than the tractor films I had to synchronize for the Russians in order to pay the rent. I'm not going tomorrow."

At ten to eleven I'm standing at the gate of Twentieth Century Fox. The house looks like a granary, the stairs are narrow and stuffy. Two men are sitting in a dimly lit room; one is telephoning, the other drinking a glass of milk. They grin at me jovially, inspect my entire length as though I were a map of the city, the milk-drinker takes a pillbox from his waistcoat pocket, selects first a yellow, then a blue capsule, stifles a belch and says, "Ulcers, like everybody in this business, I got ulcers." He smiles contentedly, one of the chosen, opens his case and fingers a cigarette; the other man offers him a light, he pushes the hand away and yells, "I don't smoke for Chrissake." His neck puffs with anger, veins dance across his temples. I sneeze. His eyes open wide; "You gotta cold?" I nod. He

tears open a drawer and brings out a spray with a length of
rubber pipe and a bulb attached to it, squirts an oily substance into his throat and nose, smooths his hair and says,
"Start." The other one strokes the script, wipes beads of
sweat from his upper lip, supports his head on two fingers
and says, "I'll read Harry." The door opens and a thin lady
with a mousy face rushes in with a glass of milk, puts it
down on the desk and rushes out again. The telephone
rings, the milk-drinker picks up the receiver and bellows
incomprehensibly for a good five minutes, slams it down
again and says, "London." I have to grin because I think of
the old UFA joke: "What's he shouting for?" "He's talking
to Vienna." "Why doesn't he call them?" My grin has been
noticed, eyebrows are raised, the stare goes glassy; he puts
his hands on the desk, spreads his fingers as though awaiting a manicure and says, "What's so funny?" "Nothing."
He leans back satisfied, gazes up at the ceiling, says, "Before you begin, let me say a word concerning the character
of this girl. This Irene is decent. She's clean. Harry is her
first man, you understand, but Harry is not all she believes
him to be. Harry is not a man to take affairs of this kind
seriously. He's had a tough childhood and——" Oh my
God, he wanted to direct and didn't make it; now he sits
behind a desk and works it off on the auditions. If only
Barlog were here, or Jugert. Slowly he comes to the end
and then stares intently across the room as though hearing
an echo and says in a trembling voice, "You may begin."
As we finish, my temporary costar says, "Great." The milk-
drinker nods his head and says, "Great." Behind him are
glossy photos of the Fox stars: Jeanne Crain, Betty Grable,
Linda Darnell. Their heads are haloed in glowing back
light, features smoothed and ironed, hair glistening super-
naturally. "We'll let you know. Who's your agent?" he asks
and sips a little milk.

Four policemen on horseback are swaying through the
mass of automobiles behind Rockefeller Center; they sway
past the pedestrians, past their colleague at the intersection
who's unraveling knots with his thumb and whistle, bobbing up and down among the car roofs, bringing the
stampede to a halt with his leveled thumb, jerking it on
with a flick of the wrist. The four riders sway on aloof like
giraffes in a herd of nervous zebras. We sit in a drugstore
among lipsticks, pills, lotions, newspapers, books, hairpins,

greeting cards, and rubber bands eating sausages wrapped
in blotting-paper rolls; no one seems to mind their being
called hot dogs. We haven't much money; Kurt Hirsch has
given the little he's saved to his parents to look after. The
shoes I would like to buy are a luxury; they are livid green,
but much had been gray at home—the turned field-gray
army coats we made into skirts, jackets, dresses, the worn-
down sandals—I want the green ones, look like a stork in
the meadow, a parrot, feel wonderful in my new plumage,
almost forget the milk-drinker in my ecstasy.

Steam gushes from the drains as though there's a devil's
kitchen down below, as though the skyscrapers go on growing in the other direction. We ride down to Greenwich Village; neat, ordinary-sized houses and a square with gaunt
trees and empty benches which resembles many I had driv-
en through in London but whose names I never found out.
This one's called Washington Square. It's as quiet as a Sunday morning in the provinces, Europe's not so distant now,
not as far as from Times Square or Astoria, or from the
nineties and hundreds at the other end of the island, where
Harlem begins, where blue-black, brown-black children
shriek among the garbage cans, look up inquisitively, mis-
trustfully, where the invisible border runs between the tidy
feudal street of the whites and the dank crumbling alley of
the blacks. They'd driven trucks in Berlin, worn American
or French uniforms, and there had been only a few; the
many make me nervous, Berlin recedes, becomes unreach-
able, the Atlantic vast and endless. Here on Washington
Square it shrinks again, the distance is bearable, graspable.
Further down, at the tip of the island where the streets
have names instead of numbers, drunks are begging;
puffed, faceless, with bloodshot eyes and foul breath, they
beg for the next bottle, for a glass, a drop, scores of them
struggle up out of their beds of newspaper, stagger toward
us with outstretched hands. My knees start to wobble as we
pass the steaming laundry basements in Chinatown, the
sweat runs down my temples and neck, my tongue probes
holes where once were teeth; chunks of memory, Mongol
nightmares flicker up like slides picked at random and pro-
jected onto an asphalt surface, a pane of glass, grow bigger,
clearer, swallow the street, the fire escapes and cellar windows. I clatter to the subway on my livid-green stilts, calm
down as the train rumbles into the damp cold black station.

At Fifty-fifth Street and Fifth Avenue they're gliding

serenely, as though unaware of the others, as though the island were divided, the breeds at feud, their camps at sites unknown. In a soundproof salon before kindly matte mirrors under soft pink lights they are being bobbed, manicured, pedicured; in velvet-lined elevators they slide through noble department stores; a clicking sound, like muffled castanets, signals departure and stop; distinguished ladies with blue-white hair and night nurses' voices show the way. They're hastening to lunch, to tea, to their first Martini; they sign instead of paying; their carriage says my appointments have been planned, my day designed, social standing impeccable, life synoptical, temperature regulated, footfall hushed.

At five o'clock the porter in the Hampshire House whispers, "You're to go right up."

> Starnberg, Upper Bavaria,
> July 21st, 1969

"What in the name of God . . . ?" asks Tonio, my husband, as the alarm clock rings at 6 a.m.

"The astronauts are getting out at seven."

"So what?" he says and yawns.

Half an hour later two well-rested journalists from a daily newspaper arrive to photograph us sitting in front of the TV as the first man sets foot on the moon. "Terrific, what?" one of them says.

"In case something goes wrong, we've got a black-edged front page all lined up," says the other.

Tonio sips his tea testily and lights a cigarette. I get up to close the window since our neighbor on the left is mowing his lawn and the one on the right has been erecting a prefabricated house for three years now; today is no exception. Our daughter wakes up; Tonio maneuvers his six feet five inches out of the chair and brings her into the living room. "You're probably very wet," he says, looking at her inquiringly. She stares at the screen, squeals "Gaga." "You're so right," he says and gives her a smacking kiss.

The TV commentator is talking excitedly to his colleague in Houston; in between one can hear the astronauts' voices, cool, impersonal, like pilots preparing to land at Munich airport in perfect weather conditions. "In a few seconds the American banner will be plunged into the surface of the moon," someone cries excitedly. "this is a great and moving moment which will go down in the annals of man, perhaps we should stop to think for a moment . . ."

"Christ Almighty," says Tonio and goes out to inspect his geraniums. Now here's the Statesman, delivering his speech well-stirred and strained, spitting words of peace like cherrystones to the moon. Here it comes, the heroic tenor's clammy fervor, the club chairman's annual report, the emotional world of centuries past; the conglomeration of thoughts and words accumulated over thousands of years, goulash that is brought out, warmed, and served, absently chewed at Christmas Football Protest Birth Death Moon. Boris Vian would have grinned, stretching his wide mouth even wider. "We have to take language apart," he'd have said, "destroy it. It blackmails us, hustles us into feelings we don't have any more and don't need . . . rapes us with words that become thoughts, become feelings." He'd have laughed and gulped pills to level the hammering of his sick heart. He had a crazy apartment, right behind the Moulin Rouge, Prévert lived on the floor below. When he wasn't writing he repainted the walls or made records or played the trumpet. Nobody bought the record we made together in Paris; the lyrics, the plays that he wrote were not understood. Ahead of his time, it's called—they're all ahead of their time, those as gifted as he is, or was. A letter arrived from Britanny: "I've finished the scenario and am trying to rest, I'm not well at all." He died shortly afterwards. Aged thirty-nine, the newspapers said.

I call Else Bongers, dial 0311 for Berlin, click click click, then the other numbers, quiet chattering, then click again. "Yes?" Aggressive, disturbed, was probably in the bathtub.

"I'll call back."

"No no."

"How are you?"

"Don't ask."

"I did already."

She'll be standing in the big room: bookshelves on the left, fireplace in the middle, telephone book and unopened letters on the window ledge. Strange that she never writes—yes, once, when Christina was born: My child has a child. . . . Thank God the cocker spaniel's gone, that ankle-snapper. It's over a year since I was there last; she came to my concert but the doorman wouldn't let her through to the dressing room: against the rules and regulations. . . . I was even more nervous than usual, set great store on her opinion. I ought to put water in the ashtrays, stop them from smoking—it's me who should stop. . . . She wants to come during her holidays—how does she stand it, that herd of acting students, what do they want to play, Hedda Gabler? Egmont? Hero and Leander? Or the contemporaries—horse on the stage, tape recorders, copulation. . . .

"Did you watch?" I ask.

"Yes, I stayed up." Click.

"Was that your lighter?"

"Yes."

"You're smoking again?"

"Of course. I was alone and overwhelmed by it. One can't endure a thing like that alone. It's impossible to grasp." There's a ring in the background: "Wait a moment," she says. Door slams, dog yaps. "One of my students, she helps me."

"With what?"

"Cooking and the like. My daily left me, housekeepers are a thing of the past and since the operation——"

"What operation?"

"Now stop it, at a certain age the repairs start. Child!"

That's the voice that jolts me, stabs me awake, that says if I'd wanted you to know you'd have known.

"There's only one question," she says, "can it and will it change the world? Everything else is uninteresting. I'm not caught up in the mass hysteria but I can't cope with it, just as I can't cope with a lot of things any more—my pupils with their endless dissertations, reproaches, narrow-mindedness; they spend a whole day discussing Gropius and the Bauhaus— whom are they telling? Dessau, the Bauhaus—I grew up with the whole circle. Well, it's enough. I'm ready to quit. . . . Child?"

"Yes?"

"I'm thinking of suicide. I've no interest for my

contemporaries any more and they've none for me.
They've never had to take a stand on anything. When
I spoke against rearmament in '49 I was attacked for
expressing sentiments which had been praised and
honored in '45, attacked because similar voices were
now being raised in East Germany, which proves that
liberals and Communists are basically one of a kind,
attacked because of my influence on young people.
Many advised me to retract my statement. What the
hell."

"Don't."

"I want to sleep."

"Do you mean it?"

"I shall sleep, I promise you."

Why this fear, why do I want to stop her—for her
sake? For mine? Why do I say "don't"? Because it's
not done, because we're brought up on man proposes,
God disposes? Asiatic religions allow it, suicide per-
missible when one-way street becomes cul-de-sac, life
a burden for yourself and others. Grandfather's death
was never discussed.

"I'm coming to Berlin."

"You stay where you are."

"If you were a Brahma——"

"If I were a what?"

"Brahma, Buddhist—you'd be just beginning. Your
obligations would be fulfilled, duty done, meditation,
contemplation can begin, it would be time to take account, the blank page would be the beginning—we
turn red when we jump off the conveyor belt, when
we're not churning up foam like an outboard motor."

"I am not red, I just don't have any money and I
can't manage on one bowl of rice daily. Enough now,
it's getting too expensive."

"That's exactly what Henry said yesterday."

"Henry who?"

"Miller. He's in Paris." Tough, resilient Henry, I always forget how slender he is, delicate; it's grotesque
the way the camera distorts, inflates him . . . his order-
liness, when he stayed with us, his room spotless, the
bed smooth, as though he'd never slept in it. And the
bunch of asters he brought—or were they dahlias? It
was hot and they hung their heads like praying brides-
maids. "I'll be damned," he chortled. You'd think his

forefathers came from the Urals, but no, Minden,
Westphalia; Heinrich Müller's Sexus, Plexus, Tropics.
Eyes like Else's, not so blue, face like a horse, sometimes a cheetah, voice like a Canadian bear. He's se-
venty-eight; four years ago he beat us at table tennis,
wiped the floor with us, Gauloise stuck in the corner
of his mouth. He rumbles when he's listening; at first I
always looked around, thought it was the dog or the
plumbing playing up again. Yesterday too, that deep
easy umm that says I'm listening, know what you
mean, know what you want to say. Does he still vitu-
perate? Or does he stand looking at the Playboy clubs
like Einstein at the bomb? Ten years ago, when we
were broke, bailiffs panting down our necks, the bank
manager said, "I'd always thought you were pecunious, after your many successes." I thought I'd start
shrieking, he sat there polishing his pince-nez saying
pecunious, but then he made us a loan and we went
straight away with Henry to the best restaurant in
town. Driving home he said, "The most beautiful Gei-
sha in all Tokyo was attacked one night by a maniac.
He chopped off her right arm and slashed her face.
Three years later she was more sought after than
ever." He had grinned like a Buddha and stroked his
smooth head.

"I'll come down the weekend after next, I want to
see your child," said Else.

"Is that a promise?"

"Yes yes." Click.

FIFTEEN

The room is beige, overrun with beige; it drifts over fireplace ceiling floor table couch wall, looms from the mirrors lampshades doors, sterilized, uninhabitable, entry forbidden, as pale as Sehmisch's prewar rolls; it will snap shut and swallow, chew, digest me beigely. Chair like a pudding; it expands, retracts, draws me down, folds itself around me, over me. Stage set for a drawing-room comedy: the lady of the house will glide on in a negligee bearing a bunch of freshly cut rattling daffodils, rattling because they're from the prop room; she will graciously fill the vases, humming a little tune, her entrance applause will fade away and the telephone will jangle unnaturally as the stage manager commences his nightly battle with the bell board. "Hello," she'll say sweetly and her bright-silver little bell-laugh will tinkle. An Adonis in white tennis shorts will ease through the French window and kiss her hand, wrist, forearm; her initial reaction will be haughty but it will slowly mingle with sly delight and she'll say, "You're incorrigible, Percy." Something's missing, of course, the piano, a small white grand, we'll need that for the second-act curtain. In comes the housekeeper, portly, motherly, bringing the letter on the silver tray—she'll have all the good lines later, blunt, no-nonsense, and they'll clap when she enters, to the annoyance of the others. "The governor's coming to lunch," madam will say, and "One o'clock, on the dot, Percy," waggling her little pink index finger.

"If he says something you don't understand, don't give yourself away," says Kurt Hirsch. A sunburned gentleman pokes his head into the beige and says, without looking at us, "Selznick will be arriving shortly." A glass clock on the mantlepiece goes ping ping. In the mirror I see something crumpled, cramped, with damp hair and red nose and livid-green feet. I'd like to smoke, but ash in those crystal bowls? Fag-ends with lipstick on them? He enters at a quarter to six; massive, room-filling. "Hello," he says and drops into the soft beige, exhausted, as though he had run twenty miles. Brown eyes sparkle—or is it his glasses? White hair, broad skull, flat nose. "How do you like New York?" he asks, and "Where are you living?" "Astoria," I say. He smiles, pushes his glasses onto his forehead, flicks a glance at Kurt Hirsch. Have I said something wrong? "Nice little film you made there, what was it called?" *"Film Without a Name?"* He shows me the palm of his big hand, lets his heavy body sink down even further. "Something to do with ruins," he says. "They've all got ruins." He blinks at me out of the cushions—in a second he'll ask, "What's so funny?" *"Murderers Among Us,"* I say quickly. "Yeah yeah," he grunts, closes his eyes and puts his hands behind his head as though taking a sun bath. "Your English'll have to improve," he adds. What do I do if he falls asleep? I go hot and he seems to shrink, he's disappearing into the beige, I'm looking at him, the couch, the room, through the wrong end of a telescope—I must have fever. Suddenly he sits up straight and looks at me with keen interest. "When do you leave for California?" he asks. "I don't know." "I'll have my assistant call your agent," he says and stands up.

You shouldn't have mentioned Astoria," says Kurt Hirsch in the elevator.

"Why not?"

He shrugs his shoulders. "There are better addresses."

We drive to the harbor: the dog has arrived. It barks and yelps, strains at its leash, runs around in circles, howls like a wolf. The half-starved, shivering, shell-shocked animal has been renamed Blondie.

My cheekbones are hammering, needles flicker up my jaw, stab in my ear, scalp contracts, head severs itself, floats up, balances between the posters and fire escapes, jumps down again, crushing my neck. "You got a temperature?" Kurt Hirsch asks.

The hallway is dry and stuffy, never aired, house without summer; smell of newspapers and leftover milk. I'm afraid of IT: IT is the parents, the looks, the silences, the rejection. IT is something lurking, a coiled-up snake in a jam jar. IT is what waits in cellars when you fetch the potatoes in winter, IT is the three paces between the front door and the light switch, IT is the stares, as the film ended in Pankow. I'm imagining things I tell myself as Kurt Hirsch opens the apartment door, but why do they speak Czech when I'm there? They both speak perfect German; with English and Czech I'm amputated, fish in a basin, like the trout in Zürich, right next to the cloakroom, swimming and staring, waiting for the net.

The passage is dark; on the kitchen table there's a candlestick with a lighted candle. "Is there a power cut?" I ask. The father looks up sharply, the mother mumbles something and scrapes crumbs from the tablecloth. The father's got a chair in his hand, his eyes grow round and glassy, his lips form an oval, his nostrils flare, he raises the chair above his head, a leg breaks the light bulb, splinters shower over the table and icebox, the dog howls; slow-motion ballet—slow, lazy, then quicker, in leaps and bounds the hatred splits open, bursts like a water-bomb, spits and splashes, screams through barracuda mouths, piranha teeth. Kurt jumps between me and the chair. "Grab your suitcase," he yells; the father rips the lid with a breadknife, kicks and punches, I run to the elevator then to the stairs, doors fly open, on past hair curlers, face cream, dressing gowns and aprons, toothbrushes in outstretched hands; on the street there's a taxi: "I don't take drunks," the driver says, goes back to the funnies. Kurt falls over my legs, the father's hammering at the window, shaking his fist, face convulsed in hatred, black spot behind black window. "I curse you," the spot screams.

"What was that about? I couldn't understand."

"It was Shabbes, Sabbath, Jewish Sunday and all that, not a power cut," says Hirsch.

In the eighth or ninth hotel there's a room for $4.50, dogs not allowed. We bind its snout with adhesive tape and smuggle it up the back stairs, it paws at the gag, pees on the floor. I lie on the bed shivering. "We'll look for a doctor tomorrow; hope to God we find one we don't have to pay right away," says Kurt Hirsch.

"So you're from Germany," the woman doctor says in the dark-red darkness. "Ever had any trouble with your lungs?"

"No."

"I can see something but a fluoroscope's not good enough, you'll have to be X-rayed, I'll write down the address." Her office is a back room with frayed sofa, kitchen table, fluoroscope apparatus, two chairs, and a hot plate. She prepares an injection and says, "Roll down your stocking."

"What are you giving me?"

She looks up angrily, not used to being questioned. "Penicillin," she says grudgingly. The needle is thick and I wince as it hits the bone. "Now now, don't carry on, you Germans are not usually so squeamish." She hands me a note with the name and address. "Monday morning at nine o'clock."

"Couldn't I go right away? I'd like to know—"

"We don't work on weekends."

"But today's only Friday."

"Thirty-five dollars."

"Can I pay later?"

"Do you have an address?"

"Hotel—"

"Pay now."

"If I've got TB we're really in trouble," I say to Kurt Hirsch, who has waited in a drugstore.

"I'll call home, they've got to give me the money," he says.

"You don't get a penny as long as you live with the shikse," the father screams, loud enough for me to hear.

"It's my money!"

"It's for your own benefit, believe me, son."

I lie in bed looking out the window at a view of a brick wall, the dog whimpers, there's a pincushion between my ribs.

"I'll drive over to Aunt Anna, she'll lend me some money," Kurt Hirsch says and goes out.

On Monday we go to the doctor. "Come back in the morning," he says after doing the X-ray. The father is standing in front of our hotel brandishing a letter: "See what she's written, the German mother, she's worried, she had a bad dream—didn't worry about the Jews, did she?" He chases me, yapping and yelling, has found new proof.

In the evening I ride out to La Guardia airport; I stand there watching the planes turn and trundle up to the runway, fly off in the drizzle, taillights blinking, out over the Atlantic.

"You haven't got TB," the doctor says, "that'll be fifty dollars."

"That's a dirty trick," Kurt Hirsch spits, as we stand on the stairs, "a low-down, cunning trick. They send each other their patients and split the take."

"I'm not sure that it's a good time for you to go to America," Michi's astrologer had said; but then, four weeks later, he had called again: "You most certainly should go, your aspects are excellent." And the chauffeur, the old one employed by OMGUS, the one who heard the grass growing, said, "You know that stargazer don't you, the one they all go to, do me a favor and ask him about me, I was born in July. I took him over a Red Cross package from your friend Hirsch a couple of days ago, he goes there too."

"Did you go to the astrologer in Berlin?"

"How do you mean? Oh sure, once, a lot of crap," he says nervously.

Success, I must have success, at any price, I tell myself: success is protection, asbestos, oxygen tent, magic word, like *artista* with the *muzhiks;* success is balloon, rainbow, camouflage net, foxhole.

I buy ten cans of fruit juice, orange and grapefruit, send them to Berlin with a jubilant letter. "You're such a child," Mother says three years later, "sending us orange juice when we were desperate for fat."

"Juice was cheaper."

"But you always wrote—"

"I exaggerated, like all emigrants."

Telephone call from the agency: "It wasn't easy," she says, "they know you're broke and have no passport, but I pulled it off—seven-year contract, with options of course, but that's usual. Be happy, everything's gonna be great, be in Hollywood on April first."

"Why seven years, that's much too long, I didn't want—"

"It's the standard contract, they'll need that long to build you up here," she says indignantly, putting me in my place.

We set out in March 1948 in the car that he'd had in Berlin and which the army has shipped over free of charge. It breaks down every second day but it's impressive, black with lots of chrome trim, and Kurt Hirsch is proud of his automobile. It's Sunday. Carefully groomed worshippers are climbing the steps of St. Patrick's, the avenues are deserted, the dinosaur is taking a breather, stretching, sleeping. The bridges between the island and the mainland are packed with Sunday drivers, elbows poking through the windows, fingers drumming on the roofs; whistling, chew-

ing, smoking, they flood the bridge, pour forth as though a
sluice had been opened, a gate snapped back to reveal the
escape route, ooze like paste from a tube. The sky widens,
promise of spring and meadows between telegraph poles,
billboards, exhaust fumes, promise of buttercups and but-
terflies. We drive through languid small towns, through
main streets that are nothing but drugstore, filling station,
Woolworth's, on past the glum flat clutter of houses, fire
escapes, antennae. Houses in underwear, unadorned, half-
finished; houses, but not homes where one is born, lives
and dies, houses to wait in, temporarily, by chance; outer
offices, switch yards, clearance depots on the way to the
waiting-room New York.

The beds in the motel quake with every passing truck or
bus. No one asked for our passports, origin, or religion;
room key, sleep, pay, drive on. We eat at drugstore
counters with their exultant slogans, sugar sprinklers,
doughy white bread, livid ice-cream sundaes and turkey-red
ketchup. I feel as though I've escaped, broken out of a
dungeon, been freed from the hatred and surly haste.
Through Harrisburg and Pittsburgh's smoky sooty streets
with churches like movie theaters and movie theaters like
churches, popcorn, bluejeans, haircurlers, jukeboxes, suburbs, small towns, one-horse towns—but no villages, a
country without villages, barns, chicken-runs, thatch, bright
balconies, feather bed in the window, sheets flapping
among the goats and dogs.

We reach Chicago in four days. Mother's brother, sister-
in-law, great-aunt, nephews, and cousins live on the outskirts. The living room is crowded; they embrace us, cook
German dishes, speak a goulash of English and German,
offer advice, know the ropes, are pioneers. Great-aunt
squeezes my hand, slaps Hirsch on the back and says, "I
came over on a sailing boat, it took six weeks, down in the
hold, but you don't notice when you're young and have a
good husband. Mine was twelve years younger than me and
Italian into the bargain—my God, back in stuffy old
Germany they got all worked up about it but here we were
able to make a fresh start, there's no bias here. I never re-
gretted it. Now and again I get homesick for Pomerania,
West Prussia, Schneidemühl, but that's only when you get
old and sentimental. You've got to be firm here—'tough'
the Americans call it, and 'time is money'—but you'll come
through all right. I want to see you on the screen next time,

not here." She demands success, like Else, like Pommer, like me.

"Where you heading?" asks the gas-station attendant on Route 66.

"California."

He whistles approval, pushes back his cap and nods. "Wish I could come along."

Everyone says the same on Route 66, from St. Louis to Needles. They gaze to the west as though they can see it glowing behind the telegraph poles, over the hilltops: the warmth, the ocean, palm trees, orange groves, the riches of Hollywood, the undiscovered gold mine. "Good luck," they shout before they shrink in the rear-view mirror, Coca-Cola raised to their mouths, cigarette in oily fingers, hopeful, resigned, mixture of both, ready to go, nothing binds them, neither the job nor the town, they appear to be only waiting for someone to say, "Come on, jump in."

Signpost: MISSOURI; signpost: OKLAHOMA; signpost: NEW MEXICO—new states almost every day, borders without customs or barriers, signposts no bigger and no smaller than NO PARKING or DANGEROUS CORNER. The earth becomes ocher-yellow, the sky is closer, swollen stars the color of linseed oil, honey-melon moon. Beneath the strange new sky the familiar gas stations, the same questions, the uniformly potent poster-promises, identical radio programs, weather forecast sung and swung, pills, pastilles, lotions for and against; CARTER'S LITTLE LIVER PILLS before and after Glenn Miller, sluggish bowels and bad breath treated and cured between *Stardust* and *Holiday for Strings,* supports for fallen arches, magical deodorants that transform wallflowers into vamps after *Melancholy Baby* and world headlines at a glance. The swing swings, flutters in the stomach, on the soles of the feet, plucks at tiredness behind the eyes, deadens, unites, relieves, deludes, becomes a drug, hammering euphoria. We got cocksure, have taken possession of the land we are crossing, pass judgment on fleeting impressions, pass folks busy with their day, their lawn mowers and kids, Hollywood towers before us, Hollywood with outstretched arms offering paradise; our arrival is a guarantee, the contract an insurance.

In Amarillo the car breaks down altogether. Three days of hotel and garage. It's hot. "You ought be here in summer," the waitress in the drugstore says, shaking her head at our beads of sweat. They drawl and slur, their voices distorting the vowels like a faulty telephone. My English now enables me to read the articles in the film magazines, the *Silver Screens* and *Movielands,* with their wealth of smiling, beautiful people. They wave in front of cinemas, at parties, on sun-drenched terraces, from private open-air baths called swimming pools. They are warmhearted and successful, handsome and relaxed, no different from the unknown neighbor, the man next door who is still waiting to become as rich and famous as they; happy children enjoying happy marriages and happy babies. Many of them mention God, who has been good to them and answered their prayers, sending them the husband, the wife, the undeserved success. HE becomes a gigantic ear hovering in the heavens over the West Coast, ever alert, ever ready to accept and deliver new orders for success if addressed in the proper manner. In Berlin, called upon in heaving cellars, he had seemed remoter, more terrible; here he is tangible and generous, a champion. He plays a major part in films in which nuns and priests, portrayed by stars, are benevolent, speak profound moral truths, resolve problems. And smile. I was sitting on the Austrian author Friedrich Torberg's sweltering balcony in New York three years later when he suddenly brought out his old scrapbooks. He held up photos, hiding the captions, and challenged me to guess why the people pictured were so jubilant.

"They just got married? Won the first prize?"

"No," he leered, showing the headline, "condemned to death. And this one?"

"Inherited a fortune—from an aunt he never knew in Australia?"

"He just killed his wife with an ax."

He'd collected them, the happy headliners, the "keep smiling club" members for whom BE HAPPY was the supreme commandment, to be obeyed under all circumstances. For the moment I still took it seriously, the smile, the "Hi folks," Christian names at first meeting.

On Sunday morning we drive on, climb up Route 66 toward the Rocky Mountains. Along the road outside Tucumcari, Indians are squatting imperiously on outspread rugs. "Maybe we should buy a rug, we might need it in Hollywood," I venture. "We're not the Salvation Army and we need a rug like a hole in the head," says Kurt Hirsch, ng, I guess,"

out gold or
like paper
dow has a
ith a neon
er the wall
trasse and
the shop
ur sheets
reminded
made my

at once
money,
refugee
full of

Holly-
Kurt

hing
of a
ish
es,
g
d
t

s of steam gushing from our
ngine gives a snort and dies.
d approaches us, holding out

say.

rtainly.

from the steam, bangs his head
ars loudly. The Indian returns si-
ds his rug and squats, stares fixedly
ugh seeing smoke signals, witness to
only.

rs now, gas stations few and far beat one displaying the sign: LAST
QUERQUE. They offer water for the
raveler, are solicitous, advise caution,
old Stalingraders had talked to the re-
lides away abruptly; in the sudden total
en generous country becomes hostile, nur-
es and jackals, abhors man. The dog fidgets
ries up and down searching for things famil-
finds a yucca, knee-high with prickly leaves
like a clean-picked pike; the spikes dig into its
and turns on the invisible enemy, whimpers
t the rocks, the blackness, the unknown.

e by day and by night, endless stretches between
from Amarillo to Tucumcari from Tucumcari to
que; they are as far from each other as Berlin
arsaw, Prague from Vienna; behind each main
he next desert, the next nothing. Rocks, sand, yuc-
he breadth of the horizon gives me agoraphobia. If
ad to walk, to flee, one would go blind in the sun, die
of thirst, and behind the rocks the Indians are waiting quietly, gathering strength, they will surge forward out of the
barrenness, from the empty belly of the west, swarm toward the coast and drive the intruders into the sea.

In Flagstaff I take the map and hold it on my knees, tick
off the miles, await the sign CALIFORNIA like the gates
to Elysium, a promise, a vindication. Two policemen are
standing on the road, signal us to halt. They peer at the
back seat, open the trunk, ask about oranges. There's a wi-
zened one in the glove compartment, they remove it, apologize, wish us good luck.

"What was that for?"

"God knows, afraid of beetles or somethi
says Kurt Hirsch.

Needles, California, is a gold-rush town wit
rush, adventurers gone, fever subsided, house
cups, use once and throw away. Our hotel wi
view of garbage cans and a yellow-brown wall
sign missing its first and last letters; it flickers ov
which resembles an alley between Prinzregenten
Bernhardstrasse, between the elevated railway an
with the mangle where Mother used to launder
and pillowcases—the yellow-brown wall always
me of chocolate pudding with vanilla sauce and
mouth water.

Kurt Hirsch goes off to look for a garage. All
I'm frightened; I see myself stranded, lost, without
passport, or language; I stand at the window, am a
once again drifting down to the bottom of the sea
serpents, toads, and hairy monsters.

"I called the agency, they've got us a room at the
wood Roosevelt and an apartment's in the offing too,"
Hirsch says and pulls me back on land.

Paradise has palm trees. That the ones on Pers
Square in Los Angeles look like the dusty remnants
discarded stage set, their leaves hanging like damp
cloths, doesn't bother me at all. Palm trees are palm tre
and Hollywood is near. The setting sun is a broken e
yolk seeping across the sky, the streets are sticky an
humid, faces gray and flaccid, bear no sign of the adjacen
ocean. The city looks like an impoverished relative of Nev
York, smaller, duller, consumptive. On the corner of Hol
lywood Boulevard and Vine Street we brighten up, comb
our hair, blow our noses, recognize the picture palaces
we've seen so often on newsreels. There's a traffic jam in
front of one of them, searchlights sweep the sky as though
seeking enemy airplanes, a loudspeaker crackles, the crowd
screeches: film première with red carpet, thick cord, and
police cordons to keep back the fans, separate the wheat
from the chaff. A policeman with a whistle threatens us
with his rubber truncheon as though we had tried to sneak
in, peeked under the counter, boarded the train without a
ticket.

From the eighth floor of the Roosevelt Hotel, Hollywood
is at my feet. Looking out over the boulevards, the ropes of

light, the hills and there where the sea must be I say, I've
got to make it. What, exactly, I don't know, apart from
fame, recognition, adoration. Our school in Schöneberg
had been named after Friedrich Rückert, and one of his
aphorisms had served as our slogan: "I will; the word is
mighty. Uttered in earnest, perfect still, 'twill move the
heavens, this one small word I will." Not one word at all, I
think to myself, and have to laugh, have to think of Fraulein Weise and Lerche and the gymnastics teacher and of
Skin of Our Teeth—the première in the Hebbel Theater
next to the ruins of the Anhalter railway station. We had
sat there as though anesthetized, paralyzed, unable to clap,
to react in any way. The play could have been written for
us, for Berlin, for the half-starved who had recognized each
other, two hours long.

In the morning Miss Patterson arrives. She is sun-tanned
and wears no make-up, has short hair and long legs, is
boyish, cheerful, matter-of-fact, says neither great nor
Garbo. She takes me to a department store, buys a white
dress, says, "Put it on," and drives me out to the Selznick
studio in Culver City. In the car I try to keep the conversation going and she says, "Main thing at the moment is your
English. Your teacher's name is Miss Cunningham, paid by
Selznick." The policeman at the studio entrance questions
us and goes to the telephone, finally raises the pole and
writes down the car number carefully. Suspicion, mistrust,
at every step. Secretaries like clams: "Mr. Wilson will see
you now," says our tightly clenched one. "Let me do the
talking," Miss Patterson whispers, "Wilson's Selznick's
right-hand man."

Dark office in a white timbered house: out of the glare
of the sun into chilled stillness behind lowered blinds.
Leather sofa, leather chairs, brass oil lamps with green
glass shades, virgin note pads, empty ashtrays. Mr. Wilson
wears a dark suit, white shirt, and tie, is slim and young
and looks at me as though he can't remember sending for
me. Miss Patterson starts to talk and I hear my name. No
reaction. Perhaps this isn't the studio after all, perhaps we
came through the wrong entrance, he's a lawyer or an insurance agent? He sits down, motions to a chair, taps his
teeth with a pencil. I look at Miss Patterson and she
nods—I should show my teeth. I bare them like a horse,
feel ridiculous. He picks up the telephone, a secretary
enters with a shorthand pad, goes out, comes back again

and gives me a sheet of paper with an address on it. Dr. Marcus, I read. We are dismissed. "What's wrong, I've got good front teeth," I say. Miss Patterson shrugs her shoulders: "They always want something changed. Miss Cunningham expects you at nine in the morning. Her office is next to Stage Two and when you're through go down to the publicity department—they need biographical details and so forth." She speaks slowly, emphatically, hoping I'll understand. "Thank you," I say and notice that I'm hanging on to her sleeve like a child at a fairground.

"Nobody said anything about a dog," said the landlady of the two-room apartment on South Doheny Drive. She loomed, massive, in the doorway, her strawberry sweater and violet slacks filled with heavy-duty tires. "It's house-trained and tiny and never barks," Kurt Hirsch said. She shook her golden locks, earrings, necklaces, brooches. "It never climbs up on the furniture, it's terribly old . . ." said Hirsch and launched into a description of a stuffed squirrel in the hope that mastiff-sized Blondie wouldn't jump through the car window and come looking for us. The landlady listened with her head inclined, suddenly drew back her arm and thumped Hirsch on the shoulder crying, "O.K., you win, honey, I'm Sadie." She ushered us into the living room gesturing to about twenty ceramic parrots, several clusters of pink Venetian wall lights against a background of flowered wallpaper, great gingham-covered armchairs, lilac floor vases with painted garlands full of artificial cacti, a huge gold-framed oil painting picturing pale sweetly smiling maidens sitting under rich foliage by the light of the rising sun and said reverently, "Now you know why I was worried about the dog." She undulated through the kitchen, bath, and bedroom, coming to a halt in front of tiny twin beds with bird-of-paradise covers, sank her hands into her sumptuous bosom and said in a small choked voice, "I was so happy here with my beloved Dick." We stood there silently trying not to wonder how she could ever have balanced on one of those tiny cots without falling off.

The first knock came at eleven in the evening. "Sadie? It's me, honey," a bass voice rumbled.

The dog barked. Kurt Hirsch called out, "Who's there?"

"It's me, Sadie."

"Sadie doesn't live here any more."

"Oh, where's Sadie?" he whined soulfully and went off dragging his feet.

At one o'clock the next one: an anxious hiss at the window, "Come on, open up, Sadie." The third came at two and at half-past three the telephone rang: "Be with you in five minutes, Sadie!" roared a drunken voice. Two sleepless weeks went by until the full circle of Sadie's acquaintances was informed of her departure.

In the morning we made many futile attempts to get the coffee-maker to work and then drove to the studio. Except for an ice-cream truck tinkling nursery rhymes as it crept around the block and a silent mail truck which glided along the curb pausing briefly at each gateway as an arm come through the window and thrust bundles of mail into the breadbin-like letter boxes, Doheny Drive was empty. Sprinklers circled over short-cropped lawns, shutters and windows had been firmly closed. Olympic Boulevard was full of Buicks Cadillacs Pontiacs Oldsmobiles Chevrolets; they cruised at a smart pace, keeping their distance, not overtaking, unwavering, as though on rails.

Selznick's huts and stages were modest compared to the UFA lot in Babelsberg and Miss Cunningham's office was no bigger than the dressing rooms in Geiselgasteig. She sat behind a small table and looked as though she was always frozen, as though heat and California sun had not been meant for her. She had soft, slightly pink eyes, which made me think that she had just been crying. She wore a gray wool jacket over a long-sleeved white blouse, a heavy wintery skirt, and solid shoes, just right for a long march across barren rain-sodden fields. She was like many elocution coaches: Madame Henriette in the Rue du Mont Thabor, Miss Ross in New York, Miss Blythe in London. The exactness and correctness of their clothes and coiffure are in perfect accord with each gently formed syllable. They are lonely and lead an ordered life with orderly holidays at the same resort each year, they like health teas, etchings, and sometimes cats and canaries. They wear an accurate wrist watch, are punctual to the second, and are always friendly and helpful in a reserved manner. Their books are old and cared for, carefully numbered. Their habit of writing in small notebooks in small handwriting during the lesson is irritating for the student at first but he very soon realizes that in this manner each mistake and everything in

need of attention has been thoroughly perceived and re-
corded.

A man as big as a cupboard was standing beside Miss
Cunningham; he was young and pretty and his limbs
seemed not to belong to each other, as though they'd been
provisionally tacked on and hurt at the joints. "Mr. Hudson," said Miss Cunningham softly. "Hi," he said, and
grinned sheepishly, fumbled with the doorknob, said "So
long," and went out, the walls of the shed shaking as he
passed by the window. "He was put under contract two
weeks ago. Mr. Wilson changed his name to Rock Hudson," said Miss Cunningham, drawing a minute handkerchief from the sleeve of her jacket and dabbing her nostrils
delicately. "He was a truck driver and his speech presents
veritable problems. Do you understand anything I say?"
she asked, concerned. One and a half hours later she closed
her books and said, "Tomorrow morning at nine o'clock.
We must work on your *th's* and be so good as to learn
these vowels." She gave me a piece of paper: I was dismissed.

On the way to the publicity department I bumped into
Mr. Wilson: "A lady does not run," he said sternly and disappeared into the main building, leaving me perplexed, unclear about what was expected of me. Vague memories of
the first English films I had seen in Berlin came back to
me: "Ladies" sat on settees drinking tea, bore strokes of
fate, or incidents presented as such, without batting an eye-
lid, wore the same never-varying expression of pride and
boredom from the first foot of film to the last, and, of
course, never ran.

The head of publicity sat bowed over a coffee table
munching around the toothpicks of a three-story sandwich
with tomato, egg, and strips of bacon hanging down its
sides and dripping mayonnaise onto the table, attempted to
wipe his glistening fingers on a scruffy paper napkin while
chewing desperately on an enormous bite which distended
his cheeks, swallowed with relief and said, "Sorry" and "Sit
down." Without the lump in his mouth his face was thin
and sad. He reached over to his desk and extracted a cardboard folder from which news clippings slid and fluttered
to the floor; he watched them with a worried expression,
like someone who wages a constant but hopeless battle
against disorder. He picked them up and took a large pad
from the table, rubbed his sleeve over the grease stain his

thumb had made on the shining white page and offered me
a cigarette which, before I could take it, dropped from the
package and fell into a pool of mayonnaise. He smiled
knowingly as though he'd expected this, as though goblins
were at work plastering his way through life with grease
stains and soggy cigarettes. "Welcome to Hollywood," he
said softly and took out a pencil. "I have to have your life
story for the press and all that." He looked around apologetically: "How do you spell Knef?" ("Kaneff," he said.)

"K-N-E-F."

"I've got orders from Mr. Selznick that the name's to be
changed."

"No," I said.

He looked up in astonishment, admiringly, as though I'd
said execution yes, blindfold no. "But I've got the list of
suggestions already," he said and gave me a list of names;
Gilda Christian was the first.

I shook my head, said, "No," once again and gave him
back the list.

"But nobody can pronounce 'Kaneff' here." He leaned
forward anxiously, wanting to protect me from a dreadful
fate.

"Please," I said, "I should like to keep my own name."

"Well," he said dismally, "that can wait." He looked
down at his pad. "Where were you born and where did you
grow up?" he asked in a tone that already made a clear dis-
tinction between the two localities, as though no one had
ever been born and raised in the same place.

"Born in Ulm."

"How do you spell it?"

"U-l-m. On the Donau."

"Donau?"

"The river."

"River?" he murmured troubled. "Rhine? Danube?—
blue Danube!" he cried. "Vienna!"

"Vienna?"

"Vienna, Austria!"

"You mean Wien?"

"Probably." We nodded at each other like two inventors
who have hit on the solution.

He sat up very straight, aimed his pencil at me and said,
"Wait a minute, there was another guy came from Ulm,
who the hell . . . Einstein! But naturally—Einstein!" His
enthusiasm quickly subsided as he saw that the name meant

nothing to me. "Yeah, but that's a great gimmick—Hildegard and Einstein both came from the romantic little town
on the banks of the blue Danube . . ." He sagged again.
"No, that won't work." He picked up a match and struck it
on the sole of his shoe; it broke in half. "You have any
family in Austria?"

"No."

Again his face took on that "never count your chickens
before they're hatched" expression. "But we could say that
your folks came from Austria?"

"Why?"

He buried his face in his hands and pressed his cheeks
together so that he looked as if he'd been caught in the
door of an elevator. "We can't use Germany," he squeezed
out.

"But I am a German." He groaned tragically and I had
to restrain myself from stroking his head. "Selznick knows
I'm German."

"Just your folks, if we could just have your folks come
from Austria," he pleaded.

I became agitated and my English forsook me: "I am
German and living in Berlin!" I managed finally, much
louder than intended.

He got up and closed the window, came back to his seat.

"Why not Austria?" he asked warmly.

"Because it's not true." He smiled. "And Austria had
Nazis too and Hitler was an Austrian."

"I believe you, sweetheart, but nobody knows that here."
He took another match and scraped it across the underside
of his desk; it flared and he gazed at it in astonishment,
blew it out and continued, "But maybe you were a victim
of the Nazis, or your parents—weren't they tortured or
something, put in a camp, at least?"

"I was in a camp."

"Tell me all about it." He slid forward to the edge of his
seat.

"A Russian camp."

His mouth puckered as though he'd swallowed a dose of
castor oil. He stood up heavily, looking at his big practical
wrist watch. "I'll take you down to make-up, you gotta do
some photos," he said.

He walked along silently beside me, only once did he
shake his head and whisper a preoccupied "Hildy, Hildy."

The midday sun was chalk-white, filtered, shadowless,

like the light in hospital corridors, the air heavy and damp. Weather for dozing, for licking ice cream, for staring into the water but not going in; obtrusive weather, forcing one to talk about it, mention it in postcards.

The hairdresser laid her cigarette on the edge of the wash-basin, said, "Hi, how ya like Hollywood?" and stuck my head under the tap before I could reply. She washed, combed, and curled and then led me into another room where a man with a beard said, "Hi, how ya like Hollywood?" pushed me into a barber's chair, tilted it backwards and started rubbing my face. When he had finished he passed me a mirror. I was confronted with a stranger: nose long and noble, shaded with brown, upper lip heart-shaped, cheeks feverish red, brows pencil-thin. He regarded me thoughtfully and then nodded as though he'd done everything humanly possible. The hair lady was waiting in the photo studio and lacquered my new locks, which stuck out from my head like loops. Another woman picked at my clothes, brushed my collar and back, went over every inch of my person as though looking for lice. The make-up man dabbed my chin and my forehead once more and then the trio stepped back and surveyed its various duty areas: the hairdresser my hair, the make-up man my face, the wardrobe woman my dress and shoes. I stood there feeling divided up and allocated and obliged to say something rewarding them for their pains. I couldn't think of anything. Then I remembered a studio joke: before the lights went on in the studio, or whenever a take had been underexposed, the Berlin technicians had called out. "Negerkampf in Tunnel." "Nigger fight in the tunnel," I translated. Three pairs of eyes stared at me glassily, disappeared abruptly. The photographer arrived and said, "Smile, open your mouth, teeth, more teeth." The studio was full of spotlights, big ones, small ones, clean new ones. I thought of the ones we had at home, tied together with string and bits of wire, of how the electricians had carried them like raw eggs; I longed for Jugert and Söhnker, for Minna, who had made me up and done my hair, sewn on buttons and complained of hunger, for the production manager who had encountered all ill tidings with "It's all a matter of nerves," longed for the chuckles, tension, and familiarity of a film family.

Miss Patterson picked me up and we drove to Sunset Boulevard. Right next to a funeral parlor offering a dignified and unforgettable funeral for sixty dollars was the Arthur Lacey agency. Mr. Lacey was lying on a couchlike chair behind a bare desk the size of a ping-pong table, telephoning. He beamed, waved, pointed to the receiver, ended the conversation with "Great" and jumped up: that is to say he sank behind the desk—at first I thought he'd fallen into a hole, or was kneeling, but then he trotted around the corner of the desk, small and round with outstretched arms. "She's the new Garbo," he chortled, "she'll be the greatest, the greatest of all, she'll make the greatest career Hollywood's ever seen." He blinked at Miss Patterson but she was lighting a cigarette dispassionately. "I'll take any bets she'll be the greatest," he continued, pulling out a handkerchief and blowing into it noisily. Lying on his chair again he said, "I spoke to Dave—Dave Selznick—and he's having your last film sent over from Germany. We'll make a big show in the Academy, invite everybody, all Hollywood'll be there an' you can explain the story before we run it."

"My English isn't good enough."

"Relax! No problem, you'll learn easy enough. We don't need Wilder—he explained that other movie you did, what was it called? Somethin' about murderers and us, and ruins——"

"*Murderers Among Us?*" I don't know that the film had been shown in Hollywood. I fidgeted around on my chair —"Don't fidget," Else Bongers would have said, "you're so intense you'll explode some day."

"The film was here?" I asked.

"Sure, in the Academy, members only. It went over great, everyone laughed like hell 'cause Wilder's comments were so funny."

I had seen Billy Wilder in Berlin. He had shown his *Lost Weekend* and invited questions afterwards. It had been something new for us, discussions at the end of a film; we had sat there uncomfortably not knowing what to ask, struck dumb in the presence of a successful Hollywood director. After what seemed an age someone plucked up courage and asked, "Please, Mr. Wilder, how much did the sets cost?" "The set was the most expensive in the world— New York. Any more questions?" We had stood up meekly and crept out.

The telephone buzzed discreetly. "Who?" Arthur Lacey yelled, "O.k., put her through . . . hi honey, how're things?

Great . . . great, they looked at your test last night, great talent, they said, just right for the part, couldn't do better—sad thing is they've already cast it with one of their contract artists . . . yeah, that's what I told 'em, you're gonna regret it, I said. . . . I'm working on Paramount right now, big part . . . relax . . . relax . . . relax I tell ya! No, don't call us, we'll get on to you as soon as we have somethin' . . . everything's gonna be fine—be happy!"

He slid down from his chair again, ran around the desk and said, "Come by whenever you want, call me day or night, you're gonna be the greatest in all Hollywood!"

In the evening we went for a walk, Kurt Hirsch, the dog, and I. A car drew up beside us and two policemen jumped out. "He's bothering you?" they asked, glaring across at Hirsch. "What're you doing here? Where you going? Why? How long?"

"We're walking the dog."

Irritated, they went back to their car and crawled along behind us, waited until we'd gone into the house. In Hollywood, Beverly Hills, Bel Air, and Westwood, suburbs in which nearly all the inhabitants were connected in one way or another with the film industry, you didn't walk. You drove, parked, and strode resolutely into your residence. Dallying pedestrians were suspect, were immediately held to be autograph hunters, burglars, or sex maniacs.

A mewing cat was sitting in front of our door; after drinking a little milk she decided she'd stay. Three weeks later she bore six healthy kittens and Sadie showed us the door. "I've got the address of a couple of emigrants," said Kurt Hirsch. "perhaps one of them will know of a house."

One of them indeed gave us the address of a German director who was looking for a tenant for his house in Benedict Canyon. The house, glued to the side of a cliff in an overgrown, wild garden, was large and inexpensive. The rattlesnakes caught our attention only after we had moved in. They peeped out of cracks in the cliff wall beside the kitchen, took their sunbaths on the porch and windowsills, drank the cat's milk with relish, and accepted me after a short trial period as a tolerable breadwinner. The fact that I had to drive them from my bed each evening, that one of them, apparently misinformed, raised its head and rattled at me as I was emptying the garbage cans one day, causing

me to freeze and wet my underwear in anticipation of the
lethal attack, that only because it was shedding its skin and
therefore handicapped did I avoid becoming a customer of
the dignified funeral parlor, that their children lived in our
mailbox turning each collection in a hair-raising adventure
—all this I could have stood; but that our cats (there were
now fourteen) had developed an interest in crocodile-sized
lizards, bringing them proudly into the house and stuffing
them under chairs and sofas, overtaxed even my strong af-
fection for animals. A Japanese gardener, recommended to
us as fearless and engaged at great expense, grew visibly
whiter during the course of his first day in our service and
didn't return for a second. Our idyllic subtropical country
life was rounded off by a wild mountain lion who sprang
onto the flat roof in the middle of the night, progressed to
the communal saucers of milk and then scratched at the
door like a dog one had put out and forgotten about. The
police had offered a reward of fifty dollars for the carcass
and so I spent several hours each night trembling as Kurt
Hirsch went from window to window brandishing his service revolver. The lion had apparently expected this lack of
charity and, after incurring our neighbors' displeasure with
the continual sirens, barking, and caterwauling, we finally
abandoned hope of the fifty dollars. The garage, shunned
by the snakes, was full of black widow spiders. My short-
sightedness probably spared me many a shock, but it was
sad to note that our small circle of new friends gradually
stopped visiting us.

Across the street lived a couple called Lustig. They invited us to visit and Frau Lustig, appalled at my scrawniness,
plied me with enormous helpings of home-made apple stru-
del. Lustig means jolly in German and the name didn't fit
Herr Lustig at all; after greeting us shyly and absently he sat
down in the dusky corner of the living room and gazed at
me with an expression of extreme anguish. As we were
leaving he gave me two books: Proust's *A la Recherche du
Temps Perdu* and Thomas Mann's *Faustus*. "You should
read these books, my child," he said and closed the door of
his library. It was the beginning of the great supplementary
course which was now to be granted me and for which I
hardly showed the appropriate gratitude, since I realized its
importance only many years later at a time when I had lost
contact with my tutors. I did meet Herr Lustig again, twenty years later on the Maximilianstrasse in Munich. His lean

face had remained unchanged. "My God, when I think how long ago that was when you visited us, soon after the war," he said. "You were the first to come from Germany and you were so different from the picture we had built up for ourselves of the young Germans, the generation that had only known Hitler. And you spoke a Berlinese—it was like a fresh breeze, it brought everything back again, everything that was good about Berlin. Perhaps we can see each other? I live here, right around the corner." In the twenties he had been a theater critic for the paper *Tempo* and like so many others he had signed a lifesaving contract as a scriptwriter with an American film company and like so many others he now drove to the studio in the mornings, sat down in his office, and wrote in a new, hard-won language. Few were as successful as he, for his manuscripts were often filmed. Most of his compatriots went unnoticed in the mill of the huge industry and, thanks to the clock which punched their cards at the studio entrance and a reliable administration machine, they received their weekly checks year in and year out without ever even seeing a producer. Although their ideas were not used and their talents wasted, they adhered to a loyal, almost humble gratitude to their mentors, for without their contracts and the assurance that they would not prove a financial burden to the country, their treasured United States visas would never have been granted. They accepted the fact that their toilets were equipped with forty-watt bulbs to discourage them from reading newspapers or other literature not connected with the film industry just as, during the war, they had accepted the fact that they were not allowed to own radios or leave the house after dark. They led a European life without whiskey and constant music, without card and parlor games, swimming pools, and crowded parties. They all said, "America was good to me," as though speaking of a cherished aunt, of a personified, all-embracing brotherly love, and appeared to forget that without the company pledge their stay would have been a short one.

The Academy Award winner Billy Wilder lived far from humility, melancholy, and memories. He had arrived, and owed his first successes to Hollywood. He was the embodiment of all that I held to be desirable at that time: a conqueror in the New World. As we stood in front of his house that first evening, I was as agitated as if I were about to face a test. We were invited for drinks and dinner and I had spent the whole day doing my hair and hands, trying to decide what to wear. The tiny, delicate tinkle of the doorbell was a quite inappropriate prelude to the high-tension, power-packed man who yanked the door open. The round close-cropped head, the taut blank face and eyes that missed little and proscribed much, the cynical, ready-for-sarcasm mouth, the nasal voice and staccato dialogue presented a picture of an alert sovereign, a victor mistrustful of the vanquished. He drained me and spurred me on, made me uncertain and bombastic at the same time.

His house was beautiful in an unfussy way, with bookshelves to the ceiling, African wood carvings, Toulouse-Lautrecs, and a built-in, well-stocked bar. Standing behind it was a dark-haired apparition named Audrey who looked like the immaculate beauties in the film magazines. She was as self-assured as only a woman conscious of her youth and beauty can be. "Speak German!" Billy Wilder commanded and looked at her like a lion-tamer certain of success. She thrust out her chin, puckered up her lips, planted her clenched fists on her hips and assumed the stance of a defiant, snorting Mussolini. She then made gargling guttural noises which sounded like the hoarse barking of the oddly dressed officers in the anti-German films—"Verbooden" and "Schtillgestanden" and "Sieg Heil" were recognizable. I tried very hard to smile dutifully, felt guilty and responsible, ashamed, for myself, for her, for all who found it funny. Her face relaxed and she grinned like a cute tomboy, without malice.

The terrace door opened silently and a little man came in. His melancholy eyes, long nose, and big ears gave him the appearance of a woebegone, maltreated cartoon animal; even his positive-sounding "Hi" did nothing to change his gloom-filled countenance. I immediately had a bad conscience. He shook my hand and gazed at me with commiseration, it was as though we'd gone through hell somewhere together but he couldn't remember where. "That's Max," said Billy Wilder and busied himself with an awe-inspiring record player which could turn the records over automatically and crush them into the bargain. Max lived over Wilder's garage. He'd spent the war in Swiss and French internment camps and the years had formed him into a permanent refugee, one could never imagine him owning an apartment, let alone feeling at home. At a time when other emigrants were already putting out feelers toward Europe and some even timidly played with thoughts of happy homecomings, Max started the five-year waiting period necessary for trading in a stateless passport for an American one. Max became a friend who had an answer to anything in general and a piece of advice for everything in particular and whose pessimism was so annihilating that one could only pray for a happy release. He registered tidings of greatest joy with pursed, pain-filled lips like someone who already glimpses the beginning of the end and whose counsel can at best delay the inevitable gruesome tragedy. His spontaneity and the endless stream of muttered puns became outriders of the unavoidable. One worried about Max while being worried about by him; he prompted a never-ending series of doubts.

"Marlene's coming tomorrow," said Max, assuming correctly that the Christian name sufficed; "she'd like to meet you."

A white iridescent triangle shimmered from the darkest corner of the Beachcomber, the murkiest and most expensive restaurant in Hollywood. "Hello," the triangle breathed over the wailing Hawaiian guitars, and smiled an amused smile. The face seemed independent of the body, seemed to float, to preside over the tables, excluded all else reduced the other diners to entourage, court society. It was a spacious face, designed for display, casually shown: "Of course you may look at me, if it pleases you," it seemed to say. A few years later, over his fourth Calvados, Erich Maria Remarque related, "I couldn't forget the face. I went walking, for days and nights on end. Once I saw sprats lying in the window of a Jewish delicatessen, the first I'd seen in New York; saliva started to flow and I was just about to enter the shop when the face suddenly appeared above the sprats; it smiled and I forgot to go in. Before, in Hollywood, Garbo had invited me to her house. As I left she stood at the gate waving to me, a supernatural being. When I got home Marlene was cooking hamburgers, and her face, leaning over the steaming frying pan, just edged the supernatural being at the gate aside."

She ordered rum drinks and sweet-and-sour spareribs and dismissed the obsequious head waiter without so much as a glance. Rice was served and chopsticks placed beside the bowls. In my excitement I relapsed into Berlinese and blurted: "I'll be a bag of bones in no time if I have to eat with those." She leaned forward over the table as though she hadn't understood, then started to laugh, a long soft laugh that grew bigger, fought for breath, controlled itself, erupted again. She took a cigarette; Max struck a light but she'd snapped her Dunhill shut again before his hand was halfway across the table. Over the dying flame she said, "She's the way I was, when I was young." She said it as though I'd long since departed, a statement, inviting no argument—the Prussian officer's daughter Magdalena von Losch had passed judgment, indisputable, irrevocable. The comparison took my breath away. "Tell me about Berlin," she went on. She spoke very softly, the breath scarcely brushing the vocal cords, the warm tone seeming to stem from under the breastbone. She was a good listener; she gave me the feeling that everything I cared to say was of the greatest importance to her. "When were you born?" she asked and lit another cigarette.

"In December."

"When in December?" laughing, as though she knew the answer already.

"On the twenty-eighth."

She turned to Max triumphantly. "Marlene was born on the twenty-seventh," he said and waggled his head like a metronome.

"I must give Carroll her dates," she said, again in that tone which denied my presence, surgeon lecturing assistant at bedside of tricky case. I didn't dare ask who Carroll was.

"Carroll is Marlene's astrologer," said Max, making small effort to hide his distaste.

"The oceans move in accordance with the rhythm of the moon, man's destiny is clearly influenced by the position of the planets," she said languidly.

A man appeared at the table. Standing behind him was a full-breasted girl with a deep neckline and cheeks gleaming like a polished California apple. For a few seconds she managed to look over and past Marlene, then the blank, arrogant pose of self-assurance crumbled and gave way to bovine adoration. She would gladly have sacrificed vital inches of her bust measurements just to look once like that pale triangle. The man was talking at Marlene. He appeared confident and relaxed although Marlene betrayed no sign of having noticed him, a vulgar page prattling into the regally deaf ear. The smallest of nods sent him on his way.

"Carroll advised me to go to war," she continued, making me wonder if I had dreamed the interruption. " 'What would I do at the front?' I asked him." The 'I' she puffed out like a soap bubble, it drifted over the table. " 'Sing for the soldiers!' he said." She shrugged a slender shoulder. "At first I laughed at him . . ." Again the whimsical smile, liking herself, forgiving herself her little faults; then she opened her eyes very wide, feigning mock speechlessness: "At that time, after Sternberg's last film, everyone was saying I was box-office poison. . . ."

Max grinned a he-who-laughs-last grin and looked about him as though surveying the fallen army of skeptics, then let his eyes rest on the tiny ribbon sewn to the breast of her dark dress.

"May I ask what that ribbon means?" I asked.

"The Légion d'honneur," said Max promptly.

She drew three of the many small bowls of sauces toward her and began to mix the contents. This was the signal for the head-waiter to approach again, clapping his hands and driving before him two boys bearing trays of bottles and dishes. She made her choice swiftly and certainly; she stirred and added drops and made known with a weak wave of her finger that the three should retire. She put sauce on our plates, selected a sparerib and dipped it in. None of us had spoken. Her activity had been of an either-or consistency, like a chef at work or a child at play. Having dabbed her fingers on a napkin, she lit a cigarette. I felt hot from the rum, the sauces, everything. Marlene sat cool; there was no hint of even the mildest flush. Gradually but insistently my thoughts were drawn to a toilet; here too she seemed far from all human needs.

"I'd love to drink Badoit now," she said. "Badoit is the best thing about France. Gabin wanted to bring crates of it to Hollywood—they are not acquainted with mineral water here," she added disparagingly. She took her chopsticks and laid them down beside a bamboo holder on which was written "Miss Dietrich," sucked once again on a straw sticking out of a hollowed cocoanut, and got up. She left the table without anyone having mentioned the bill and without the slightest warning; lika conjurer she swept her cigarettes, lighter, compact, with one movement into her bag and left. Eyes followed her, devoured her, bored into her, envied, wanted to take possession, break through the majestic aura, the uninterest in surroundings and interest

caused. She hovered along on legs that appeared too long
to fulfill any function other than decoration, straightening
the knees at every step, striding widely; she walked the way
she ate, or stirred sauces: with absolute concentration. Like
a haggard mastiff I walloped along behind her, my feet
plonking stubbornly onto places quite opposed to my will,
my hands flapping around my knees. The hatcheck girl,
white and gasping for breath, pushed a piece of paper over
the counter. Marlene took a pencil and wrote an almost
legible "Marlene" and orderly "D," followed by a long
curved flourish which ran off the edge of the page. Without
turning round she said into the night, "Have you any coffee
in the house?"

"Yes," said Max.

"It hasn't been cleaned," he mumbled as he opened the
door to his garage. She went through the living room, up
three steps and disappeared through a door in the wallpaper. We heard the rattle of pots and water running. Max
stood forlornly on the straw matting and said dimly, "She
never sleeps; always stays with Billy when she's in Hollywood. In the morning, before anyone else even dreams of
opening his eyes, she's already read the papers and made
soup, aired the rooms, cleaned the ashtrays, and told the
maid which soap she should use for the doors and which for
the bathtub—and on top of it she smokes like an industrial
development area and has fittings and appointments the
whole day long." He shrugged his shoulders as though confronted daily with a fresh and insoluble mystery, then took
off his gold wrist watch, wound it up, gazed at the dial and
said reproachfully. "A present from Marlene." She came in
with pot and cups, scuffed off her shoes and settled onto a
shaky couch. "I'll bake a cake tomorrow," she said. As I
stifled a yawn at four in the morning she exclaimed aghast,
"One cannot be tired when still so young." At five we stood
under the harsh light of a streetlamp breathing the stale
shallow air and she looked as if she'd just been for a brisk
refreshing walk around a Brandenburg lake. At eight o'clock
a delivery service brought me a hamper full of mushrooms,
a bottle of vitamin tablets, and a recipe for goulash; shortly
afterwards Max called: "Marlene wants to see a movie this
evening, she'll pick you up."

In the afternoon I called Marlene to thank her. I heard a
"Hello," but breathed so softly that I feared she must be ill;
a toneless "Yes" assured me she was still on the line and a

click informed me she had hung up. I stared at the receiver and tried to remember what I had done wrong. In the evening she came with fresh supplies of tablets which she spread out over the table with the professionalism of a qualified druggist, two bags of sweets and a headscarf, which she tied around her head in front of the cinema. All sign of a the woman whose silence could terrorize was banished. A few sailors were lying around the otherwise empty balcony. The main film, in startling Technicolor and starring one of Hollywood s first bosom phenomenons, had already started. The tremendous mammae filled the screen, burst the frame, strained at the blouse, heaved sideways and forwards, and, in a telling scene accompanied by celestial choirs, settled around the shoulders of a youth who had been wounded in the struggle for freedom. "The one in the middle is the head!" bellowed a sailor right behind us. Marlene went into her long low laugh; it folded her over, drew her hair down over her knees, made a square of the triangle, gradually subsided.

"If we were in New York we could go and eat pastrami sandwiches and sour pickles," she said as the pink houselights went on, disclosing the alarming Chinese interior decoration. In the theater courtyard groups of silent people stood staring devoutly at the ground. They were examining slabs of concrete with the imprints of stars' hands and feet. The bearing and contemplative attitude of the multitude suggested a crowded cemetery being visited by all the bereaved at the same time. "And we could walk too, in New York," Marlene said and looked glumly down the fast-emptying boulevard. Although the very thought of New York filled me with dread, I felt obliged to share her longing, ignorant as I was at that time that comparison and dreams of faraway places formed an integral part of an emigrant's life. They loved New York in Paris, sang London's praises in Rome, roamed Switzerland in search of the California climate, had visions of snow-capped Alps while lying on Pacific beaches; rummaging through the boutiques of Milan, they sighed for New York's department stores and lauded the virtues of American maple syrup over palatschinken in Vienna. They had become mid-Atlantic citizens who cited Molnar s "It's a little crummy wherever you are," and whose endless possibilities for comparison eclipsed the most fleeting sense of belonging. The exception, the Garden of Eden from which one had been evicted, the nonpareil that one had forfeited, was and remained Berlin, the Berlin of the twenties, the wonders of which I was now acquainted with, got to know without having seen it, and which lay like an astral body over the contemporary ruins.

"Look after the child," Marlene said to Max as we stood in Los Angeles' main railway station the next evening. Doors were slammed, porters drew back, whistles sounded—only Marlene appeared not to notice the apparent preparations for departure. I craned my neck and looked for the stationmaster. "They don't have the fellow with the flag here," said Max with the air of a man who had missed many a train because of this outlandish custom. Before the sparkling silver carriages suddenly swept silently from the platform she came to the window, looked first at Max then at me, then turned without a smile or a wave and entered her compartment. "Four days on a train," sighed Max, rolling his eyes, "And all because Carroll Righter said she shouldn't fly this week."

Mr. Fry was always tanned and freshly shaved and his mode of dress was ground for assuming that most of his waking hours were spent on the tennis court. He owned a Spanish-style house with a swimming pool, a Cadillac, and a farm near Palm Springs, and was somehow connected with the Lacey agency. One Sunday he invited Kurt Hirsch and me for brunch, drinks, and barbecue—an American invention where the master of the house makes a fire on the terrace, disappears amid clouds of smoke, and emerges with steaks either still totally raw or burnt to a cinder. When we arrived at noon, his enthusiastic blue eyeballs were clashing violently with the red clouds surrounding them and the general unrest in his house made me feel that a Hollywood weekend must be far more enervating than all the Christian workdays put together. After a "Hi" and a "Great" he handed us two vase-sized glasses of milk and my first gulp—a good one, in anticipation of milk—was followed by a mighty upheaval; stars burst like fireworks and a chicken leg seemed trapped in my windpipe. Sight and sound slowly returned and I heard hearty laughter and a shout of "That'll put lead in your pencil!" Then he went and refilled our glasses from five different bottles of rum. Around the pool oiled profiles lay tilted to the sun, others were half obscured behind copies of *The Hollywood Re-*

porter, a paper no bigger than a ship's journal which gave exhaustive information on every film planned or in the making in strange elliptical English and which everybody read and swore they didn't. Others were grouped around a swing with a sunroof and were listening avidly to the measured tones of an unsightly obese gentleman in a polo shirt and sailor cap. They all swung around eagerly upon hearing our footsteps, looked at us with undisguised disappointment and went back to their original positions. Only the fat man had ignored our approach. He was a producer.

After my second glass I began to recognize the charm of my surroundings, changed into my bathing suit and slipped into the water. I set off with the sedate breaststroke I had learned in the municipal baths in Schöneberg but was soon overtaken and swamped by a crawling champion. Kurt Hirsch sat on an outspread bath towel watching two perspiring gentlemen playing badminton, grated his teeth and muttered: "Goyim naches."

Further drinks in smaller vases followed and fresh guests streamed in as others left. There was a continuous coming and going with enraptured greetings and heartfelt adieus, "Sooo thrilled to meet you" introductions camouflaging glassy eyes already forgetting the new face, the unknown name before it even registered. The departing friends were one and all late already for urgent appointments with invariably prominent hosts whose names were trumpeted across the patio. They were doing the rounds of the Sunday parties as they did the rounds of the agencies and producers' offices, in search of the wink, the lucky deal, the film or contract that would catapult them to the top. They all peered over the shoulders of the people they were talking to for fear of missing someone more important, of gossiping through their moment of fate. Heads of studios were accorded reverence in that they were mentioned only after careful looks around and assessment of earshot. A nonstop record player provided gaiety in keeping with the constant blue of the sky. At six it was turned off in favor of the radio. Everyone hurried into the living room and huddled in a semicircle to listen to the staccato outpourings of a New York show-business reporter named Walter Winchell; he spoke as though the radio station were surrounded by tanks, as though this were the last chance to gabble messages, mobilize the army, raise the alarm. I did indeed become alarmed as I hardly understood a word but was still none the wiser after careful translation since the informatin was concerned only with divorce rumors, engagement announcements, and who'd-been-seen-with-whom-in-which-night-club gossip. The torrent at an end, the semicircle broke up and ran to the bar. Some left as new waves poured in, the ladies now appearing in mink capes and cocktail dresses followed by absently peering pipe chewers announced as promising authors, or by pert pretty youths who gleefully challenged the ladies' prerogative as centers of attraction. A Hungarian lady, cooingly greeted by everyone as Zsa Zsa, wafted from kiss to kiss and darling to darling in a haze of chiffon and a blaze of jewelry and just in time stopped herself from embracing the butler. Catching sight of me she squealed: "Oh what a pretty dress—and so cheap!" and proceeded to finger the material like the woman at the clothes stand on the market behind Wilmersdorf railway station. Already heady from so much alcohol, I found myself wishing to be just once as bubbling, prattling, and self-confident as she.

After dinner the gentlemen left the room and didn't return. The ladies jiggled their girdles, powdered their noses, painted new lines around their lips, and settled down to discuss the retired escorts. "George loves me dearly," one of them purred, "he'd better—a fourth divorce would ruin him." They giggled and clucked and I thought of the old regulars who had brought the world back into sync with a "Shit," whose obscenity had been a lifesaver; I thought warmly of their simplicity and straightness, tried to remember a world without barbs, beauty I couldn't describe couldn't compare, prayed for independence and the joy of being alone, the joy that had driven me onto the Griebnitz lake at night.

"Where you from?" a woman with ringlets and nails like rapiers asked me.

"Germany," I said in a small voice.

"Which studio you with?"

"Selznick."

"Selznick?" she echoed incredulously. "He's getting divorced, he'll be taken for half of everything he's got, so how's he gonna make movies then, huh?" She leaned forward and looked at me pityingly: "Selznick—ha!" she rasped and slammed the gates of hell behind him; "I wouldn't let him wash my panties!"

One of the pipe smokers staggered through the door,

stopped unsteadily, and contentedly surveyed the cackling ladies like a cock squatting on the farmyard dungheap. "Jimmy's so happy since we had our baby," a peach-skinned damsel chirruped; "I had the doctor sew up my vagina right away and now he says I'm like a virgin, don t you, darling?" He poked his pipe with one finger and turned his attention to a wooden box which the butler had been banging and turning this way and that for some time; their combined efforts were rewarded after a further ten minutes and a milky picture of two wrestlers appeared. "There's Gorgeous George!" they chortled, pointing at one of the wheezing giants. "Isn't he cute?" As the doorbell rang and new recruits appeared, the ladies lost interest in Gorgeous George and each other, fixed their sights on the new-comers, and broke apart.

Among the late arrivals was a tall man with gray hair who was quickly boxed in; he smiled to all sides, thereby stretching his scarred skin maliciously over an otherwise curiously soft face. His clothes and paleness contrasted sharply with the carnival costumes and spa complexions of the other guests. "Hello Aries," he said, and "Hello Moonchild—how's Miss Aquarius this evening?"

"Carroll, I'm doing a test tomorrow, will I get the part?"

"When can I have another baby, Carroll?"

"I gotta talk to you about my stock."

He stood there like a lighthouse amid flailing combat units, raised one hand benevolently, smoothed the waves and said, "Now now children, I am not a clairvoyant." He made for the bookshelves I had been examining, which held film manuscripts bound in leather, *Life* and *Look* magazines, and a beautiful set of uncut Dickens volumes and said, "May I ask your name, address, and birthdate?" He pulled a notebook from his pocket and looked at me paternally. A maid in cap and apron brought him a cup of coffee. "Have a whiskey!" commanded a drunk, holding a glass under his nose. "No, thank you," the man they called Carroll said amicably and firmly, "I don t drink." The drunk glared at him punishingly with pursed lips, then, realizing that this was not having the desired effect, sagged back against the bookshelves crowing, "A tee-totaler—I'll be damned!" and slopped his whiskey over the carpet as he

"Miss Dietrich was going to speak to you about me," I doubled up with laughter.

said, hoping to gain importance and thinking simultaneously of my previous experiences with astrologers.

"Miss Dietrich?"

"Yes."

"Oh."

"She said she was a client of yours."

"Yes, well, I'm not at liberty to name or discuss my clients, do you understand?" I didn't but nodded affirmatively. "I'll work on your chart."

"I don't have enough money."

He spoke rapidly and softly and I had to lean forward to hear him. His slanted eyes, like the eyes of some Russians I had seen, didn't fit his head or his body, just as the scarred skin didn't fit; a high, smooth forehead, oversized flat ears, sloping chin, soft mouth. A controlled face, a sensitive one.

"I don't have enough money," I repeated.

The face tightened, became cool and dignified: "It is an honor to be of service."

I forgot my doubts and blurted, "What about Berlin? My mother's there and they've got an airlift and it's cut off——"

"We'll talk in three days' time, I'll call you," he said, waved at the pandemonium and disappeared.

Three Mexicans were sitting at the side of the pool plucking guitars; a blond Goliath seized the one in the center by the scruff of his neck, held him up like a rabbit and bellowed, "This here's the best goddamn guitar player in the whole of Mexico!" dropped him and said, "Play!" The Mexican grinned shyly and took his position, but before he could begin his admirer cupped his hands to his mouth and roared, "Quiet, for Christ's sake! I want everybody to listen now, and anyone who don't think he's the best goddamn guitar player in Mexico I'll bust his teeth in."

I crept off to find my bathing suit and, crossing the hall, bumped into the small friendly gentleman who had praised my English and the color of my eyes only two hours ago and who now leered at me viciously and snarled, "You ain't tryin' to tell me you just learned English now, are you? Liars, all women are liars." He stuck a finger into my shoulder and tried to bore a hole. A plump woman in a too-tight satin dress and dainty high-heeled pumps hobbled up to him and whined, "Henry, please, Henry."

"Shut your trap," said Henry.

Her mouth opened, letting out a hiss, and the voice, now

here until you have returned to Europe, worked there and come back again. Then you will find the prospects here better at first, and later excellent. Your basic chart reveals great tensions but also great success. You will always have to fight and you will always be impatient. This you should attempt to control since only later will you be able to realize the ambitions you are now trying to force. You will always have to deal with intrigues and malicious gossip and your lack of feeling for money will make it easy for certain people to exploit you. What happened in June 1945? My calculations indicate an extremely dangerous situation."

"I was in a Russian prison camp."

He nodded. "It's hard to believe that you lived through it. May I use your chart for research and for my pupils?—without revealing your identity, of course."

"Yes, of course," I said, feeling flattered.

"I thank you," he said formally. "Should you ever need my help, this is my telephone number, please don't hesitate to call me at any time of the day or night."

He left, and since much that he had said had been negative, I didn't believe him.

SIXTEEN

Late summer, 1949

If only it wasn't so unbearably hot, and so early, too—I haven't been up this early for ages, except for tests, must have tested for just about every studio, Warner's, Paramount, MGM, then always Lacey's phone call: Great, they said, but they've cast a contract artist, scared to be the first to use a German in Hollywood—they'll regret it, don't worry. . . . Then that audience with Jack Warner: sits at the end of his throne room surrounded with Oscars and watches to see how you make out on the hundred-meter dash from the door to his desk. His personality doesn't quite match the size of the office; if you hadn't been unnerved by the five secretaries and his chair weren't lit like the high spot of a museum you'd never notice him. He's got a thing on war, no doubt about it, he showed me fifty or more photos of himself in silver frames in colonel's uniform, camouflage, Eisenhower jacket, steel helmet, peaked cap. He was delighted to find someone who hadn't seen his pictures: Here, that's me in Africa, '44—fearless stance, steely eyes scanning the Sahara—and here, that's me in Italy, beside a donkey, trusty steed. Then in a jeep, windshield turned down over the hood, boot planted on the seat, and then that overexposed shot of him sitting on a gasoline barrel, farm ruins in the background. He got all excited: Great fighters, our boys, he said. Makes pictures about the war now, stands in the glare of the special-effects fires, starts drooling when the mines go off and the extras yell Help. If the Nazis had been only half as dumb as they're played in the movies the thousand-year Reich wouldn't have lasted a week. . . . Still can't believe that Fox took me—my first American film with location in Berlin, in forty-eight hours I'll see Mother and Stepfather and Else Bongers, Carroll Righter was right after all, return to Europe, work there first, he said, and here I am on the plane with a contract in my bag. What if I've lost my talent, after two years of doing nothing? We were invited everywhere but never to work. The people who could have done something didn't and those who would have couldn't; every night parties and drinks; I hardly ever ate just forgot about it except cottage cheese and oranges; during that last test my stomach rumbled so much the sound engineer stopped the shooting and went looking for the dog. I forget to eat, don't cook when I'm alone. . . . They were right about Selznick; divorce, sold the studio. . . . As long as I was still at the airport I wasn't afraid, the Fox man was there and the photographers, the mix-up with my papers and vaccination stamps—God the cholera shot nearly killed me. . . . I've got stage fright too, the sweat'll soak my only suit if I'm not careful, be thankful not to have to look at that eternally blue sky for a while, and the palm trees, always the same, firs don't change either but at least they sometimes have snow on their heads, or rain, palms are crashing bores. You're an absolute good-for-nothing, Mother would say, lying around the beach the livelong day—as though everlasting leisure were a holiday. I'd rather run from UFA to the Schlosspark Theater, play morning noon and night and do radio shows on Sunday, than this sitting around, I'm as brown as you can get—I'd probably never be able to make a film again if it weren't for Dr. Jonas, falling asleep on the beach like a beginner, face covered with blisters the color of red peppers. Treatment, vitamin shots, lotions and bandages, and never a bill. They won't go back home any more, he and his wife; we've found a new home, they say—five years' study to become what he'd been in Germany for ages already, got angina pectoris doing it, too. Incredible that Americans don't recognize European doctors, they'd have sent Freud, Jung, Pasteur, and Koch back to school. . . . I'm going to miss the emigrants, I'm only three hours in the air and I miss them already, would never have thought it. . . . I start to shake when I think of Berlin—I'll have to watch that I don't use English words, I hate that, and jokes are out, too, never used to tell them but the Berliners in Hollywood love to hear Berlin jokes, I never realized how funny the Berliners are till I came here. . . . There'll be another Fox man in Chicago—and photographers, and I look like mustard. Marlene's always cool, I'll see her in New York. Must write to Bobby Koster and Peggy, thank them for the farewell dinner and the talisman. Changed his name from Hermann Kosterlitz to Henry Koster and everybody calls him Bobby;

his English still sounds like Berlinese even though he's married to an American—hard to believe that Peggy's nearly thirty. I wonder if it's easier for the ones who married Americans? The old films he always showed on weekends: Hildchen's got to find out what went on in the world. Garbo, Griffith, and the stories he told about Lubitsch with a lisp like Barlog's; they all used to go to the Romanische Café in Berlin, that must have been next to the Marmorhaus, there where the hole is. . . . Max got so excited you'd have thought he'd got the part, not me. Funny I'm so afraid of Billy Wilder, maybe because of what he said about his mother in front of everyone. He looked straight at me and said, My mother was murdered in Auschwitz. But he never stopped inviting us, even took me to American football, stupid game, couldn't get the hang of it at all, never could see the ball, once I pretended to get excited and yelled Hurray—at the wrong moment, as it turned out. Then driving back he said, Would you stay in America if you had a success? and I said Yes and I still don't know if I was lying or not. Make my home here? Never go back to Europe? What do I mean Europe, I don't know Europe. I know Berlin. . . . Montgomery Clift will be there already, My God, what an actor. The director's called Seaton and the producer Perlberg, better get that into my head, mustn't mix them up. . . . Robert Siodmak scares me too, eyes like an owl and his Saxon accent makes your teeth chatter. Sweet of him to tell me about his new film and the part I'd be terrific in and end up by saying, Too bad I've discovered a new American girl for it. . . . Lilli Palmer at the pool, toes in the water: You'll make good, I have a feeling for these things, it was hard for everybody at the beginning. And Harrison, her husband, every time he gets drunk he roars Bloody foreigners, the Englishman abroad. The English tried to blow up the Zoo bunker, Mother wrote, it didn't budge an inch and the Berliners stood behind the barrier laughing. . . . Christmas was a nightmare, rose-colored Christmas trees in Beverly Hills—who thought that one up? Christmas cards, everybody sends them, Christmas Eve's the big event for us at home, here it's Christmas Day. . . . Jesus, that strip joint the other day—where was it? Gardena City; grilled chicken and striptease—the dark one beat her breast like an orangutan and half the audience had hair curl. . . . do they take them out to go to bed? I'm thirsty but they won't serve drinks until we're out of the

rough patch. . . . That's where we must have driven, down
there, head still full of dreams then, big film star, take the
world by storm. You feel so important when you fly, so active, but you might just as well be sitting at home staring at
the rain. What on earth made me go to church at New
Year's? The priest screeched like a fishwife: Valley of Sin-
Repent—Reckoning, afterwards that Really-gave-it-to-'em-
that-time look. Strange, I always cry at organ music, can't
look at the crucifix either, Christ crucified, thorns, torture. . . . Americans get more foreign for me every day, perhaps it's just Hollywood—America's like smog, the longer
you stay the worse it gets—who said that? Can't remember.
But they don't revel in others' misfortune the way they do at
home, and they're not envious either, just foreign. . . . All
they talk about now is the Nuremberg trials; Mother hasn't
mentioned the subject once. That house Kurt Hirsch lived
in on Sophie-Charlottestrasse in Zehlendorf, the requisitioned one with the garden chairs and the piano—ten
notes, the white ones from middle C to E an octave higher
still worked—of course Mother had to be there the only
day the MPs called: Any Germans here?—us in the attic.
And now they shoot films about the airlift, bombers dropping raisins, Mother calls them. . . . Just why do I get so
angry when the emigrants talk about Roosevelt? "When he
died we embraced each other on the streets and cried." Or
the patriotic nonsense; that radio author recently who
smacked the steering wheel of his new Cadillac, jammed
the horn and said, As long as we build automobiles like this
we're the greatest. . . . Curt Goetz, sitting in Frascati's little
garden. He looked tired, lined. I was in your play *Hocus
Pocus* right after the war, I said. He just nodded absently,
as though it was none of his business any more. It's easier
for Axel, he's not a writer, no bother with language or producers' whims, cuts films for Warner's, drinks his Chilean
wine and plays Gustav Mahler—Listen to the second
movement, he yells and jumps around on the sofa; they're
all shit compared to Mahler. They stick together, the Hun-
garians, whenever one of them is successful twenty others
get employed. . . . God knoqs how they stomach those
rocking-chair heroes in their studio bungalows, the
Warners and Cohns and Zanucks—Zanuck: beaver's teeth
pronged into the cigar, gnaws on it like a dog on a bone,
tinny voice, lid scraping across a saucepan—Wanna see my
soundproof bedroom? Thank you no. Still, I prefer him to

the others—big deal, it's his film you're making . . . If I can get a card for the PX I'll go shopping for Mother—oh, Christ, now my jacket's soaked. . . .

Chicago's like an oven. God, I crawled to them, would have stood on my head if they'd asked me. They've changed you, child, Ludwig Marcuse says. He's right, I have changed. I've become everything I hate—well not quite, but almost. Marcuse can belly-laugh like Grandfather, flaps his arms like a sea lion, loves to talk, sets up a barrage like a Stalin organ, says Neien when he wants his Nein clearly understood, wide long-drawn-out Berlin Neien. I get hungry when I watch him eat, never seen such pleasure, looks at his full plate like a cat at a barrel of fish, big ears go red, body rocks to and fro, picks up his spoon and fork, looks over at his wife and winks, she smiles and he falls on the soup knödel meat cake pudding cheese. Can't imagine him sitting at a desk alone, always see him surrounded by a lot of people when I think of him, whole lots of people. Although you hardly get a word in edgewise he always gives you the feeling that he's listening, knows already, knows what you think and hope, wish for; makes you feel ridiculous with your film problems, money and passport worries. Sometimes he says what I should read, what not—I've never heard him speak a word of English, can't possibly do his university lectures in German. How do they all manage to live in the film resort without film salaries? That first time I was taken to Feuchtwanger, I didn't really know who he was, never read a single book—he doesn't look like a rebel, but then what rebel ever did, only the camp followers dress the part. Gentle, fastidious, in front of high bookshelves in an old-fashioned, un-Californian house. . . . It's no cooler up here either, I'm as sticky as a postage stamp. It's night already in Europe, be home day after tomorrow.

I saw them as I stepped down the stairs: Mother, Stepfather, half-brother. Just like Gatow almost two years ago, shy, startled, paler, no frost to color the cheeks this time, not quite so scrawny. Half-brother had grown, blond hair combed with water, slicked down to the side, elbows threadbare, arms too long for the rest. Mother's eyes light gray under light-gray sky and black hat, over a bunch of flowers, hair still tight from the hairdresser. Stepfather's clean pate, chin scratched from recent shave, collar, tie, heavy hands.

"Hug each other!" the photographers shouted. "Once more!" The director came up and said "Hello" quickly and with ill humor, then kissed a woman who had been on the plane and who turned out to be his wife.

"What did you learn in America?" an untidy woman reporter with bitten-down fingernails asked, propelling her pencil.

"Can you still speak German?" asked another.

"And how," I said in slang, trying to laugh away the hostility.

"I asked you what you learned in America."

"Well, English and how to open cans and the meaning of patience."

There were five or six of them; they regarded me coolly, sarcastically. "How long will the filming last?"

"A very long time, I hope."

"Why hope?"

"I'm so happy to be back in Berlin."

"Really," one of them sniffed and gave me a "Tell it to the marines" look.

"The way you carry it off," Mother said when they were gone. "Your father—" She hesitated, looked at Stepfather.

An American production assistant was waiting outside with a chauffeur-driven car. "Hi," he said, "have a good flight? Mr. Perlberg got held up, he'll call you this afternoon," he added and drove off in another car.

"I've been told to drive you to the apartment," the German chauffeur said.

"What apartment?"

"Out in Zehlendorf, requisitioned villa." We got in. "Well, I don't know about that," he said, glaring at Mother Stepfather Half-brother. "This here's a Yank production car."

"We'll take a train," Mother said nervously.

"We'll all take a train."

"Oh well, nobody need know, I suppose," the chauffeur said doubtfully, and off we went.

Stepfather started to cough, couldn't stop. "Perhaps I can get you a permit for Switzerland," I said, "it should be possible by now."

"No no, it's only a cold."

"I thought you'd be fatter." Mother said.

"I want to fly too," yelped Half-brother. "Mother thought you'd be coming to our place, she's got something to eat."

Dudenstrasse, Kolonnenstrasse, Hauptstrasse, on the right the church where I was confirmed—Perrwitz, the vicar was called—the church reminds me of the water tower out at Priesterweg, right behind the cemetery where Father and Grandmother are buried. The ruins look seedier, crustier. Streets swept, craters cleaned, stones sorted. Rags bottles and bones scrubbed and stacked. Laundered leftovers, polished waste land; bandaged, set to rights, spring-cleaned. More desolate than I remember, down in the mouth like a military cemetery with a fresh wreath placed by a leading statesman. Taps blown soft and flat on the bugle, bowed heads, then off to lunch in the escorted limousines. The wind blew mortar dust from the mountain of bricks, spun it across the pitted street.

The car stopped in front of a turn-of-the-century house. "Here's the apartment," the woman said without looking at us and opened a door: two rooms, large and dim, tables with crocheted doilies, walnut cupboard, double bed. "If you need anything, I live upstairs in the attic."

"She must be the owner," Stepfather said. Mother took her hat off and patted her waves. They were almost white. "Can't be easy, in your own house . . . they don't get any rent either." We stood around as though waiting for a request to be seated; no sound other than Stepfather's shrill shallow breathing. Across the road was a leveled ruin, blades of grass between the stones, a ruin that looked as though it had resigned itself to remaining one.

"Why don't you stay here tonight?" I asked as it grew dark.

"I wonder if it's allowed?" Mother looked around, probably thinking of MPs and our hide-out on Sophie-Charlotte-strasse. "Heinz has to go to school in the morning and Father to the doctor. I'll have to tend the shop alone." I went with them to the station. "If only you could stay in Berlin," Mother said.

The sky was turning gray as I fell asleep, between the firs, over the ruin and its merry sparrows.

A breathless production assistant came in the morning: "Here's your PX card and some army dollars. Mr. Perlberg was held up, he'll call you today."

"I'd like to move to a pension."

He stared at me. "Why? The crew and the electricians and the like, they're all in a pension, but not the actors," he said, indignant at my lack of dignity, showing me my place.

"I'd still prefer it."

"As you like," he said and cocked the corner of his mouth.

Every door in the requisitioned pension on the corner opposite Zehlendorf-West railway station stood wide open. Members of the crew in baseball caps sat on their beds playing cards, drinking beer, and listening to AFN. They looked up in astonishment, then at each other, then back to the game in hand. At midday a jeep took me to Dahlem. In front of the PX, American soldiers were standing, behind the fence a few children chanted, "Chewing gum, cigarettes, look—there's a Buick."

"How many cans of meat and fruit am I allowed?" I asked the German saleswoman. She leaned against the counter and said haughtily in English, "What do you want?"

Müller, my driver, beckoned to me: "Gotta get a move on, lookin' for locations and all," he said proudly. He drives too fast, the tires squeal, the windshield rattles, he sees the dachshund too late. Front wheel back wheel jolt over it. The man is standing holding the leash and the collar, raises his stick and shouts, "Damn Yanks, damn you Yanks, you've killed my little one!" He sits on the curbstone, holds the dog in his arms. "We might find a vet," I say. He doesn't notice that I speak German, only says, "Damn Yanks, you take away everything."

They couldn't hear for the noise of the old lathes, so I tapped him on the shoulder. "Hildekind," Stepfather cried and was Stepfather again in his brown smock with patches of glue and lacquer stains. We carried the cartons upstairs. A photographer stood at the door. "Can I take a few pictures?" he asked and snapped Mother's delight at the cans. Across the road, in the bar where I used to fetch Stepfather's beer, a telephone. I call Else Bongers. "Child," she says softly, "child, where are you living? I'll come tomorrow afternoon." Then Barlog: "Christ, it's you, now you're a Hollywood star. Furtwängler's first concert tonight in the Titania Palast—Beethoven. Bring along your Mum. I've got tickets."

The old barn with its too-high stage, Rheinstrasse, Steglitz, was still standing, along with the Ministry of Internal Revenue on the corner. "You missed a couple of smashing parts," Barlog hollered, skirting any danger of sentimentality, "you had to go off to America. . . ." His eyes rolled, as if to say: the moon, darkest Africa. "Hollywood, God, who needs it, missed all those lovely parts." Herta, Barlog, Mother, and I were sitting next to each other. American and English officers were all around us; some I knew—Peter van Eyck, George Salmony. "Where's Mr. Pommer?" I whispered into Barlog's ear. "Not a clue, London or something like that." Everything that takes place outside the Schlosspark Theater is "something like that." "You don't look so hot, much too thin and those painted nails . . ." He shakes his antennae. The lights dim. Furtwängler sways top-heavily onto the stage, stretches, bows. Da da da daaa. The old Philharmonic comes back to me, the sirens, tears stream down my face, don't know why. The longing again—for Berlin, too.

Perlberg and Mr. Seaton came the next afternoon, sat down on the old pension sofa and looked at their shoes. "We've rewritten the part, had to rewrite it. We're sorry about bringing you all the way to Berlin but we gotta recast, you're not right for the new version." Mr. Perlberg produced an air ticket. "We'd like you to stay a little longer, coupla days, for the press and so forth. We'll settle the financial side with your agent."

"There's a German lady to see you," says the German concierge. Else Bongers is standing in the doorway. Senses something, knows something, says nothing. We both say nothing. Talk about the weather, theater, say See you tomorrow or the day after. We stand waiting for the train. As it rattles into the station she says, "Stay here, child. Just stay here."

"I can't, not until I've got a passport."

To Mother I say, "They don't want me to wait around while they're shooting the scenes with the others. I'll be back in three weeks."

"Are you sure?"

"Yes."

Stepfather was sitting at his lathe. Two customers came in. "There's the daughter," they say in chorus, "we saw you at the Schlosspark Theater and in the films, you're doing another one, aren't you, we read all about it." They shook my hand and looked at me thankfully.

"I have to go now, Mother will explain." It was the last time I saw him; he died before I could return to Berlin again.

In Frankfurt a reporter was waiting. "I hear you've been replaced," he said cheerfully and wrote something down although I hadn't replied. "Well, is it true or not?" The newspapers reported: "The sophisticated former medical student XY was chosen in favor of the cobbler's daughter HK."

I had two years to wonder what had happened. Then I heard about the Demandowsky file. Marlene telephoned me in Hollywood after the New York première of the airlift film. "You didn't miss a thing," she said, "it's a bad film," and hung up.

"You can stay with us," Henry Koster said, "if Kurt's called up, of course you can. . . ." He peered through the magnifying glasses of the farsighted and was embarrassed. Helpfulness embarrassed him, his own especially. We were sitting under an etching of a piqued-looking Shakespeare in a dark brown frame, part of the furnishings of the Benedict Canyon snake pit. "What happens if they send her to a factory to make grenades?" barked Axel, the Mahler addict. "And why the hell did you have to stay a reserve officer?" he added, turning to Hirsch. "I'd rather start a war as an officer than peel potatoes all day," said Kurt. Axel glowered at the etching: "How big is Korea anyway?" Since nobody answered he said, "Shit," and sat down again. Max studied his thumbnail, conversed in monosyllables, relied on his face to express what he'd known all along. Only once he'd said, "You hear the joke about the speared Indian? 'Does it hurt much?' 'Only when I laugh,' " and, pointing to the cat draped around my shoulders: "Ever since Zille peed in the heater it stinks here." The doorbell rang and Robert Thören stood in the doorway fighting for breath. "Am I a mountaineer?" he gasped angrily, glaring at the steps, and slipped an empty cigarette holder—empty since his heart attack—behind the immaculate handkerchief in his breast pocket, took a second one from another pocket, went through the routine of lighting up and inhaling like an actor rehearsing without props, then, erect and constantly aware of being a handsome man, stepped into the living room. Robert Thören, an author much more at home telling stories than writing them, raised his eyebrows, surveyed

the congregation and said, "Korea!" Inherent in this
"Korea" was: "Tsores usually comes in threes," and/or:
"Are you telling me?" Walter Slezak happily stroked his
rounded middle, giggled, deigned to share the joke at last:
"I kicked out Oblo, my astrologer. I asked him to do Hildchen's horoscope. 'This is a banner year, a milestone,' the
baboon said." Then, turning to me: "Ah, our girl Himlet
. . ."——"Himlet?" Max echoed, rampant for a new pun.
"A mixture of inlet and Hamlet," said Walter contentedly
and waddled over to his fragile Dutch wife. Ursula, wife of
the Swiss actor Paul Hubschmid, stood up. "I'll make us a
few sandwiches," she said, knocking over her glass in her
boundless myopia, wiped a dry patch dry, left the wet
patch wet and went into the kitchen. I followed and
watched her thread her way through the thirteen cats, then
settled down to examine the bandaged and splinted right
hand I had rammed into a glass on the previous Sunday.
"Let's go up to Lake Tahoe for the weekend," Ursula said
as she picked through the near-vacant icebox.

"I don't think we have any money."

She held up a hand: "They have those cheap cabins and
we have to get out for a while. By then Paul's breaktaking
adventure story should be finished."

Paul entered, slammed down a glass, slapped the quivering table with the flat of his hand in complete and total
contrast to his otherwise placid and peace-loving disposi-
tion and snorted furiously, "How is a man supposed to
work without Bircher Müsli?" In the ensuing pause, during
which Ursula continued to smear butter onto crumbling
crackers with utmost concentration, Sasha, a Russian ballet
dancer who had been stranded in Hollywood with the
Monte Carlo company all too long ago, sprang through the
door, saw to his horror that the leap must end in disaster
and tried to curtail it, thereby landing on three cats instead
of two. "Let's have a banquet," he said from the floor, "I
had a day's shooting at MGM today. I'll cook you sauces,
sauces as they make them only in the Camargue."

"We don't need sauces with crackers," said Ursula severely and stepped over him.

"What happened to Minna?" Max asked, pointing at one
of my cats whose fur looked strangely chewed.

"She did two laps in the washing machine," I confessed
bleakly, "she'd snuggled in between the sheets."

Peggy and Henry Koster made to leave. "Have to get up

early," he said somewhat guiltily in view of those present who were not expected anywhere in the morning. "Let's go to La Rue tomorrow night, we'll pick you up around eight." La Rue was a restaurant, one of the best on the Sunset Strip. The rule was, when you're in trouble, you go out; when not, paint the town. Not to be seen meant sick, unsuccessful, written off, written yourself off. To discuss failure meant admitting it. Nobody had asked what happened in Berlin. Nobody wanted to complain, sympathize, weep and think, "Thank God it's her and not me" on the way home. Reticence about crucial matters meant something else will turn up, I'll be ready, I'll take it and turn it to advantage. They had all known crises, and respected those who bore them according to the rules of the land. "A great girl," an American author had remarked one evening at the Mocambo as a girl with one leg came in on crutches. "She's got cancer, may have another three weeks to live, but just look at her." She was beautiful, had smiled toward the stage and tapped her one foot to the music.

Invited by Miss Patterson, we ate a cheerless lunch, the conversation flagging with each mouthful. Back at the office even Lacey's "Great" lacked its former conviction, was more a reflex, chewing the cud, irreparable vocal defect. His parting "I'll call you" marked the end of a fruitless relationship.

Two weeks later Erich Pommer arrived: "I can offer you a contract for two films. I hope to be able to produce the first by the end of next year."

"Where?"

"In Germany."

"I don't have a passport, I can leave the country only for an American production."

"Apply for permission right away." He stood in his coat and declined my offer of coffee. In his reluctance lay an almost commanding petition to change immediately my surroundings, circumstances, way of life. Standing on the overgrown steps, he addressed his weighty remarks to trivial objects, as was his custom. His long-lidded eyes resting on a listless salamander, he said, "Frau Zuckerberg is back in Europe, she's telling everyone she's your agent. Be careful. You can always work in Europe again; don't let her persuade you that only she can salvage your career. Agents are worthless when no parts are offered, and producers are

not in the habit of letting themselves be forced into things."
Then he went off, leaving behind him hope and uncertainty, anticipation and fear of anticipaton.

Inactivity 1950 had nothing to do with Weltanschauung,
protest or pleasure, wasn't a synonym for meditation or
narcotic euphoria; unkempt hair and ragged clothes were
not badges of freedom or declarations of an inner need to
change the system, but rather depressing signals of failure
in a society geared to furs, houses, diamonds, cars, and
bank accounts. The voluntary outsider has little to do with
the unwitting one and the involuntary and passed-over rev-
olutionary must soon see that the cause is lost. Labeled ill-
starred, parasite, bringer of bad luck, with no herd to comfort him, he succumbs to fright. Mine began to manifest itself in peculiar forms. Having given up storming rubber
walls which sent me sprawling before I'd even reached
them, I lapsed into leaden lulls of sleep relieved by hectic
insomniac bouts of trying to blend myself into a community I could find no contact with and rejected. I paraded,
sought celebration of my womanhood, cut capers where
none were asked, and finally wound up echoing sentiments
I had learned from plays and films; I walked the shaky
plank beloved of so many actors: play the play at home. J.
D. Salinger's signposts, Henry Miller's flaming swords were
still unknown to me; my reading till then had indeed informed me, broadened my vocabulary, warmed my vanity,
but was nothing I could put to work, imparted no dynamic
peace. Fear dictated my actions and I would have given
much to achieve affinity with others. I agreed with everyone, regardless of theme or opinion, and it required ˙ ttle
effort to take advantage of such somnambulism, prᴑ ided
one offered an alternative. I have nothing more in common
with the Hildegard Albertina Hirsch who flew to Europe
late in 1950, not because she shames me but because she
disappeared—no, not entirely; she bequeathed me a fickle
susceptibility to Angst, like someone who has recovered
from acute pneumonia and must always beware of a cold.
"I know myself, I know that I am not," writes André Gide.
Detours and changes, periods of development and meta-
morphosis, are a good foundation; they clear away the
mists that cling around the term "standpoint," the heroical-
ly defended standstill. What I had learned was fright; what
I had to forget was that I had been acquainted with it. The
moment I landed at Frankfurt airport there began five

years of idiotic haste, unmade decisions, dependence on others, and dread of being alone. The Angst decreed that the void make way for a void.

I hate hate. I hate the fact that I know hate, am at its mercy, hate gritty-scratchy like tarred sandpaper, bilious, stinging-nettle, breathless, as though it has to break out, get going. Angst, hand in hand with the guilty knowledge of being The German abroad and The Emigrant at home, started it all. "Hate is good copy," wrote a German author with many standpoints. What will he do when his inkwell of complaints runs dry? Call on hate to lend brilliance where competence is already squandered? I know beauty, I hate the hate that is left over from that time. Hatred of parasites, time-stealers, life-stealers, the blood-flukes that pierce your pores and course through your blood stream. Hate those who kick the man down and deplore the absence of bruises. Hate the sycophant beginners who blossom into tyrants with minor success, swell from worms to boa constrictors. Hate the "I meant well" whiners, ever ready for enmity. Hate those who know only a universal ME and a microscopic YOU, the fervor of their pettiness, their greed—I loomed into their sights like a clay pigeon. And I hate the hatred still in me.

Shortly after Erich Pommer's visit I received one of those stampless yet postmarked envelopes that augur officialese. The letter informed me in the concise brusque terms befitting a State Communiqué that I should prepare myself for an examination which might eventually lead to my citizenship. The date given left three weeks and I spent them with black coffee, Alka Seltzer, and several tomes of very comprehensive history which made monstrosities glorious, chaos orderly, and battles locations with dates. As I walked through the Los Angeles courthouse to the Immigration Department, the presidents and laws, senators and wars were humming and hammering, scurrying and flurrying like epileptic bees in a hive. I took my place in a glass cubicle and the questions, eighty or more, were launched at me, mussing my parrot-talk, uprooting the tracks of memory I had laid: Who was the nineteenth, the fifth, the first President; who signed what, where, and, above all, why; how many senators, how many states; could you imagine the United States ever naming a Minister of Propaganda? A Yes would have erased my name from the list of applicants forever, my No permitted me to become an American citizen. I was free to wander where I pleased, except in Communist-occupied territories, and sojourns in my native land were limited to five years, whether enjoyed consecutively or in short bursts.

At Pesach, the Jewish peace festival, Kurt Hirsch called his parents. The reconciliation was terse in view of the long-distance charges and the whens and wheres of a possible meeting were left open.

A new agent had taken me under his wing; his name was Kurt Frings and he spoke a Cologne-tinged German and English to match. He had spent the pre-visa years in Mexico earning his living as a boxer and other things and, thanks to his influential wife, had now progressed to an office, clients, and stomach ulcers. Sharp and wiry, he weaved his way between Early American furniture and engravings of English race horses; using his desk chair as a springboard, mounting it, bouncing forward, gaining speed and interest, he read the telegram I had brought and which Willi Forst had sent me requesting my presence in Germany within forty-eight hours for a new film. His somewhat dented boxer's eyes narrowed, became slits, the arms went up protectively, then he spoke: "Tcha Hildchen, I've got an offer for you from an independent outfit, American, good script and the German one you haven't read. I'd advise you not to go, they'll murder you after what happened in Berlin."

I called Carroll Righter. "I need an hour to look it up," he said. Once again in the hotel lobby we had used before, he sat down, straight, correctly dressed, motionless, as though preparing himself for a difficult task: "The American production will fall through. If the producer's dates I was given are correct, I see problems which will hold up the starting date and consequently become impossible to surmount. The European film will gain you a big name again although there'll be scandalous aspects, attacks and intrigues; and although the film will not quite fulfill your artistic demands I would nevertheless advise you to accept."

"They haven't sent a ticket, I have no money and I owe rent, not to speak of the contract I signed for the house——"

He interrupted my oral diarrhea: "I'll take over the house. See that you're on the morning plane."

It was the beginning of a deep friendship which still

holds today and in which he was often the giver and I the receiver. And it came to pass as he had prophesied: the American film fell flat.

"Has something happened?" Henry Koster asked anxiously as I stepped into his living room panting for breath. Just as in Berlin it had been an unwritten law not to burden your friends with bombed-out problems except in cases of extreme distress, so in Hollywood at times of pecuniary embarrassment. "I'm not poor, just broke," Mike Todd, one of the first producers to seek independence of the big studios, put it, and one resolved the problem of being broke alone and single-handed. But I, bereft of the most meager possessions, would have had a hard time persuading a bank to advance me the price of a local call, and so I was left with no alternative but to plump for Henry Koster and against principles. "Tell me, what's wrong?" he insisted. "I need money," I finally stammered, "a lot of money, I've got to go to Europe, a film with Willi Forst, Kurt wants to come too, enough money for two tickets and God knows when I'll pay it back." He gave me a check. "Send us a postcard," he called out and shoved me to the door.

I didn't like to ask the stewardess but I was sure that we were going the wrong way in the wrong plane; it flew out over the Pacific as though bound for Hawaii, Tokyo, Korea. Then it slid into a turn, a long one, with grinding motors and shuddering wings and came back over white-capped waves, beach, hot-dog stands, filling stations, movie-house towers, studios, over the Prussian blue of the swimming pools, over Mulholland Drive on the ridge of the hills, brittle-yellow fields, sepia rocks, tempera tones losing luster, drying into desert sand.

"Well now," said Marlene, like a doctor taking off a plaster cast, "I spoke to Carroll, he says it's O.K. for you to do the film with Willi Forst." She smiled, enjoying a secret joke. She put on a pair of horn-rimmed spectacles and studied a list. "I have to go shopping, want to come along?" From the furnace of the New York streets into the Department store deep-freeze, we scramble from the first to the second, the third to the fourth floor; she buys a belt, a dress, a scarf and a suit. "Shoe size—what's your shoe size?" "Marlene, I can't possibly——" She reproves silently, sucks her cheeks between her teeth; looking neither right nor left, disregarding climate, gaping pedestrians, buses missing us by inches, she walks, wholly taken up with walking. I wheeze, feel as if I'm swathed in hot towels. "Here, take a salt tablet," handing me one she has ready. She lives in a hotel, nothing luxurious, exorbitant. "My daughter's expecting a baby, I have to be close, that's her house over there." Between the tall ones two or three meek two-story brownstones with tiny gardens, brass knobs on the doors. She mixes drinks, packs cartons, bags, and packages full of tablets, pastilles, drops, oils, I'm all set for an expedition in head-hunting territory, equipped against cholera and fish poisoning, lockjaw and circulatory failure, colds, inflamed nails, insomnia, aching back, liver damage, duodenal catarrh, constipation, neuralgia, allergies, toothache, seasickness, bronchitis, loss of hair, twitching eyelids. Instructions: "This you take in the morning, this before lunch, and that in the evening; these three times a day and these twice, that only in an emergency." "I'll mix them up," I say, "I'll stand on my head at night and faint during the day." She chooses not to hear, the consulting doctor, no time for pleasantries. She dictates the names of surgeons and specialists she has auditioned in Paris, Zürich, London, Amsterdam, and found adequate. "Call them if anything happens," she says and closes the clinic. Her beauty in the bleak daylight, under the brute bulb of the elevator, by heat and by cold—where are the hordes of men who should be hanging on her eyelashes? "That's my husband," she says. Rudi Siebert stands in the hullabaloo of Fifth Avenue, expectant grandfather expectant grandmother exchange gentle signs of friendliness; apologetically he calls, "Got to get back to the chickens," waves, is swallowed up. "He has a farm in California," says Marlene. She looks at her hands, practical hands, don't match face, shoulders, beauty. "I'm doing the chores while Maria's pregnant, the daily woman's no good, American women have no idea of how to keep house. When does the plane leave?"

"Tomorrow morning at seven."

"I'll send the car. Where are you staying?"

"With the parents, in Astoria." Raised eyebrows. "They made up at Pesach."

It is after midnight as Kurt Hirsch and I turn into the sweaty street and enter the peeling house that still smells of spilt milk and newspapers. The father gives vent to his feelings about high life, riches, Marlene's limousine that brought us. Thyroid trouble, probably, I conjecture to myself, Marlene's model pupil; enlarge my diagnosis: high blood pressure, risk of a stroke. The mother raises a Kleen-ex to her eyes, sniffles: "Taking my boy back to the Ger-mans, the Nazis, they're all Nazis, the Dietrich woman too and a whore on top of it." She grasps her son's hand, sinks her head, goes on sniffling; it's like Thespian Night at the village hall, improvisation hour. Hero-Father finds his form: "Just wait and see where it gets you, going to the Germans!" "The war's in Korea, not Germany," I say. The scene derails, explodes into Czech, excludes me, knocks me flat, counts me out with pointed fingers, raised fists. I call Marlene: "Sorry, but I can't stay here, and I've no money for a cab or train." "The car'll be there right away. Mazel tov for Germany." The scene threatens to become a repeat of the Sabbath drama but I'm quicker this time, and the neighbors need longer to take their places. The liveried chauffeur is deaf to the ranting and raving, back-porch tu-mult, packs cartons and cases, pushes past and through, climbs in, purrs away. That does it, I say to myself, what-ever happens you stay in Europe.

A large cardboard box is lying on my seat in the Pan American plane. Hats and dresses nestle in silken paper. A card: Wear the linen coat with the black velvet cap on ar-rival. Underneath a playful M. After Bostom comes Gander, then the Atlantic, then Shannon. Shortly before we're due there's a grunt from the right, whistling and gur-gling, then still, the propellor blades standing straight up and down and sideways. We lurch on to Ireland, are thank-ful for the landing strip, shed, and Irish whiskey, stay thankful and patient although the connection for Frankfurt has already gone. Erich Pommer is waiting in London: "I would have asked you to stay here tonight anyway, I have to talk to you." He dampens the ardor, the Sturm and Drang. "I want you to know that I'm against this part."

"I haven't even read it," I try to say but don't get very far.

"You're not a vamp and shouldn't become one. You'll be typed, pushed in the wrong direction. At all events it won't be easy, the German press is against you, they're going to attack you."

"Why?"

"Because they expected you to repeat your home suc-cesses abroad, and since you haven't, they can't trust their own judgment any more; apart from which it's a sign of character at the moment to run down Germans and praise

foreigners." I hardly register his pessimism. I shall work,
the rest will take care of itself. "And beware of the advi-
sers. You have great gifts, don't destroy them." The praise
I hear, the warning is forgotten by the time we land at the
Rhein-Main airport in Frankfurt.

The photographers and reporters bustle and shove, shoo
me back up the gangway: Wave again, smile, laugh, over
the shoulder, bend the knee—they know how it's done
now, have seen the right movies, are more American than
the Americans, complete with second person singular,
"Hildes," and back-slaps; here and there a "Forgive me,
Miss," and "May I ask" make me think of two photos
printed over each other, of two radio stations hogging the
same wave length. "What sort of film is it that Forst's making?" "What's the theme?" "Tell us the story." "What's so
special about it?" "Did you accept because you didn't make
it over there?" I grin coyly, try to get by with "Mr. Forst
has asked me not to disclose the subject matter."

In town a hotel, no longer requisitioned, with beds and
sheets, curtains and towels, rugs, warm water, and telephone. Down on the street an old man is pulling a cart
laden with bananas, there's a flower stall at the corner,
three cars with German license plates. I call the bar in the
Bernhardstrasse: "Would you call my mother to the phone,
please?"

"That's our Hilde—all right, hold the line. . . ."

Mother's voice, breathless, thin: "What's happened?"

"I'm in Frankfurt."

"Where?"

"Frankfurt. I'm going to Hamburg tomorrow—can you
come?"

"Yes, yes, I read something but I don't trust the papers
any more."

Someone from the production is waiting outside the
booth. "We have to be in Bendestorf tomorrow, Herr Forst
is expected from Vienna." "Bendestorf?" "That's where the
studio is, and your hotel too." In the evening there's a film
première, the theater is new, the owner excited. He invites
us to his office: German champagne and potato chips, pea-
nuts, and orange juice. The film shows the Berlin I know,
the people I know. The stringy man picking his way home
through the ruins is called Otto Normalverbraucher.* "You
sure the public'll still buy that?" one of them says afterwards; "what we need now is operettas, comedies, some-

thing to laugh at, warm the heart." Heart is a word I hear
often, together with soul, contact, potential public, repara-
tion, comeback, controversial, undercurrent, theatrical license, upkeep of occupational forces, demilitarization, aid
to Berlin.

South of Hamburg, down the autobahn left creased by
tank tracks to Hittfeld, then country road, village street,
sleeps Bendestorf, a tiny health resort at the edge of Klecker Forest and Lüneburg Heath, its prehistoric stones and
graves a Sunday magnet for the nearby towns. The pension
is called Meinsbur; it's an old farmhouse, lower Saxon with
pewter and fireplaces, massive locks, peasant bunks, polished stone floor in the hall. A somewhat nasal high hoarse
voice says, "That's what I call punctuality, flies halfway
around the world and gets here on the dot." I had seen his
films; in *Bel Ami* he had put his arm casually around the
lovely leading lady's waist, at fourteen or fifteen I had been
shocked.

* Normalverbraucher: Average Consumer.

SEVENTEEN

Willi Forst stretches out his hand, comes toward me, smiles. He walks rhythmically, musically, in time with an old-fashioned swing, accent in front of the beat. His rosy morning-dew face bears no trace of war or famine, occupation or stress, is insensitive to tragedy, wants no part of chaos and destruction. A sprightly monarch returned from exile, confident, charged with energy and ready to reign. His smile settles over other people like a tea cozy, like blinkers on a horse. If there's anything worth looking at it's me, the smile commands. I settle down, my feelers curl back, bristles grow velvet-soft, hubbub center starts to purr; there'll be no mistakes, rejections, or recasting here. I shall follow and defend blindly, ask no questions. The crew assembles: Venda Vich, peeping at the studio and the outside world through a built-in view finder; Jupp Paschke, the make-up man, sealing each occurrence with a broad captious "Better luck next time"; Schurli Marischka, one of the few first assistants not to give the impression he knows better than the director; Gustav Frölich, who will be my costar in the film whose title I now hear for the first time, and André, whom I had last seen as the Merry Widow in the Don Juan bar in Berlin, engaged here as costume designer and introducing himself as the "wardrobe mistress." Soundmen, electricians, carpenters, cutter. I know them all and I've even seen the studio, tucked between the trees a hundred yards away from the pension. What I haven't seen is the script. It remains the Forst mystery, the conductor's score with no orchestral parts.

Two weeks after my arrival and only a few days before shooting started he led me into the parlor of the Meinbur, placed a tome on his knee, lit a cigarette, folded back the cover and read: *The Sinner*. Admirably restraining Forst the actor, he read every word of the manuscript, including the technical directions such as dissolve, fade, close, medium, long shot, pan, pausing only as he reached the broadly typed "End." He remained immobile for a few seconds, during which I sat listening to the clumsy ticking of the wormholed grandfather clock, then he stood up, uncorked a bottle of schnapps and drank off two thimble-sized glasses, saying, "Is that a part or isn't it?" Words failed me so I nodded briskly. Erich Pommer's warning seemed precipitate and Carroll Righter's forecast of scandal exaggerated, since the story was about a girl who had strayed from the straight and narrow as a result of family complications, war and displacement, found her way back through a love affair with a mortally sick painter, and finally followed him to the grave with the help of poison. The fact that she often posed for him during their blissful alliance and that for these sessions he generally requested her to shed every vestige of clothing seemed to me, after my short-lived artistic training under Klemke's censorious tutelage, neither extraordinary nor worth mentioning.

"Spic and span" or "fresh as a daisy," Mother Blocken from the Bernhardstrasse would have said warmly of Willi Forst's faultless exterior as he strode through the outskirts of the Klecker Forest each morning on his way to superintend the delicately built Jupp Paschke's work. Forst inspected each brush stroke, the arching of the brows and the shading of the lids, with the concentration of an engineer watching his calculations become reality. I had never experienced such emphatic interest in myself and my appearance; his knowledge of the silly secrets of make-up, which actresses usually share only with their make-up men and mirrors, exposed me, forbade all possibility of feminine hide-and-seek games, and, at the beginning, left me with the permanent feeling of being caught with a hole in my stocking. With a last desperate attempt at resistance and timid sarcasm I nicknamed him The Maestro.

There was no familiarity in the studio, the tone was formal, the coffee-sipping assistants barking "On your marks" were either silenced or evicted, the press banned. There were no long-winded discussions about how a scene should be played; the soft-spoken dictator ruled the studio from the lighting bridge to the fireman, from the actors to the camera crew; his charm and repose left no doubt about the infallibility of his detailed commands, excluded all thought of individual interpretation and not one of the cowed would ever have dreamed of spitting at his tamer. His reactions to dim-witted actors and extras were violent, often uncontrolled and terrifying and no apologies were forthcoming. The lava of his rage bubbled and glowed, gushed over trembling heads. For me he remained infallible, impeccable, the force of his fury excused by his aims, an ersatz father who released me from responsibility. I harbored the suppressed adoration of a fifteen-year-old with unbalanced hormones. My closely guarded brittle secret didn't go unnoticed, however, but the mature object of my ardor reciprocated graciously by guiding the tensions into the platonic passion of our work.

In the late autumn an inflated voice called from Munich, stating that it represented Twentieth Century Fox and informing me that they had decided to test me for an American film called *Decision Before Dawn*. "No," I said, amazed that it came out so directly and conclusively. A subsequent conversation with the director, Anatole Litvak, swayed my attitude only a little and only to the extent that my ambition had grown porous because of the American defeat and that I knew I was still no match for the malicious innuendoes of the German press. The Maestro declared himself willing to show Litvak a selection of rushes which up to this time no one, not even the distributor, had seen. I muttered my gratitude, felt rejected and passed on. I was suffering from a very conspicuous cold when Litvak arrived from Munich and I greeted him with puffed eyes and a red nose, my *m*'s all coming out *b*'s. I still possessed nothing other than Marlene's summer coat, whereas Litvak seemed to have prepared himself for a sleigh ride through the tundra. With the temperature several degrees below, sneezing and sniffling, I followed him into the unheated projection room for my first view of scenes from the film I had been working on for many weeks. The meeting between European star director and American star director was one of choice propriety, like an unexpected confrontation of two ambassadors of warring nations. They knew each other from the Berlin days which had been described to me as golden, from a time when the American Litvak was still a Russian from Kiev with a Nansen passport. I sensed a mild superciliousness on his part, concluded that he deemed it warranted since he'd made his career on the winning side, and took up my position behind The Maestro. The uncut rushes stuttered across the screen and meant little to me; I had no opinion of my own and the undisguised pleasure on The Maestro's face relieved me of the need to express any. In one melodramatic episode I threw a scene in a bar and collapsed, sobbing and heartbroken (I "did my nut," as actors put it), and this seemed to convince Litvak of my capabilities, just as hysterical screaming, torrents of self-pitying tears, and globs of passionate ooze often impress even the most respected directors more than sensitivity and controlled skill. I only half-noticed the cool, humorless, arrogant face, the white hair, the light eyes, the scratchy strained voice. Before he went back to the Four Seasons Hotel in Hamburg he favored me with a friendly smile which set me to wondering what skulduggery Fox would think up next.

The contract that arrived shortly afterwards did nothing to disperse my anxiety. Confusion, doubts, suspicion, and the wish to be able to trust implicitly and without criticism were relics of the wrong decision, the pigheadedness, the recklessness, that had sent me scurrying to America. Totally lacking in self-confidence, I expected awful strokes of fate to follow each happy phase of professional recognition, as though every sunny day must be paid for with weeks and months of desperation and indecision. My hopeless lack of feeling for money and my lack of interest in the size of salaries, which I put down to the postwar years in Berlin, my inability to read contracts or to enter a shop without feeling uncomfortable, my impatience, which at that time served to camouflage my horror of people, questions, and decisions, left me continually searching for someone who would take over the unfathomable task of dealing with the mechanics of living, with life itself. Nagging and boring its way through every waking minute was the fear of America, of having to go back, of the wasteland, dread of not getting another film, of not being allowed to play any more. The only therapy against this panic was the days of work in the studio, the reconciling warmth of a director who believed in me. Sundays were cement blocks of boredom, as endless as they'd been during the Meixner epoch; only a rainy one seemed to offer protection and insurance, solace far from California's great blue sky.

Except for a few locations in Italy and the recording of a monologue which was to accompany the almost silent action of the film, my work with Willi Forst was at an end. We had talked of another production together but there was no script as yet, only a vague idea, more a casual promise of a meeting someday somewhere. Our imminent departure for Italy was a last buffer; I concentrated on it and dared not think beyond it.

Kurt Hirsch had taken a job as assistant and translator with Fox and drove to Munich in a newly acquired car. I didn't miss him, thought about him with a sad mixture of sympathy and hopelessness.

As we arrived in Positano a tomato-red sun was sitting on the sea, coloring piled-up tumbles of houses chocolate-box gold, splashing flames over window-panes, conjuring Chagall children from fat clouds. A dot the size of a pin circled and touched the same nerve time after time and whispered that it would be good to throw oneself from the cliff one was sitting on, good since the long-sought-after and finally found beauty might then decide to stay.

The next morning it rained. After fourteen days of waiting in vain the winter-sleepy hotel went into an uproar: a call from Munich had been announced. After a lengthy shouting match with the operators, countless interruptions, fresh connections and hopeful "Prontos" it turned out that Kurt Hirsch was the hardy communicator. "I'm calling in a professional capacity for Fox," he bellowed. "You have to be in Munich the day after tomorrow, Litvak needs you for the first scene."

"I can't get away, we've had bad weather and haven't shot a thing yet."

"The American film's more important."

"I can't let the Forst production go up in smoke just because the Americans suddenly need me."

A row developed, concentrating on film schedules but signifying something quite different.

St. Moritz
December 27, 1969,

I never did like clowns, or trapeze artists, the drum roll before their bodies vault through the Big Top, the stares of the people below, white between lid and iris, fingers cramped in bags of candy, sighs of relief, of disappointment as the feet touch the platform. The animals, led, drilled, displayed in circles, leaping through hoops; the smell of sawdust; the glory of courage, the pluck to thumb your nose at death. It all terrified me; I cried at the top of my lungs and was removed during intermission by a perplexed mother, bewildered by a child that turned fun into grief, wouldn't see the joke in kicking the staggering clown. The same at school when they brought in the giant snake: "Don't be a ninny," the teachers said as I couldn't bring myself to touch it, couldn't believe that it wanted to be touched, cringed at the thought of its skin; teacherfaces all agog: make her, make her, make her. Make the tiger jump through the burning hoop, let's see if she flinches when the knife thuds beside her face; elephant raising its knee, bear on a bicycle, ape in collar and tie, marching tunes to round it off, tunes for watching the troops go by. I saw no beauty, felt no equation between ugliness and reality, saw only duress and failure. Our sole vocation should be the quest for beauty, it seems to me, for affinity and peace in the sense Henry Miller describes in his passage on Epidaurus. That I find it so seldom is my own fault, the price of my impatience, as Ludwig Marcuse uses the word in his *Obituary for Ludwig Marcuse.* By chance and too late I discovered that Marcuse had been my neighbor in Bavaria for many years; apart from casual meetings at receptions I hadn't seen him since the early fifties in Hollywood.

Shortly before we moved from Starnberg to St. Moritz this autumn, Tonio and I went to a reading given in Munich by the writer Anaïs Nin. We went because Miller had often spoken of her and we therefore thought we would meet a friend of his.

The hall was full. A young man mounted the podium and introduced an old man in the throes of bronchitis, the old man introduced Madame Nin, Madame Nin introduced the lady translator, and, just as the matter of identities had been settled, the microphone went dead. Everyone smirked, as though the insidious whims of technology were

water on a duck's back for the intellectual mind.
Ludwig Marcuse was eating vanilla ice cream. He
noticed neither the breakdown nor the repair of
the loudspeakers, nor me, his immediate neighbor,
nor the condescending twaddle now being bandied
about the podium on the writer Miller—coy narra-
tions of how one prepared him a meal, stilled his
hunger, encouraged him, that unpredictable gifted
child that one had gently but unrelentingly guided
to success. ("A man should neither be praised nor
criticized," says Henry Miller.) A young man in
frayed velvet jeans elbowed his way forward and
said, "Why can't we have a discussion, just talk to
each other? I met Miller in a bistro in Paris, he
was clear and unpretentious. We talked until we
were tired, or bored maybe. Why can't we do that
here?" The actress Käthe Dorsch could have
matched Madame Nin's expression; I had seen her
play Elizabeth of England and Dürrenmatt's *The
Visit*. Madame Nin spoke, but her tone had that
grain of prep-school reproval which would have restricted Dorsch's performance to the provinces:
Perhaps this isn't the right place for you, young
man. Ludwig Marcuse scraped the runny remains
from his bowl and looked about him like someone
who awakes from a narcotic, tests his surroundings, finds them not to his liking and goes to sleep
again. He left in the intermission; Madame Nin exchanged words with me, about Henry's age, his
weaknesses, about the people he now associated
with and who were wrong for him.

Where are the right ones for someone like Miller, and does he need them anyway? Perhaps he
needs them no more than the mountain now facing
me, the one I have loved since my first visit to St.
Moritz, as I love the Baltic, Grandfather's shed,
and the shores of Lake Griebnitz. It's a fat mountain, indefinite in shape, immalleable, has nothing
of the attraction of its neighbors whose ragged
peaks prick into clouds; it has a cumbrous back
like a dozy hippopotamus's, no good for skiing,
climbing, walking, whooping tobogganers, building
houses. Its imperviousness seems to say, "The parasites of the earth, that's what you are. Without

our trees, plants, algae, animals and seas you couldn't exist, but we'd get by without you." It should then turn over, toss off its name like a horse its rider, squash the inanity that has spread across its feet, disrupt the parade, end the performance, stifle the circus fanfares. The valley where one once licked one's wounds, recuperated and found haven would be still again, the mountain without a name would straighten up, shed an avalanche, nod off anew.

On the afternoon after Madame Nin's loquacious soirée came Ludwig Marcuse's telegram. I called him. "You must think I'm crazy," he said, his voice bubbling nasally as if issuing from a storage room, filtering through blankets and cartons. "I live alone, never go out, it alarms me to—I wasn't aware of anything last night." He came to dinner, the house was full of nothing but packing cases, he wanted to talk, to eat stuffed red peppers, to see our daughter Christina. "The girl with the blond tongue," he called her in his letter, describing her coquetry which knew little deference to his years. "I used to love to go out, in the evenings when work was done. In Hollywood we played silly guessing games with Werfel and Thomas Mann, but today . . . tons of tedium have been poured upon me." His gentle sadness that we were leaving moved me; "It's not that important," I wanted to say. Next morning in the Munich paper: "Knef leaves Germany!" And in Berlin: "Knef turns her back on us—not good enough any more?" In foreign lands I had always been ashamed of Germans who were ashamed of being German. The snowball plunged through the press jungle yelping betrayal; united Europe had been the theme on TV a few nights before, students bearing a coffin because a national anthem had been played. Anonymous threatening letters arrive in the mail; they've been part of my life since the première of *The Sinner* but I still find it hard to shrug them off. Where to live is one of our problems: we set up camp like gypsies and lay intricate plans for a permanent residence until we remember we don't have the money to buy it without mortgages, and mortgages are debts and I can't face debts since the time we had so many.

"Not even Hitler got reviews like this," A friend said on November 10, 1959. For the price of a cinema ticket they all felt obliged to teach me a lesson. And living with Tonio had won me a banner headline: MARRIAGE WRECKER. The chief editor of a film magazine went so far as to write an open letter on the first page, his moral feelings were so upset. The machinery of getting a divorce in England was complicated at that time. "You have to be caught in flagrante," our London lawyer had said. We drove to the specialist hotel he recommended, wedged ourselves into the tiny bed, and rang for the waiter. Most of the staff turned out to be German or Austrian and when the detectives came they said, "Frau Knef? No, she's never been here," and that was that. Before our lawyer could track down a hotel that still employed British waiters Tonio's wife changed her mind about granting the divorce and didn't change it again for another three years. And although I was awarded a federal film prize in Berlin the headlines gained the upper hand, contracts were canceled, and a producer said, "You're on the Catholic black list, dear child, if I had a contract for half a million with you I'd rather pay you off than make the film —you're forbidden in sixty-four towns to date." Back in London the long narrow buff-colored envelope from America cried out for attention: $65,000 back taxes for the years 1955/56 engagement *Silk Stocking*s plus so much interest payable immediately" we read before the flames lovingly swallowed the letter but not the debt. My New York lawyers had deducted the taxes from my weekly check but where on earth had they sent them? Tonio summoned all his reserves and said, "As long as the English don't get petty there's no need to get excited." The telephone rang the next morning: "This is the Inland Revenue. We see that you have made a number of films in England. Could you be here at nine in the morning?" London airport two hours later: "Where's the next plane going to?"

"Tangiers."

"Why not?" said Tonio. We stayed six beautiful weeks, financed by the casino which Tonio developed a feeling for. In Berlin my pale mother confronted us: our most recent bank statement showed a credit of thirty pfennig. "Was it suicide?" asked the article in the morning paper, reporting that I'd been admitted to the hospital. It was meningitis. Our problems with money and domicile began during this period—oh yes, once we did take the leap and bought a field but our application for a building permit was turned down; at the meeting a member of the council had said, "I hear she's chummy with Jews, we don't want that here."

A month ago Frau Landstorfer said, "Just think, I was just taking my schmalznoodles out of the oven as they landed on the moon, they were right on time." Then she took out her old-fashioned German playing cards, acorns and leaves instead of hearts and diamonds, her work-worn hands reached for the piles I had cut, counted, turned the cards face up. "Dear me, I see you in a foreign country and there'll be lots of excitement." We had met her for the first time in the summer of '61, soon after the evening when the stage-door keeper of the Kurfürstendamm theater had burst into our dressing room and babbled, "They say there's something going on at the Brandenburg Gate, they're building a fence." West Berlin policemen at the victory column: "Keep the peace now, keep well back," they called like the stationmaster in Wilmersdorf. "Be reasonable now," this solicitously, as though they had an accident to screen, must measure the skid marks, sweep away the glass. Soldiers were sitting on English tanks and smoking, looking as though they'd forgotten the password, lost the maneuver plans, missed the tea break. "Why don't you shoot!" a boy yelled, pointing at the Russian panzers, great immobile whales washed up with the tide. Groups chanted about butter, milk, and Ulbricht, stopped and hastily thought up new rhymes, petered out again;

a couple of adamant bleaters blistered obscenely on alone, kicked the curbstones like sulky kids, shrugged their shoulders, and went home. Two days later a lead article in the London *Daily Express* "The Germans thoroughly deserve to have a wall in Berlin."

Mother cried; she'd grown thin, her skin opaque gray. "It's nothing but gastritis," the three doctors had said, "circulation, nerves, nothing to worry about." She steadied herself on the edge of the kitchen table and said, "I'm staying here; we belong here even if the papers do pull you to pieces— I'm ashamed to go and visit my friends any more, they talk of nothing but the articles. Even so, we're still Berliners."

"You've got a German passport, Tonio an English one, and I'll soon have none at all," I said. I had been to the authorities: "What do I have to do to regain my German citizenship?"

"Well," said the stiff official, screwing up his thermos flask, "as far as we're concerned you're still stateless. Go down to the third door on the left and ask them. Oh, and seeing as you're here, would you give me an autograph? Not for myself, of course, it's the wife, she's always going on about our Hilde." The third door on the left bore the legend DISPLACED PERSONS.

In September 1961 we moved to Starnberg and brought Mother to the Munich clinic. Then I drove to the Dankwartstrasse, ground floor, Landstorfer on the name plate. "Holy Maria, it's bad, your mother is sick, very sick, don't drag her from quack to quack, she won't live till Christmas. I'm sorry but you did ask." They operated in the morning: twenty minutes later the professor reappeared: "If she'd come a year ago, even six months . . ."

"How long does she have?"

"Three months, four at the most." A church, dark red and rejecting, stood opposite the clinic. It never helps, I thought, neither during the war nor now. Someone touched my sleeve; a nun was standing there looking at me. If she so much as mentions God I'll knock her bonnet off, I promised myself. "You're alone now, no one can help you," she said.

She died three days before Christmas. In the afternoon I had fought for morphine as usual. "It is our duty to prolong life," said the nurse. I stayed until she had filled the syringe and given the injection, until I saw the relief on my mother's face, the wet forehead smoothing out again. They called at two in the morning; she was dead when I entered the room, her face set in pain and despair.

On the twenty-seventh of December a man from the local tax office telephoned: "This is Dr. Kessler, I hear your mother's dead. The lease of the house will now run in your name, making you fully liable to federal taxation."

"I'm a Swiss resident——"

"Not any longer. Income tax is payable in advance in the Federal Republic——"

"But I don't have any money, the hospital——"

"I will expect you here between nine and twelve in the morning."

"How proud our Maker must be of us," said Else Bongers, "put the furniture in storage and come here."

The priest said, "It's come to this, I see my congregation only at baptisms and burials." In front of the crematorium the funeral director said, "You must pay a deposit for the music before we go in." As the organ died away an attendant nudged us: "Time's up, I've got another big crowd coming in."

A week later we flew to Los Angeles. The Berlin senate had chosen me to represent it and the mayor, Willy Brandt, at an exhibition; I was to cut the ribbon, make speeches, give interviews, convey greetings, inform the unenlightened about the divided city, its waterways, air corridors, inhabitants. Boarding the plane in Tempelhof I heard a shrill voice: "Ooh look, there's Hilde Knef, she's wearing a white hat and her mother's not dead two weeks." The use of colors as a barometer of one's grief is another of those tricky problems. Frau Dunke, Hedwig Dunke, Bernhardstrasse 5, had two daughters and a husband who played the clarinet. He played scales, nothing but scales the whole

summer long, windows open wide. He doodled
through the octaves; they bluntly stabbed their
way along the railway tracks, held their own
against bicycle bells and "Throw us down a penny,
Mum." The daughters married, left home. The
husband died in August, just before the war broke
out; a year later the elder daughter and, soon after,
the second. Hedwig stood in her doorway contem-
plating the neighbors and cried: "Can't anyone die
in winter, for God's sake? Every damn summer
I'm stuck here in black."

Mayor Yorty of Los Angeles kept hold of my
hand until the flash bulbs and TV cameras had
finished, then said, "Here's the famous actress
who's going to tell us about the heroic behavior of
the Berliners." After reading the prepared speech I
found myself hustled from TV studios to radio stations, from women's clubs to diplomatic functions
and back. One midnight I was confronted by a
testy host on a coast-to-coast show. "Isn't it rather
ridiculous, not to say stupid, of the Berliners to
want to stay in Berlin?" I let him hang, snubbed
the microphone, savoring the pause, nation-wide
stillness, needled him into further conjecture.
"What I mean is, aren't they rather like the citizens
of Pompeii, sitting at the foot of Vesuvius?" "If
the Russians are looked on by the Americans as a
natural disaster you're absolutely right." The range
of colors that appeared on my host's face must
have looked beautiful on the home screens.

In Germany little had been heard of my mission: still registered as an eyesore in the federal
landscape, I returned to the Berlin town hall after
the ten-day tour of duty and made my report. I
then received a letter informing me that my work
as an honorary ambassadress had been favorably
noted. I added it to my collection: Foreign Minister Heinrich von Brentano's card which had
reached me at the Imperial Theatre on Broadway
some years before: "You are doing more for
Germany than we ever can." Professor Hallstein's
letter with a similar text; Theodor Heyss's auto-
graphed picture; Otto Suhr's etchings of Berlin,
signed and dedicated, and the manuscript of a

speech given by the President of the Bavarian County Council, Dr. Hundhammer, following one of my film premières: "If it is now possible to make and exhibit films such as *The Sinner* with financial guarantees from the state, then it is high time something was done to protect the chastity and morals of our youth." This last I had kept because I thought it was significant that it had been written, printed, and delivered six years after the war, the concentration camps, and ravishment.

December 1950

It all started ludicrously. A man with a frosty nose was standing on the platform in Innsbruck banging on the steamed-up window of my sleeping car and calling my name, which percolated through wads of sleep. "Telegram for you," he shouted, pointing at the station, "over there." The cold nipping at my naked legs woke me up. The fat official stirred his coffee, sipped, blew on it, drank, stood up, rummaged through drawers and pigeonholes, gave me the envelope. On platform I, where the Verona-Munich train was standing, loudspeakers were crackling. "You'll have to prove your identity and sign the form even if you are an actress."

"My passport's on the train."

"You won't catch that one any more anyway," he said cheerfully.

I hurtled off. "Boarding the train when in motion forbidden!" bellowed frosty-nose as I lay in the corridor with a broken high heel and twisted ankle. The telegram was from Anatole Litvak: "Delighted to have you on the film. Have a good trip." His assistant picked me up in Munich. "Mr. Litvak wants me to go through the script with you on account of your accent—it's your first American film, after all." Kurt Hirsch arrived. "Litvak expects us for dinner."

"I'm tired."

"It's important."

A string quartet was dismembering Kreisler. At the head of the only occupied table in the restaurant of the Four Seasons Hotel sat Anatole Litvak. He wedged a chair between his own and those of the long row of his collaborators, introduced me, and called for a waiter. "You must be hungry," he said and I suddenly knew where I had seen the face before, where I had mistaken it for someone else's, where it had confused me to such an extent that I had thought I would never forget it again but did; I hadn't recognized it at our meeting in Bendestorf. In Beverly Hills, right behind the monstrous post office, in the street with the shops that always looked as if they were clubs for which you needed a membership card, he had stood with his right hand around a street lamp (or was it one of the spindly palms?), arm outstretched, foot raised against the post or tree, swinging rather than standing lost in thought, playful, someone who couldn't make up his mind to move on, someone without plans and waiting for no one, who had got up that morning, carefully shaved and dressed, and set out to keep his appointments but now couldn't remember which. For one shattering second I had thought it was E.v.D. "That's Litvak, the director," Miss Patterson said and rolled down the window. "Hello there," she called out. The face slammed down its shutters, became adult, mistrustful, guarded. "This is a new client of ours, just in from Europe." He had nodded and said, "Pleasure."

"Why did you come?" the same voice said. "I can see that you don't feel well." He felt my pulse, counted. "You've got a high temperature, I'll send for a doctor." He led me to the elevator squinting through his cigarette smoke and pressed the button impatiently. Standing beside the reception desk was a woman; her short blond hair lay softly around her face like a cap. It was E.vD.'s wife. We looked at each other. "Come along, get in," he said and waited until the gates clicked shut.

The next morning, cool, arrogant, and often sarcastic, relishing all efforts to please, he stood like the eye of a hurricane surrounded by assistants, costume designers, actors, and journalists. He edged his chewed cigarette from one corner of his mouth to the other while directing his pale eyes at the foreheads of those who addressed him, forcing them to straighten up, to balance more and more unsteadily on tiptoe as he gazed absently, his attention seemingly rooted elsewhere. In direct contrast to the seclusion and isolation I had experienced during the weeks with Willi Forst, the studio that Fox had rented for Anatole Litvak's war film was like a Foreign Legion outpost under siege. Replacing the bedraggled fag-end with a clean whole one he proceeded to examine my German women's army uniform, boots, bag, coiffure, ignored the advice proffered by his swarm of assistants, and demanded a rehearsal. Like Forst he insisted on exact conformity to his directions but couldn't formulate them with the same precision since he had never been an actor. The takes interrupted the euphoric agitation which inexplicably seized everyone working on the film the moment he entered the studio, and they all seemed to regard the actual filming of the scenes as an irritating but necessary detail. Litvak's personality was ideally suited to the bedlam of mammoth production; he blossomed, shed years with each confrontation with danger, scaled walls and clambered up vertiginous chimney stacks, goaded his court to suicidal feats with his example of zealous idealism and absolute dedication to the job at hand, sparing no one, least of all himself.

In the evening after shooting he was a different man altogether; it was as though in discarding the baseball cap and the furlined army jacket he had discarded himself, becoming an easy host with apparently nothing on his mind but the well-being of his guests. Only the voice, racked by asthma, remained tetchy and ill-disposed, made his small talk strenuous and his humor aggressive, prompted sympathy.

A telegram was lying at my place at the table. "Neff rushes great. Zanuck." His smile and the compliment acted like a transfusion, filled me with self-confidence.

During the day I worked on Litvak's film; in the evenings I synchronized the monologue for *The Sinner*, and at Christmas I drove up to the mountains with Kurt Hirsch. It was a fiasco. The last hopes of rescuing the mortgaged puberty-marriage were dashed. An elderly lady sitting in the hotel restaurant looked up from her needlework, raised a gnarled finger, and said with a remarkable lack of perception, "When I look at you two young things I wouldn't mind betting that you've run away from home and are causing your parents a great deal of worry." That was the day I knew that I would never go back to America with Kurt Hirsch again. The next weeks seemed bent on making up for the lost time of the past three years and exposed Hildegard Albertina Hirsch to turning points and attacks which she didn't recognize or didn't want to recognize as such, and for which she was at all events no match.

January 1951

Munich station full of slush, unchanged since the war. Hotel room full of roses: bundles, heaps of roses. The agent says, "I wish I had been loved just once as you are, all those great men fighting over you." Sometimes my own reflection startles me—I think I'd be less surprised if it weren't there at all, if when I came into the bathroom the white of the wall behind me weren't broken by my head and shoulders, if the white were to remain intact and the mirror not register me. "Be happy—enjoy these years, they're the best a woman ever gets," says the agent, her hands like claws, grabbing, snatching, take-what-you-can-get hands. Sometimes again I think the New York milk-drinker from Fox must be directing the burlesque going on around me without a script. Perhaps happiness is self-effacing, is what doesn't cloy the memory. Speak Write Silence —Tucholsky's staircase. He didn't mean happiness. Rejection of everything, everyone. I'm passive—lame excuse; words are like life belts, deflating at the touch. Slides of memory come to a halt, move on jerkily, stop again one or two frames further on: Litvak's eyes—one lid longer than the other: "You're a child, one must take care of you." Monologues prologues necrologies, they've painted themselves a picture of themselves, it's important to them to be like that picture. One wants me because the other wants me, the man I'm married to wants to keep something which never existed, the agent wants to arrange and command, wants power. "Grow up, be more demanding, take the presents they offer." Grown-up logic grown-up organization, lunacy idiocy, connivance contrivance, wrong reckoning wrong balance, overestimating life's span a life long. Possessive grown-up cannibals, wanting to gobble up every yard of the earth they plant their feet on, at loggerheads with themselves and all else—trash-can voyeurs, fanatics for ugliness, only happy when they can break the bad news: Now I'm going to tell you the truth. Make way for the sadists proudly bearing the banner of truth at half-mast. Even the old charwoman in the studio at six in the morning: "Did you hear about it? He's got cancer and then the floods in Italy, three hundred dead not to mention the air crash, the whole lot of 'em burned alive—you see?—didn't

I tell you?—can't fool me—he who laughs last laughs
longest." Heard it all seen it all foretold it all, don't hold
with John Donne: "No man is an island . . . therefore
never send to know for whom the bell tolls, it tolls for
thee." I was clever, or canny, with my Bernhardstrasse
dream, my "I will" dream, clever the way kleptomaniacs
are clever, canny-clever until I went to America, until the
men burst in wanting to be men with their versions of loyalty and woe, their notions of when you should be happy or
unhappy—like bad actors: at "gay" they gaze at the heavens, at "sad" at the floor; as Mephistopheles they fold their
arms and as Parsifal they spread them wide. How good it
would be to fall asleep on someone's shoulder—whose?
Why can't I enjoy the fawning? Men were once friends. I
must grow up; if I only knew what that means apart from
crush or get crushed, the either/or ax. Hate peters out, is
short-winded—is it? Not mass hate. When one flags the
next starts sprinting, like wild dogs hounding a sick cow.
The young photographer recently—I would have liked him
as a brother, a friend, a *copain:* "I tried to gas myself. I
had always thought it would be different after the war, better. But they're really only waiting for a new one and until
it comes they dream about the old one and kill time by
sleeping with someone they don't respect—that's why I
wanted to bow out. I shall have to live many lifetimes to
make good the things I've botched in this one and all the
previous ones. I believe in reincarnation, there's no other
explanation for Mozart and Shakespeare, the last stages of
incarnation. And the only explanation for evil, for crimi-
nals, is that they're living their first life and have nothing
they can orient themselves by, they remember nothing, recognize nothing, and so they plump for the easiest and most
banal path. I believed in Hitler when I was fifteen, until I
was fifteen."—They live in shame for having worshipped
false idols—guilt is the password, inexpiable guilt. . . . Gifted people attain beauty, no matter what they look like, the
gift makes them beautiful; beauty with no gift becomes
ugly. How beautiful Heinrich George could look, for all his
fat. How few names stand out, stick up, crop up, go down
in history, up and down synonymous, what goes up must
come down, the higher they get the harder they fall, fall
from grace, from your high horse, keep your feet on the
ground, walk before you run, crawl before you walk,
know your limits, live within your means. Those first

Americans in Berlin: "We volunteered of our own free will." And we believed it; I wonder if they're saying the same thing in Korea. . . . The Germans are geared to order now, take a realistic view, are terrified of anything that can't be resolved by an adding machine—the young photographer won't get far with his theory; the supernatural, the paranormal are taboo. " 'Phenomena defy explanation,' Hippocrates said, 'the fact that we can't explain them is no fault of theirs but due only to our lack of understanding,' " says the young photographer. . . . Memory is a prism: Kurt Hirsch leaves the room and five minutes later I hardly know how he walks or laughs or eats. The prism is brittle, frail, unreliable. Life is sometimes like Sundays in a strange town; one doesn't know whom to turn to. They're all busy with something that is strange and therefore hostile. And when you get to know it well it turns hostile again, the ferry of one's hopes shuttles in between. Like intermission at the theater: you've lost yourself in the darkness among all the others, become one with them up there and then: Well, what do you say to that? Orange juice Martinis cigarettes verdicts. Queasy heaves go through me. . . . Litvak wants to go away with me. I don't like traveling all that much, too busy with myself, hardly notice anything, I'm that busy. You can only absorb the impressions if you forget yourself and I wouldn't know where to begin, I must be like a kaleidoscope inside, shake me I'll make you a new pattern. Why do I wish I'd had a potential suicide case as a brother? Or a friend? Else Bongers always thought I was self-sufficient—I'm not capable of being alone, except when I'm working. One's alone in the studio, on the stage too. It's up to you. Sometimes I'm afraid of being recognized, other times afraid of not being recognized. I want success and fight it. If I could drive I'd keep one foot on the brake and one on the gas. . . . At the gallery with Litvak I stared at the woman standing beside the heater warming her hands. Forgot the pictures. "What are you doing?" he asked, "you're forever looking somewhere where there's nothing to see." I didn't know Chirico. "But you used to paint— how can you possibly not know him?" They forget how much we were not allowed to see, read, listen to. We go out to eat in the evening. People entering a restaurant: they fidget around at the door, finger their ties, watches, handbags, stick their hands in their pockets. Up comes the waiter. They gain stature, stride valiantly after the leader.

Tucked in behind the table their courage grows, eyes survey the scene: My money's as good as theirs, come on now, show us what you've got to offer. They expand with each new waiter, flow over their chairs, after the first gin they own the room, after dinner and cognac the house; lean back, accept a light from the *garçon,* wife powders her nose—swiftly, as though she didn't really mean it—then exit, proud, they've nourished themselves in the most civilized manner possible, they're proud. Litvak eats quickly. He orders for me like a dietitian. I can tell now from his intake of vodka just when he'll start to sing the song about Stenka Razin and how he chucks his mistress into the Volga so that the revolution can proceed.

At the beginning I was excited by the huge posters splashed across cinema walls, billboards and piles of debris—long tresses, naive, vampy, to live up to the name *Sinner*—impressed by the tour of premières from Hamburg to Vienna, amazed at the press conferences, the reporters' embarrassment at exposing themselves to their colleagues, filled with admiration for Willi Forst as he delivered flaming speeches in defense of his well-made but coyly melodramatic film, and bowled over by the hordes of jubilant fans.

By the time I left Munich with Anatole Litvak a few weeks later the success had become persecution; I had lost my name, was now referred to exclusively as "The Sinner," threatening letters, detailed and illustrated proposals from countless sex maniacs, made up the bulk of my morning mail. The film was attacked from the pulpit, rent asunder by the clergy, shown amid clouds of tear gas and stink bombs, protest marches and processions, and had nevertheless or therefore been seen by two million Germans in its first three weeks of release. Priests preaching tolerance were branded as "yellow-livered bastards" or "black dogs;" others, singing descant in the protest choir, had set up barricades in front of the movie houses and demanded that the negative be burned at the stake. Piles of people who had fainted or been trampled on were a common sight in the foyers. Wherever I went the shout went up: "The Sinner!" If I ran I heard: "Now she's doing the teen-age act." If I walked normally: "Look at the slinky slut." If I laughed: "She's got a nerve." If I didn't laugh:

"Too late for penance now." They blithered and blathered and the film made the rounds of the courts. The bishop of Luxembourg, like so many others of his faith, had ordered his flock to boycott the theaters. Leaflets were distributed proclaiming, "This film makes a mockery not only of Christian morality but of basic human decency; it ridicules the honor of our women and endangers the sound integrity of our community." And Cardinal Frings, distantly related to the wiry ex-boxer agent in Hollywood, appeared as a witness and testified against a chaplain in the Ruhr who had advised against interference. President Gockeln of Westphalia trumpeted: "I expect and await further demonstrations against *The Sinner*." Member of Parliament Heike felt obliged to lecture a crowd on the subject and landed in the hospital and finally Dr. Hundhammer of the Bavarian County Council capped it all with his announcement.

I realized pretty quickly that I was being held mainly responsible for the *Sinner* nuisance. Having missed the formative years of moral renaissance, Wirtschaftswunder, and a society striving to reinstate virtue and order, I completely failed to grasp that stable currency, regular nourishment, and heated bedrooms had returned hand in hand with a prudery of the most insipid and nauseating sort, ignoring and disclaiming recent history. The reaction to a naked girl shown for a few seconds on the screen led me to believe that a lobotomy must have been performed on the majority of the demonstrators, relieving them of the memory of a diabolical past. "The Sinner finds war funny," was the caption of a picture of me in uniform laughing during a break on Litvak's film. *Der Mittag*, a Düsseldorf newspaper, commented about a photo showing Litvak from the back and me from the side: "This broad back belongs to Anatole Litvak, who plans to return to the U.S.A. accompanied by Hildegard Knef, here pictured standing demurely at his side. She began her career in the intimacy of Demandowsky's film paradise under Goebbels' wing; after the collapse she found her way into the arms of the American soldier Hirsch, and now she has finally become a resistance worker in a film which will probably not be shown in Germany."

Erich Pommer: "Revolutions start with films, not with gas chambers. I am ready to begin production this autumn; as a producer I shall profit by the publicity, you will not. By the way, Kurt Hirsch visited me. He's going to try to finish you."

"How and with what?"

"After this scandal everyone's in the right except you. A divorce will pour oil on the flames." Deviating from his usual habit of being cool or censorious he thumped me on the shoulder as though I were a comrade being sent off to Siberia. "Don't underestimate the divorce. It'll drain you, not just financially."

"Litvak will help me," I said, happy in the knowledge of having found an impatient Professor Higgins who appeared to have saved up all the finer points of his otherwise prickly character for me.

Erich Pommer slid down in his chair, became the testy eagle once more: "Don't be such a child, you can't afford that any more. You've a lot of time until our film begins. Go off alone somewhere."

He might just as well have recommended suicide. Alone was unthinkable, alone meant coping alone with threatening letters, cranks emerging from hotel closets swinging their members, whistling crowds, children squealing "Sinner," youths winking and squeaking with changing voices, ambiguous suggestions from portly gentlemen with air-raid-warden faces, vinegary wives standing up in restaurants at the sight of me and muttering, "Come along, Fritz, we're leaving," or "Don't go putting on airs now, we've all had a look at your fanny."

Willi Forst was preparing a new film and rode the waves of success and uproar with equanimity, was pleased about the protests and queues, seemed happy to have made me famous, and most probably had no idea of the consequences of this sort of fame which for years to come, whatever I did or didn't do, animated the popular press: "The sinner sins . . . again . . . still sinning . . . goes on sinning . . . will never stop . . . can't help it." Fame brought troops of sycophants and not-at-any-price know-it-alls, of the cow-eyed and the reformers, the yes-yes sighers and the no-no snarlers. In Germany The Sinner, abroad The German, I swung on a rickety see-saw, became a yo-yo, an aspen leaf, shivering from euphoric optimism and the need for fame to self-destructive depressions and floods of prissy tears.

"Don't speak German here," said Litvak as we arrived in France. "Why not?" I stuttered, "my French is miserable." Fräulein Weise's "Les nuages sont gris" was always torture because my "gris" emerged as "grease" and made her turn turkey-red flamingo-scarlet and start bellowing like a bull. "Les nuages sont gris" and "Je suis allemande" were the sum total of my knowledge of a language which, since it is spoken somewhere between the base of the nose and the edge of the upper lip, as opposed to the mumbling gullet-grumbles of Berlinese, was not for me. Litvak shot me a glance that would have transformed me into a frog if I had been a princess and the loops and rolls of films and photos went sliding across the screen of recollection, freezing at the scenes of Auschwitz.

"The hairdresser thought you were American," he said two days later, much happier, almost complimentary, making me into a centaur whose feet have been hidden with the help of an excellent couturier.

"So that's how one must live," I thought to myself as I observed how easily he dealt with severe concierges in plush hotels offering rooms like polo fields and bathrooms like gymnasiums, insolent maîtres d's in overfull restaurants, "Rien ne va plus" barkers in casinos, and tried to follow his example. Sacrificing sense of time and all resolutions, he spent whole nights at the baccarat table returning gray-faced with the rising sun and brooking no inquiry. He went to the seashore but never swam, to the mountains but never to ski, and in every town there was a casino. In captain's uniform in summer and ski outfit in winter he reviled all forms of sport and went from shop to shop in a buying mania until the next casino tragedy stopped him short. Where the tumult of the studio had relaxed him, leisure made him nervous; he would dictate and telephone, secretaries and messenger boys came and went, new trips became imperative the moment we had unpacked. The wonder of Europe, which I had only recently discovered, tarnished rapidly. I understood less and less the rhythm and standards of the life of luxury, felt bored stiff in the fashionable restaurants and bars, saw no thrill at meeting the same faces at every turn and rekindling yesterday's gossip. More and more it seemed to me that the proud halls of ancient Europe had been sold to the shieks of Hollywood. His sudden warmth and paternal interest would then compensate for many hours of severity, just as the unexpected congeniality of a person who tends to acrimony will often excite more attention than the friendliness of someone who is generally amiable.

The majority of the directors who attained fame at a

time when the film industry was the zenith of the entertainment business were permanently in danger of suffering from bloated self-esteem and lack of temperance. Not the intemperance of fantasy as a release from materialism, in the manner discussed by Salinger, but the sort that has to do with surface values and success. The splicing and welding of the most contrary professions in a studio demands a leader, an All-Seer who gathers and holds together the threads of the story, which is more often than not shot out of sequence; demands a man whose word is law and whose taste and *niveau* set the standard. Determining the daily lives of so many people may lead him to regard himself as a ruler, or even a creator, and will certainly present problems in his private life. As in no other profession is a film director able to regard, observe, sound out, and see through people. Actors' stage fright, which makes them vulnerable and childish, the agitation and change of character that take place when the camera rolls and penetrates their façades like an X ray makes for a lopsided relationship, as in an interview; the one judges, the other must allow judgment. But the actor is used to being observed and to guarding his own powers of observation; the observer often forgets that he too may be observed. This is exactly what a director reared on the old patriarchal system cannot abide. And although I had sought a mentor, I couldn't accept a demagogue, had no use for a round-the-clock director and he none for me. We got on each other's nerves and very soon thought fondly of each other only when we were apart. His earnest endeavor to teach me what to wear when, his hopes of persuading me to part company with baggy trousers, sweaters, and Marlene's summer coat— which I still stubbornly wore—and awakening my interest in fashion magazines was like a dog breeder's wanting to lace up his Afghan hound in a corset. My disregard for money and the "right" places made him so furious that he began to cite the virtues of my predecessors. Taking him at his word I became monosyllabic, obstinate, and gloomy. My excitement at hearing Beethoven's Ninth conducted by Furtwängler (we had arrived late; the Meister had shot first a threatening, then a thoughtful, then a forgiving glance and lifted his baton) was quashed with a sarcastic: "That truly stirred up the German Herz"—relegating Beethoven to Weltschmerz and Viennese pops. And then when a chauffeur in Cannes said, "I could tell you were German right away, I really love them—those were the days when we had a bit of law and order around here," the beam in his eye was lodged deeper and the incident was a model example of how one is often admired by the wrong people for the wrong reasons.

Paris for the first time: the Arc de Triomphe, approached from the Avenue de la Grande Armée in an open cabriolet in May. "Ein Glück, dass das heil geblieben ist" (Thank God that's remained intact), I said in German. At "heil" I thought of the photo of Hitler at the victory parade on the Champs Elysées, his knee raised as though he were about to begin a Tyrolean country dance. The profile over the steering wheel became sharper, called me to order, implied: I might have known you wouldn't stick to the agreement. Cussed out, I said, first murmuring, then gaining conviction: "German was also spoken in the years before Hitler. And Russian before Stalin." The first statement undermined my popularity but the second bordered on blasphemy. This was at a time when no victor would tolerate criticism or argument. "You were all delighted," he said, assessing three generations.

"Ja."

American films were running in the cinemas on the Champs Elysées. "When I come home on leave we'll go to the UFA-Palast," Martin had said, Martin my cycling chum, the one with the long black girl's eyelashes. We met on Sunday mornings fetching the milk, swung the battered pails, rattled the loose lids, pretended they were super gadgets, not something our parents had pushed into our paws saying, "Go get the milk and don't dawdle." Martin, with the watery blue slop in the pail, breath white with frost, said, "Been called up." "Your boy hasn't picked up his shoes," Step-father had said. She had pulled her scarf up over her face and her sobbing had been audible in spite of the lathes. Stepfather sent me over to the bar across the street: "Get her a stiff one." "Martin fell on his second day," she said, sitting on the stool in front of the sewing machine. The same night a cousin of mine had arrived; I knew him only from photographs. He was twenty-three and his hands shook like the old man's at the newspaper kiosk at the station. "Why are you in the air force?" Mother had asked him. "Had no choice. I've been flying Stukas for six months now." Two weeks later we got a postcard from his mother: "He crashed." That was all. Nearly all of them from the Treitschke School were dead, and everyone I had known in the Bernhardstrasse. Only Mucke was still there but he was five years younger than I. And Helmuth Weidke, he had bad lungs. His brother had been blown up in a tank near Kharkov, they couldn't even find his dog tags. We used to practice foxtrots and waltzes together in the Antoine dancing school on Kurfürstendamm. "Lift your feet up," the teacher always said, "you're supposed to be dancing, not polishing the floor, Herr Weidke."

From now on, whether at the race track or at parties, in a bistro or the Bois de Boulogne, everything when I arrived was under occupation by memories. They hovered over Longchamps and summer hats and Balmain's best and showed me Biesenthal and old nags pulling carts; they sat in the Méditerranée by soft lights and tender fish and brought back the taste of the first soup in the camp, set lice and rats scurrying about Maxim's red plush, settled Russian T-4 tanks in front of the Louvre and the Tuileries, laid land mines at the entrance of night clubs. Between visions I heard drunken chats about war and victory and the liberation of Paris; war became safari, men became heroes, in a world where the man has problems and the woman tantrums; they told stories of women and other men's wives, all blessed with skin like alabaster, all reacting in the same accommodating fashion to the perfume and nylons they'd brought back from the front, the Spanish Civil War was only just over and Hamburg still one great big bonfire, the bombs for Dresden were loaded once more, Hiroshima seemed to have no great appeal and Korea was hardly worth mentioning; death was here a man of action, prairie pioneer, tomahawks, cowboys and Indians. And I also got to know the snobbish liberals who professed to know exactly how workers should live without ever having asked them, behaving aloofly rather than sociably in their presence, and choosing the leftover aristocracy and millionaire social whirl as topics of conversation more often than factory strikes or union deadlocks. And up would pop the picture of Stepfather, bony and smeared with glue, lacquer under his fingernails, cutting leather with a short curved knife and saying, "I can judge a man by his shoes." I was sure that he wouldn't have welcomed life under these salon Communists.

EIGHTEEN

"May I speak to you a moment, Mr. Albers?"

"Come in, little one." Hans Albers, one of the biggest stars in the history of German movies, stood in his undershirt, baggy trousers, slippers, and truck driver's cap swizzling his champagne with his finger. "How can old Hans be of service?"

We had been shooting Erich Pommer's *Night on the Road* for some ten days.

"Mr. Pommer says it's for you to decide."

He went to the door and shouted down the corridor, "Sukrow, open another bottle." Sukrow, his dresser, shot in with an already fizzing bottle as though he'd been awaiting the call for days now. "What decision?" Albers said.

"We started shooting four weeks late and we've got another six weeks to go but I signed to do a film with Tyrone Power in Hollywood that begins in three weeks' time and if I'm not there I'll have to pay damages for breach of contract and I don't have the money."

"So you want to shoot day and night, eh? What does the director say?"

"He's willing."

"You know what? There was an actor at the little provincial theater where I started out—you weren't even a twinkle in your father's eye then—and he was a far better actor than I. But he hadn't been kissed in the cradle, he had no spark, and that's why I became a star and he didn't." He emptied his glass and pierced a cigar with a pair of nail scissors. "You've got it all before you, and I'll soon have it all behind me."

After two weeks we had eyes like elderly bull-terriers', make-up slid off our burning skin the moment it was applied, the director had regained his wartime girth, Venda Vich, the Bohemian cameraman, was having difficulties with the few scraps of German he had once called his own, and I was suffering from stomach catarrh. Only Albers seemed unchanged. We had left until the last night one dangerous scene, in which I had to fall from a moving truck and be rewarded for my pains by a box on the ears from Albers. He was very worried about hurting me, drank another cognac to steady his nerves, and forgot to take off his signet ring. I arrived at the airport and, somewhat later, the Fox studio punctually but with a black eye and a knee the size of a pumpkin and promptly fell asleep in my canvas chair on the set of *Diplomatic Courier*. Henry Hathaway, the director, and my costar Tyrone Power shook me to my senses and explained considerately that I must take a seat in a studio-built railway compartment and exchange a few lines of dialogue with Power. Hathaway, a stickler for realism, was convinced that European trains sway and rattle more than the domestic ones and had commanded several workers to shake the mock carriage during the take; he took, they shook, and two large suitcases flew from the luggage rack knocking me cold; shooting was held up for some days.

Hollywood 1951 had changed considerably in the fourteen months I'd been absent. A Senator McCarthy had succeeded in placing the whole community under suspicion of harboring Communist ideals; authors, directors, and actors were forced to bare their political pasts in front of a committee and those found guity of leftist tendencies were ordered to name comrades still at large. Suspicion aroused by "the Germans" was now greatly alleviated and redirected at the more suspect Communists, and I was cross-examined sotto voce by reporters about the iniquitous treatment of the poor Berliners at the hands of the Bolshevik hordes in '45, and about *The Sinner*. The iron front of the women's clubs loomed behind every question about the latter and before I realized what was happening I found myself back under the headings of "femme fatale" and "sophisticated." The two fire-breathing archangels Louella Parsons and Hedda Hopper, whose daily newspaper columns on Hollywood's private life enjoyed nationwide circulation, informed Fox that they were ready to interview. Although they were deadly enemies they saw eye to eye on one point: people who worked in the film industry had better conform to their own unimpeachable standards of morality or reckon with printed fire and brimstone. They had boost-

ed a number of careers and ruined many others and their
most recent success at that time was Ingrid Bergman, who,
thanks to their perseverance, had been forced to leave the
U.S.A. because she fell in love and bore a child out of wedlock. Not to speak of the less prominent victims, who were
legion; they were already on the train bound for Hades before their name could become a name.

Louella reclined on a floral couch with her heavily ringed
hands folded and would have made a perfect model for the
Queen Mother at Toad Hall. With her head held regally to
one side, her questions stepped in sympathy and understanding, she quickly led her wary audience to believe in
mistaken identity or malicious gossip, and so loosened their
tongues:

"My dear, how nice to see you. I hear you're so talented,
dear sweet Tyrone told me about you in the most glowing
terms—there's nothing going on between the two of you, is
there now?" She waved a finger back and forth as though
I'd got my nursery rhymes mixed up.

"No," I said, conscience clear.

"Well well, all right, I'll soon find out about it if there is,
nobody can hide the truth from me. You know that dear
Tyrone's married, don't you?"

"Yes."

"Yes, well I often worry about him, not sure that dear
Linda's quite right for him. Poor Lana Turner was so upset
when he married dear Linda." They were all either "dear"
or "poor" and she kept me on tenterhooks wondering
which she would apply to me or whether she had another
adjective up her sleeve which would qualify me for the
one-way ticket to purgatory. "But then I hear you were
very friendly with Anatole Litvak?"

"Yes."

"And is my information correct that you're still married?"

"Yes."

"Well how am I to understand that?" Inquisition glit-
tered through Grandma's comfiness.

"The one had nothing to do with the other."

"Ah ha, I see. And don't you want to get married
again?"

"No."

"Oh, so you don't want to have babies?"

"Yes."

"And how do you think you're going to have babies if you're not married?"

"That's true."

"You see?—and now tell me about the scandal. I hear you were naked?" ("Don't be flippant and always count to ten before you answer," Tyrone had said.) "How long did the nude scenes take—you're not going to tell me the crew was present?"

"The scenes took several days and the automatic camera has yet to be invented." I had a clear vision of Tyrone throwing up his hands and told myself don't lose your nerve, you've still a contract with Pommer.

"Oh, I'd no idea you could be so witty," she said, just as I was wondering whether to go by boat or plane. "You're very like Marlene Dietrich, don't you think? Of course she comes from Germany too."

"All Germans don't look alike and Miss Dietrich is more beautiful than I am."

This returned me to favor. "Modesty is a precious virtue, my dear." ("Don't worry about it," Tyrone had added, "let her write what she wants as long as she spells your name right—Hopper's much worse.")

Hedda Hopper wore hats like cartwheels and had been an actress. Five years later, when I was playing on Broadway, she came to New York for a prize-giving and delivered a despicable rabble-rousing speech inciting her audience to smoke out the ever-present Communists and purge the theater of its current decadence. Despicable speech, despicable audience that listened intently. The witches Hopper and Parsons both died before *Hair* and *Oh! Calcutta!*, the Beatles and the Rolling Stones, saving themselves much chagrin.

The sleepy-looking girl with the transparent plastic shower cap over her white-blond hair and a thick layer of cream on her pale face sits down beside me. She glances up at the peeved hairdresser with wide troubled eyes. "I'm late again, aren't I?" she whispers and leans back under the hand spray. She digs around in a faded beach bag and takes out a sandwich, a pillbox, a book. She smiles at my reflection in the mirror. "Hi, my name's Marilyn Monroe, what's yours?"

"Hildegarde Neff." I still stumble over the "Neff," can't get used to it, have no sense of belonging to it, feel confronted with defeat each time I hear it; one can make one name famous, not two.

"You're the new girl from Germany, aren't you?" The big blue eyes stare at me unwaveringly, blank surprised admiring unenvious, overestimating other people. Face of a child. Grew up among Quakers, or in the gardener's cottage, watched the gentry's carriages sweep up the drive to the castle. "I'm reading Rilke," she says, pointing at the book. "It's the first one of his I've read. Can you tell me about him? When was he born?"

Thankful for my emigrant tutors I say, "Same year as Thomas Mann, 1875."

"Who's Thomas Mann? Could I read him? Could you get me some of his books? How long's your schedule this time?"

"About four weeks."

"So we'll see each other mornings, yeah?" She gets up and scuffs over to the make-up room in old sandals, a child with short legs and a fat bottom.

One and a half hours later I bump into a girl in the corridor; only the eyes are still recognizable. She seems to have grown with the make-up, the legs seem longer, the body more willowy, the face glows as if lit by candles. "Till tomorrow and thanks again," the little voice whispers. That same evening there's a gala; awards are announced, new discoveries introduced. Marilyn Monroe and I are placed at the same table. She's wearing a red dress that's too tight for her, I've seen it before, in the Fox wardrobe. It isn't becoming to her and although it's too tight it looks like one of Mum's old ones dug out of mothballs with lipstick and rouge it'll look swell. Eyes half closed, mouth half open, hands tremble a little. One glass too many, child's first go at the punch. The photographers hold their cameras up high, flash into her cleavage. She leans and stretches, turns and smiles, is willing, offers herself to the lenses. Someone bends forward and whispers into her ear. "No, please," she says, "I can't." The trembling hand knocks over a glass. Finally she stands up, the people snigger, the tight skirt presses her knees together, she trips to the microphone, the walk is absurd and she's got miles to go, they stare at the dress, wait for it to burst and liberate the bosom, the belly, the bottom. The master of ceremonies roars: "Marilyn Monroe!" Great gag, hell of a joke, they chuckle as she steadies herself on the mike stand, closes her eyes, leaves a long pause in which one hears her amplified breathing, short, panting, obscene. "Hi," she whispers and starts the trip back. A man beside me says, "She's so dumb it's not true."

"She's frightened," I say.

"She's giving us the star nonsense already, comes to the studio late every morning."

"You've acted in the theater, haven't you?" she asks one morning.

"Yes."

"I'd love to act on the stage but I'm afraid, I'm afraid of the people, know what I mean?"

"We're waiting, Marilyn," an assistant calls.

"Oh please, my hair's not done yet, and my make-up and the dress . . . it'll take just a few seconds."

"Come on now."

She turns to me and says, "Till tomorrow, yeah?"

The camera loved her. The camera registered the honesty, candor and naiveté which disarmed her audiences and made her a star after a few appearances in mostly bad films. It registered the naiveté which later destroyed her. There exists an absurd and grave misunderstanding of the acting profession in that every Joe Doakes who knows he's a good liar believes he would make a good actor. The great film stars, consciously or unconsciously, used each part as a pretext for expressing their own particular truth. They raped the characters, requisitioned them, and remained, whether as Camille or Anna Karenina, Garbo—or as a band-singer, dancer, or secretary, Monroe. They reached the people with their strength or vulnerability, with the extraordinary quality of their truth. They were the *monstres sacrés*, the sacred cows, the indomitables whom no make-up, costume, or character could change and whose mystery was wrapped in an incorruptibility which only the camera was capable of measuring and which would have been lost on a stage. They were more reliant than other actors on their directors, on the man who guided and yet served their personalities, effacing himself, like Garbo's Maurice Stiller or Dietrich's Josef von Sternberg. Stars no longer exist because the director no longer exists in a supporting capacity; he has himself become the star, his style unmistakable and his performers interchangeable, as likely as not green unknowns.

I have worked with great actors and with actors who

thought they were great; with fanatical and impassioned actors, with flaccid ones and ones who had slowed with the years; with actors who churned out their evening performances and only took first nights seriously, and with actors who died every night. With actors who had seemed weak during the take but were then breathtaking on the screen, and vice versa, with precision actors who understood their trade as thoroughly as the cutter or cameraman, and with a few who regarded the job as an extension of the psychiatrist's couch or the political forum. But it was not my fortune to work with many stars, stars equipped with personalities that took the audience by the scruff of the neck and owed nothing to publicity and image build-ups. Whether to be a star in the almost outdated sense is still worth striving for I don't know. Many who had the gift went under in the disrupted industry, the tragicomic distributor dictatorship, in nitwitted supporting roles and money troubles.

A good stage actor is not necessarily a good film actor, nor is the reverse any more likely; very seldom is an actor both. A number of actors who have become world-famous in recent years appear to have been trained in gymnasiums rather than drama schools and tend to be ineffectual and soporific in scenes which do not call for physical prowess. Cinematic bloodbaths and horror orgies are just as uniform as cinematic acts of copulation. The nipples and thigh measurements of the interesting players hardly differ from those of the uninteresting ones; the thrusts and joggings of sexual coupling make no great demands on acting talent and star quality can weave no spell in close-ups of bunched buttocks, heaving bosoms, and hairy legs. The love scene becomes a gymnastic display and both types of film seem to want to convey one message: that in bed and violence people are pretty much alike. And Else Bongers' "Talent is a stipulation, it's uninteresting; the question must be: What else has he got?" takes on today a meaning quite different from what she originally intended. Acting schools, whether bad or indifferent, whether of the type which has just hit on Stanislavski or the other dedicated to developing sonorous voices, are springboards at best. The lunacy which festered on Broadway during the fifties and insisted that real artistry can blossom only in an atmosphere of soul-searching crotch-scratching introspection has died out. One recognized the disciples of this dogma by the fact that the psychological intricacies they had found in the depths of the character they were portraying invariably outweighed the importance of the lines (which had been designed by the author to let the public in on the secret too), causing them either to mumble or forget them completely. But this never seemed to bother them, and their genius no doubt sparkled within a two-foot radius.

In Europe at this time there were actors who turned the studio into a classroom. Historical films were particularly suited to their lectures. I once played with such a student prince. In a scene where a door was to be opened and then closed again, nothing else, he explained to the assembled crew that at just this moment in history the Prussians had carried the day at Langensalza and Leuthen, that Nymphenburg had started producing porcelain, that Mirabeau and Voltaire had made the following statements and that without the Polish wars of inheritance world events would have taken a quite different course and for this reason the door must be opened like this and not like that. These nuances did not come across on the screen. At the same period I met an actress who told me that the way she played the developing stages of her parts must be determined by the ending. The laughter this provoked classified me as a philistine but I was loath to explain that Else Bongers had once commented about my Gretchen in *Faust:* "If you play the Easter scene as though you were already in jail Heinrich would say to himself, 'Hands off, mate, she must have the clap' and the play would be over." Still other actors relied on emotion and felt they were giving their best in scenes charged with stress only if they demolished the set; they scoffed at the idea of expressing passion within the choreographic corset of the director's requests. But the balance was in my favor and with most of my costars I was more than fortunate: with Oskar Werner in *Decision Before Dawn*, with Hardy Krüger in a less successful film, with Söhnker, James Mason, Viktor de Kowa, O. E. Hasse, Gert Fröbe, Daniel Gelin, Don Ameche, and Tyrone Power.

The Cardinal's distant relative was even more agitated than usual. He paced up and down between the protruding table and the chair legs in my tiny stage dressing room, three yards up, three yards down. "As sure as my name's Frings," he panted, "this has never happened! Zanuck wrote a letter saying that it had been worth it to change the

shooting schedule and wait for Hilde. And something else
—she was supposed to be nominated for an Oscar for *Decision Before Dawn*." He looked about him as though he'd
just triumphed through a knockout.

"What do you mean 'supposed to'?" Tyrone asked.

"Well, use your head, the war's only been over six years
and whether she's good or not she is a Kraut, after all."

Tyrone fiddled with the record player and put on the
record he played every morning in the studio. "Enjoy yourself, it's later than you think," blared out above the shouts
of the workers.

"But they've got another good idea, they're gonna im-
mortalize her in front of Graumann's Chinese, feet and
hands. And they've come up with a new film—*The Snows
of Kilimanjaro,* the Hemingway story, with Peck. You've
gotta play a countess, give you a chance to get away from
the refugee rags for once, and she has to sing, too."

"I can't sing."

"Then you'll learn—by the way, is that your car outside,
the one with no fenders?"

"Yes."

"What happened this time?"

"What do you think happened, she can't drive, that's
all," said Tyrone. ("When you turn the ignition key, remember you are releasing the safety catch of a loaded machine gun," my driving instructor had said.) "There's no
holding her now, she'll be a world star—I'll throw a party
for you Saturday night," he added and arranged his face
into a bristling smile as he turned to a group of elderly ladies who had won some sort of contest awarding them a
whole day with their favorite star.

Marlene Dietrich and the French actor Jean-Pierre Au-
mont sat doubled over with their hands raised protectively
to their faces. "It's awful," groaned Jean-Pierre.

"I've never been so frightened in my whole life," Marlene breathed as we came to a stop on the parking lot.

"I had the brakes checked especially for you."

"You'll take taxis from now on," she said, paler than
ever.

Tyrone and Linda stood beside their Roman-style swimming pool, the fairest of a fair gathering. They represented
the Hollywood of the rich, famous, and lavishly frivolous
and their guests could have been selected from the latest

film calendar. Nothing indicated that the industry was in crisis, that the age of long-term contracts was at an end, that Tyrone and Linda would shortly be divorced; no one who knew him could know that Tyrone's daily reveille, "It's later than you think," was to become macabre truth in a few years.

"Garfield's finished," I heard someone say sadly. John Garfield was one of Hollywood's best actors, his aggressive melancholy face unforgettable; he had come from Broadway, from the group run by the director Elia Kazan. Marlene glanced first over her left shoulder, then over her right and said, "He refused to give names . . ." She caught her breath and added loudly. "We're all whispering as though we were living under Hitler." Her remark was lost in the rumba music and laughter, in the rumble of approaching cars.

"This is Mr. Zanuck's secretary. Mr. and Mrs. Zanuck would be delighted to have you spend the weekend with them at their residence in Palm Springs. Eight o'clock tonight for dinner."

"But I'll never make it," I said, but she'd already hung up.

Tyrone was sitting beside me on a canvas studio chair and said, "Of course you will, that's no invitation, it's an order and all Hollywood'll envy you."

Palm Springs. desert oasis, health resort, and several hours by car from Hollywood, was still nowhere in sight by eight o'clock. I have been night-blind since the end of the war, so I hung onto the taillights of another car which seemed to be heading in the same direction. After a further hour it suddenly stopped in the middle of the desert. The driver got out, scowled at me furiously and disappeared behind a yucca tree. It seemed an inappropriate moment to ask him the way so I pressed on along desert tracks in the darkness and eventually found a filling station with a friendly attendant and a little while later the house. The host was already sitting over coffee and liqueurs with his guests but the warmth of his welcome soon dispelled my anxiety and I thankfully sipped the whiskey he offered. He resumed the monologue which my arrival had apparently interrupted and I tried to catch the rhythm of the nods and grunts of agreement from the others. With a jolt we suddenly realized that he'd paused. Looking up I found his face within inches of mine, front teeth locked around a cigar, sparks flying: "You know what Communism means?"

"What?"

"Communism!"

"No," I said.

"Sure you do, you suffered at the hands of Communism."

"Well no, that was war . . ."

"War or not, the Communists are the enemies of civilization, of our free country." His face appeared to melt shrivel, only the cigar stayed whole, shrunken head-hunter head, abracadabra—gone. "I'd like to see people like Garfield rotting of cancer in jail," the grotesque head says. "And every one of my friends here tonight'll agree with me. Whaddaya say?" I hear again. His wife stood up and clapped her hands. "Time for our little game!" she said gaily.

"C."

"Animal, vegetable or mineral?"—quiz terror, Fräulein Weise crowing, "Give up, you don't know."

At midnight they all went to their bedrooms and at seven in the morning a masseur came and pummeled my back; as I turned over the elderly gentleman closed his eyes and said, "I'm only allowed to massage ladies' backs, otherwise I'll lose my license."

Mr. Zanuck was treading water in the middle of his pool, chewing a sodden cigar. "Hi, sleep well?" he called out, his face back to its normal size. "You don't need to drive back tonight, I got my plane here; we can leave in the morning an' I'll have a driver bring your car."

"Thank you, Mr. Zanuck."

"She's got good legs," he shouted to his wife, who was reading a newspaper. She looked up, said "Yes," and went on reading. "The voice coach says you can sing. You're gonna get two or three Cole Porter songs." He seemed happy to tell me the good news. He bobbed his head up and down, a sleek, contented, friendly sea lion. Tilting his cigar upwards, leaving a trail of ashes behind him, he swam to the side of the pool.

Four months later I flew to New York. I had made three films and imprinted my hand and shoe sizes in cement at Graumann's Chinese Theater, had gotten to know stars and clubs and parties, was divorced.

One forgets the sea that lives off Hollywood's shores, that, gray like a northern November day, gently slaps old palaces in Santa Monica and gurgles across the broad sands of Malibu. A beach without basket chairs or sand castles. Unloved beach, unloved sea, odorless. "If you're prone to homesickness, you shouldn't come here," Jean-Pierre had said. He made films at MGM and lived for a girl who was his daughter and looked like the wife he had lost some months before. Often in the evenings after shooting we would tour Hollywood's "must" parties together, he desperate, I scatterbrained.

During the day I soaked in the chlorinated water of a diving school run by a Tarzan type with the patience of a lamb, for Hemingway's novel called for me to glide up like a mermaid from under a sailboat and confuse the hero sitting there pondering war and justice. Color cameras tracked after me on cranes, faltered, lost sight of the siren, found her again almost choking, hanging on to the rudder for dear life—everyone confused but the hero. Or I practiced Cole Porter's evergreen "Just one of those things" and "You do something to me" in the coach's bungalow for hours and days on end until the morning when I was supposed to enter in a gold-yellow evening dress waggling a yard-long cigarette holder and coo them into Gregory Peck's ear.

They had accepted me in the assured, accent-free Hollywood, honored me with candlelit dinners and English silver in Merle Oberon's house, Charlie Chaplin acting out his anecdotes from coffee until the small hours; with balls under red and white awnings on balmy nights, orchestra hidden away among the bushes; with evenings of chamber music at the author Harry Kurnitz's, Ava Gardner lying on the carpet with her shoes in her hand, floored by the chamber music; cocktails with Gary Cooper's cool estranged wife, Cooper present, a shy, reserved, ever-surprised guest; a party thrown by one of the leading agents, his agency like a department store: first floor leading men, second floor leading ladies, top floor newcomers and restaurant. His house amid hills and artificial waterfalls, Klee and Miró in the lobby, Montgomery Clift standing beside them staring into his glass for five hours together, standing staring drinking, Judy Garland brushing hair from her eyes, looking, searching, going from room to room, Joan Crawford, always in white, always ready to parry stares

with the camera, delighted till ten, then off to bed; an
American actress with an Italian husband: "Beats me why
he's always going on about Rome—we got churches too,
ain't we?" A producer invites me to a party, table for two
at the pool. other guests can't make it, Neff beats a hasty
retreat; host shows the way to the exit, bedroom with bed
like a football field: "Why not? It's healthy." Farewell
party at Max's. his garage as full as a bunker, Gary Cooper's sauerkraut sliding from his plate into Merle Oberon's
silver lamé, hanging there between her breasts; Marlene in
long velvet at the upright. Friedrich Holländer burrowing
in the keys, thoughtfully blissfully whispering the words as
she sighs, "Falling in love again." Tyrone in frilled shirt,
prettier gayer than any movie poster. Carroll Righter's soft
warning, "I'd advise you to take care of your salaries. And
as soon as the film in Europe is finished you should come
back."

Then ten days of New York. Sardi's, "21," premières,
photo-sessions, interviews watched over by Fox.

In the hotel lobby an Italian director is waiting, offers me
a film. Beside him a chain smoker with a suit like an unmade bed. "Name's Garfield," he mutters, "saw you in *Decision Before Dawn.* Liked it."

The sudden smile retreats, creeps behind clouds of
smoke and a glass of gin-and-tonic. The director leaves.
Garfield stays. "You doing anything? I'd like to talk.
Haven't worked for a while, feel alone. You know what's
going on here?"

"Yes."

"It's not good to be seen with me."

("What are they afraid of?" I'd asked Jean-Pierre as
many people decided to evade McCarthy's firing squad and
left Hollywood to await developments. Jean-Pierre, who
had been in the Resistance, had shrugged his shoulders and
said, "Beginners.")

Garfield's deep-set eyes over the flame of a match: "How
long you staying?"

"I'm flying to Germany tomorrow morning."

"I'd like to go along. I don't have a passport . . ."

"To Germany?"

"You still got a lot of Nazis? I'm a Jew."

"Don't know, they're quiet for the moment."

"Ours are deafening, it evens things out. Can't you stay
in New York a few days?"

"No."

"Come on, let's have a drink."

"Skouras is throwing a party for me at nine at '21.'"

He rubs his stubbled chin. "You're on the way up, eh? How long you have to listen to his bullshit?"

"Why don't you come along?"

"Me? I'd love to see their faces."

"What about after?"

"I'll call you, we'll meet someplace. I gotta talk."

Champagne caviar smoked salmon white wine red wine fish meat cognac. Skouras gets to his feet. Oxlike package, voice like a child's rattle. "We have a great actress with us tonight, gonna make a great career in our great land. I'm a little Greek, started with nothing in this great country and look at me now." He plops back onto his chair, tears in his eyes. The waiter comes and whispers, "Urgent call."

"Can you get away? I feel like the ceiling's coming down around my ears."

"It'll take one or two hours."

"Jesus. O.K., I'll call back."

"If you've got a friend have him come over," Skouras shouts and winks.

Garfield's voice is thick at one o'clock: "I have to see you, gotta talk, walk, speak. Hurry it up."

"Another hour."

I call him at two. There's a click but nobody answers; another click: disconnected. I try again, let it ring for several minutes. The Pan Am flight leaves for London at seven. I write him a note but I have no address, only the telephone number. I dail again. No answer. The plane flies via Boston, I buy a morning paper. The headline: "John Garfield dead! The well-known actor was found this morning in his apartment . . ."

Hubmann the photographer is standing in the closet of my suite at the George V. "Why don't you knock? I'm changing film."

"How am I to know which closet you're using?"

He glares and shuts the door from the inside.

Wherever I have gone in the past weeks Hubmann's been there too; he's working for a German magazine which is running a series of six cover stories and is eager to report on my meeting with Erich von Stroheim.

First comes a bouquet of flowers, then a phone call, then

his wife, then himself. The monocle absent yet tangible, back straight as a die, as though on horseback, civilian uniform impeccable, each soft word a command. The corner of the mouth on the monocle side arches ironically; "So this is my Alraune," he says, rolling the *r*, letting it rumble deliciously into "aune." We sit down on the balcony; Hubmann does his routine. "Are you free this afternoon? I'd like to show you one of my films," he says. The projection room in the Paris museum smells musty and damp, like a boathouse in winter. He slaps down the seat of his chair, waits until his wife and I are seated, looks down the empty theater and calls, "You may begin." The title *Greed* pops up palely on the screen. From then on I forget that it's a silent film, that the frame wobbles and jerks for four hours. As the lights go up he takes a cigarette from a case, taps it against the lid, taps and taps as though it were responsible for something that is irking him. "You have just seen the shortened version," he grates, "they forced me to cut: The première in New York ran twenty-four hours." The projectionist whistles and bangs lids onto tins of film. "Why don't you direct any more?" I ask. "Why, why?" The eyes bunch as though each were holding a monocle. "Because I had a fight. With MGM. With Louis B. Mayer. One doesn't have fights with Louis B. Mayer. One must bow to the demands of the industry." He said "bow" as though he were presenting them with his bare behind. "Bow," he repeated and marched out of the projection tomb into the warm summer evening.

"Why did the production cast that old imperial relic for the part?" a young journalist asks on the first day of shooting in Munich. "I looked him up in the archive, born in Austria, played military officers en masse."

Jupp Paschke mutters, "Better luck next time," and Ilse Müller hisses streams of excruciating Saxon without ever moving her lips. Ilse, Jupp, and I go from one studio to another, Jupp makes up, Ilse dresses. Only England and America forbid them to accompany me: union rules. We meet at five in the morning, know each other's waking and somnambulistic moods intimately, make ourselves understood with half-sentences and scraps of jargon. Ilse used to dance in the ballet at the Berlin Scala and can still do splits with perfectly straight knees. Now she drinks heavily and her beautiful, high-cheekboned face is puffed. She mothers me like a concerned hen but when I eat bread dipped in linseed oil on an empty stomach at breakfast, as Grandfather had always done, she turns her back on me and tussles with her heaving nausea, saying, "Only Polacks have guts like crocodiles—but mark my words, that stuff'll make you fat." In the evenings she lays cards, sweeps them angrily aside and says, "Off to bed now, tomorrow's another day." The young worker she lives with deceives her. One morning a very pregnant girl turns up bawling, "You've got to help me, your friend did this!"

"There are certain limits," snorts Ilse and pours herself another schnapps.

Alraune, or *Mandragore,* as it was called in English, and the French film *La fête d'Henriette* begin simultaneously. I shoot from Monday to Thursday in Munich, from Friday to Sunday in Paris. The director Julien Duvivier presents me to the press: "First German in a Paris studio since the war." An actress curtsies tó me and giggles something I only half understand, something about "vedette Allemande" and how happy they all are to have the Germans back. Champagne is served and Duvivier translates the more harmless and polite questions for me and ignores the others; I think I hear a "Boche" from the rear but they finally back down in the face of Duvivier's *noblesse,* he sips at a cup of tea and complains of *crise de foie,* then we all go home.

We start filming in the Médrano circus. Duvivier and I are leaning against some wooden bars, smoking and waiting for the lights to be set for the next scene. I am dressed for the part of a bareback circus rider, gold leotard and laced-up boots. Duvivier more like a director of savings banks than films in his gray suit and somber tie. The stallion plods in, eyes us, paws the ground, eases its bowels. I feel hot air blowing passionately down my naked back. "Keep calm," Duvivier murmurs, "we're leaning against the tiger's cage." Out of the corner of my left eye I see its jade-colored right one sparkling among gay stripes, something that feels like wire wool scrubs my back, the wooden bars between us are bending like spaghetti. I launch myself, land in the stallion droppings, the nag neighs and starts to climb a ladder. Duvivier takes the stub of his cigarette from his holder, inserts a fresh one, changes the filter, clicks his lighter, moves away from the cage without looking at the tiger, comes over to where I'm lying and says, "You're still too young to be this nervous."

When I speak French his cheek twitches as though he
had trigeminal neuralgia but he's gentle and patient and on
the last day he embraces me and says words of praise.
When both films are over another one starts. During lunch
breaks I read manuscripts which have been recommended
by the agents, read on trains and planes. I let them influence me, decide for me, welcome their excited suggestions
with relief. I am reckless, negligent, have no time to be otherwise. I work with a series of illustrious directors on a
series of lackluster films which nevertheless often show lus-
trous box-office receipts for their shareholders, among
whom I unfortunately do not belong. My salary is paid into
a blocked account in Frankfurt, since foreigners are still
not allowed to spend cash in Germany; from there it is
transferred to Mr. Brom, an agent in California. He and
other managers attend to things from there, saying, "Leave
it to us, you need all your energy for your work."

Film fans barricade every hotel door and squeal the moment they see me. They storm the lobbies with drawn fountain pens, shatter windowpanes, are grateful for every button or lock of hair they can get. I visit towns I have never
been to before and am greeted by everyone. I receive prizes
and am driven through streets in open cars like a victorious
general; I make my first phonograph records, synchronize
the German films into English and vice versa, contests are
organized to find Knef's double, girls wear my hair style,
fetishists steal my underwear from hotel and dressing
rooms, a New York model agency names me "The woman
who best represents Europe in the U.S.A." and my friends
from the German press nail me with a home-wrecking *af-
faire* with Gregory Peck whom I last saw while working on
Kilimanjaro and then only at times prescribed by the script.
On days when I am not shooting I travel from première to
première accompanied by Karl Klär, a film publicity manager. Karl has asthma, is nearsighted and much too intelligent for the job. When the film is over we climb onto the
stage; Karl stays behind the curtain and when I ask him,
"Where the hell are we?" he answers, "Say 'in your lovely
town,' that's near enough."

"I'm so happy to be able to visit your lovely town . . ."
After my speech the theater owner pours German champagne, kisses my hand, and says, "Bet you've no idea how
old I am," stroking his middle lovingly. "Always knock ten
years off your estimate, then he'll keep the film running,"

says Karl. When Karl and I leave the theater the doors are hastily locked behind us, leaving us at the mercy of the mob. One evening the charge is so vigorous that Karl is shot up into the air like a champagne cork; he finds a foothold on a first-floor balcony and dangles there minus his glasses and one trouser leg bleating "Help " Three stalwarts link hands to protect me from the fountain-pen stilettos, a gnome ducks up from under their outstreched arms, opens his trench coat which is all he's got on and whines, "Please touch it just once, it's my birthday." Karl falls from the balcony and breaks his foot, continues the journey in plaster.

Six weeks later I'm in the hospital. "You're lucky you landed here." says a young doctor who finds each vein at first jab, "I'm an expert on nervous disorders." After eight days I'm well again. "I have to stay in this dump," he whispers as I'm leaving, "I was in the SS. Guinea pigs are no substitute, you mark my words, medical science'll bear me out one day." He waves and smiles, calls after me, "and don't forget to take your drops."

February 1953

Location work for an English film, *The Man Between,* directed by Carol Reed, begins in Berlin. Ruins have become a popular backdrop for foreign companies, whereas German productions avoid them avidly; they prefer to set their tales in cozy woods and hamlets, or in the villa of a consul/surgeon/conductor who is charitably involved in delicate problems of human nature and apparently missed out on the war with all those candlelit home concerts.

Sir Carol, raised to knighthood by his sovereign, looks like someone who has ripped his trousers and shirt from a neatly packed suitcase, put them on in a trice, and torn off without his breakfast; moist hair and traces of toothpaste underline this impression. He walks the way a shark swims, his hands invariably raised as though he were about to catch a ball. When he thinks he rubs his forehead briefly with a cocked thumb. He drinks gin and is never drunk, eats seldom and without interest, sleeps only if he must.

At work he takes his time. The film lasts five months. On the first day we are shooting in the ruins of the Lützow riverbank. He has me get out of a taxi and walk up to a lonely house fifty-eight times. After the fortieth take he calls out, "Are you cold?"

"No."

"Are you tired?"

"No."

After the fifty-eighth he walks up to me, grins and says, "All right, you win." From then on we are friends; I had stood his test. We walk down the Kurfürstendamm that evening: hot-dog stands in place of bomb sites, feeble neon signs, night clubs, pathetic window displays, jewelry, clothes, flowers. In four of the five cinemas my films are running. He looks at the posters, shoves his hands into the pockets of his flapping overcoat and says, "Even if they were all good it's a bit much."

Mother looks about her in the hotel room. I follow her gaze and only then see what's going on: Ilse Müller has balanced a board between two chair backs and is ironing a dress I wear in the film, Jupp Paschke is cleaning his make-up case, a record is playing, the agent is telephoning, two chambermaids are waiting for an autograph, Hubmann is still taking pictures, an English assistant brings tomorrow's schedule, a doctor from the insurance company writes a prescription. Mother says softly, "You can't go on living in this madhouse." The agent puts down the receiver. "That's something mothers don't understand—she's a world star." She beams broadly. Mother's eyes assess a world star's world. Wallpaper flowered and spattered, shoddy bed and cupboard, window overlooking the kitchen, used make-up tissues between glasses and jugs. "Come down to the Bernhardstrasse if you get a moment, we can talk there." An hour later there's a press conference. The crowd chants "Hilde Hilde" in front of the hotel, Sir Carol, James Mason, and I grin at the flashbulbs, I translate questions and answers. The reporters are friendly to me, even those who have to remind me that we've met before, four years ago when I was last in Berlin.

Else Bongers is waiting in my room, sitting quietly and smoking. I rush over to her, gush like a waterfall. "Sit down, take a deep breath, breathe out again," she says. The door bursts open, the agent comes in with several film people prattling ecstatically. "Throw them all out. I have to talk to you."

Her lighter clicks in the sudden stillness. She looks at me as one looks at a photograph. "This can't go on," she says, "you've become shallow, completely changed, it's high time you remembered who you are." Her voice is dull, coated, the blue eyes glint sadly. She gets up, closes a closet door, turns around. "Since when are you nice?" she asks, cracking the "nice" around my ears. There's the aggression again, the clarity. "Since when are you ingratiating? Does everyone who comes through that door get fed and entertained? Since when do you care about praise or criticism? What has happened?" She paces beside the bed, the weak lamp lights her face. It is still gaunt, sunken postwar cheeks among prosperous Wirtschaftswunder jowls. "Since that day in Zehlendorf, in the American hotel, when you were caught between Hollywood's cold shoulder and the Germans' delight at your flop, you've been selling yourself. You were never hectic. During the war when the other girls were sighing, 'Who knows how long we've still got' and hopping into bed at the drop of a hat, you didn't take part. Have you eaten?"

"At noon, yes."

She picks up the phone and orders.

"Aren't you hungry?"

She waves her hand sharply. "I didn't come here to eat."

She takes a full ashtray and tips the ends into the toilet, washes it and returns it to the table half full of water. "What can you call your own? I don't want to see you having to live as I do one day. And we won't go into the fact that you have never written or been in touch at all. You know when you're on the wrong track." She pushes her hair back. A lot of gray among the titian. "Child, you don't need this circus. Why are you running from film to film? Who told you you have to live like this?"

A waiter brings chicken soup. She opens the window and looks down into the yard, waits until he's gone. "Eat," she says. "You're not a mannequin, I'd rather see you a little less chic but fatter. You're living off your own substance."

"And you?"

"We are not discussing me. I am uninteresting, fat or thin makes no difference."

I suddenly laugh, spit the soup across the table. "I just remembered the last time you said 'nice'."

"When?"

"I called you once and told you that a young actor had been cast opposite me and you said, 'But he'd dreadful!' I said, 'Yes, but he's so nice,' and you said, 'Nice! He should bring you orchids twice a day!' "

She doesn't laugh. "It's perfectly true," she says and clicks her lighter. "I am not judging, I am passing sentence—on everything that is going on around you." She raises the lid of the tureen and says, "Eat that meat. You don't need these famous directors who invariably overlook the important points. You've no need to be in awe of them." She leans back and stares at the wall, no delight at being right is in her. "You will always listen to men because you trust them."

I fumble with a box of matches. 'If you have to smoke then at least you should have a lighter," she says and gives me her gold one.

"I saw your picture and the article in the paper," I say.

"Yes, they're spying on me, photograph me whenever I go out onto the terrace. I've been branded a Communist because I spoke against rearmament."

"Who started it?"

She shrugs a shoulder. "What difference does it make? The English officer who was billeted at my house at the end of the war sent me the newspaper clipping. In the margin he had written: 'I should have thought one could rely on one's friends'—'Me too,' I wrote underneath and sent it back. You must sleep now," she says, embraces me suddenly and goes to the door, her back like a young girl's going off to ballet class.

I sit on the bed and remember the Englishmen who had sold black-market margarine in the café next to the radio station. They insisted that you hand over the money before they produced the tins. On one occasion the military police had startled us in the middle of the transaction; I'd paid the money but hadn't received the tin; he dashed off with a week's salary. Would be nice to meet him in London one day and say, "Would you mind giving me my margarine?"

It's almost midnight. I walk down the Kurfürstendamm to Wielandstrasse and stand in front of the Don Juan. The OFF-LIMITS sign is gone, the door has a new handle, the piano is where it always was and Ricci is playing Viennese songs in C major. ". . . denn er lebt in Mödling und sie in St. Veit, und sie komm'n net z'samm und sie komm'n net z'samm, denn der Weg wad so weit . . ." One fat man is leaning on the bar, another with a checked suit and three rings on a finger like a banana is dancing with a long-haired damsel, two others are drinking German champagne at the table next to the toilet. They all look up irritated as

Ricci stops playing. "Hildchen," he says, as though he's
been expecting me. The bartender rattles the cocktail sha-
ker and attempts to engage the five sleepy guests in scintil-
lating conversation, makes as though business were flourish-
ing. I sit down on the piano bench. Ricci says, "Glad you're
back," and plays the old chestnuts from "Stardust" to
"Dream." At three we are eating pea soup and saying, "Do
you remember . . . ?" He's given up photography; the
Yanks all have their own cameras now. He wants to open a
restaurant with a bar, "Bei Ricci" it'll be called and must
have a piano.

At five Ilse Müller and Jupp Paschke are waiting in front
of my hotel room. "Good evening," says Ilse and, "Better
luck next time," is Jupp's solid contribution. We shoot until
the morning of the next day on the Kantstrasse, behind the
Savignyplatz, in front of the new Schiller Theater. Someone pulls my hair. "Still churning out films?" says Barlog,
rolling his eyes. He looks up at Carol, shakes his hand,
nods half impressed, half disparagingly at the sound trucks,
generators, cranes, points his thumb over his shoulder and
says, "That's my theater now, what do you say to that?" He
pulls me to the stage door, up dark stairways and down
passages, shouts, "Stay where you are!" Two spots blind
me; I'm standing on the stage, the auditorium is a black
nothing, a toothless gaping mouth. "Don't you get the old
longing? Wouldn't you like to act again?" I am rooted, frozen, a waxworks dummy. Actor's nightmare: standing on
the stage and can't remember the lines, never knew them,
don't even know what play. Our theater was as wide as a
noodle, the first row orchestra right under the stage, the
rest of it the size of a hand towel, without balconies or
boxes. "Well, what do you say, little one?" I nod, tears roll
down my throat. The spot fades, under an exit sign I see
the antennae-hair, the puckered forehead. "Turn the
bloody films in, you're famous enough now, come back and
do some decent parts again."

"I've signed contracts."

"Contracts, contracts, if you came back to me you'd act
again." He says "act" as though he meant "live." If you
came back to me you'd live again.

After four weeks' shooting Carol Reed asks me, "Heard
the news?"

"What news?"

He balances on the curb, winds a thread around a loose

button and grins. An English and a German assistant hover in the background with furrowed expressions. The workers are drinking tea; a few spectators have sat down on our canvas chairs and are discussing us openly. "Don't you listen to the news?" He folds his hands behind his back and jigs along merrily.

"No."

His nose wrinkles as though he's about to sneeze, then he says, "Stalin is dead." He looks at a billboard on which there's a giant poster of the deceased and which has been the background of the scenes we have just shot. He plays a silent but considerable part in our East-West espionage story, his mustache and big-daddy comfort are present in almost every take. "Now we can reshoot half of what we've done," the German assistant says, "but next time we just use the hammer and sickle, otherwise another one might die on us."

"Maybe they'll become a democracy now," crows a German extra, "then your whole film's down the drain."

"Alex is going to be delighted," Carol Reed says and goes into paraoxysms of laughter. Alexander Korda is our producer. He is Hungarian-born and has advanced to "Sir" in England. In his penthouse at Claridge's he has one of the finest art collections and a first-class French cook. But above all he has charm. And, like Erich Pommer, he can't live without film.

When we arrive in England for the studio work my appendix inflames and I shoot with an ice-pack strapped to my stomach. It's still there as I stand on the balcony of Alexander Korda's office and watch the gigantic procession which follows Elizabeth II on coronation day. The rain pours into champagne glasses and onto carriages, statesmen's heads and spectators' stands. Carol Reed whispers, "It's like wonderland, like a fairy tale, don't you think?" I don't. I already feel excluded from exultation and jubilation, am shaken by repulsion and limp rage, a little envy and much mistrust. Pomp and circumstance, flags and processions, torches and fireworks were the overture to war and bombs, ruins and prison camp. The column slows down. Churchill's coach halts directly beneath the balustrade. He waves to the left and right, chewing on his lower lip as though missing something—he has no cigar. He then contents himself with short nods as though to say it's all very well and good but now let's get down to business.

"Bravo," I murmur. Carol looks astounded. "He wanted to attack Germany from the Balkans," I say, "and if a couple of others hadn't thought otherwise, perhaps you could have set your film in Frankfurt on the Oder, in the Russian zone."

"Or not at all," Carol says and grins.

"Did you see the parade?" a journalist asks me at Shepperton studios the next morning.

"Yes."

"What did you feel, as a German?"

"I was impressed."

"Were you in the Party?"

"Which one?" I ask innocently.

"The Nazi Party."

I nod.

"You were a member?"

"No."

"But you just said you were."

"I didn't say anything, I nodded."

"It amounts to the same thing, wouldn't you say?"

"I nodded because I'd been expecting the question. Your colleagues have been asking it for eight years."

"Does that surprise you?"

"Yes."

"May I ask why?"

"If I had been a member I wouldn't say so and if I told you I hadn't you wouldn't believe me. So why do you ask? It also surprises me that you have so little faith in your authorities."

His expression signifies that aggressive questions posed by an interviewer in no way entitle an interviewee to like answers. "Would you mind telling me what the British authorities have to do with my question?"

"They gave me a work permit."

"There are rumors about missing files."

"Born of wishful thinking, most likely."

"You appear to find it all very amusing."

"I wish I could. And I wish I could once have a cozy show-business interview like any other actor in this studio instead of a political cross-examination."

The eyebrows went up and promised no good; his article delivered what the eyebrows had promised.

My dialogue coach, Helen, who had been engaged for

the Reed film to try to breathe a whiff of Kensington into my American accent, says, "Why can't you have a normal little chat with them instead of always charging into the arena like a bull?"

"I'll learn."

"No, I'm afraid I don't think you will," she says, passing me a cup of tea. "Every time a reporter comes I'll have to hold a pad of chloroform under your nose." She hesitates, lights a cigarette, and then adds, "Present company excepted, I don't like the Germans either."

"Nobody expects you to."

"Please don't misunderstand me, but I can't even look at an Alsatian dog since those films of the concentration camps were shown."

"Why do you except present company?"

"You're the only German I know."

After the last evening's rushes we sit in the studio bar drinking gin-and-tonic. Carol Reed is depressed. "The film's over," he says, "let's be plastered when we say good-bye."

In his house in Chelsea Ljuba Welitsch sings, "Ich habe deinen Mund geküsst . . ." She has sung it twenty or thirty times now since Carol always pushes the needle back to the same groove. He is reveling in memories of the endless nights of shooting in the Berlin Opera, where *Salome* had formed the background of a chase scene. We sit on the floor silently gazing into our glasses; only the parrot (which Carol had bought during the filming and which had taken a good-sized lump out of his index finger by way of welcome) remains unimpressed and measures his volume against Salome's. At last Carol covers the rowdy up and turns off the record player. With his head resting on both hands he says, "I can understand painters not wanting to part with their pictures. Months of work, perhaps years of preparation, suddenly it's finished. What'll I do next, what'll I do between films? I don't know." He says it half amused, as though he were standing beside himself watching his grief, rather surprised, somewhat disdainful at this slack upper lip. He thinks, lives, breathes "film" as Barlog does "theater." Wars, disasters, illness, and private life are hurdles and obstacles on the fringe of passion. At dawn we drive to Covent Garden. The vegetable carts are being unloaded, the workers stand in front of a van drinking tea, stamping their feet to keep them warm. We play football with a cabbage, it shatters a pane of glass, two friendly policemen advise us against further larks of this sort. "I wish I could live the way you do," Carol says, "a hotel room and two suitcases, no possessions." He stands in front of the hotel and waits until my taxi drives off to the airport. I see him through the rear window: lost, a little tired, and still amused, as though he'd made fun of everything and everybody.

On the plane to Hamburg the pain in my right side eases; my appendix is about to burst. A surgeon friend of mine is waiting in his operating gear: "But none of your games here, please. This is a Catholic clinic and the nurses are nuns. I'm operating here for the first time."

"What is a 'papillon d'amour' and what does it look like?" I ask him as the shots begin to take effect. A few minutes later one of the nurses brings me a gold-wrapped chocolate bug about three inches long and says, "The doctor asked me to give you this. He said you'd know what he meant." I have just enough time to fish out some eyelash adhesive from my make-up case, smear it on my belly, get the bug to stick and slip on one of my transparent black vamp film nightdresses before I go under. Three hours later I recognize my friend's mauve face; it seems to be steaming and his breathing is uneven. I feel worried about him but drift off to sleep again. "Very funny," I hear through the haze, "you were nearly conscious again by the time we got the glue off. And don't ask me what the nurse had to say." A flash parts the curtain of mists and freezes my dopy smile, makes me aware of pain and nausea. Two reporters have smuggled themselves in as laundrymen and got the picture; its stark beauty informs my mother in Berlin of her daughter's distress. Arriving at the hospital in Hamburg she is told by the receptionist that she is already the tenth mother to turn up that morning demanding to see her poor Hilde. Crying bitterly she enters my room flanked by two sturdy male nurses; one of them asks, "Is this your mother or isn't it?"

"Auguste," I say.

"Oh so she's not your mother?"

"Yes yes, I just call her Auguste sometimes." She comes over to the bed. I don't tell her that her hat's on backwards and that her shoes don't match.

The wire from New York reaches me at the pension in Schleswig-Holstein. Cole Porter and George Kaufman have written a musical called *Silk Stockings*. They offer me the lead. "You need a holiday, not a musical," Mother says. I still limp; it's as though a length of wire was fastened between my navel and my knee; the scar is long and it hurts. When I sit here with Mother on the pension balcony—in front of us three red geraniums, two white, lower leaves dry like moth's wings singed by an oil lamp—I think I can hear the Wilmersdorf stationmaster's shouts of "Aaaall aboard, keeeep well back," the whistle of the lathes, the ping of the cash register as you pressed the knob under the handle to get at the coin drawer, think I can smell leather-dust and bone-glue, see green shelves and tickets attached to heels with paper clips.

"Why don't you give up the shop," I say, "sell it."

Her right thumbnail is black and ripped from the half-moon to the top; the three-edged sewing-machine needle has gone through it. She looks at her hand and says, "It's not all that bad, I've found a good apprentice and the shop's still a security. He wouldn't have liked to see me give it up so soon after his death." She plucks at the geraniums and then continues, "We got on well together at the end, when we were older; in the early days it was mostly fights, but I don't have to tell you that." She strokes her long legs, draws circles with her left toe. "I miss him very much, the shop gives me the feeling that he's not completely gone from my life."

Once he'd struck a plate so hard with his fist that blood had spurted onto the wallpaper. It was on a Sunday morning, shortly after their wedding. "Will you get divorced now?" I had asked her hopefully.

"Before he died they put a bronchoscope down his throat, to look at his lungs. Without an anesthetic. He was crying like a child when I visited him. When you can't fight any more you're done for," she says and screws up her large eyes.

"I must go back to America before the next film starts, otherwise my passport will lapse. Why don't you come? You could see your brother again."

"You must get well first," she says, "later, perhaps . . ." Her hair is almost completely white. In the light of the low sun she looks very young. "America," she says suddenly and clucks, "I'd have to summon up all my courage."

Back in California I meet Mr. Brom, the agent. He places his arm around my shoulders paternally. "Hildchen, we're doing everything humanly possible. Your money is well invested."

"An actor I know in Munich said I should buy land with one of my salaries at least. He says the lakes and summer resorts around Munich are still quite cheap."

Deep hohohos rumble through him, shake his feet and hands. "What do actors know about money? Zuckerbergchen in Europe and me here in America—no no, you couldn't do better."

I meet Carroll Righter. Unchanged, jacket pockets stuffed full with ephemerides, he climbs out of an automobile that looks as if it'll fall apart any second. "I don't understand technical things," he says equably as the parking-lot attendant calls his attention to a flat tire. We have lunch at his favorite restaurant; its leather couches and black lampshades look as if they belonged in a rainy, wind-swept city rather than in the subtropical suburban film colony. The head waiter flurries around us. "He's a Gemini," says Carroll.

"Yes," the man confirms and stops flurrying, "is that good?"

"Provided one can counter one's nervousness." Carroll nods like a resigned doctor who knows full well that the patient won't stick to his diet.

The head waiter looks crestfallen, fixes his eyes on my plate and says, "Remember a French jeep that gave you a lift in the Schlosstrasse? Your leg was bandaged."

"Yes, I'd stepped on a nail on the stage. Were you the driver?"

"Sure was," he says and stretches himself. "I'm from Alsace, I was in the French Army. You got out on Zehlendorf, how's that for memory?" We shake hands like old buddies.

Carroll's short cough gives me to understand that his Philadelphia upbringing doesn't approve of this intimacy. "I have to speak at a convention in New York. We can fly together, I'll study the Broadway offer on the plane."

"It'll never come off anyway, I can't sing on a stage."

"We shall see," he says.

At the airport that evening we see Marlene standing between mountains of luggage. "Why wasn't I informed?" she asks loftily. "Which plane are you taking?"

"American Airlines."

"Then I'll transfer, I bore myself silly on night flights."

"Why don't you sleep?" Carroll asks.

She looks at him as though he'd run afoul of amnesia since their last meeting. "I rarely sleep," she says, her eyebrows disappearing into her hat.

At five Carroll giggles like a child who's caught Momma fibbing. "She's sleeping like a dormouse."

"We ran into a storm two hours ago and are going to be ten minutes late. Your flight calculations are getting slack," she says, never raising a lid.

"Tut tut," says he and waves his hands as though conducting an adagio, "and Capricorns are never satisfied."

NINETEEN

I'm sitting in front of them. One is called Cy Feuer, the other Ernie Martin. They are in their early or middle thirties and have been the most successful production team on Broadway for some years now. Cy Feuer shifts around on his chair as though it were an uncomfortable bicycle seat and puffs at a cigarette like a nonsmoker, like a boy giving it a first try in the men's room. He breathes out before he speaks and further taxes this lack of oxygen with speeches of such length and pace that a lesser man would pass out, I'm sure. His energy saps me, makes me feel frail, invalid, senile. His round head jerks backwards and forwards, he chops the air with his index finger and hammers his thigh with his short broad hand, pulverizing the forgotten cigarette. His mutilated vocal cords produce hoarse wild tones which spring across the room like shuttlecocks. Although he uses slang he is in no way vulgar. Above the short nose and wide mouth his eyes are brown and love a brawl; they stayed leveled at my face, unblinking, sizing up. Ernie Martin, by contrast, is long and slender and expends energy only as a last resort. He is sitting beside his partner but gives the impression of waiting in the background. Nothing about him betrays participation or interest except the big dark clever eyes which occasionally flicker behind the threads of his frayed eyebrows. Like a ventriloquist he keeps his long cigar immobile when he speaks, and he speaks even faster than Cy Feuer. Flabbergasted, I follow the tempo of the sentences which stream from his mask and then stop as though they'd never been spoken. Squatting behind Cy Feuer and Ernie Martin is Arthur, always referred to as poor Arthur. He is the production assistant, errand boy, and jack-of-all-trades and his gray eyes peer into private sloughs which reflect their unalleviated gloom onto Arthur's face and fashion it into a permanent expression of dread and foreboding.

"I can't sing," I say for the third time.

"Cole Porter says you can."

"In a film perhaps, but not on the stage, and I've never done a play in a foreign language."

"Ninochka has to have an accent," Cy Feuer says.

Silk Stockings is the story of Ninochka, the female Russian Commissar who falls into the hands of a capitalist in Paris and revises her Weltanschauung. It had been a play before it became a musical, and Garbo had played in the very famous film version.

"We'll get you a Russian to work on the accent. This afternoon you've got a date with Herb Greene, he's our conductor and does voice coaching. Day after tomorrow you can sing on the Imperial stage, then we'll know more."

"I've got three films to do in Europe."

"How long'll they take?"

"Till the fall of next year."

"Jesus Christ," says Cy Feuer, "can we buy you out?"

"I hardly think so."

"Maybe we should postpone," Ernie Martin mutters.

"Hell," Cy bellows, "you know what that means?"

Ernie Martin rips the cigar from his mouth and holds it like a dagger in his clenched fist: "She's Ninochka—provided she can sing."

Their confidence and the challenge prickle on the skin. My ambition takes the hook, ignores doubts and the certainty of only two possibilities: success means a run of up to two years without a vacation, a flop means two days.

Herb Greene's apartment is on the seventh floor of a house exposed to the deafening traffic of 58th Street and Eighth Avenue. His studio contains nothing but a sofa and a grand piano and to make oneself understood one must close the windows. Herb is in his late twenties; he is small and his corpulence adds maturity. Sitting on the piano stool with his legs crossed, his left hand cupping his right heel, now and then plucking at the too-short sock, he grins: "Cy and Ernie say you're scared. You're right, I wouldn't trust myself either."

He employs tricks he has learned from his psychiatrist. His forehead is framed by tousled black hair which joins the temples to the brows and the brows at the center and he has a number of lines which look as if they've been penciled in on his chubby round face. He opens the window and yells above the din, "Sing this note so that they'll hear it across the street!" He bangs on an A, hammers it and screams, "Get your mouth open and your tongue down flat, let the tone come out. You're not breathing right. You'll never come across like that. Don't pull your stomach in, you're squashing the note. Breathe in, belly in, breathe out, belly out—not the nasal operatic crap, the exact opposite!" He slaps me on the stomach and I roar like a bull. "Better already!" he roars back.

"I've got a fresh appendix scar!"

He slams the window shut and shouts, "Sarah, bring in the whiskey, I've murdered the Kraut."

Between ten-minute bouts of mouth-open-tongue-down-give 'em-hell-across-the-street I have to sit down and not talk. He grins at me. "When I'm through they'll hear you in every last seat."

"How many seats does the Imperial have?"

"Around two thousand."

"I'll never make it."

"Course not," he says and plays the *Pathétique* so that the walls start to shake. "If I didn't have to go to my headshrinker every three days I'd take a trip to Bonn, take a look at old Beethoven's house. But the way it is, I need every cent for the soul-peeler." He laughs, is contented with his lot. "Tomorrow you'll sing for Porter and Kaufman," he says in one of my mute intervals, "their ears are gonna waggle."

"Or drop off," I say.

"A couple of complexes less would do you no harm either, my fair Prussian maid," he whinnies.

"I've got a toothache," I say in the morning in front of the stage door.

"That's fine, it'll feed your masochism," he beams and clambers down a ladder into the orchestra pit.

One light bulb is hanging over the imperial stage. The floor is gray and hard, pitted like old asphalt.

"I'm the stage manager," says a gray-haired gentleman and mumbles, "You'll be O.K.," as an automatic afterthought.

"I don't want to be O.K.," I counter.

"For the very good reason she can't sing," says Herb and bangs the piano lid back. I howl rather than sing and the song we have prepared seems as long as the whole of *Salome*. I finally get to the end and stand there festering with thoughts of "You see, I told you all along it wouldn't work."

"O.k.," someone calls from the darkness. I hear doors slamming; someone moves across the top balcony. In the front row of the orchestra I can make out a man who is looking up at me with slightly protruding eyes as big as fried eggs that express neither delight nor disappointment. He is wearing a white carnation in his buttonhole and holding a silver-topped cane in delicate hands. He cocks his head to one side and says, "Wouldn't you like to come and sit down?"

"Yes, Mr. Porter," I say in the hope that it really is he.

Two rows behind him sits another man I don't recognize. His long legs are crossed, tangled and spliced like a sailor's knot. Slowly and yet impatiently he unravels his limbs, seems to keep finding feet that are still not in a position to take him where he wants to go. He pulls at a scarf which, although it's twisted around his neck several times, dangles below the hem of his overcoat, tugs with one hand at the rusty fingers of the other and then bends down awkwardly to pick up a crumb which he carefully places in his coat pocket. He strokes his thick gray hair and gingerly rubs his neck as if to reassure himself that they're still there, takes a pair of thick spectacles and lets them fall onto a fleshy nose which looks like a mistake in the otherwise lean face; lost in thought and moving stiffly, he comes down the aisle to the edge of the orchestra pit and begins to polish the balustrade with one end of his scarf. "Hmm," he says and bends down to tie a perfectly tied shoe lace.

Climbing down the stairs from the stage to the auditorium Herb says, "That's George Kaufman, in case you didn't know. He's directing, and he wrote the book too."

September 7, 1954,
New York

Erich Pommer had been pessimistic, as always: "You're putting all your eggs in one basket, you can't keep a flop on Broadway a secret; from Honolulu to Bitterfeld everyone will know what happened. Did you have to choose a play in which you must bear comparison with Garbo? And do you have to be the first German to play in New York? I think even in Israel you'd meet with less resentment than in New York."

"Feuer, Martin, and Kaufman are all Jewish." I had

caught my breath at "Jewish" as though I'd put my foot in it, had said something that would hurt him. Why?

"I sincerely hope you know what you're doing, for your own sake."

Else Bongers wasn't sure: "After a certain time one is no longer judged by one's performances but by one's decisions. I can't advise you, I don't know Broadway."

I arrived at midday today. It's nearly a year since I howled at the empty Imperial balconies. Until two months ago I had always believed-hoped-feared that they'd find another Ninochka and dispense with my services.

September 14

I went to see Cole Porter at the Waldorf-Astoria this morning. Dreaded bumping into Kurt Hirsch's father. My costar, Don Ameche, was there. Very polite, very friendly. Tiny mustache. He plays with a rosary in his trousers pocket the whole time; he bent over once and it slipped out. We were photographed for a good hour, Porter at the piano with us behind him. As he showed us to the door I noticed that he limps; they say he had a car accident ten years ago. "I'm so sorry it was so ungemütlich," he said, "but we'll be seeing a great deal of each other in the coming months." Then my daily routine: from eleven till one, and again from three till five, Herb Greene. In between I learn lines. Ninochka would have outtalked Hamlet. Additional scenes arrive every day; if it goes on like this the play will last five hours.

September 26

We were at George Kaufman's apartment last night. Herb Greene played the music from the overture to the finale. Kaufman and his wife Leueen, who also worked with him on the book, Feuer, Martin, Porter, Ameche, Yvonne Adair, who's playing the hysterical film star, and I all sat on the white carpet growing more and more desperate.

October 10

Today was the first reading. The whole cast sat in a half-circle on the stage with the manuscripts in their hands, a paper cup of coffee beside each chair. One after the other the empty cups fell over and rolled into the footlights. Kaufman, Feuer, and Martin sat opposite us with their back to the auditorium. Kaufman didn't say a word.

Cupped his hands over his ears like earmuffs as though he couldn't stand it, as though the whole thing was hopeless and degrading. One of the three Commissars is a radio actor; he purred his lines as though he'd already played the part for years. To begin with we laughed at the gags and funny business but the sight of Kaufman gradually dampened our ardor and by the first cigarette break we were all standing around as if we were rehearsing Strindberg's *Dance of Death*. Nobody had a pencil. Unbelievable that actors never have pencils at first readings. Henry, the stage manager, lent his and it went from hand to hand until finally Cy Feuer's temper snapped. "I'm well aware that you don't get paid till the opening but you could at least buy one little pencil, for Christ's sake. We've wasted hours already." Tomorrow we block the first scenes.

October 16

Rehearsals have been postponed for a week, the opening in Philadelphia hasn't. Kaufman's writing a new beginning and changing some of the second act.

October 27

We rehearse the songs and the dialogue separately. The stage manager yells "Song" when we get to a place where one is supposed to be, then we go on with the dialogue as though it were a straight play. Haven't seen the ballet at all as yet, they're rehearsing in a warehouse at the docks. In the evening we go through the songs with the chorus in a dance hall that has pink Chinese lanterns and lots of dirt. Between rehearsals: radio shows, interviews, photos, fittings. I spent a whole night doing photos with Richard Avedon. He stuck my head under a shower and started work when all trace of make-up and hair-do was gone. At seven he dismissed me and went to bed; I went straight to rehearsal.

Herb Greene has a cold. We work with an accompanist who plays as if he would like to chop the piano, the theater, and Porter into little bits. New pages of dialogue daily. Whole scenes are thrown out and replaced by new ones. Songs from the first act are moved to the second and the other way around. I start to say a line and somebody bawls, "That's been cut since yesterday, for Heaven's sake." Kaufman whispers his directions as though he were slipping hot tips on the races. Porter hasn't been in the theater for days; they say he's writing new songs and will come when we run through with ballet and chorus.

November 5

After my "J'accuse" monologue Kaufman rested his arm on my shoulder and whispered, "Pity it's a musical, you're too good for musicals." I must have looked at him like a startled cow. It was the first sentence of any length I'd heard him utter. The one who's playing the Head Commissar can't remember his lines. I'm sure if he had to say "Saks Fifth Avenue" he wouldn't get further than "Saks." He keeps giving me wrong cues. How does he think he's going to get by without a prompter? Beats me why the Americans won't use them. Perhaps nobody ever pointed out their advantages to them. That they don't have a *Dramaturg*, or literary editor, is understandable and more than a relief. If I ever go dry the curtain'll have to fall. I can't improvise in a foreign language, and if I forget a line in a song they're not going to stop and wait for me.

This morning at three o'clock, after the rehearsal, Ameche and I drove down to an Italian restaurant in the Village. He quietly drank a whole bottle of Jack Daniels with his fettucine and then strolled back with me as though it had been cocoa. Before and during work he won't touch a drop. He's very easy and disciplined. Has great humor. Only on Saturdays he goes on strike, no night rehearsals, no conferences. Saturday midnight he goes to church and I realize that another week has gone by.

November 9

Ameche blew his top today. Porter was there: first run-through with songs and ballet. Massacre. The missing sets are marked by strips of plaster stuck on the stage; a red strip is the back wall, a white one the cupboard, and so on. Doors we have but they stick. I tried to kick one open and it fell over and nearly brained one of the Commissars. My suitcase wouldn't shut. I made my entrance, the lid fell open in the middle of my first line and all the props I need for the next scene went leaping about the stage, making Ameche and me miss the cue for our duet. The revolver didn't work and the costumes aren't ready; some haven't even been designed yet. The costume designer must take Seconal; she totters and dozes and when you speak to her she starts and says, "It'll all be all right on the night." Two actors were fired. They went without a word. Faces gray-green. Suicide candidates. One had three children. New ones are being auditioned tomorrow.

They wanted to cut Ameche's best song. He became very chilly. "Why don't you get yourselves another boy?" Pause. "Be reasonable, Don, you must feel it dragging just as much as we do." Palaver palaver. For the time being it stays where it was.

The ballet—there are thirty or forty of them—couldn't get used to the stage. It's wide but has no depth. One of the boys did a high kick and knocked a girl unconscious. Another twisted his ankle since he had no way of knowing that the chorus would storm the stage just as he was executing a pirouette. The love song I have to sing lying at Ameche s feet was interrupted by his chair falling apart. Cy screamed for the stage manager. Henry strode forward and planted himself in the middle of the stage like a tin soldier and said, "I hauled this junk up from the cellars, otherwise we'd have nothing. When're the sets gonna be ready? What about the backdrops?"

Yvonne Adair sobbed like a baby. They'd copied her only song in the wrong key. Every time he has a free minute the Head Commissar goes to the telephone, dials a number, puts down the receiver beside the phone without listening, waits for about a minute, then hangs up again. Wish I knew what it meant.

November 10

Ameche has found out. The Head Commissar lives alone with a German shepherd that gets up only when the telephone rings. To keep the dog from getting too fat he calls whenever possible.

I blew my top today. Three times they've taken my head measurements and the fur hat is still so big that it comes down over my eyes. The leather coat is enormous and the uniform much too tight. Whenever I raise my arm the seams rip. Two run-throughs at three and a half hours apiece. Nothing went right. "Don't stop, don't stop!" Cy bellowed, "we wanna get a time on it!" We stood there on the stage when it was all over. No word from out front. Cy Ernie Porter Kaufman slumped in the back rows bickering. I lashed out at a chair and it skidded across the stage. "We yell our guts out and they can't even say boo." Don put a lighted cigarette in my mouth and said, "Kraut, you're not getting the shakes?" Julie, one of the dancers, brought me an orange. "You have to eat fruit, you won't get through otherwise."

Have lost ten pounds. Could just as well give up my hotel room, for all I see of it. Someone told me about a penthouse on top of a hotel at Tenth and Fifth Avenue. Who knows how long I'll be in New York.

November 13

Kaufman raised his voice today. "Eat a steak, you've no attack and I can hardly hear you." "Who me?" "Yes you!" Wanted to ask him when he thought I would find time for such a luxury.

Vorkuta in January must be warmer than the theater and there's still only that one bulb. Like a prison. Ninochka's first evening dress, at the sight of which the audience is supposed to go berserk, hangs like a rag. When I proudly spin around in front of Don it flaps like an old mosquito net. I fell flat on my face today because they'd only tacked the hem. And during the quick change from uniform to evening dress the zipper broke. "Why isn't Hildy on stage?" Cy thundered. "Because the zipper broke!" "Come as you are, you're holding us up!"

Cy Ernie Porter Kaufman sit through the best gags as though they were watching their mothers being led to the gallows. Only poor Arthur sniggers behind his hand. The solitary titters make it even worse. The sets were promised for today. After the second run-through Ernie said, "Even without the finale we're too long already. An' if you add the intermission we might as well do Wagner's *Ring* and be done with it."

I'd love to be able to invite a German student of Theatrical Science to attend rehearsals.

The Head Commissar is a Vivaldi fan and between entrances reads books on harpsichord construction in the time of Bach. The dancers pass the time with crossword puzzles. One of them stands on his head the whole day long, another collects sailboat catalogues. The prettiest of the girls has four children but no husband. She knits sweaters and stocking caps day and night. One of the other Commissars kept developing fever from an inflamed appendix and was fired. "Sorry, but we can't take risks before the opening," Cy said. Every time he goes near one of the actors, singers, or dancers they go red, expecting the ax.

November 14

Ameche has met the Head Commissar's German shepherd. Somehow during a break he got hold of the Commissar's door key and tore off. As always the Commissar came from the stage and went straight to the phone. He dialed the number, heard the click of the receiver being lifted, gasped, and said, "Bodo? Bodo?" At the other end panting, woof woof, panting. Not until the evening did Don confess who had done the panting and then only because the Commissar blew his lines altogether and Cy started stalking him.

The sets arrived at noon. There are so many that no one knows where to start. The distances and measurements marked by the plaster strips weren't even close to being correct. The backdrops fell down the moment they were put up, the Russian kitchen is the size of a telephone booth, and the chorus, twenty dancers, and I trample each other to death. On the other hand the airport telephone booth, from which Ninochka bids her capitalist adieu, is as spacious as a hothouse in a botanical garden. But the telephone itself evened the score because it wouldn't be lifted; the whole box came away and the back wall collapsed when I tried. The tapes got mixed up and instead of airport noises and "Passengers for Moscow to gate seven" my "I love you, I love you" was accompanied by a jingle about the evils of dandruff. The Paris hotel-lobby set for the opening scene looked as though it had survived an earthquake and the settee on which Ameche reclines while singing the title song, "Silk Stockings," had only three legs and toppled over backwards during the refrain; all you saw of Don was his feet. The sides of the fashion salon set didn't fit and the finale reminded me of some street battles I had seen; finally Yvonne got entangled with a length of cord and lay trussed up on the stage like a bundle of laundry. Shortly before midnight Kaufman said, "Let's at least go through the finale once more." "To hell with the finale!" Cy raved. "The critics are already at their desks by the time the finale comes up, at twelve midnight their death sentences go to press!" And Ernie said, "If I'd had to pay eight dollars for those three hours and forty-seven minutes I'd demand my money back."

Tommorrow is the lighting rehearsal. We don't see the

orchestra until the day of the opening. Thirty-two pieces and no microphone. And only a piano till now.

November 16

We were supposed to rehearse the new songs with Herb this morning and start the run-throughs at two. "Change of plan," poor Arthur called out, "act one, scene one, curtain up."

As the curtain gave no sign of going up Cy screamed from the back row, "Where's Henry?"

"Not here," I said.

"Waddaya mean 'not here'? Is he sick? Is he dead? Waddaya mean 'not here'?"

"He's at the zoo," I said.

Even Cole Porter looked up.

"At the zoo?" they repeated and stared at me. "We're opening in six days. Would you mind telling me what for the love of Jesus Henry is doing at the ZOO?"

"He's at the zoo with my turtle."

Cy and Ernie came slowly down the center aisle. Kaufman got up, Porter lit a cigarette. Cy leaned his elbows on the edge of the orchestra pit and said gently, "Look Hildy, I know the last weeks have been tough but let's all make an effort to stay reasonable, O.K.? Just tell us quietly why Henry had to take your turtle to the zoo instead of COMING TO REHEARSAL???" This last made him angry again. Veins bulged on his forehead; he spluttered. Ernie eased him aside and said, "Hildy, let's start at the beginning."

"He had to have a home," I said.

"Who had to have a home?"

"Tino's a talisman after all," I said.

"Who's Tino?" Ernie asked, taking my hand.

"My turtle."

"You fond of turtles?"

"Not very."

"Why do you worry about them, then?"

"I told you, she's—he's a talisman."

Cy gave me a cigarette, then Ernie gave me a light and said comfortingly, "Now sit down and tell us all about it, we got lots of time." Cy let out a strangled gasp; Ernie dealt him a punishing glance.

"I'm not crazy," I said.

"We know that, Hildy," Kaufman whispered. Ernie nodded and said, "Go ahead."

"When I left Germany a reporter I know came out to the plane, presented me with a cardboard box, and said, 'This is to bring you good luck.' At first I thought it was flowers but then when I tried to lift it I found it was too heavy for flowers and also it was wet underneath and made funny scratching noises. The stewardess wanted to put it in the icebox—'You can't hold the orchids all the way to New York,' she said every time she came past. I went to the toilet and opened the box and found a turtle with a note stuck on its back: 'My name is Tino and I eat salad and bananas. I also need damp earth.' I didn't take my eyes off the box for the whole eighteen or twenty hours, only I had no idea how I was going to get him through customs and the health inspection—I knew it's forbidden to bring in any plants or animals."

"And how did you get him—her—Tino through?" asked Ernie.

"The photographers were waiting for me on the tarmac and I gave one of them the box. I told him it was a cactus and asked him to wait for me in front of the airport, otherwise I'd probably have been put in quarantine with Tino, or sent back to Shannon even."

Porter lit another cigarette, Kaufman inspected the carpet for crumbs, and Cy was now lying full-length on the stage sunning himself, his hands behind his head; Ernie alone remained unchanged. "And then?" he asked.

"The chambermaids at the hotel refused to clean my room, they were afraid of Tino. I couldn't take a bath either, since he lived mostly in the tub—I'd been down to Central Park and got the earth he needs and the bath seemed the best place to keep it moist. And then it was very difficult to find the kind of salad he likes, he'll only take crisp fresh hearts of lettuce. Just as rehearsals were starting the hotel manager came and told me that Tino must go within twenty-four hours. I found a pet shop on Seventh Avenue but the owner was away. His assistant, Mr. Blau, comes from Vienna. He asked me, 'Is the turtle Greek?' I didn't know. He said it'd be very dangerous for him to take a Greek turtle since they're banned in America so I had to swear to him that it was a German turtle and leave my address and phone number before he'd accept it. A couple of days ago he called me. 'My boss is back,' he said, 'you get over here right away.' When I got to the shop he was standing in front of the door crying. 'The turtle she is Greek,' he said. 'I have a wife, four children, and a sick mother and now I lose my job because your turtle is Greek.' I had to talk to his boss for a half-hour before Mr. Blau had his job back and I my turtle. Henry offered to help me and said they'd probably be crazy about Tino at the Central Park Zoo."

"But it can't be taking him two hours," moaned Cy.

"Maybe they've arrested him," said poor Arthur.

Cy got up, groaned, "Jesus Christ," and disappeared into the john.

Ernie released my hand and called out, "From the top everybody, Arthur'll give you the cues."

The run-through was a bigger catastrophe than ever. Arthur mixed up ballet and lighting cues, telephones rang instead of doorbells, the curtain fell at several wrong moments, and after a backdrop had been lowered too early, hit the hotel lobby, and broken in two, splitting the nose of a member of the chorus, we decided to stop.

At six in the evening Henry appeared.

"Where were you?" hollered Cy.

"At the zoo."

"For ten hours???"

Henry turned to me questioningly; I nodded.

"It was on account of the turtle."

"We know all about it, Henry," Kaufman whispered.

"At the Central Park Zoo they asked me whether it's a Greek turtle." He turned to me again. "Is it Greek or isn't it?"

"I don't know."

"Well, they said they couldn't take it if I didn't have any papers on its origin, so I called the other zoo out on Long Island and they said I should come over."

"Why didn't you throw it in the Hudson?" Cy screamed.

"Now listen, what d'you take me for—a murderer?" Henry screamed back. "Anyway, it took me hours to get out there; I took the wrong train twice—you ever try getting out to Long Island by subway? By the time I did get there the director had gone to lunch, of course, and some smart-aleck assistant comes up and asks me, 'Is this a Greek turtle?' "

"NO," Cy thundered. *"I CAN'T TAKE IT."*

Porter was tapping the floor with his cane, Kaufman was

leafing through the script, and Ernie had ordered a whiskey.

"Well you wanna know why I'm late or don't you?" Henry shouted.

"O.K., O.K.," Cy whimpered and sank his head into his hands.

"Did you know for instance that Greek turtles are absolutely forbidden in the U.S.A.?"

No one answered.

"No? Well me neither," Henry continued. "O.K., to cut a long story short, the director took three hours over lunch and then he came and examined the turtle and turned round to this high-falutin assistant of his and said, 'You should be able to tell by now that this isn't a Greek turtle.' "

Ernie finished his whiskey and asked, "So how do you tell whether a turtle's Greek, Catholic, or Jewish, for Christ's sake?"

"I didn't ask," said Henry.

"Maybe some of 'em are circumcised," said Herb.

November 20

Marlene came to rehearsal. It made us all nervous knowing that someone was out front who wasn't part of the production. We managed quite well up to the intermission; the second part was a debacle. The spots clung faithfully to actors with neither songs nor dialogue, the set changes took ages, Herb Greene had to play some of the interludes several times over before the next scene could begin, the stagehand forgot to sweep the stage, and I leaned my elbow on a thumbtack while singing my love song. Ameche and I got hoarser with each rehearsal; from the tenth row on one can hardly hear us, apparently. The doctor says our vocal cords are the color of ripe tomatoes; during the break he sprayed them with oil which then trickled to my empty stomach, where it was not welcome. Herb Greene will have to conduct the opening after only two rehearsals with the orchestra. Kaufman rewrote three scenes during the night and we were obliged to read them; when we are supposed to learn them remains his mystery. My dresser is a colored lady named Lela. She says my costumes are so badly sewn they'll drop off me after three performances. Marlene thought the Russian uniform abominable and the evening dress laughable—"For the hicks," she said, and "There's such chaos on the stage that you can't judge a thing. Two

or three moments are promising." We open in Philadelphia
in two days' time.

November 21
Philadelphia

Cy swears that no New York critic will be here, it's a
"gentleman's agreement." But a flop in Philadelphia is the
end anyway. More shows have closed after their out-of-town
openings in the past few weeks than have gone on to
Broadway. I took the train last night after rehearsal. The
East Coast is snowed in from Boston to Washington and all
the trains were late; I just had time to learn the new scenes
and sleep for an hour before the rehearsal started. We live
on coffee, tea, and woolly white bread and peanut butter. I
feel as though I'm spending my last night in the condemned
cell. I can think of nothing but my lyrics, cues, and entrance lines. In the three hours and forty-five minutes I
hardly leave the stage. I don't know how I'll do it.

November 22

We rehearse single scenes in the foyer of the Shubert
Theater. There's a draft. Yvonne has a cold. One of the
Commissars has a temperature, another an ear infection.
Nothing works. They're nailing up sets on the stage, a
piano tuner's at work in the pit, the charwomen vacuum
the floor around our feet. You can't hear yourself think. At
every corner there are posters with the name I can't get
used to: HILDEGARDE NEFF AND DON AMECHE IN *Silk
Stockings*. I'd rather be anywhere than here. Through the
glass door I see the wide street. Every passerby seems to be
looking forward to our downfall, the whole town seems to
be preparing for the slaughter. I want a family, a home,
children, even a drunken husband, anything, just no first
night. Marlene arrived this morning with Noël Coward. Carroll Righter's here too. Kaufman sits on a fireman's flap-
seat and looks at us without the slightest reaction, as
though he can't remember ever seeing us before. Poor Arthur says, "We'll be a lot wiser in ten hours' time." We all
stop whatever we're trying to do and look at him like cannibals trying to decide whether he'd taste better boiled or
fried. The orchestra rehearsal begins at two. It's worse than
anyone had thought possible. Thirty-two men trumpet at us
like a herd of elephants stampeding. Our mouths gape like
goldfish; we hear neither ourselves nor our fellow actors.

Cy stands in the dress circle, his face like a farmer's after the flood. At seven he takes Ameche and me across to a bar; Ernie and Arthur follow a few minutes later. They try to talk us into steaks and whiskey but I can neither eat nor drink, my throat is the size of a needle's eye. Cy says at least twenty times, "Relax, it's not New York." Porter and Kaufman come and sit with us. Ernie is reticent, Porter too, Kaufman even more so than usual. Thirty minutes later we get up and totter past the long queue of people waiting at the box office in the hope of getting returned tickets. "At least we're sold out," Cy says. We have two communal dressing rooms, one in the cellar for the ballet and chorus, the other for the actors behind the stage. Gentlemen to the right, ladies to the left, in the middle a sheet. The corridor is full of buckets of flowers: funeral parlor for a prominent citizen. Henry tries out the backstage loudspeakers: "Fifteen minutes, fifteen minutes," it crackles. "fifteen minutes to the overture." Herb Greene peeps around the sheet; he's yellow-green like an unripe lemon. He wants to speak but can't summon enough spit, squeezes out a "Fuck 'em," after several tries, makes a V sign, and drops the sheet again. Porter puts his hand on my shoulder and blinks like an owl, Kaufman's bow tie sticks up vertically under his chin, he stretches, drums on my dressing table with his fingers, and stalks toward the sheet on his stiltlike legs.

Cy stands in the doorway and calls out, "Listen kids, treat it like a rehearsal, whatever happens go on playing. And don't lose your nerve if they don't laugh, Philadelphia's famous for it, they always sit on their hands. New York'll be different." His attempt to say something comforting goes wrong at the words "New York," his voice cracks, the syllables get jumbled. his right eye twitches. Arthur is standing behind him and his whole head is twitching, bobbing sideways as if on a spring.

Ernie comes and stands behind my chair. We look at each other in the make-up mirror. He places his hands around my neck as though he might massage it, his mouth is wide, the upper lip jerks up and down over the teeth. "Ninochka," he says, "Ninochka——" Abruptly he turns away, as if to say "No long good-byes."

I hear voices coughing and gargling, then the loudspeaker announcing, "Five minutes, five minutes." "The mob's in already," Ameche murmurs. My hands are cold stiff frozen. "Come on," he says and pulls me up from my chair. Ameche, horse-addict, baseball fan, former film star, Italian, father of six children, and bourbon drinker, says, "You can tell a good horse by the way it relaxes before the big race. Show 'em, Kraut."

"Clear the stage, houselights, overture!" Henry roars.

They're playing like a fire brigade. If they're this fast in my song about Commissar Kamichev—"When the electromagnetic of the hemale meets the electromagnetic of the female"—I've had it. "I won't make it," I say. Don gives me his handkerchief, my hands are hot now, dripping.

Entrance of the Three Commissars. After their "Hail Bibinski" song I'm on. I am not me and she who is not me hears applause, hears me talking through the applause, treading on it, hears me singing and then talking again, sees Ameche, recognizes the Head Commissar's uniform, sees emergency light high in the balcony, then: backstage, Lela. She tears off the coat, holds up the evening dress, ratsch the zipper, cold leather cloth on my face, on again. Just before the end of the act Don opens a bottle of champagne, to make sure it does open Henry had always loosened the cork during rehearsals and synchronized a perfect pop from backstage. Not tonight. Don makes the grand flourish—nothing. The first bars of our love-duet waft up from the pit, I open my mouth to sing—pop. The audience chuckles knowingly. I step down to the footlights for the "J'accuse" monologue, am blinded by the spots, lose the horizon, seem to be dangling, floating somewhere between the flies and the stage. The curtain brushes my face as it falls.

Cy is there already. "Jesus Christ," he barks, "it's a peachy audience, if the second half goes this well . . ." he runs back and forth. Ameche nudges me. "Well, Kraut, what did I tell you?" Lela rubs me down like a dog come in from the rain, hands me tea, Marlene's vitamin pills, gargle mixture, throat lozenge, dresses me, sticks my hat on. The bell tinkles in the auditorium, once twice three times. Henry shouts, "Clear the stage, houselights, curtain!" Divided stage: on the right the hotel room, on the left the telephone booth. Ameche right, me left. The spot dims on the booth as I finish the call, another fades in on Ameche and he sings the title song, "Silk Stockings." He sings the first verse and the backdrop behind him starts to wobble and then sails up revealing a stagehand sitting on a ladder

drinking a can of beer. The audience rocks with laughter,
Ameche doesn't know why, checks his fly, goes on singing
halfheartedly, the backdrop thuds down again, Henry's
voice from the wings, "Which son of a bitch was that?"
Two hours later they're clapping throughout the finale,
though it still plays like Thanksgiving Day on a Moroccan
marketplace. "Bravo," they shout, "Hildegarde, Don," clap
and sing to the music like Gospel singers, whistle the tunes,
shout "Kaufman" and "Porter."

The iron curtain grinds down. We stand on the stage,
shake each other, laugh, kiss, cry, the ballet girls are drooping like used bananas. Cy is beaming, he runs up to me and
yells, "If you hadn't guffawed like a drunken marine they'd
have thought the guy on the ladder was part of the show!"
General laughter. Lela sniffles, "Baby baby, that sho' was
somethin'," and holds a whiskey up to my face.

Kaufman comes into the dressing room. He puts his long
arms around me. "You were excellent, excellent," he says.
It takes some time for me to realize that he has said it in
German. "You speak German?" I ask stupidly. He blinks
and grins sheepishly, sits down on the edge of the table,
crosses and plaits his legs. "We're still dragging in a couple
of spots, two ballet numbers have to go, I'll rewrite the
ending and restage the finale. But if you're as good in New
York as you were tonight I'll be content."

"Do you know Fritz Kortner?"

"The name, yes."

"I didn't care to mention it until now but just before I
left, Kortner asked me to talk to you about releasing one of
your plays for Germany. He'd like to direct *The Man
Who Came to Dinner*."

He looks at his shoes and pulls at a wrist. "Please understand me correctly. I don't wish to entertain the Nazis,
don't want to make them laugh. My plays will not be performed in Germany or Austria. Can you understand that?"

"Kortner emigrated."

"The audience didn't."

Marlene comes in and says, "Fabulous, fabulous." She
embraces Kaufman, who is still sitting on the table looking
at his shoes.

Carroll Righter is standing in the corridor. "I am happy
you were able to have your first great theatrical success in
my home town." I try to detect any uncertainty in his face
but it remains relaxed and sincere. His advice had been

negative: "There will be delays, difficulties—I see no
catastrophe, only I'm against your being bound for so long,
especially during the next years and for reasons of health.
If you insist on playing the show you must reckon with obstacles and disappointment, not so much professionally as
privately and financially."

Noël Coward kisses my forehead and says, "Good God I
was nervous, might have been one of my own. The soliloquy at the end of the first act is perfect, sheer delight. They
tell me the show cost half a million dollars, in which case I
wonder why you have to wear clothes my charlady
wouldn't be seen dead in." The costume designer leans
around the door and says, "It'll all work out." "I sincerely
hope so," Noël snaps. "But never mind that, you were
splendid, quite delicious. Your first entrance has no build-
up, has to be changed. But before you get to New York
they'll change pretty well everything anyway. Dear Lord,
don't I know it."

At two-thirty we are sitting in my hotel room. Marlene,
Porter, Kaufman, Ernie, Cy, Ameche, and I. Noël Coward
has taken the last train back to New York. Poor Arthur
comes running in with the first papers. "Take a look at
that!" he bubbles. Cy reads aloud: "Smash for Feuer and
Martin, Kaufman and Porter, Neff and Ameche," is the
first headline; the review ends with, "Hildegarde Neff steps
into Garbo's shoes and walks away with them."

"Work can begin," Cole Porter says and smiles like
someone who is acquainted with every nook and cranny of
hell. He sits small and delicate in his chair, straight and still
as though awaiting reproof from his governess, a tap with
the cane for incorrect posture. Cole Porter is rich and successful. It is sometimes hard to believe. He listens intently
to every reservation made by the producers, who are his
juniors by many years, and fulfills every demand. He works
as though his daily bread were at stake, as though he must
still prove himself as a composer, lyricist, dependable
teamworker. Nothing about him signifies that this is his
twenty-fifth Broadway show, that almost every one of his
songs has been a hit throughout the world. They say he
never travels without his servants, his silk sheets, his crockery and cutlery. We know that his injured, often operated
upon leg causes him constant pain. Cy has said so, and
Ernie. Porter has not. We know little of him other than his
discipline and discretion, to us his only coquetry appears to

be the carnation in his buttonhole. Like George Kaufman, who had been an editor of *The New York Times* before he became one of the best and most successful writers on Broadway, he disguises his preeminence so well that he has apparently forgotten about it himself.

Ameche nips at his bourbon and says, "It couldn't have gone better, apart from a couple of sticky patches."

"They're after our scalps in New York," Cy answers, "the whole show needs more pep."

"It's a play with music, not a musical," Marlene says, "and that's exactly its charm."

Ernie, who is still poring over the reviews, grumbles, "Yeah, that's all fine and dandy but we need the four and a half weeks till New York badly."

"When will we be able to rehearse, if we play eight performances? I mean Wednesdays and Saturdays we have matinees, so they're out to start out with," I say.

They all look at me, crestfallen teachers who have caught their model pupil cribbing. "My dear child," Porter says, "apparently you have not been informed that each day has forty-eight hours from now on."

Ernie stretches and yawns, "Let's catch a little shut-eye before it's banned. When's rehearsal?"

"Nine," Kaufman whispers.

Marlene, Ameche, and I are left alone. "What on earth do they want to change?" I ask them.

"Everything," Ameche says and drinks the last third of the bottle sip for sip in a tiny glass, washing it down with tap water.

I can't sleep, the music throbs from the pillow, I hear myself missing cues, see myself stumbling. At five I think I hear a click at the door. "Who's there?" I scream, sure it's my murderer, and push an armchair in front of the door. Eleven stories down a brown paper bag skips from one side of the street to the other, inflates, sails up, falls on the roof of a car, dances around a streetlamp. The street is empty, nothing moves but the bag and a colored woman dusting desks and wiping her brow with the back of her hand, lifting waste baskets onto the chairs of an office on the fifth floor opposite. The room gets blacker, narrower, becomes a corridor, cul-de-sac. The light switch sparks and gives me a shock; in the bathroom mirror I see a swollen, blotchy face and inflamed eyes. I fall asleep at six-thirty. An hour later the telephone rings: "Your call, dearie."

November 23

Cy, Ernie, Kaufman, and Porter are standing on the stage like blocks of ancient granite. They hear nothing, see nothing. Finally Cy breaks the spell and throws himself onto the sofa. He slaps his forehead with the flat of his hand and exclaims, "Why the hell'd she have to marry a millionaire in desperate need of an heir?"

"Yvonne's expecting a baby," Arthur mutters, as though announcing the outbreak of war, "her husband just came with the certificate."

The dancer who's going on for Yvonne tonight comes running out of the dressing room bathed in perspiration and sneezing. "You got a cold?" Cy erupts. "No, no, I'm sure I haven't," she sniffles. Henry runs after her with the script but the choreographer says, "Let's get the dance routines straight first."

"We're sold out for four weeks," Ernie says.

"And she has to have a baby," Arthur adds, as though he'd known it all along.

In the evening Henry stands in the wings and hisses the lyrics at the girl but she doesn't hear, doesn't see, looks as if she's sinking in quicksand. At intermission they all slap her on the back and say, "Good girl, you'll make it." Otherwise it's a typical second performance; slack, dreary, lacking any tension, and the running time is eight minutes longer than on the first night although applause and laughs are shorter and one song has been cut altogether. Cy spits, "If you all start droopin' now what're you gonna be like in four weeks? Run-through tomorrow morning, we'll soon see who's dragging his feet. In the afternoon we'll block the new scenes."

Ernie says, "The gal can dance but the voice isn't big enough." They're looking for a replacement.

November 26

To have played Yvonne's part on Broadway would have been her big chance. Now she sits in the stalls and watches Cy and Ernie auditioning other girls. No tears, no protest. She still plays in the evening and improves with each performance but they remain firm: "The voice isn't big enough."

We rehearse from nine until six-thirty, make up, eat a

sandwich, play the performance, rehearse again, then go home to learn lines.

November 28

At the intermission Lela says, "I don't like your looks, you look awful and your back's full o' spots." We rehearse till one in the morning, then stop, as Kaufman has to write two new scenes. Ameche and I walk to the hotel. The cold boxes our ears, we've almost forgotten what winter air tastes and smells like. Ameche hops from one foot to the other, shivers and shakes. "I can't stand the cold," he says, "it makes me ill." I'm hot, so hot that I'd like to take my coat off. Ernie and Cy are in the elevator. "You got spots on your face, what's the matter, nerves?" Cy asks me. Ameche puts his hand to my forehead. "You've got fever," he says. Cy calls the clinic; two doctors arrive a half hour later and examine me in the bathroom. They shine a flashlight into my eyes, into my throat, tap my chest, listen, look at each other, go out.

Cy is lying on the floor laughing so violently I think he'll choke. Ernie has forgotten his rule about conservation of energy and is striding from the door to the window, from the window to the door. Ameche's invisible right hand is clicking the rosary, his left is undoing his collar. The doctors are leaning against a chest of drawers; one has the blood-pressure thing in his hand, the other an untouched glass of whiskey. "What is it?" I ask.

For a moment, no reaction. Then Cy goes to the telephone: "Get me Mr. Kaufman," he gurgles. "Come on over, eleven twelve."

"Well come on, let me into the big funny secret—what have I got?" I say.

"You tell her," Cy wheezes.

Ernie passes the buck to the doctors. The one with the blood-pressure thing rolls the wide tape up and down, the other one tinkles his ice, then they both look up and say simultaneously, "Measles."

"I don't believe you."

"Looks like you'll have to," says Ernie, slowing down on his tour.

"I had measles. As a child."

The whiskey drinker glances narrowly at his partner: "As far as we can tell it's the measles."

George Kaufman opens the door.

"Jesus Christ," Cy howls, "you won't believe it."

"I'll believe anything," whispers Kaufman.

Ameche says, "Our Kraut's got the measles."

Ernie resumes his trudge, Cy goes back to the floor, Kaufman buttons his waistcoat, catches sight of a spent match in the corner, picks it up and studies it closely.

"How long do measles last?" asks Ernie.

"With medical supervision thirty days, one month without," the pressure-measurer announces. He hasn't got a good audience.

"And with measles you have to stay in the dark, don't you?" Ameche asks.

"We can turn the spots on the audience, we'd probably get a prize for being avant-garde," Cy splutters.

"Can she go on playing?" Ernie asks.

"No," they answer.

Cy brings his knees up to his chin and groans, '$490,000 down the drain, a few hundred people out of work just because she——"

"O.K.," Ernie snaps, "we got the message."

"Perhaps I can go on playing. Maybe you can help me with shots or something?"

"It's catching," Ameche says.

"Couldn't we say it's an allergy?"

"For four weeks?" says Ernie. "And three hundred people get the measles?"

November 29

The whole cast is there. Julie distributes orange slices. Under her black winter coat she's wearing tights. Her ballet shoes are new, she walks as if on boards. The other dancers have long woolen socks over their calves, the girls have smeared their faces with cream, mascara smudges on their cheeks, hair pinned up and covered with scarves. They rub their knees and ankles, try to keep warm, prop their legs up on the cold radiators, bend their trunks over their thighs. The actors stand in the shabby working light with their overcoat collars turned up; the morning of a long day which will not end till the morning of the next. Lela searches for the hook on the rear wall of the set, finds it and hangs up the evening dress, places shoes on the floor, spreads a towel and the leather face cloth over the back of a chair, checks the zipper, zips it up and down, checks the hem, checks her flashlight. She picks up the shoes again and inspects the soles by the light of the flashlight, takes a pair of scissors from her apron pocket and scores the leather three times lengthways and three times sideways, rummages in her shiny bag and finds her metal nailfile, rubs the tips of the high heels with it. "Better to file 'em ten times than fall down once," she says before each run-through. She moves slowly and gently; her black, short-cropped hair is brushed back, framing her round baby forehead and tiny ears. "Wanna coffee, honey, 'fore it starts?" She moves toward the dressing room, stops after two paces as though she'd forgotten something, turns back to me and says, "You got dem spots on yo' face now."

Cy claps his hands and yells, "Everyone here? I got somethin' to say to you all."

"Close the doors!" Arthur barks.

The iron door clangs shut. Nobody moves or even dares to breathe, it seems, cheeks full of orange bulge at each other. There's a clattering in the balcony; a cleaning woman leans on her broom staring down at us.

"Get the hell outa here," Henry shouts.

Cy pushes his chin forward and says, "Hildy's got the measles."

Their heads go from Cy to me, then back to Cy, as though watching tennis in slow motion.

"We all know that your unions would close the show. You got a choice—measles or no show."

"Could be just a rash, couldn't it?" one of the dancers calls out.

"Make up your minds. You got fifteen minutes."

They form small groups, then a large circle; one of the Commissars steps forward from the circle and says, "O.K., it's a rash."

Cy says, "Don't go too close to her if you don't have to."

"We're awful sorry, Hildy," one of the ballet girls says, "like you to know we appreciate your going on."

"Cut the chatter, we go from the top!" Cy roars.

My make-up table looks like a village apothecary's. Between the Kleenex combs rouge mascara Factor-panstick there are bottles of fruit juice lotion eyedrops and scraps of paper telling what Gradma used to use. Someone has written "Chin up!" on my mirror in lipstick. When they're not on stage they all stand in the wings next to the fireman watching me anxiously. Squashed together in the Russian kitchen they whisper, "We'll cover for you if you get dizzy." I toss and bob from friendly foam-capped rollers to unfriendly chasms, Ameche stays beside me, ready to catch me if I fall. A doctor stands beside Lela and gives me shots during the changes.

December 20

I know little of what has happened in the past days and nights, can hardly remember what was rehearsal and what performance, remember only the sore throat, itching back and shoulders, burning eyes. Can still see Marlene sitting on the toilet seat supervising my bath in the green ooze, feeding me with drops and tablets between snoozes— "Open wide, eat this, drink that." Remember a Wednesday; after the second performance remember slipping from my chair and saying to myself, "The floor can't be that far away, I've been falling quite a while now," and "Funny that I still think in German when I speak English all the time." Then Lela's face, her otherwise light-brown eyes darker than her skin; the doctor digs around in search of the vein, jabs me awake. I yell at him. Lela's eyes go back to light-normal; I hear her say, "She's O.K. agin."

George Kaufman refuses to go on rewriting and adding the crude gags that Cy and Ernie insist on. He is more taciturn than ever. Cole Porter doesn't leave his hotel room at all any more. "We locked him in," says Cy. New songs every day.

The New York opening was to have been on December thirtieth. It has been postponed and the money refunded. The newspapers seem to have no theme but *Silk Stockings*. German articles prophesying disaster reach me by air mail, those reporting the Philadelphia success come by boat. The measles secret has remained one and no one else has caught them. Cy has rented a theater in Boston. That means a further four weeks of rehearsals, rewrites, performances. They have engaged what is called a "play doctor," a man who specializes in repairing shows, adding gags and whole new scenes, getting them fit for Broadway.

January 7, 1955.
Boston

It was a bad first night. I overplayed, was out of step, and the many changes have done Ninochka no good.

The choreographer was fired, dancers, actors, and singers have been replaced. The tension before each per-

formance borders on panic. Glassy-eyed we pick our way
through each scene, thinking only of the lines, trying desperately to remember what was cut and what has been
added. Each evening is an oral examination.

The "play doctor" has arrived. He is slicing through the
play like a snow plow, peppering it full of rancid Capita-
list-Communist corn, strangling Ninochka with mouthfuls
of partyese.

This morning Kaufman came onto the stage with his
wife Leueen. She said, "We're sorry to have to tell you
that Mr. Kaufman cannot continue his work on the show
for reasons of health." She turned abruptly and ran out
through the auditorium onto the street. Kaufman remained
motionless, whispered, "Please forgive me."

Cy will now direct.

Mother had planned to come to New York on New
Year's Day if *Silk Stockings* survived the opening; now she
cables: ARRIVING BOSTON 9 JANUARY.

January 8

There's a park across from the hotel. Children in red
green blue bonnets toboggan down little slopes. I can't hear
their cries, nor the clip-clop of the two horses being led
down the path by a groom. The Grandma Moses picture is
obscured at the lower right corner by Cy's head; by Ernie's
ear, temple and black hair at the upper right.

It's early morning, before rehearsal; my breakfast tray is
on the floor, milk has slopped over the toast. Blue-white
light from the winter sky turns the edges of yellow light
from the table lamp greenish.

"I would like you to release me from my contract," I
say. "Ninochka has nothing more to do with the part I
signed for."

Cy: "We still got three weeks till New York, a lot'll be
changed."

"Too much has been changed already," I answer.

A girl with long red hair falls from her sled and rolls
over in the snow; a woman runs to her, brushes the white
from the red. I'll be attacked, the press will write that she
was afraid, incapable, but this will be later, not tonight.

"You can't duck out," Cy says.

I'll fly to Chicago with Mother. She'll see her brother
again.

"You're tired, give yourself a chance," says Ernie.

"We'll give you a day off rehearsals," says Cy.

The hill in the Schöneberg municipal park was steeper; if you went down on your stomach you had to watch that you didn't bang into the low railing with your head.

"Try to sleep a coupla hours, we don't need you at the theater till twelve," says Cy.

"Believe me," Ernie says, "we all want the same thing. A hit in New York."

The agent was here. "I need money for my mother," I said, "for the trip to Chicago, hotel, and all that."

"I can give you a hundred dollars, that'll be plenty for Mama."

It was before rehearsal; I was holding a teacup in my left hand and an eggspoon in my right. I slam down the spoon on the white shell, soft-boiled yellow spurts on the table and carpet; I take her by the collar, want to speak, can't, my tongue sticks to my palate, spittle runs dry, I pull her up and press her to the wall. "I haven't stopped working for years. When I say I need money I mean I need my money and not a loan." I let go of her. My heart thumps in my throat.

"You're going to be sorry you did that," she says, slamming the door.

January 10

The plane was due to land at 9:30 in the evening. Arthur had offered to pick Mother up and bring her to the theater; they'd be there shortly before the finale, he said. "Flight's delayed twelve hours," he whispered as I was changing from the uniform into the evening dress. "There's a storm over the Atlantic, they haven't left Shannon yet."

In the morning I drove out to the airport. The frosty-salt east wind piles up mounds of snowflakes, prompts thoughts of lentil soup with chunks of bacon, of potato pancakes straight from the pan, rollmops and sour gherkins, flabby ones spilling their juice down your hands.

The four-engined plane crawls out of the milky blue mist, hovers over the runway, the wheels touch down and hop up again, the body shivers, shakes itself like a steaming wet horse, twitches like cowhide bothered by flies, quiets down. A fat man runs down the gangway carrying newspapers, an attaché case, an unfurled umbrella. The wind catches the umbrella and blows it open, bending the spokes.

Then a stewardess appears leading a boy with a red fire engine pressed to his chest; then Mother. Her gray cap takes off as though she had thrown it, bowls back again and dances under the belly of the plane. A frozen-looking airport photographer takes his snap and brings her cap. Mother says, "Thank you" in English. She blinks and makes her we'll-manage-somehow face. On Saturdays, when all our regulars came for their shoes and casual customers wanted a seam stitched in a hurry, she'd say, "We'll manage somehow."

"You look awful, child," she says in the terminal building, "you've lost so much weight."

"I'll get it back," I say.

"You flew to Boston that first time too," Mother says.

I had forgotten. The customs officers are as good-natured as St. Bernards, the suitcases stay shut. "Good luck," they say.

"On the way to London one of the engines broke down, the propellor suddenly stood still. Lots of them didn't get back on again." She rubs the steamed-up window with her glove. "Doesn't look like America at all," she says. "Don't worry about me, now, I've brought a dictionary."

"Would you like to sleep first?"

"I don't think I could."

"Then come to rehearsal."

Ameche puts his arms around her and says, "Welcome to America."

"How do you do?" Mother asks and quickly peers down at her dictionary.

Some of the dancers smile at her and say, "Hi." One of the Commissars tries out his German: "Das ist 'mama, ja-woll," he says several times.

"Why does he say 'jawoll'?" Mother asks.

"It's what all the Nazis say in American films."

After the performance she comes to my dressing room. She twiddles her narrow wedding ring and says after a while, "You're not happy. Funny, I felt it more as you came on the stage than at the airport this morning, even though I understood very little. Else Bongers told me to tell you you should back out if you're not happy with the show; you should take all the money you've earned in the last years and take a vacation. Yes, that's what she asked me to tell you."

"I've signed a contract."

"How long?"

"Run of the play—that means as long as the show lasts on Broadway."

"I sometimes wonder whether I should hope it's a success," she says.

January 12

Yvonne's part has been recast for the third time. Cy and Ernie asked Moss Hart, who had written several plays with George Kaufman, to come from New York. They wanted to hear his opinion. "You have to let it settle." he said and looked at his watch, still hoping to catch the last train back "They're all playing as though they were under ether, only thinking of cues, lines, cuts, and so on. If you don't let it play unchanged for at least ten days in a row then don't be surprised that it looks like Saturday night at the ball game. And you can't come to town the way it is anyway."

"Maybe we should forget *Silk Stockings* and do *The Merry Widow* in Alaska instead," the play doctor cackles.

He cackles alone. Since Kaufman left we are thin-skinned and not at all receptive to the play doctor's sense of humor. The atmosphere has grown abrasive, the tone is louder. When they railed at Henry for fading a spot too late yesterday he stalked onto the stage and yelled, "Fade it yourself!" Cy and Ernie fumed and snorted but Henry's still there.

January 14

New York has been postponed again. We're going to Detroit at the end of the month. "Oh you'll love 'em," Herb said, "they're as solid as the bumpers they build for General Motors, and instead of laughing they dip their fog lamps." It's the longest out-of-town tryout a Broadway production has ever had.

The dressing rooms are small, hardly bigger than a disrobing room in an X-ray office; the dividing walls start at the ankles and end two hands above the head, the dressing tables are built into the walls. We feel spied upon, though no one spies; we call out to each other, a little stiffly knowing that everyone hears, spin the gags out further and further, milk them to death. Twenty or more eaux de colognes team up under and over the partitions, challenge odors of peppermint and burnt sulfur, sweet smell of tinted talc. Henry begins his implacable countdown. At five to eight the loudspeakers click: "Half hour, half an hour, please." The first call sounds bored, remote, still lots of time to play with, is more a query about possible absentees, treadmill tone. The next is crisp and curt: "Fifteen minutes, fifteen minutes, please." Categorical, incorruptible, threatening: anyone still not made-up shaved dressed had better watch out. Then: "Five minutes! I repeat, five minutes, please." This is bellicose, this smacks of fall in on the parade ground, company halt, right turn, objective viaduct, prepare to open fire. "So let's go," a cellmate mutters, "hats off and pray." Then there's a cease-fire stillness until the speakers click for the last time and Henry's furious: "Place for the first act, please! Houselights! Overture!" detonates. And away they go; the trumpeters fight to rid themselves of all frustration before they have to show consideration for our puny instruments, the drummer thwacks his skins and cymbals as though he were in a strip joint, the strings get the edge on the brass, all the strains are stewed by the speakers, music ground through a mincer.

Mother sits on my "guest stool." "Why don't you take a taxi back to the hotel?"

"If I'm not in the way, I'd rather stay here."

During intermission she stands squashed against the partition. Lela rubs me down, pulls on my dress, dries my hair with a hand-dryer. "I'm glad you've got Lela, she's so calm," Mother says. Lela has understood "Lela" and smiles at her.

Shortly before twelve we clatter down the corridor like a herd reprieved from the slaughter, noisily, chattily, the show over, rehearsal about to begin, New York ever present like an iceberg looming out of the ocean. I am just smearing cleansing cream on my rouge and brown panstick when there's a knock at the door. "Come in," I shout over the dressing-room din. A woman enters. She has round blue eyes, dark blond hair, is impeccably turned out like all American women who give a damn. I look at her in the mirror, turn around, knock against Mother's knee. "Remember me?" the woman asks in German.

"Yes."

"Hilde Jansen," she says, just in case.

She shakes Mother's hand, embraces me, her diamond brooch gets tangled with my bathrobe, pulls a long thread. "I've been living in Boston for quite a while now, I married a Bostonian," she says.

Duwe's charcoal-burner in front of the Deutsche Theater, the bunker in the Friedrichstrasse, "La Paloma" in
E.v.D.'s home cinema, air-raid shelter; we wear the same
size shoes, she lent me a pair of brown pumps once, suede.

"I'm giving a small dinner party for a few friends tonight, why don't you both come?" she says.

"We've got a rehearsal. They often go on till three or
four in the morning."

In the corridor she asks, "Have you heard from E.v.D.?"

"No."

"I heard he was dead."

"I don't know."

"Weren't you with him when the Russians came?"

"Everyone on stage, please," Arthur calls.

"Good luck for New York. Sometimes I get the urge to
act again. But only sometimes." She laughs and waves. At
the stage door she turns back once more. An attractive,
neat American in a mink coat.

Mother and I get back to the hotel at three o'clock. "Do
you want me to be there for the opening in New York?"
Mother asks.

"No. I'll call you the moment it's over."

"Before you go to Detroit I'll go and visit my brother.
It's a funny feeling—we haven't seen each other since
1928."

January 20

Now we're swapping songs. I had to sing Ameche's "Silk
Stockings" song. I stood in the Russian kitchen crying for
my silk stockings.

Tomorrow Ameche gets his song back.

Cole Porter observes each disfiguration of his work with
the reserve of an English butler.

February 5
Detroit

After the first performance in Detroit—one couldn't call
it a première—even the otherwise optimistic Ameche came
to the conclusion that all we'll see of New York will be the
railway station when we change trains. Kaufman's soufflé
has become hash, liberally salted. I can't help thinking that
the audience endures the three and one-half hours only to
be able to say, "We saw it before it folded."

Herb Greene murmured, "Cy and Ernie are wondering what other far-flung outposts we could grace with a visit. I caught 'em looking at a globe." Cy on the other hand swears that, barring earthquakes, deluge, or the outbreak of pestilence, the New York opening will take place on February 24 at 8:30 in the evening.

February 9

The few of us who have been with the show from the first day are beginning to resemble the pitiful creatures on posters appealing for relief in famine areas.

Tyrone Power called from Washington, where he's playing Christopher Fry's *The Dark Is Light Enough.* It's his first theatrical venture. He opens in New York in mid-February, he and an infectious hepatitis he picked up he doesn't know where. "I'm divorced and cleaned out," he said, "if you stand me on my head and shake me a gallstone's the most you'll find." His contract with Fox has lapsed.

February 16

Several scenes from the original version have been reintroduced. Cy says the show's running a great deal better and one can tell we're beginning to enjoy it. We regard him with the indulgence one shows to an obstreperous octogenarian.

February 17

From my hotel window I see the Huron River, the long bridge, the border between Canada and the United States. I know that the bridge is a bridge, the Huron a river, the border here and not there. I know that I should eat the steak under the warm tin cover, the green beans as well, but I stand at the window and look at the river bridge border, think: Fluss Brücke Grenze. I say the words in English: river bridge border. These are the only words I can remember, the last words of a language I am losing, word for word, phrase for phrase, a language I had understood and understand no more.

February 18

Someone from the agency has rented the Fifth Avenue penthouse for me. For four weeks.

My stage fright gets worse at every performance. During

the overture I hope for a theater fire, typhoon, revolution in the Pentagon.

Poor Arthur announces with a serves-her-right expression, "Yvonne's in the hospital, had a miscarriage." Cy and Ernie have finally decided on a plump blonde with a voice like a fanfare.

February 22
New York

We arrived on a sleeper from Detroit this morning. We reckon in hours, saying to ourselves: forty-eight hours means two breakfasts, two steaks, two nights' rehearsal, two evenings without an audience, a few hours' sleep. Means time. I could have gone on traveling for weeks in the train, in the clean compartment with the wide bed and my own shower; would have let myself be rocked from Canada to Mexico, from San Francisco to New Orleans, lying on foam rubber staring at the black gray blue sky. Generous train, not like ours in Europe, sooty, musty, too hot or too cold, flea-bitten brown plush, chamberpot under the saucer-sized basin, customs officials groping in suitcases at three in the morning.

The taxi that took me from the station to the apartment was the usual beat-up lopsided yellow one with no ashtrays. The license displayed a photograph and the name ISAAK LOEWENZAHN in capital letters. On Forty-first Street we stood for a quarter of an hour wedged between a Greyhound bus and a garbage truck. "Is that a life?" Isaak Loewenzahn said, "I ask yuh, what sortova life is that?" The garbage truck edged in on us inch by inch until Isaak Loewenzahn rolled down his window and yelled, "Anyone int'rested in a tall thin Chevvy?" Looking into his rear mirror he said, "An' you ain't feelin' so hunky-dory either, huh? Two days to the openin'?"

"You're right."

"Reconnized ya right away from photos and the movie— what was it called again? Show gonna be good?"

"No idea."

"Has Peck got bowlegs or ain't he?"

"Didn't look."

A pencil was balanced on his right ear, a cigarette on the other. A morning paper was lying on the seat beside him; during the ride he leafed through it, at red lights he settled down to read, changed gears and accelerated without looking up, knew exactly when red would turn green. In between he chatted with his rear mirror. I missed a great deal of what he said since he was chewing gum, adding a fresh piece every few minutes and munching them like old crusts of bread.

" 'Nother show folded yesterday," he said between chewing, leafing, reading, changing gears, and bawling out the window, "an' the one they say ain't too hot at all—that gets raves." He shrugged his shoulders and made galloping noises on the dashboard with his fingers. "Folks talk when they come outta the theaters, that's how I get to know what's goin' on. An' sometimes I go to a mat'nee. Tallulah's show's crap but she's great, an' *Can-Can*—that's from Porter too, ain't bad, ain't bad. Is that a cough I hear?" For the first time he turned around and looked at me directly. His eyes seemed to hang in his face, the outer corners flopped down onto his cheeks and two deep lines ran from his eyelids to his throat; beside them the ears stood out like handles on the cropped head. It was a hastily assembled face; it must have come about under strange circumstances. "Isaak Loewenzahn, get ready for birth!" someone probably called at the last minute, and there was no time to match things up. The nose encroached on the mouth and there would not have been space for three hairs on the upper lip, whereas the chin was as big as a prize fighter's fist.

"Did I hear a cough?" he repeated threateningly as his eyes sagged lower and lower.

"I cleared my throat," I said.

"Don't gimme that, I know a cough when I hear one," he insisted. "We're gonna make a little detour, my brother-in-law's gotta drugstore, stocks the best cough drops in town."

"I don't have time, I have to be at the theater in an hour."

"Don't worry, from Tenth to Forth-sixth takes me eight minutes, you'll be the Imperial on time—you're at the Imperial ain't ya?"

"Yes."

He trampled on the brakes and the clutch, I slid from the seat to the wet corrugated rubber mat on the floor, then he banged into neutral, ran into a crowded shop, pointed at the taxi with one hand, at a shelf with the other, threw money over people's heads, caught the paper bag thrown back, ran out again, bumped into the waiting policeman, grinned nervously at the pile-up of hooting traffic behind the wrongly parked taxi, pointed at me, rolled his eyes and held his hand to his throat in a somewhat overplayed portrayal of heart attack plus asphyxia, jumped in behind the wheel, tossed the bag over his shoulder and said, "Suck 'em slowly."

"How much were they?" I said, sucking bitterly.

"Forget it," he said, raised his right hand casually at my "Thank you" and took a curve with his left.

In front of the hotel he stretched his arm over the seat-back, opened my door and said, "Loewenzahn'll be waitin' in thirty minutes." I tried to read the meter. "Gratis," he said, "for Broadway greenhorns it's free." He opened the paper at the funnies, laid them across the steering wheel and drove up to the red light at Fourteenth Street on squealing tires.

The hotel manager with silver-gray hair and matching tie showed me the penthouse. It's on the eighteenth floor, has a terrace on all four sides, a stainless steel antiseptic kitchen, an icebox in which three people could stand comfortably, two bedrooms and bathrooms. "The staff and faculties are at your disposal, otherwise this penthouse is independent of the rest of the hotel, apart from the elevator, of course. We rent it only to reliable guests," he added gently. "You're German, aren't you?"

"Yes."

He nodded happily.

I set my alarm clock, lay down on the bed and fell asleep. Five minutes later the door bell rang. "Who's there?" I called.

Through the closed door I heard a muffled, "Open up, it's Hardy."

"What are you doing in New York?"

"I've come to hold your hand." Hardy Krüger said, still standing in the door, still looking as though he'd recently come of age, blond hair short and spiky. Two years ago we had made a film together, *Illusion in Minor* it was called, and had become good friends.

"I've got a ticket for the first night, center balcony. How long do you rehearse?"

"God knows, sometimes it's two or three, or four."

"I'll take a look at the town, then I'll pick you up and we'll go and hear some jazz. Do you good." In Isaak's cab he heard me run through the lines of a new scene. "If we fold I can fly back with you," I said at the stage door. Hardy stood on the steps and looked at me, stood as he would have done in Berlin or Hamburg, said, "Sorry," as someone bumped into him, and then, "You'll make out."

February 24

Dress rehearsal with stops and repeats is at one o'clock. There are no fights: bad sign. A hairdresser named Ronnie has been engaged. At six I lie down on a camp bed— my dressing room is so small that I have to get up and lift it against the wall if someone wants to come in. Opposite my make-up table there's a door to the john, on the other side of the john there's another door to Ameche's dressing room. Lela has brought me a steak. It's red and raw in the middle, blood runs over the plate. "Yuh gotta eat it," she says, knowing that I won't, and goes out, turning off the light. I try to sleep. "Relax the left leg, now the right leg, put off all thoughts till later——" "Later" brings on a stomach cramp, a nerve taps on my jaw, light wells up behind my eyes, belly large and hollow, nudging my heart, thumbnail picks at the skin under the half-moon of the index finger. Telegrams are heaped on my dressing table, Lela has opened them. The top one is from Käthe Dorsch. That she remembers . . . light-years since Lake Atter. Lela says that every star on Broadway has wired, even Tallulah Bankhead.

Don is pacing in his dressing room. I know he's frightened. I'll smoke one more cigarette, only one. It's suffocating in here, hasn't even got a window. Ronnie comes in, combs my hair, fumbles with the tongs. We don't speak. Lela is gray, even her eyes are gray. Don warms his voice: "O mia bella Napoli . . ." "Why didn't no one murder him till now?" asks Ronnie. "Silenzio!" I holler. "Deutschland, Deutschland über Alles," rumbles through two doors, then he's standing behind me, cigarette holder between his teeth, says, "Whatever happens, Kraut . . ."

In the toilet bowl I see the word ELBA, the makers have named their model ELBA; Elba, Napoleon . . . there have been worse bust-ups. . . .

Henry goes from door to door saying, "Half hour." No loudspeakers today. Cy's there, tuxedo, Ernie too. "There we are," Cy says. Ernie buttons and re-buttons his jacket. They go out. Porter sits down on Lela's stool, stands up

again, says "Yes," closes the door carefully. It is absolutely
quiet. It's as if I were lying in an operating theater,
strapped down, all prepared, doctors and nurses gone. I
have my uniform on. There's nothing more to do. Someone
yanks the door open—"I'm from *Life* magazine, we wanna
get a cover photo, face just before the curtain goes up, the
tension——" "OUT," Lela screams, "OUT!" In the corridor I hear, "The Trumans are out front, and Skouras. The
lobby looks like Tiffany's. . . ."

I start to shake, from the bottom to the top, feet knees
spine head chin, shake, it won't stop, tears shake off my
cheeks. "You'll make it, Honey," Lela says, picks up her
flashlight and pulls me along behind her. We stumble along
the wall behind the set over to the left side where the spiral
stairs go up to the ballet dressing room. High up above between the backdrops hanging in the flies the hooded lights
wink like stars behind streaks of clouds. The curtain hurtles
up, whoosh, takes a layer of skin with it. "Help," I want to
say, "Help." I hear my cue. The Head Commissar is miles
away, I walk and walk and walk and then I'm at his desk,
stop, salute. He gapes at me—dries, no idea what to say,
where he is, what to do. Applause breaks out, they go on
clapping. He opens his mouth, I hear nothing. I speak, hear
nothing. I miss a line—which one? Too late, the Commissar
gives the wrong cue, I jump two speeches. Then Ameche.
Applause for the duet. Quick change, leather cloth, zipper,
Lela rubs my wrists with ice. Three hours late I'm sitting
on the piano in the Russian kitchen, dancers, chorus—over
their heads I see Ameche, silent love scene in the midst of
the tumult, Ninochka and Capitalist fall into each other's
arms, finale, curtain. We stand in a long line like on Olympic team, bow in groups, singly. We'd rehearsed it last night,
with the music, bar for bar, step for step, just in case.

Don puts a lighted cigarette in my mouth, the fireman
passes us, says nothing, Lela hands me a glass of whiskey,
we stand behind the curtain. Photographers storm the
stage, photograph our streaming faces. Marlene embraces
me, says, "Smile." My sweaty hands leave smears on her
shimmering white robe. The corridor is stuffed full, the
buckets of flowers have been knocked over, the wall telephone next to the stage door rings continuously, Marlene
says, "See you at Sardi's." Otto Preminger's bald dome
bobs in front of me. "Bravo," he says, "you've arrived." Cy
picks his way through the buckets, Ernie's stuck against the

cupboard. "All depends on the papers," says Cy. "But they
gotta say it's a hit, even if they chew their typewriters," Arthur yells over the coiffures, earrings, fur shoulders, tuxedo
lapels.

Autograph hunters are crowded in front of the stage
door clapping and singing the songs from the show. Lela
packs bundles of flowers into the cab, Hardy pushes me
onto the seat, we drive two blocks to Forty-fourth Street.
Cars are standing three deep in front of Sardi's, two cops
blow furiously on their whistles, mink and chinchilla jostle
at the door, the doorman stands with folded arms letting no
one in or out. "Miss Neff?" he whispers uncertainly, opens
the door and holds up the curtain. Success signal. They are
sitting reading on the first floor. Look up, go on reading.
Marlene says, "Atkinson's all for it." She folds up the big
Times and orders champagne. Suddenly I don't care. No
joy, no excitement. Tired, empty, dead. Marlene says, "It
was better in Philadelphia, it was a play set to music." Preminger says, "Enjoy the success. I didn't see it in Philadelphia, I liked it and so did everyone else." He raised his
glass: "Two years at least!" The champagne makes me
drunk, harebrained, sadly drunk. An agent says, "Be
happy. You're the greatest." Hardy takes me home at four.
The concierge congratulates me, the telephone operator
looks out from behind the switchboard with her earphones
around her neck and says, "Great." The penthouse looks
like a florist's at Easter. On the coffee table there's a package, in it a gold Cartier traveling clock, engraved: "To Hildegarde with love. Leueen and George Kaufman." They
weren't there tonight.

Hardy says, "Sleep it off. I'll call tomorrow afternoon."

Mother is still awake. "I heard the news on TV," she
says, " 'great success' I was able to understand, my brother
translated the rest. Be with you in a week."

The terrace floor is slippery. Over the tips of the iron
railings I look down at Fifth Avenue and the corner of
Tenth Street, see the flat roofs of the three- and-four-story
houses, high above me the Chrysler Building and the Empire State, the Hudson is invisible, and the docks, the ships,
their sirens like sea lions barking. Two police cars shoot
past Washington Square, their sirens like an air-raid warning. In between, swelling for seconds then fading: Thelon-
ius Monk, grunts from the tugboats.

This evening at 8:30 the curtain goes up. Tommorrow at

2:30. Tomorrow is Saturday, two performances. At ten in the morning the overseas exchange says, "Call from Germany for you Miss Neff, and congratulations on your great success." The newspapers call, the voices faint, scratchy, like old phonograph records: "What's your reaction? What are you wearing at the moment? Are you still celebrating? We're proud of our Hilde."

Success. Broadway success.

TWENTY

Broadway is not "Broadway." Broadway has everything except theaters. Squashed together in the side streets, wall to wall between Seventh and Eighth Avenues and Forty-third and Fifty-third Street are the theaters that are "Broadway." Broadway is the street with the tin-pot carnival atmosphere of a bustling port, with its peepshows, dirty movies, middle-class cinemas, bars, and rooms by the hour; it runs diagonally from the top of Manhattan across the tidy parallel streets, crosses Seventh Avenue and becomes Times Square, slices arbitrarily across the island and dwindles to a stop near the southern tip between garbage dumps and Battery Park.

New York spoils me, shows me that success is welcome, doesn't envy or pick holes. To be a Broadway star means permanently reserved tables in crowded restaurants, dentist on Sundays, our only free day, cabs stopping when hailed, even in sudden showers, laughing into lenses arm in arm with Presidents, interviews, radio shows, TV shows, singing lessons, dancing lessons, keep fit, be on time, save the voice. Never "Hildy," always "Miss Neff," printed invitations four weeks in advance; eight performances a week, show sold out for months to come. On Mondays, Tuesdays, Thursdays, Fridays steak and salad at 4:30, sleep from 4:45 until 6:15, tea with honey at 6:30, cab 7:10, theater 7:20. Make up, dress, warm up the voice. Wednesdays and Saturdays the same, three and a half hours earlier. Matinee over at 6, tea in the dressing room, sleep on the camp bed. Everyone must be at the theater half an hour before curtain, even dancers who don't appear until twenty minutes before the finale. Latecomers are wanred the first time, penalized with a cut of two-thirds of their weekly salaries the second, and fired on the spot the third. Understudies have been engaged for Ameche and me. They have rehearsed our parts and now hope and fear we may break a leg.

They arrive punctually and remain in the theater until the last curtain. Cy and Ernie attend two shows a week without warning, creep into the back row of the balcony and whisper points of displeasure into portable tape recorders, order a morning rehearsal if the performance runs longer than the opening. For anyone to build up his part or start to improvise is out of the question. There are no squabbles and no intrigues, no stars or bit-players. Everyone visits everyone else and no one takes umbrage when Henry yells, "Shut your big mouth when the curtain's up!"

I'm still nervous. When the loudpseakers click and Henry says, "Fifteen minutes," my fingertips go dead, something moans between my ribs. I call it chicken, it moans on until I step into the spots and report to the Head Commissar. "If the chicken feeling ever leaves you, you'll be no good," Henry says, "you can't say 'Good evening' to Fredric March backstage, he goes crazy."

My suitcases are in the cellar gathering dust. I now have keys to the street door as well as to the apartment, carry credit cards and a telephone book with the numbers of the doctors, the tradesmen, the police and fire departments, receive monthly bills from the butcher, the drugstore, the supermarket. I live in New York. We live, Mother and I. She crosses Fifth Avenue as though it were the Kurfürstendamm. Now she goes to the German neighborhood on Eighty-sixth Street only when she needs black bread, liverwurst, Westphalian ham, or Danziger Goldwasser. In the evenings she takes English lessons or goes to the opera, the movies, the theater. She has Hungarian, German, Dutch, and Swedish friends. Between Central Park and Geenwich Village, the East River and the Hudson, Wilmersdorf has gotten lost.

Tyrone has been playing Christopher Fry for nine weeks now. The reviews were middling. After our respective shows he, Ameche, and I walk through the wind up to Fifty-first Street and sit on the wooden benches of smoky Basin Street, hear Mulligan and Chet Baker, go on to Reuben's and eat blintzes, or take a cab to the Village Vanguard. Baker's trumpet ricochets around nocturnal Manhattan's brawling streets and quiet avenues, mingles with New York, the sirens and horns, belongs here as the rumble of elevated railways and creaks from heavy front doors belong to Berlin; Brubeck's 'Take the A Train,' Paul

Desmond's threads of sound, Erroll Garner, Peterson, and
Max Roach die with the dawn, with the spluttering hose
trucks sluicing the curbs. Farewell Mulligan, sand-colored
in the white-yellow light of the shallow stage, stepping
aside, turning off when the chorus is over, no interest at all
in applause, take it or leave it. One of them is always fid-
dling with the cables or speakers, microphones and mouth-
pieces, doodling, stepping out to play, remote, almost in a
trance, then doodling. They seem to have time, like the old
men who play chess on the benches in Washington Square.
Unheeding, shifting their levels of consciousness over the
furor of leisure, over the corporeal go-getters.

I get to know people who are just visiting and drop into
the dressing room, and people who live in New York and
for whom everything of value in life is to be found in Manhattan. They need neither cars nor weekend houses, plan
no vacations or trips. They sniff through the town like
bloodhounds, forever finding something new that's worth
seeing or hearing, unearthing galleries, restaurants, li-
braries, a cinema that runs only silent films, a vegetable
stand that sells Italian tomatoes, a bookstore that stocks
Henry Miller.

Dr. Manfred George was born in Berlin; his forefathers
came from Uckermark. They had voluntarily defended
Germany's honor with saber and shako in the numerous
wars of the nineteenth century and their offspring Manfred
had served in Flanders and Russia in '14-'18 with valor, if
not of his own volition. Warned of impending arrest, he
had later escaped over the Czech mountains and landed in
Prague with neither clothes nor money. An invasion cur-
tailed his stay so he hurried on and eventually found himself in New York. Manfred George, tenacious and on the
smaller side of medium height, often cynical and rationalis-
tic, often metaphysically inclined and sometimes emotional,
had crafty eyes. Crafty and inquisitive, behind rimless
spectacles. His soft speech was accompanied by little
coughs, his long fingers were never still. Dr. Manfred
George was the publisher and chief editor of the newspaper
Aufbau and had already requested an interview during rehearsals. And because we had thought it blockish to sit in a
hotel lounge we went to the Museum of Modern Art. And
at the Museum of Modern Art we stood in front of a Rous-
seau and forgot the interview. Looking at the tiger's head
and the sofa in the middle of the jungle he said, "Do you

know Miller? Henry, I mean, nor Arthur." "No." I could have done him no bigger favor. He took me to the rehearsal and said, "You'll be hearing from me. And read the *Tropics* first."

Ninochka stood in Miller's way until after the New York opening. Then I read him and called George. Miller brought me together with George and George with Miller and later, after I had met him, I was able to tell George about Miller. After this telephone call I received J. D. Salinger's *Catcher in the Rye* and "Teddy" and "Esme" and a box of paints: "I know that you used to paint. You'll need some distraction now, you must balance the nightly monotony." Then came Orozco, Kierkegaard, André Gide, the complete works of Shakespeare, including the sonnets, with a note: "After Shakespeare nobody really need write; that some still do shows courage." Since I was never able to go to the theater, apart from the one I was playing in, he picked out films that were showing in the early afternoon, between voice lessons and steak, nap, honey-tea and cab to the theater. After viewing my first Sunday efforts in oil he praised my sense of composition and feeling for color and sent me large canvases and a comprehensive book on the possibilities of mixing oil, tempera, and water colors. In other words he held my head above water. Then came the afternoon when we visited an exhibition of photographs. The first two rooms were full of mannered shots in the pottery-class tradition; in the third was a Korean War picture of a GI holding his dead buddy. He was holding him as a mother holds her child, his face caked with dirt, his helmet pushed forward over his eyes, tears coursing in clean streams through the dirt. I didn't know I was crying until he touched my arm and pushed a handkerchief into my hands, then stood beside me looking helpless, caught unawares. We didn't speak and when I found a taxi and drove back to Tenth Street I forgot to say good-bye.

After the performance he was sitting in my dressing room. "May I smoke?" he asked and his long fingers picked awkwardly at the strip around the cellophane cover. "I took the liberty of accepting a cup of tea." He looked up at Lela and smiled gratefully. He reminded me of someone who says "With your permission" and "If I may make so bold," and knocks although the door's wide open; and he knew it. "I should like to ask a favor of you," he said, louder and more assertive.

Ameche came in. "I had a frog in my throat," he said, "did you notice?" After I had introduced them Don said, "You have to take the sign off, two reporters from the *Herald Tribune* and the *Daily News* are coming tomorrow."

"Yes, I must say I was quite bewildered," said George.

"She started it," Ameche said and looked over my head into the mirror. "If we go on losing weight they're not gonna see us any more from the back of the orchestra, maybe we should apply for jobs on radio."

Ronnie the hairdresser shot through the door yelping, "Why do the signs have to go?"

" 'Cause the press is coming," said Ameche.

"You both got no character," Ronnie said.

"What's on 'em, anyway?" a delicate black-haired youth, Ronnie's new assistant, asked and went out into the passage. He was bowled over by the appearance of a massive lady in a tiny veiled hat who strode through the door and clumped Ameche on the shoulder. "I'm president of the committee to keep our parks clean an' we're throwin' a ball Saturday why dontcha both come an' sing for us?"

"We play on Saturdays."

"Come in the intermissions."

"The intermission lasts fifteen minutes."

"Make it longer."

"You'd have to ask Cy Feuer."

"Thanks a million, you swell people," she burbled and bumped into the door. "Well what on earth's that?" she cried and stared at us.

"You see?" said Ameche.

We had both put up beautifully printed signs on our doors. One read: ENTRY IS STRICTLY FORBIDDEN TO ITALIANS. PERSONS DISREGARDING THIS WARNING WILL BE PROSECUTED BY LAW. The other: KRAUTS GO HOME.

At the same moment a liveried chauffeur entered the room and placed a tureen full of raw sauerkraut on my make-up table. "With the compliments of Mr. Power," he whispered. The massive lady was still standing there staring from one to the other and her open mouth disclosed incisors smeared with dark red lipstick.

"It's her daily ration," Ameche said, "all of us on Broadway chip in for her because her salary goes to the zoo to support immigrating turtles."

"We won't see her again," Ronnie cackled when the lady had gone.

"If you waste half your youth on *Silk Stockings* you have to kill time somehow," Ameche said and strode into his dressing room, prodding both toilet doors open with his foot. A furious grunt informed Lela and me that he had stuck his arms into the shirt sleeves she had sewn up during the last act.

Poor Arthur looked around the door and said, "We were four minutes too long."

"I had a frog in my throat," said Ameche.

"And Hildy dragged her soliloquy," said Arthur. "Which horse did you bet on?" he asked in the direction of Ameche's door.

"Nashua."

"A lot?"

"A lot."

Walter Slezak, who was playing in a hit musical version of a Marcel Pagnol play, waddled in and said, "We had two thousand deaf-mute Albanians out front tonight, how were yours?" He greeted George, whose crafty eyes were now glinting amused-confusedly, and added, "Basically they're all still wearing feathers."

Tyrone Power squeezed into the densely populated doorway. The bundle of newspapers under his arm slid to the floor, he raised his eyesbrows and said, "For reasons of fairness I'm obliged to inform you that your ad in the *Mirror* was highly successful. Fifty-two absolutely charming people willing to sell me their homing pigeons called during the day."

"We had nothing to do with it," Ameche and I cooed.

Lela suddenly caught her breath as she was rinsing the teapot and stared at the floor. Ameche came in saying, "I gotta go to a birthday party, they'll all be plastered by the time I get there anyway," bent down to pick a thread off his trouser leg, stayed bent down, staring at the floor. George too, Ronnie likewise. Only Tyrone took a cigarette from his case, lit it lackadaisically and said, "Lela, would you mind mixing me a whiskey—if the Kraut doesn't brew it herself, that is."

Lela didn't hear, went on staring at the floor, her breath coming in short doses. Slezak said, "I would be very glad to learn why you are all staring at the floor. I am the founder of the Society for Looking-Glass Balls since I can only see mine in the mirror—"

"You gotta get 'em to print that it was all a mistake," gasped Ronnie and gave me one of the papers. In banner headlines I read: HILDEGARDE NEFF TO SING AT MET.

"It ain't true, is it?" Lela whispered, almost choking.

"What?" Tyrone asked, threading his way to the john.

"That Hilde's gonna sing at the Met," said Ronnie.

Tyrone stood with outstretched fingers and said, "Which of you smeared the doorknobs with honey?"

"We had nothing to do with it," Ameche and I cooed.

"When do you ever get time to act?" asked Tyrone, attempting to maneuver a handkerchief from his breast pocket.

"And where did you have the pretty papers printed?" I asked him.

"Me?" he said.

"You're all crazy," murmured George.

"This is just the beginning," said Ronnie, "wait till they get to the five hundredth performance. Cole Porter once got six concert grands delivered to his apartment on the same day, he had to move out."

Tyrone and Don looked at each other pensively.

"What's the favor?" I asked Manfred George as we stood in Times Square. "Later," he said. We ate dripping hamburgers, walked with the crowd, stood wedged between sailors in front of a restaurant where a Dixieland band was romping on a high wide counter, jostled on again for two blocks. "I've never been to Basin Street," George said, "would you go with me? I have no relationship to jazz, even though I've lived so long in New York." We clambered over swinging legs and stamping feet and sat down under the bass, which was booming like an invitation to a macumba dance. "I bought a Brubeck record to get an idea," George shouted. After Mulligan had played an ecstatic chorus, the crowd roaring, "Yeah man yeah," and "Go man go," George said, "The favor I ask of you is—not to laugh at me." The musicians rolled off the stage and a pimply youth took the microphone, his body still bobbing in time with the last number, raised it to his mouth like a spoonful of soup and breathed, "Back in a while."

George lit a cigarette and said, "Did you wake up this morning at four and stand at your living-room window for a long time trying to think why you were so frightened?

Did you then open a can and cut yourself doing so?"

"Yes," I said, and looked at the bandage on my left thumb, wondering from where one might see into the penthouse. It was impossible. The wide terrace obscured the windows from the street on the living-room and Tenth Street side, there was nothing opposite that would have served as a peephole, and on the side facing east, facing the East River, there were no windows at all, only the elevator and an emergency staircase.

"I often write important articles at night," he said, "and I suddenly saw you walking about in your apartment yesterday. I was about to call you, then thought better of it. Did you get up, or am I wrong?"

"No, you're right," I said, "about everything."

"This is the first time I've had this extrasensory perception, I think it's called. I was beginning to think that overwork and a certain awe you inspire in me were playing tricks."

"Awe, why awe?"

He pulled the filter from the cigarette, went on smoking and picking at threads of tobacco, shrugged his shoulders, brushed a hand across his thin gray hair and said, "I once had a deep relationship with a fire extinguisher; since then I have learned to treat my nocturnal visitations with care." He looked at his hand and chuckled. "For a long time I drew comfort from the fact that a light burned in the window opposite my study until six in the morning. It was good to know I wasn't the only insomniac in the neighborhood. One day my curiosity got the better of me and I crossed the street and took the elevator to the twelfth floor but there was nothing there but offices and an emergency light over a fire extinguisher."

In the taxi he said, "When you cried this afternoon I felt like one of the heroes from the realms of Kafka, someone who has circled a closed house a thousand times trying to find the entrance, and who suddenly comes upon a door and hears a voice that says, 'What kept you?' "

"Do you eat onions?" Henry yelled as I came from the stage the next evening during intermission.

"No."

"Then tell her yourself." He pointed at the receiver dangling from the wall.

"Do you eat onions?" Marlene breathed.

"No, why?" I shouted over the babble and tramping of the ballet dancers.

" 'Cause I'm cooking your dinner," she said and hung up.

After the performance I drove to Park Avenue. The door to her apartment was wide open. In the alcove of the small hall the table was set and Marlene was kneeling on the floor of the tiny kitchen peering into the oven. "I'm sure it's spoiled, you're half an hour late," she said.

"I'm sorry. I couldn't get away."

She placed the pots on the table, took my coat and hung it up beside two black ones and a light raincoat. "Where are the minks?" I asked.

"Who needs them? Everyone thinks I've got ten anyway," she said and closed the closet door. "You want red or white?"

"White." She went to the kitchen and came back with a bottle and a corkscrew. "Kurt Hirsch was backstage," I said.

"Sit down and start. What did he want?"

"Just wanted to say hello, he'd been to the show." ("There's a man outside, Honey. He don' wanna say his name," Lela had whispered. He had grown thinner, hair streaked with gray, the youthfulness wiped away.) "His parents died a short while ago."

Marlene puckered up her mouth as if to say no sob stories please.

"His mother was taken to the hospital. After the operation they told his father that there was no hope. He went home and hanged himself. I have a bad conscience."

"You always do," she said, tasting a sauce. "What have you got to do with it?"

"A lot maybe, maybe very little. Maybe nothing at all, I don't know."

"It's a habit you have to break yourself of. You must stop apologizing. Also to yourself. That goes for the stage, for everything." She sipped the wine, said, "I think they shoot alcohol through the cork, it's much too full for a Moselle," and sat down on a fragile chair. "Eat now," she said and, after watching me with great interest for a while, "tastes better with onions."

"Perhaps they're better off now," I said, "could hardly be worse."

Marlene got up and went to the kitchen, returning with a lighted cigarette. "The electricity leaves the liver and—pfft, you've had it," she said, making the gesture the French make when they say, "Je m'en fous."

"Carroll thinks otherwise," I said.

"Carroll is sometimes naive. One shouldn't know too much about doctors and astrologers, one shouldn't become their friends, otherwise they can't help you any more." Then she sat down and filled our glasses, giving me to understand that further dissertations on the hereafter were redundant. "How was the show?" she asked.

"Ameche broke up in the middle of our love scene and got bawled out by Henry. I'd whispered into his ear, 'You scare me, Nashua.' "

She sucked her cheeks in and looked at me.

"Nashua's the horse he bet on and lost. Before the performance I asked the policeman in front of the theater to lend me his horse for half an hour. We pushed it into Ameche's dressing room backwards and hung a sign arounds its neck saying, 'Sorry I lost. Nashua.' "

The hollows in her cheeks slowly disappeared, she bent her head over the table and shook it as though she had taken off a bathing cap.

"Why don't you eat?" I asked.

"I have no appetite when I cook." She let her shoes slip off her feet, walked into the living room, looked into one of the many gold-tinted mirrors, pushed her hair back and said, "They've got fresh radishes on Eighty-sixth, I'll send you some." She picked up an unwieldy brown office ashtray from the table and emptied it.

"Who on earth gave you that?" I asked her.

"The man of my heart," she answered and smiled. "It was his Christmas present—I gave him five Vuitton suitcases." The telephone rang. "We belong to the group that has to buy its own presents," she said and picked up the receiver at the fifth ring without saying hello or the number or anything at all. I heard a distant male voice, "Hmm," she sighed and replaced the receiver. "But they still call after midnight to make sure I'm nice and safe at home, oh yes, this they spend money on." She snuggled into the corner of the sofa. "Maria's got a cold, I took the children to the park. Nobody recognized me. The children call me 'pretty Mama,' never 'Grandma.' Did you visit the Kaufmans?"

"No."

"Well, you should. Everything that's good about the show is theirs."

There was a photograph on the small writing table: Hemingway, earnest, brow wrinkled against the summer sky. "To Kraut with love, Papa" was written on it. "We're stuck with the 'Kraut,' " I said.

"Coming from him it's an honor," she answered and regarded the silver-framed picture almost adoringly.

As I got into the taxi at two-thirty I saw Manfred George standing at the corner. I looked back but he had disappeared. I called him at ten in the morning: "Were you on Park Avenue last night?"

"No," he said.

"Something must have happened at about half past two . . . you still there?" I asked, because of the long silence.

"Yes," he said finally. "I went around my block on West End Avenue at two-thirty. A man stopped me and asked for a light. He demanded my wrist watch but luckily it's being repaired. I gave him ten dollars and off he went. It was a ghastly feeling."

Simultaneously we said, "I think it's better we don't . . ."

". . . tell anybody about these phenomena," he completed the sentence. We went on to discuss the fact that it would soon get hot and that the Imperial stage had no air conditioning, that it looked as though the city garbage men would shortly go on strike, that Otto Hahn would be in New York in a few days and that Faulkner had written a new book. It took several months for us to get used to being informed by strange signs about the other's well-being. The telepathic link held for three years before it just as abruptly broke again. The turning point came as I was lying in a Zürich hotel with a temperature of 104°. It was four o'clock in the afternoon. I saw Manfred standing beside the window with his arm outstretched. I sent a cable, he called back. "What happened at ten o'clock your time yesterday?" I asked. "I was waiting on a subway platform reading a paper. I looked up and saw you standing at the barrier. I hurried toward you and heard screams and commotion behind me. The roof had caved in exactly where I'd been standing."

The Saturday matinee was like a funeral ceremony. Even the Head Commissar squinted over the footlights to reassure himself that someone really was there. They slumped in their seats as though the attendants had sold them strait-jackets and knockout drops instead of programs. A bunch of stewed-looking carnations with a note attached was delivered to my dressing room during the intermission: "The members of the New York German Club are honored to attend your performance," was written in a decorative hand. "I've seen plenty of charity shows where the audience just brooded over their fifty dollars but this takes the cake," said Ameche. In the second act Herb Greene got unnerved by the eerie silence and began to conduct as though he were playing the background music to a hue and cry and Ameche swallowed the wrong way during his care-free "I love the looks of you" and ended the song prematurely in an agonizing bout of coughing. The clarinets squeaked breathlessly and my Kamichev song contained notes that were new to everyone. We bellowed our lines as if we were playing in the open air against a hurricane, the dancers socked their high kicks so that I thought they'd come apart in the middle and although a ballet slipper sailed in a high arc through the auditorium and landed in the upper balcony the reaction remained one of rigid control. After bowing briefly and bitterly we crawled to our dressing rooms. "I almost feel sorry for you," Ameche said, "you're never gonna live this down." Cy was standing in the passage fuming, "What the hell did you think you were doing??? Those were the oil kings from the whole country! They paid two hundred dollars a seat to some charity and you give 'em a show like summer stock. Run-through on Monday morning!" Lela hung on to Ameche's sleeve. "Who sent the flowers an' the note?" "Don't," he said brokenly, "they cost me a packet."

Like lulling country rain the noise of New York steadily dripped and gurgled through the high wide halls of the Metropolitan Museum. The coolness was a relief after the heavy thundery air of the first hot day. Manfred George left it to me whether to stop in front of a picture or walk past, his quiet coughs and expectant crafty eyes prodding me to formulate immediately my impressions and thoughts. At first haltingly, then gaining fluency, as though it were philistine yet unavoidable, he whispered the painters' life stories, their place in history and the influences they had been exposed to. Interrupting my appreciation of his knowledge he said, "It's a mistake to think a scholar particularly

intelligent or particularly dumb." He took off his spectacles
and rubbed the spotless lenses, looked at me inquiringly
and helplessly, pushed the spectacles onto his nose and
plucked the curved wire carelessly over his ear, gained confidence behind glass, felt protected and ironical. "I hoard
knowledge like a computer, like most of my ante-diluvian
generation. In thirty years people like me will have to perform in circuses, we're computers who've been fed wrong,"
he said and chuckled thinly, as though visualizing a deadly
enemy's awful fate. "It's the youngsters that interest me,"
he said, so loud that two silently gliding Indian ladies
turned around in atonishment, "the ones who'll be showing
at the Guggenheim when it's finally finished." We were
standing in front of Salvador Dali's "Christ." Klemke, my
teacher, would have adored the texture and folds of the
loin cloth. George shrugged his shoulder: "His mustache
has more fantasy."

Three days later we went to the movies to see de Sica's
Umberto D. It was playing to a few limp devotees who had
escaped from the murderous heat into the air-conditioned
darkness and were now sleeping or chewing popcorn. As
we lit our cigarettes in the foyer and I attempted to mask
my red rims with sunglasses I said, "It seems to be my fate
to burst into tears in your presence, but the story of the old
man touched me so much, the loneliness of old men—"
"Why do you hesitate?" he smiled. "I came upon a quote
from Emerson the other day, 'The surest poison is time.' "
We crossed Madison Avenue. The breeze seemed to be
escaping from a boiler. "Time never stood still in my whole
life," George said, "yet I always lived close to death. He
was the constant companion who heightened the sweetness
of life." A fat man ran past us and knocked the newspapers
and paperbacks from George's hand. "Can't you watch
where you're going?" the fat man snarled and turned
around threateningly. His eyes glittering slits, George
brushed his upper lip with one finger, ready, though ill-
equipped, to do battle. He suddenly bubbled and nodded
agreement as though the man had said something delightful. "My only fear of death," he continued, as though there
had been no interruption, "is that he won't honor the contract we made at my birth, that he'll want it to mature earlier." He ran a hand over his thin flat hair and let it rest
protectively on his neck. "Up to now he's always waved me
aside whenever I crossed his path. I make certain demands

and requests of God, in keeping with the old Jewish custom of regarding an agent between Man and God as unnecessary." He took his hand from his neck, looked at his wristwatch and waved for a taxi. "I hope you don't think something's wrong with me," he said as he struggled with the door-handle. The young Irishman behind the wheel opened his monologue with, "Got any free tickets for an old cab driver?" and kept it going until Tenth Street.

"I'm addicted to life," George said in the elevator; "I'm standing in a long line with many others, and the mountain's still a long way off; I hear the drums beating at the foot of the mountain, the line shuffles forward and, because I'm small, I am able to dodge back two or three places without anyone noticing, and stay in the same spot a little longer."

Mother and I were sitting in the living room. The terrace doors stood open and although the yellow cushions on the wobbly sun chairs were wiped with a damp cloth at least twice a day, they were covered with a film of oily soot. A thunderstorm grumbled over Hoboken and Jerssey city, a streak of lightning hung in the night sky, waiting, procrastinating, a gust of wind shook the TV antennae and flagpoles, folded back the edges of the canopy over the street entrance. The heat persisted, viscid, sticky. The television set was silently showing "The Steve Allen Show," in the kitchen the Frigidaire clicked and went into its quarter-hourly chatter. Mother stood up and turned the TV off just as a platinum blonde stretched out her arms and opened her mouth. "My left eye itches," Mother said. Although she set no store by omens and took my excursions into astrology for humbug and signs of weakness, she relied on her left eye. It itched when something was good, or would turn out well. "I can't accept it, I just don't believe it," she said. "I don't suppose anyone does when he's first told," I answered.

Two days previously I had gone to a specialist. "Perhaps it's the heat, I'm not used to it, sometimes the thermometer backstage registers over a hundred degrees. I've been feeling dreadful for weeks now, I constantly lose weight." A nurse drew blood from a vein and one finger.

A half hour before this evening's performance he had come to my dressing room. He had turned the tap over the wash basin on and then off again and asked, "Are you married?"

"No."

"Are you responsible for anyone, financially or otherwise?"

"Yes."

"The test shows leukemia."

"How long have I got?" I had asked so quietly that he left the tap on and stared at me vacantly.

"Did you ever have any tests before?"

"No."

"Hard to say," he said finally, "of course you'll have to stop working but we do have medicines today—"

"That don't help either."

During intermission Ameche had said, "What's up? You're playing as if you'd like to hiss them to death."

"Call Carroll," my mother said suddenly.

"Why did you never tell me that I'd die young?" I said as the receiver was lifted.

"Have you indulged in drunken debauchery?"

"No, I'm not drunk," I shouted.

"What happened?" I told him. "Hold the line." I heard the rustle of pages and the long-distance operator asking, "Finished your call?" Carroll had a coughing attack and then said, "I'm convinced they mixed up the tests. Your aspects have been difficult since April, they show misunderstandings, intrigues, and a delicate state of health, but under no circumstances could you have an illness such as the one diagnosed. Insist on new tests and have them sent to a different laboratory."

The doctor reacted to my request with the kind of piqued that's-all-the-thanks-you-get attitude one might expect of a scientist forced to squander hours on precious research on trivialities. Nevertheless new blood tests were sent to three different laboratories.

This time he came after the performance. He benevolently took my hand and said, "I'm so happy—there's no further cause for alarm. There really was a mix-up." He shook his head and smiled broadly. "First time in the whole of my practice. All three laboratories confirm that your blood shows no sign of illness, your blood count's a little low but this we can take care of with a few B12 shots." He rubbed his fingertips together, straightened his tie once more and left.

"Who'd have thought it?" someone called out from the door. Barlog was standing under his antennae, Herta's cat's eyes blinked in the background. "We were out front, wasn't bad, wanted to take a look at what you're up to." He pulled my ear lobe, grinned at Lela silently and pregnantly as if to say, "Shame about you not speaking German," then encircled my forearm with his thumb and index finger and said, "You wouldn't be so skinny if you were in my company, my actors get vacations."

"Will you come back to my apartment?"

"If you've got a crust of bread for us, all right."

I called Mother. "What did the doctor say?" she asked anxiously. "Yes, Carroll was right." She released the air from her lungs as though she'd been holding it the whole evening.

Cy came and stood beside me. "Got a moment?" he asked.

"What's wrong?"

"Listen, the German Consulate called about tickets for a German conductor and his party. What was his name again —Yan somebody . . ."

"Karajan?"

"Could be, doesn't really matter. He's giving his first concert in Manhattan, there's gonna be trouble, protests an' pickets, you know. We can't afford to have you be seen with him, no pictures, no dinners, nothin'—it could wreck the show. If they call, you ain't home, O.K.? We gotta insist, I'm afraid."

"Yes, Cy."

"Everything was fine up till now, no one had anything against you." He traced a line down my back with his finger, clapped his other hand to his cheek as though clubbing a fly, thrust his lower lip forward and said, "O.K., Kraut, sorry."

Barlog looked out the cab window. As we turned into Times Square he gasped, "I've never seen such a heap of rabble in my life—and the drunks . . ." He slumped down in his seat and tried to make out the tips of the skyscrapers. "Christ almighty," he muttered, leaving it open as to whether he was impressed or the opposite.

"Well, Mama, how's it going with the English?" Bleating happily he embraced her and then ran out onto the terrace, nodded at the Empire State Building as though approving a set designer's first model, said, "Not bad," and came and sat down on the sofa wearing his director's expression: "Your strength comes over just the same in English but the play's a mess, seemed to me as if too many cooks have been stirring it up—and what was with the ballet? They hopped around like a seaside music hall."

"They were nervous, one of them was sacked for coming ten minutes late. She lives way out in the suburbs and her son's got chickenpox, so she missed the train. How long are you staying?"

"We're taking a look at a couple of plays but they cook with water here the same as we do." He suddenly jumped up. "Now listen: In that scene where he sings his song and you just sit there, don't look out into the audience, look down." He held his head to one side and looked at the floor with an expression of extreme distaste, as though a maggot were crawling there. "And your first entrance—take much longer before you say the first line. Then the evening dress, when you show it off don't be so sure of yourself, it mustn't be so elegant, get me?" He jerked around in circles like a seal balancing a ball on its nose. "She's gotta be embarrassed, see?—Come on, stand up, I'll show you . . ." At two o'clock Herta said, "Bolli, I think we ought to be going . . ." "Don't forget what I told you," he said at the elevator, as though the curtain were about to go up at the Schlosspark Theater.

Following the dictates of a strange cycle, the stream of visitors rose, subsided again, and rose anew. A slight elderly gentleman with unforgettable soft blue eyes introduced himself as Otto Hahn, rummaged in a brown plastic bag, brought out two bottles of wine, and asked me whether I had the time and inclination to empty them with him. Charles Laughton, room-filling and oddly shy, his corpulence opposing his yen to remain unnoticed. Maurice Chevalier's rosy apple cheeks. Piaf, tiny, undernourished, her seaman's laugh like a camouflage net, arousing doubts that she'd live to see another day. The mayor of Berlin, Otto Suhr, came, and UN delegates, ministers, students, quiz-show winners. John Steinbeck, powerful and high-spirited, his gestures straight out of a pantomime, then still and retracted, saving himself for the next gust of life. Lena Horne and Shirley Booth and many from Hollywood, and finally the guests of Lufthansa's maiden flight to New York.

The heat accumulated, nestled in concrete and stones, released the day's charge by night, made friends with an old tropical malady, regenerated it, obliged me to stagger to the theater doubled up with pain and fever. New York's reeling pedestrians all had the color of eggplant; short-lived relief in air-conditioned rooms gave way to searing neuralgia and epidemics of flu. We had abandoned all thought of make-up and, clad in fur hat and Russian military raiment, I melted under the spotlights like butter subjected to a blowtorch. My incapacity to do anything except sleep or lie in a tub of tepid water until the evening performance had allowed mountains of mail to amass. Two secretaries I had engaged on the German Consulate's recommendation livened up my summer; one drank and rasped obscenities into the ears of my unwitting telephone callers, the other forged my signature on checks. One of the countless agents had persuaded me to pose for an advertisement and felt entitled to a 100 percent commission; when I declared myself none too delighted he threatened dire consequences and eternal enmity.

One evening, after hours of ear-splitting thunder had been followed by a short period of coolness, I went to see George Kaufman.

Leueen opened the door. Her black dress against the white background accentuated the slenderness of her figure and left it to the observer to decide whether she was better described as slim or thin as a rake, willowy or emaciated. The wide red mouth in the white boyish face suggested a malevolently exaggerated El Greco. George Kaufman stood in the immaculate perfection of the living room as though he'd lost his way and were waiting for the guide to commence the tour of inspection. "My God, you've grown thin," he said, like everyone else who hadn't seen me for some weeks. With relief I noted that Leueen's cigarette ash had dropped onto the white carpet and that they had decided to ignore it; the gray spot lent the room an unexpected lived-in quality. Kaufman propped his elbow on the mantlepiece and although his appearance was one of imposing elegance I couldn't help fearing that, lost in thought, he might allow his elbow to slip off and so spill the contents of his glass, lose his balance, and skin his ankle on the heavy brass bellows. "Is the show still fun?" he asked with mild irony and a complete lack of embarrassment, as though he'd been on a short vacation. He was not the man to tell of my despair in Boston and my nightly irritation at much of the ham that had been added, and he didn't need his taste confirmed by others. Nevertheless, as I took my leave of Leueen and George Kaufman some hours later, I felt dismal and discouraged, as though I had witnessed the triumph of fatuity over aestheticism and dignity.

Years later, in the Rhodesian bush, I saw a kudu. It was standing on long graceful legs only a few yards from the Land-Rover I was sitting in, majestic and unalarmed, its gnarled corkscrew horns ending in youthful exclamation marks. "He's old, the herd's turned him out," the white hunter said. It looked at us, proud and unapproachable, expecting nothing, safe in the knowledge that nothing more could surprise or disappoint it.

Cole Porter was in Europe. My dressing-room mirror was stuck full of postcards with snow-capped mountains and hastily scribbled messages ("It's cool here," or "I'm fine, how are you?"), which turned a troupe of grateful fans a bilious shade of green.

After we had passed the 200th performance and the show was booked solid for months to come various things happened at roughly the same time: my face was found by a group of young American artists to be "The most expressive in the New York theater world," the *Journal-American* described me as an "Enrichment of the American Stage," the *Silk Stockings* LP got off to a flying start, and the biggest daily newspaper in Berlin devoted its front-page headline and two inside pages to a report on Hildegard Knef's lamentable flop in New York.

Berlin was a long way off and in a fit of largess and altruism I turned a blind eye. But, as the seeds of this journalistic dandelion began to flower in the fertile plans of the entire German press, I felt the stings of calumny.

"What's eating you?" Ameche pitched at my crabby silence.

"The tapeworm of the Fatherland's press," I growled just as Tyrone came in asking for hammer and nails. He was carrying a leather-framed picture which contained a broadly printed "PLAN" and, since this commandeered most of the available space, a squashed-up "ahead."

"Put it away and try again tomorrow, the Kraut's cranky," said Ameche.

"Tell Daddy all about it," Tyrone purred.

After I had translated a few headlines and photo captions they looked at each other. "I don't get it," Ameche said, "every other foreigner would be backed to the hilt by his country, they should be yelling hallelujah after the success you've had."

"Why don't you sue?" Tyrone asked.

"German law's different. The most I'd get would be a correction on the bottom of the back page, sandwiched in between 'Canary lost' and 'Bicycle for sale.'"

"So who cares?" Tyrone said. "Don't tell me you want to live there again?" he added, as though we were speaking of Outer Mongolia. "We have ways of making you talk," he said, aping every actor who had ever played a Hollywood Nazi.

Ameche left since it was Saturday and church was beckoning, and Tyrone and I drove to a little club run and frequented by homosexuals who greeted us with "Good to see you" and then left us alone in a corner with steaks and candlelight.

"But you haven't given any anti-German interviews and there's been no scandal, why should they turn sour?"

"No idea."

"Provincial crap," Tyrone said and ordered two Black Labels.

"The German language has a word for it which English doesn't—'Schadenfreude.' Roughly it means 'delight at the misfortune of others.' And if there's no misfortune then you have to create one in order to be delighted about it."

September 2, 1955

Ameche was ill. His understudy did his best to seize the chance with both hands. The additional rehearsals and a strange costar made the performances even more strenuous than they already were. There are evenings when I sit in the dressing room completely void and exhausted and can't find the energy to go home.

September 15

I'm painting again since it got a little cooler. Quince-yellow yolk-yellow worm squirming from the fat tube, first daub on raw canvas, clean and bristle-hard brush paints a

dented quadrangle: it turns into a flat yellow roof, underneath vermilion or carmine, salmon-pink maybe, it becomes the wall, the thumb-wide street is sienna-colored.
My New York is skyless, unpeopled, red and yellow, with
antennae like grave crosses. A self-portrait is hanging over
the emergency staircase: it looks like a poster for a revolution, and yet it smacks of a film photo.

September 20

"Three times daily" is written on the bottle. I've been
taking them for weeks now. A doctor prescribed them for
the tropical illness. I collapsed like a sack of potatoes during intermission yesterday. Too many anti-biotics. The give
you pills here as if they were gumdrops. Ameche's arms
keep going dead, for months we held our hands in buckets
filled with ice between entrances.

October 1, 1955

Mother has demanded a final statement from Mr. Brom,
she says there's a lot she can't understand. He had arranged for my salary to be paid into a lawyer's account so
that taxes and commission would be deducted without my
missing them. What remains is very little. I can't help missing them.

December 29

The dancers brought a huge cake onto the stage during
the finale yesterday. The orchestra played "Happy Birthday" and the audience joined in. A family gathering, ending with me standing at the footlights blowing out the
candles.

January 1, 1956

The New Year began in Igor Bernstein's taxi at the
corner of Forty-Sixth and Times Square. "Happy New
Year," he said in a voice that held no promise of anything
that might come close to being called happy.

January 15

I had looked forward to meeting Danny Kaye, which
made the evening at "21" an even greater disappointment.
Throughout the steak tartare, salad, and cheese he mimick-
ed first my Ninochka accent, then my normal one, and
eventually wound up doing the concentration camp Kom-

mandant. This asininity finally over, his friend. a writer, struck a stance like Rodin's "Thinker" and whispered. "I have a problem I'd like to discuss with you—you're so sophisticated and European and so much more understanding than our American women." He lowered his head, presenting me with his perfect part, and continued, "My problem is that whenever I have sexual intercourse I get this terrific cramp in my left leg. What would be your advice?"

"Don't fuck," I said.

I believe he must have expected something quite different of me since he strode off without saying good-bye, leaving me to look for a taxi by myself.

February 26

We had decided to have the *Silk Stockings* birthday party yesterday, Saturday the 25th. Ameche and I rented a restaurant and invited everyone connected with the show from the cashiers to the stagehands. Only Lela and a Negro who plays second trumpet excused themselves with weak arguments that all ended with, "You'll see, it's better we don't. . . ." Finally I persuaded them. The restaurant had a doorman. "Niggers ain't allowed in," he barked. "We've rented the restaurant," I said, louder than necessary, "I'll call the newspapers, coming from a German it'll make a nice scandal." After making a phone call he opened the door and hissed, "The boss says we make an exception just for today," then let go of the knob, slamming the door into the trumpeter's back.

March 1

"Looking forward to the tour?" asks Cy.

"Which tour?"

"Next winter, when the Broadway run's over."

"I only signed for the Broadway run."

"How do you make that out?"

"That's the agreement that was made."

"But not with us," he says.

I ask to see my contract. Cy is right, small print, last page.

Lilli Palmer is in New York, she gives me her lawyer's address. "I see no way out," he says, "except illness, a severe case. And as long as the tour is running, whether in Topeka or Denver, you won't be able to accept other engagements."

I'm twenty pounds underweight. After two years with the show I would never last a tour. I know how to make the tropical bugs flare up again. But how long can I stand the fever and the pain?

March 7

"You have to have a holiday," Manfred Geroge says, "six months at least, a year would be better."

"How would I finance it? I pay United States taxes."

His ears go red. "We have never spoken about money and your financial affairs are none of my business, but surely you must be very rich? You haven't stopped working for years and always in starring parts."

"When I parted company with the agent almost a year ago I had sixteen dollars in my account."

"Do you own any houses or jewelry? Land?"

"Nothing."

"Then you spent it all?"

"They said that I'd spent it all, yes."

"May I see your files?"

"I don't have any. I always left these things to others, just like the Broadway contract."

April 11

I have the certificates. Two doctors confirm that the tropical illness has reached a critical stage and state that a cure is out of the question so long as I go on playing. They insist on a vacation of at least six months. Cy and Ernie had to accept their verdict.

I don't know where I shall go. I only know that I feel a relief as if I'd received my conscription papers and had then been declared unfit for service at the last moment, returning me to a freedom I had already said good-bye to. Of saying good-bye to Lela, Don, Herb, Henry, and the gang I cannot think. I only think of Nebraska or Colorado or South Dakota and imagine myself reporting to the Head Commissar for the 966th time. I weigh eighty-eight pounds, most people think I'm consumptive, discreetly suggest the Swiss mountains, a quiet sanatorium and plenty of milk. My Hungarian friends have Hungarian relatives in Paris and they have friends in Basle who have acquaintances in St. Moritz who know of a house on the lake which is reasonable in price and available from spring till autumn. I have bought my first brand-new car and Mother says, "A dollar is worth four marks and thirty pfennig. If we're careful we can live for almost a year on what we've saved." No word from Mr. Brom.

April 12

"You're a child. A naive, gullible child," says Manfred George.

"Then it's naive to buy a loaf of bread without watching the baker bake it, or to climb into an airplane without a pilot's license or asking to see the builders blueprints. With the money you pay you also invest trust. You put yourself in the hands of every cab driver, elevator man, doctor, surgeon, lawyer. If we wanted to do without them and go it alone our expectation of life would have to be considerably greater. I see nothing admirable in mistrust. The mistrust I had I used up during the war."

"You haven't used up your mistrust, you just won't admit that the war never ended."

April 22

I shall play till the end of the month. The City of New York honored me last Sunday by asking me to take part in the Easter Parade sitting in an open car. We drove down Fifth Avenue and my moss-green hat flapped in the wind, flew ahead, settled on the hood of the car, hopped along in front of Bergdorf Goodman's windows, lost its brim and much of the moss-green under the wheels of a horse-drawn carriage.

Manfred George says, "I can't imagine New York without you any more."

The SS *America* leaves for Le Havre early in May.

May 3

The crates are packed. Two friends come and promise to visit me in Europe some time soon. Two films have been offered. I'm spending a year in Europe," I say grandly. It's an escape, an escape I welcome. I'm thirty years old and I'm not afraid. When the money's at an end, I'll see what's to be done. I am not afraid of starving, or of going under in the panicking herd, I'm afraid only of becoming again the person I once was. Before I came to New York. My ambition has run dry, or is satiated, is fat or worn to a frazzle. Is no longer lean and hungry. I shall make no plans, live without design, even with less purpose than the Mexican boy in Tijuana who only wanted to sell me half of his oranges and when I asked him why I couldn't have them all he said, "What would I do in the afternoon?" I'll see the fat mountain again and love the tingling cold nights, the air that's so clear, as though none had ever breathed it. Carroll Righter says I'm making a mistake, that I should stay in America. I am not even afraid of making a mistake.

May 4

Manfred George gives me letters for friends in Zürich, Paris, Ascona, Geneva, and London. "In case you're there," he says. "And go to Israel, I'd like you to. I'll write and tell you whom to see there. I set more store by the young Israelis than anyone else. Perhaps because I fell out of the nest of my generation very early and escaped the calcification and the hardening of their deep-frozen ideas. I've been fighting for this new state for years now although I must confess I don't even speak Hebrew and, of necessity, am far removed from the real inhabitants—if you don't count the fact that many thousands of years ago our forefathers built sand castles in the Egyptian desert together and that this serves as a foundation for common bonds today. Already as a young man I felt that somehow a normal community must be recreated out of this scattered and forever wandering people that would be of benefit to the coming generations."

He had never before voiced so fully his thoughts on the Jewish past, present, and future. He had sometimes attacked me. or admonished me: "If you want to share collective guilt, then you must also share collective pride," he had once said. "Pride in what?" I had asked. "They were few, but they were important, and it's just as irresponsible to forget them as to forget the others." And at some time during the winter he had said, "Don't be afraid of not liking a Jew. Those who insist that you must love them all without qualification in order to prove that you're not an anti-Semite are also Fascists of a kind, or roosters, and you can't argue with roosters."

May 5

"We were happy to have you stay with us," they said at the hotel, "we only accepted the Jewish agent on your account, we don't usually take them because . . . well, you understand." I don't know why everyone thinks I understand.

The boat rolls good-naturedly, the stewards put up deck chairs, distribute cushions, the shock is still with me. Faces, hands, handkerchiefs, skyscrapers, evaporate and sink, go their way, leave you behind, complete the full circle, move on. New York was part of the friendship.

Mother rearranges the cabin as though we were embarking on a world trip. "We'll be there in four days," I say.

"So we will," she says, "Europe always seems so far away." She turns off the air conditioner, looks out at the water, blows her nose and adds, "I was happy in New York."

"Yes," I say, "perhaps we will be again someday."

"It's difficult to make new friends at my age. I never had so many and such good ones as in New York. They're nearly all immigrants. And they know that my generation, more than any other, let them down. I think I'll go for a breath of air," she says and sits down on the bed. "It's awful, I know, but I have to say it—I'm dreading going back to Berlin, and Germany, the stuffiness, the pettiness, the grudging, the narrow-mindedness. Your father was right. 'Out,' he always said, 'let's get out and on the double.' "

TWENTY ONE

They take their time at seaports. We reached Le Havre at five in the morning; at eight we were allowed to go ashore. I went to the purser responsible for car freight three times and pleaded for gentle treatment of my first-born, of which I had been delivered at cut-rate and with the words, "We are honored to have you drive it in Europe."

"Europe," I whispered as I stepped onto the dock, and felt a warm wave welling—which immediately plummeted to the back of my knees and turned to ice for there, swinging out of the belly of the boat on flimsy chains carelessly draped around its four wheels, was my automobile—baptized "The Snowgoose," in keeping with its white exterior —swinging helplessly between heaven and the harbor; it jerked forward, dangled trembling, hoisted itself up, gave a jump sagged back on its four grips, bunched itself for a mighty spring, described a half circle, hung creaking over the asphalt of the quay showing its four tires and the practical black of its posterior, found itself deposited, freed of chains, stood. Ignoring the friendly German magazine photographer who had been sent to photograph our landing, I went around the Snowgoose, felt its wings maternally, reassured myself of its general condition, promised solemnly that nothing of this sort would ever happen again, slid behind the wheel, pressed a knob which surprisingly opened the hood, pressed a second which activated the windshield wipers plus washing facilities, ducked as the ice-cold shower spurted over the windshield and washed everything within washing distance and ignored all knob-pressing attempts on my part to interrupt its program. After I had dried myself, combed my hair, beckoned to Mother and sat down again, a foul-tempered blodge entered our field of vision, darkened the bright blank May sky, slammed our four suitcases to the ground and trumpeted out of a mouth full

of a squelchy fag-end and brown-black tooth stumps:
"Vingt dollars!"

"What does he want?" asked Mother.

"He wants twenty dollars."

"What for?"

"That's what I'd like to know."

He scratched his bull neck thoroughly and repeated frog-
gily, "Vingt dollars!"

"Ecoutez!" I yelled and left a pause in which I endeav-
ored to combine the French I had acquired from Fraulein
Weise and my few French films; "Ecoutez!" I said again
for this reason and went on with, 'Nous sommes Alle-
mandes, pas des Américaines! Vingt dollars!" and tapped
my forehead with my my index finger. Our poison-Yves
now became choleric, went lots of vivid hues, finally decided
on dark Burgendy red and howled "Boche" and other
things and did something which cut me to the quick—he
slapped the Snowgoose with his filthy mitt. Mother gripped
me by my pleated skirt, the photographer, who had felt the
sting of the "Boche," entered the fray, the garage man, who
was filling the Snowgoose's belly, let go of the gasoline
hose, which danced around our wheels, the blodge
screamed something ending in "SS," the garage man con-
tributed his father and Verdun to the discussion, and rather
than wait until they got around to Grandfather's outrage of
1870/1 I handed the attendant five dollars, fed the Snowgoose gas and, employing my abdominal muscles in a manner that would have made Herb Greene glow with pride,
roared, "Va manger les bacilles!" which was meant to
convey the equivalent of "Go swallow a germ."

Once out of the dock area, I reduced our speed to twelve
or fifteen miles an hour, since the Snowgoose was not yet
broken in. I also stopped at another filling station and had
the tires, oil, water, and battery checked, and the photographer worriedly asked when I thought we might get to Paris
if we continued at this rate I could only look at him with
disdain for not appreciating the beauty and intricacies of a
new automobile. We sighted Rouen at midday, I looked for
a shady haven for the Snowgoose since I had heard that
sun was not at all good for the enamel, and only then was I
prepared to savor the cathedral, the people, and spring.
Pulling over to let tractors, bicycles, and donkey carts over-
take me safely we reached Mantes and, toward sundown,

Paris. And in Paris I forgot my passion for the Snowgoose, looked right and looked left and was called to order by the malevolent squealing of a braking bus and the shrill whistles of an unstable policeman. French and German reporters were waiting at the hotel and after entrusting the Snowgoose to the dependable-looking garage man and repeatedly impressing upon him: Wash Polish Grease, I went to the lobby and answered those questions pertaining to New York and *Silk Stockings* and tried to evade the others dealing with my futue plans—I had no idea how to explain that I neither could nor wanted to work again for a long time. French, German, and Italian film scripts were piled in my room, together with stage plays from London and Vienna, flowers, telegrams, invitations. Mother said, "I can understand your being pleased but a rest is more important."

In the evening we drove to the Place du Tertre. It was completely empty except for a shaggy black animal that could have been a mixture of sheep dog and mastiff and whose dimensions were difficult to ascertain since most of him was lying in a dark doorway. He yawned at us several times, looking very much like a hippopotamus in so doing, stood up—that is to say unfolded himself attaining astonishing height and breadth—and let his bored but perceptive eyes sweep around the square, reminding me of an ancient stationmaster checking his provincial station before shutting up shop, changing the signs, and turning out the light. He then trotted off to the opposite side of the square, knocking over a bicycle in the process, and disappeared into a bar. After less than three minutes he came hurtling out of the bar and across the square, slithered to a stop, turned and tottered like someone who has sunk too many Pernods too quickly, sat down and looked at us as though awaiting a suggestion about how to brighten up a dull evening. Quickly sensing that we were uninitiated and pliable, he assumed leadership. In the very first bistro, which with its red and white gingham tablecloths and accordion player was geared to tourism and gay Paree, we found the key to his soul: he was a beer drinker. He ignored food and water and made his preference clear by springing over the bar. Midnight found us sitting on the steps of Sacré Coeur with the mammoth lying across our laps; we gazed down at glittering Paris and listened to our companion's uninhibited snores. Although the parting was painful, we left him at one o'clock there where we had found him and, looking back, saw him making a crooked beeline for the nearest bar.

The Julier pass was still full of snow. A thick bank of cloud billowed up from the Maloja, over the Corvatsch and the Piz Nair, over Sils Maria and the fat dogged mountain, dipped into the lakes, the trees, and the houses, sprayed rain and sleet a whole day and a whole night long. Then, the next morning, summer began; hot, dry and crisp, the heavens glacier-colored, the lakes green and blue and black; and I was happy, happy as I had been in Zossen and on the Baltic, and sometimes on Lake Griebnitz.

St. Moritz
April 7, 1970

Seven or eight hours a day for the past four months I have been looking up from my typewriter and seeing a yellow house. It's on the other side of the lake, right behind the dairy. It looks somewhat neglected and the yellow is a dirty yellow, like dried mustard. Since it once belonged to Wilhelm Furtwängler it is known as "Das Furtwängler Haus." At that time, in the summer of '56, the director of the Zürich theater, Kurt Hirschfeld, lived there. The great actor Gustav Gründgens was spending his holidays in Pontresina and the three of us would often go for walks around Lake Staz and then drink coffee and eat apfelstrudel from Hanselmann's Konditorei in the dark living room. They spoke of theater, the Berlin theater, and of the fact that no other theater could compare with the theater which had existed there. They spoke of new plays and new productions, of the first night on which . . . of that evening when . . . They are dead, as are Manfred George, Erich Pommer and Alexander Korda, Boris Vian and Tyrone Power. My mother. In Berlin the houses died before their inhabitants or with them; here they remain, almost as solid as the mountains, in remembrance of the people who lived in them.

When the money was at an end I signed the contract. It committed me to make a number of films over a number of years for the newly formed UFA. A distributor I knew well had been appointed head of the company, but he resigned again after a few weeks and a gentleman I did not know, Arno Hauke, was entrusted with the financial and artistic management. Herr Hauke's breezy forthright manner was apparently born of the conviction that the success of the major concern was already guaranteed; his opening gambits, "Don't worry about a thing" and "Be nice to each other," dispelled all apprehension on the part of hesitant colleagues and encouraged them to work in an atmosphere of heady festivity. The walls of the reception, conference, and projection rooms of the UFA-Haus in Dusseldorf were hung with bishop's-purple silk and left no doubt that money and confidence were united here to create a new realm, which would nevertheless be erected according to the principles and aims of the old: a German film industry that would declare war on Hollywood and saw in television no cause for alarm. One owned cinemas and studios, offices and cars; all that remained to be done was to make a film.

On my arrival in Berlin I was given a grand reception. Helicopters circled over the Russian checkpoint in Zehlendorf dropping balloons and towing streamers, sending the Russian and East German guards into an uproar; West Berliners shook my hand. Mayor Otto Shur invited me to tea, a squadron of white-clad motorcycle police ("white mice") escorted the Snowgoose through the city to the town hall on Rudolf-Wildeplatz, and I found myself with a new title: UFA Star No. 1.

Shortly afterwards my new company sent me a film script I had already declined five times. The incipient monotony of our young relationship was broken by the Berlin film festival. I represented UFA as No. 1, dancing and smiling at every ball, and the firm silence maintained on the question of the planned production slowly became unsettling. When Herr Hauke's chauffeur then brought me the same script for the eighth time I began to have serious doubts about UFA's future and my own. The story was as follows: A French schoolteacher in Algeria (me) is opposed to the Algerians' fight for freedom. She gets mixed up with three escaping Foreign Legionnaires, falls in love with one of them (a German) and promptly sees the whole political setup in a different light.

I made many futile attempts to interest Herr Hauke in a theme which didn't deal with our neighbors' colonial problems and was then invited to a dinner at which I was confronted with Herr Hauke, the complete board of directors, and Wolfgang Staudte, with whom I had made *The Mur-*

derers Among Us. He said, "I'm going to direct the film, rewrite the whole script of course, and we'll make a wonderful picture. Do you trust me?" "Yes," I said sweetly and with conviction. "Here's to a great film," they all said and drank a toast. Since no one ever drank to a bad film, a certain skepticism remained with me.

My mother had rented a house in Berlin and I bought furniture and my first bed of my own with an advance from UFA. I was reasonably optimistic as long as I didn't ponder the fact that neither a new script nor the synopsis of one had been forthcoming. I was informed that the location work would take place in Morocco and the studio work in Berlin, and that they had agreed on the title *Madeleine and the Legionnaire.* Herr Staudte told me that he intended to make an "ensemble" film, quite the opposite of what everyone would expect after the "Star No. 1" publicity, that the photography would have a newsreel quality, and that he would like me to wear my hair in a crew cut. I then flew with him and the rest of the team to Tangiers.

Just how much successful films owe to improvisation is almost impossible to ascertain, since their directors are understandably loath to enumerate the chores of the daily treadmill but prefer rather to talk about the magical creative force which seized and inspired them by the hour. But one thing does seem fairly certain: that to work successfully as director and running script writer while making a mammoth production involving half the Moroccan army is virtually impossible. If there have been cinematic masterpieces that were evolved on the spur of the moment, I am able to state with a clear conscience: This wasn't one of them.

So long as we remained in Morocco the mood and morale of the crew was high, almost euphoric, since the daily batches of exposed film had been sent to Germany to be developed and we had yet to view the results. When we returned from balmy Tangiers to wintry Berlin, the fall in temperature was not restricted to the climate. My threats to walk off the film unless I was told how the jumbled story would end or at least continue fell on either deaf ears or the durable "Be nice to each other," which did nothing to placate me and so was followed by the company lawyers citing my contract and the awesome consequences of a breach on my part. My director seemed to be suffering from a round-the-clock hangover by now and I gradually saw his point and followed his example. We shot scenes in which I had to address German-speaking legionnaires in German with "Thank God—you're French!" and one morning our director surprised us with a Brechtian song deploring the wickedness of the generals which he had composed in the small hours and seriously insisted we should sing. Finally I suggested to UFA that they make the second film stipulated by my contract right after the legionnaire epic and bring it out before, but since an actor's influence on a film is extremely limited his intelligence is generally held to be comparable and the smirks on the faces of the UFA bosses left no doubt that they shared this opinion. Moreover they clapped me on the shoulder and spoke: "This will be one of the greatest films in the history of the German cinema, it will bring you many prizes."

The première took place in the newly built UFA Palast am Zoo. The publicity and public relations offices had excelled themselves and the evening was launched with colossal pomp and ceremony; when the houselights went up at the end, however, the atmosphere was very similar to Pankow 1946, at the premiere of *Love at First Sight*. Gingerly I took my bow and was heaped with UFA flowers by the cinema attendants and then sat in the manager's office behind the stage listening to the doleful reporters' sporadic efforts to say something comforting. No other representative of UFA was present at this conference. I then went to a Russian restaurant in the Kantstrasse called the Mazurka, partook of a lot of cold Polish vodka and warm Russian music, and then rode my Snowgoose up and down the Avus autobahn crying loudly until I realized that a pair of headlights in my rear mirror had been there since the Mazurka. At Halensee station I braked hard, the other car did too, and a man jumped out and ran toward me; before he could reach the Snowgoose I stepped on the accelerator and saw no more of him that evening. Two days later the same car was parked in front of my house. Friends called and said how sorry they were that the papers, which, in a fit of self-preservation, I had not read, had placed the blame for the UFA catastrophe on me, surmising that the poor director had not a chance against the headstrong star and that therefore the bad script, amateurish camera work, inferior lighting and sets, could also be held against me.

From UFA I heard nothing and was henceforth spared Arno Hauke's "Don't worry about a thing." The film didn't recover its production costs and UFA's next projects were noticeably humbler, and also their last.

The work had lasted many long months and was followed by an even longer period of unemployment. I had time to go for walks, visit my friends, and work out how long the money I had received for the film would last. "An actor's only as good as his last film" is an apt Hollywood adage and, applied to my situation, it summarized my chances as grim if not altogether hopeless. The regular hikes around Lake Grünewald, Krumme Lanke, and other Berlin beauty spots were possibly beneficial to my health but did nothing to bolster my morale, and were abruptly terminated when I saw the car again. It was the same dark-blue shabby old Opel that had followed me on the autobahn and parked in front of my house, and, in view of the threatening letters I was constantly receiving from maniacs in general, and thinking of one in particular who had squeezed himself into the Snowgoose, loomed up in my rear mirror as I drove down a dark street, and run away when I threw myself out of the moving car and screamed, I was frightened.

At a time when my whole situation had gotten critical my friend René came to Berlin. He couldn't have come at a better time, for René, a Swiss-born Russian, had had a number of professions of which two were ideally suited to the said situation. He had been a boxer in Paris, a psychiatrist and publisher in New York, and had then done nothing at all in Portugal for several years. I had met him in St. Moritz. He skied like an Olympic gold medalist, was apparently bursting with energy and joie de vivre, and when I asked him, "What do you do?" he answered, "Nothing. As a boxer I found myself going goofy, as a psychiatrist screwy, and as a publisher I looked up one evening and saw myself sitting with two telephones, one at each ear, two manuscripts open in front of me, and an unhappy wife behind me, and a fatherless son tossing about in bed, so I dropped the telephones, closed the manuscripts, packed our suitcases and went off to do nothing." René always wore dark-blue suits, at whatever time of the day, and had a friend called Baron Schniebel, whom I think he had met when he was a psychiatrist. Baron Schniebel was two feet six inches tall and was visible only to his friend René. A place was set at dinner for the Baron, vodka poured, and all the day's problems were thrashed out with him during

the meal. Schniebel helped to curtail the otherwise lengthy
and lonely thought process, René maintained. The fruits of
his Paris career manifested themselves in crisp uppercuts
which were applied to anyone who either willfully or acci-
dentally caused me displeasure. Today René lives in Geneva and, as a result of a spate of industry quite out of keeping with his former character, is very rich, and may be consulted at any time on any matter: "Which publisher should
I go to?" "It doesn't make the slightest difference, you'll
only communicate with them through your lawyers once
the book is out."

"We've got tax problems." "Marvelous, if you hadn't
you'd be broke."

"We're broke." "Marvelous, if you weren't you'd have
tax problems."

"Which magazine should get the first-serial rights?" "It
doesn't really matter, they're gonna fuck it up anyway."

In Berlin René spoke thus: "You have to find an agent
who looks as criminally inclined as possible, so that you
never hit on the idea of trusting him, and tell him to get
you a film in France." Then he called Baron Schniebel and
the three of us went out to the Mazurka. At five in the
morning René started swapping punches with a Russian
and after pausing to finish the bottle of vodka, they exchanged visiting cards and invited each other to step outside, indicating a duel with pistols at the very least. When I
hurried after them I found that Berlin's fresh morning air
had meditated already and drawn them into a convivial chat.
I settled down in the Snowgoose to await fraternal developments and heard someone whisper, "Don't be afraid, I only
want to tell you something. Whenever you feel like working
again call DEFA. We're very sorry you had to suffer with
the rest of the UFA crack-up but we had no choice."
DEFA was the Russian-licensed East German film
company that had made *The Murderers Among Us.* "Who
authorized you to tell me that?" I called out, but he was already getting into the dark-blue Opel and driving away.
Rene hurried across the wide Kantstrasse and said, "Didn't
I see somebody at the car?" "I've been mixed up in an
East-West B picture," I answered. "Off to France," said
René.

They live in a large house made almost entirely of glass.
A house that was modern ten years ago. Now it's worn, out

of style, neglected-looking. The rooms on each floor are of equal size, the passages equally wide. There are no carpets and no curtains, no flowers or pictures. In front of the house there's a street, across the street the water of the English Channel, farther north the town of Brighton.

The head of the institute, an actor, a television producer, and I are standing in the hall. "Come along upstairs, the men will be pleased," the director says. They come down the stairs toward us, come straight at me, I try not to bump into them. A hand touches my shoulder, another my face. "We've got visitors," they way and turn their heads this way and that, "isn't that right? We've got visitors." Their eyeballs are white, without pupils or irises, only a few are wearing dark glasses; their skin is scarred and charred, covered with dark-blue spots, as though someone had spattered it with ink. A young man with black hair is standing at the window. The scar begins at the brows, under the brows are holes; he hastily pushes up his glasses, takes the director's hand and taps at the palm with his fingertips. "Give him your hand," the director says. The young man feels each of my fingers, feels for my face, carefully strokes my temples and mouth. He says something that sounds like a dog's bark, hoarse and harsh. The director says, "He's deaf, it caught his eardrums as well as his eyes. He was a pianist before he became a bomber pilot. Just four weeks ago he took a piano apart, tore out all the strings." The hand strokes my arm. "He's happy to be able to touch a woman," the director says. The young man smiles. One can see that he had been very handsome.

"What is this film you're making?" the head of the institute asks.

"It's for an American TV series," the producer answers. He points at the actor and me. "They're both playing blind people."

"We get so out of touch here," the head of the institute says, turning to me. "You're a foreigner, aren't you?"

"Yes."

"Scandinavian?"

"German."

"Yes," he says, looking at the colorless sea, "they're all war-blind here, some still from the first one."

Grandfather had stayed behind in Zossen and I had gone back to town with mother, to the Sedanstrasse. In the afternoon she went out and left me with the woman who lived on the ground floor. She wore thick spectacles and a yellow armband with three black dots on it. She didn't turn the light on as it got dark, just sat there quietly on the sofa. "It's dark," I said. "That's all right, dear, it doesn't matter." Then she stood up and walked into my chair, knocking it over. She still had gas lighting and it took a long time before she turned on a light. In the semidarkness she had groped at my face and I screamed and ran out into the street.

The actor gives me a cigarette. I don't even know his name. He was already in the car this morning when they came to pick me up for the ride to Brighton.

That was on May 8th, 1959.

YOU: No, it was the ninth.

ME: The eighth.

YOU: O.K., the eighth.

ME: Today's the twentieth, I have to fly home to Berlin tomorrow.

YOU: If it wasn't so hot I'd shut the windows. Your next-door neighbor's been washing up for three hours now, seems to be doing all the plates in London.

ME: Don't run the bath too full, if the water gets up to to the overflow it runs down into the courtyard and from there into the hairdresser's. How old are you?

YOU: Twenty-six.

ME: I'm thirty-three. Did you break your nose?

YOU: What makes you think that?

ME: It's got a bump.

YOU: This is a classic Greek nose, as most erudite people are quick to see. My forebears on my father's side were Greek.

ME: I thought you'd broken it.

YOU: Why did you do that TV film?

ME: I don't know. Roy said I could use the dough.

YOU: Who's Roy?

ME: My agent.

YOU: I don't like to act any more. How do you get mad?

ME: What do you mean, "How do you get mad?"

YOU: I've got to play a man who's continually furious.

ME: You've never been furious?

YOU: No, I've never been furious. . . . You looked awful that morning we went to Brighton. I was very disappointed.

ME: I hadn't slept, I'd been out all night with some actors. Superdrunkards.

YOU: Do you live in Berlin?

ME: Yes. What sort of shirt is that?

YOU: I like it.

ME: I'll call it the piano shirt. It looks as though you're wrapped in a keyboard.

YOU: Are you coming back to London?

ME: I don't know. Do you have any children?

YOU: No, just a cross-eyed cat.

When the door slammed behind you and the security chain rattled against the frame I took my suitcases, packed them slowly and neatly, then threw the door keys into the hairdresser's mailbox and drove to the airport.

Three days later I borrowed Baron Schniebel and took him for a walk around the Schlachtensee. "I've been talking to myself for days now," I said. "That's why I've asked you to give me four hours of your time. I'd like you to listen to me carefully. Nothing more. I've bought fifty sleeping pills, although I never take them—yes, I did take one in London last week, so there are only forty-nine. Can you tell me what that means? Good, I have problems, worries, troubles, that's fairly obvious. But I tell myself that I'm not stupid enough to be unhappy and that's ten percent true and ninety not. Since we've already mentioned the pills I have to tell you that I've been sleeping badly for over a year now. My brain chatters like a telex and I also have two dreams which aren't dreams at all because I experienced both of them. First of all there's the boat pond in the English Garden in Munich. It was neither big nor deep and on Sundays it was full of rowboats with young couples or fat women with wavy perms or men with knotted handkerchiefs on their heads. One Monday morning I walked down the path that led to the pond. There was a rotting smell and great flies were buzzing and there was a bloop bloop sound like frogs croaking sadly. I could find neither the pond nor its banks. They'd drained off the water, as one empties a bathtub. Bubbles the size of soup plates were welling out of the quagmire, greenish and shimmering; they swelled until they burst, it was like a sick bowel. In between raked paths and trimmed hedges this swollen, stinking bowel. That's one of the dreams, or half-dreams. I'll tell you the second one later. My troubles are the following: I don't have anything

I can pawn and everything I touch for the past two years is bad, or goes bad when I touch it. It's as though I'm in one of those eternally revolving elevators and it never gets to a floor. And I don't know any more where I got on. I'm exaggerating a little, but still it's something like the story of the black-market butter after the war. I was living with a couple called Alike and Fritz and I'd given them the salary I'd earned at the theater to buy butter with. When I came home after the performance they led me into the kitchen. We were very excited and more or less on tiptoe and hardly daring to breathe we went up to the washbasin where we'd put it to cool, but all we found was the silver paper and a yellow streak running down the drainpipe. The landlord had taken delivery of the first load of coke in two years and had lit the hot-water boiler. But apart from the troubles which are all too obvious other things happen to me which are upsetting, to put it mildly. For example the Paris hotel room. Every night from one till five someone marched up and down above me, first in the middle of the room, then up and down the walls, then back to the middle. And it tinkled as if he were wearing spurs. The concierge looked at me as though I'd gone crazy, said the gentleman above was seventy-five and almost a cripple. One night I went and got him—the concierge, I mean. 'Now please listen to this,' I said. The concierge had a mustache and it started to shiver. 'I don't understand it,' he stammered and ran out. Then in London: I'd taken an apartment and one cold and foggy evening I came home from the studio and as I opened the door I heard the telephone ringing. It was someone from the publicity department who said that three Italian journalists would be dropping by and that she was sorry no one had told me about it during the day. A short while later the three arrived. Within two minutes I realized that they weren't journalists at all, let alone Italians. They spoke Cockney and looked like Scandinavian wrestlers—if there is such a thing—and the one who said he was the photographer dropped his Rolleiflex case and it jumped back up like a rubber ball. They all looked at me to see if I'd noticed and just at that moment the telephone rang and the third assistant started to tell me which scenes we'd be doing tomorrow. I interrupted him and said, 'Oh, my God, how terrible, you mean we'll have to shoot all night? Whatever happened?' but the silly bastard merely said, 'What on earth are you talking about?' and hung up. I turned to the three and told them that something had gone wrong with the camera and that we'd have to reshoot everything we'd done that day during the night and that I was terribly sorry to have to put them off till the next evening. When they'd gone I called the police. They arrived, within seconds it seemed, with ten uniformed men and two detectives. I described the so-called journalists. They were the most sought-after band of crooks in London and had several murders to their credit. From then on until the film was finished, two detectives lived in the apartment and another two came with me to the studio every day because they said the gang would certainly pay me back. We never saw them again. Anyway, I was terrified of every visitor at the studio and of every noise in the night. The detectives stayed close until I boarded the plane for Berlin, which they had gone over with a fine-tooth comb before I got on. Then four weeks ago, in another apartment in London, the lock was sawn out of the door, I heard the ratsch ratsch in the night and called the police again. A day later somebody painted a swastika in my dressing room and cut all my clothes to ribbons. You must admit that all this is not exactly designed to soothe one's nerves in the long run but then again it's also no reason for carrying forty-nine sleeping pills around. And as to work—there was the film in France your friend René advised me to do. The script, the director, and the actors were all good and we were all determined to make a good film. It was probably more important for my costar then for the rest of us, it was his first job after his seventh attempt to kick heroin. He had his agent to thank for the addiction; years previously this gentleman had accepted for his client two films to be shot simultaneously and when he collapsed after four or five weeks of shooting he was given an injection and then another and again the next day—first morphine, later heroin. After his fourth spell in a sanatorium one had hoped he was cured but then his son died. With this film he wanted to prove that he could work again. When it was two-thirds finished the producer ran out of money and the rest was shot on a shoestring. Back in Germany I heard rumors that I might be sued for libel; I had told somebody at some time that someone had done something odd with my money—you must know that I tend to recklessness and appear to invite duplicity. And my mother was depressed, not to say resigned. Her friends had cut out all the negative articles about me, pasted them neat-

ly on sheets of paper, and presented them to her in an
enormous carton. Telling her that she shouldn't get worked
up over a little brood of vultures didn't help. I'm going
round the bend, was all she said. You and I know how
many people are ready for enmity. I must tell you about
the film producer who lives here in Grunewald. I'd never
worked for him but I heard that he was running around
telling everyone, 'She's finished, done for, out for the
count.' I climbed in the Snowgoose and drove to his house:
'You neither made nor lost a penny on me, so why do you
talk about me?' I said. He fidgeted like a dovetailed chaf-
finch. 'Lies, all lies, please believe me,' he said, the color of
our roof. And then there was my dressmaker here in town.
He'd made my film dresses for years, even for the English
ones, where the unions howled blue murder, but I got him
through. 'We are not accustomed to being treated as an in-
stallment establishment,' he told Mother on the telephone
after she'd sent him part of the bill. But I wanted to tell
you about work. Now listen. In January I was offered a
part in a German film. A walk-on, more or less. I accepted.
When it was finished I went on a promotion tour with the
male lead and saw again all the cinema owners I knew so
well and who had become even fatter in the meantime and
now spend their vacations in houses on Majorca they'd
bought with the profits from my old films. They were reluc-
tant to shake my hand and hedged around me as though I
had leprosy—one in Osnabrück took my name off the poster to be on the safe side and asked me not to go on the
stage. And not so long ago I was having dinner in a restaurant with your friend René when a director named Kurt
Hoffmann came up to our table. 'Good evening' or 'Hello'
or perhaps it was 'How are you?' I wanted to say but didn't
get that far since he pulled out the vacant chair, said, 'I'm
in rather a hurry,' and carried it away. I know it's stupid to
mention it and to tell you the truth I hadn't even thought
about it again till now—success and failure are both greatly
overrated but failure gives you a whole lot more to talk
about. Else Bongers for instance hates failure: 'Why aren't
you at the film festival?' she asked me last summer. 'What
would I do there? I haven't been invited,' I answered.
'That's going too far,' she hissed so intensely that her toothless poodle had a heart attack.

"As I say, none of this is destined to make my beauty
rest a tranquil affair and I'll admit that now and again it's

the gnashing of my teeth that keeps me awake, for even the silliest, stupidest film doesn't justify such behavior. That's my opinion. And yours too, probably. I know which question must come now, logically and yet as black as your hat: Why don't you go on the stage again? Yes, I thought so, and that's a tricky point I've been trying to talk around all the while. Shall I tell you the second dream first? All right. There's this camp near Nuremberg, I shot a film there before I went to New York. In the mornings the children would stream out of the huts and walk beside our cars until we parked and then stand there the whole day staring at the cars. They were Russian, Polish, Rumanian, and Bulgarian children and their parents had been interned in the camp since the end of the war because they had no papers. One day a chauffeur opened the hood of a car and unintentionally slammed it down again on one of the boy's fingers. He pulled and in the excitement no one could find the catch to the hood. The boy didn't cry or say anything, just tugged at his fingers with the other hand. By the time we'd freed him all his fingers and the bone in the middle of the hand were broken. We wanted to take him into town to the clinic but the women shook their fists at us and the medical orderly at the camp slammed the door in our faces. The boy had just looked at us. At night I see his face, at first vague and streaky, then clearer and sharper, and the more I try to get away from it the clearer it gets. Look at the swans. Of course it's all nonsense what they say about them. They say they commit suicide when their spouse dies; they fly up as high as they can, tuck in their wings, and let themselves fall, plunge to the ground like a stone. I wouldn't put it past them, they seem to have no friends apart from each other. Look at them. When you hand them a piece of bread they wave their heads about as though it were an insult to feed them with garbage. They could knock our heads to pulp with their wings. My grandfather loved swans. 'They're so contemptuous and mean,' he'd say and laugh when the ducks flurried away from them. I was never allowed to make fun of them when they waddled along the shore. 'That's their sore point,' he said, 'but it's no reason to make fun of them.' Once he took me to Lake Müggel. He had a rucksack full of bread crusts he'd gotten from the baker in looked like fat featherbeds, or meringue pies. We ate sour crabapples and threw crusts into the water. In between I Sedanstrasse. The swans were sleeping in the reeds. They

had to look at the meadow: 'Green's good for the eyes,'
Grandfather said. Swans remind me of crabapples and the
red currant jelly Grandfather used to make with sago,
clear, see-through grains of sago, and of corn-poppies and
chickpeas and the primulas and dill in the bed to the left of
my swing. We grew everything except tomatoes in the garden; 'I can't abide nightshade plants,' said Grandfather. To
the point: the very thought of a stage première makes my
hair stand on end, it's as though I'd lived through a death-
or-glory beachhead landing and must do everything in my
power to duck a second. Perhaps my courage will recuper-
ate one day; at the moment it's dilapidated, run dry, as dry
as sawdust.'

We walked on for an hour in silence. We got into the
Snowgoose in the Goethestrasse and said farewell in front
of my house. "Your friend René once said. 'One must
choose one's enemies with care,' " I said before shutting the
gate.

When David Anthony Palastanga arrived in Berlin he
was wearing the piano shirt.

That was on a Saturday.

On Sunday I was awarded the Federal Film Prize for the
best supporting performance. The reaction of the gala audience couldn't have been more surprised or stupefied if
they had announced that a hit-and-run driver had been
elected chairman of the local Knights of the Road.

On Monday I was offered several films.

On Wednesday word had got round about David
Anthony and I was a "marriage wrecker," according to
many front pages.

On Thursday the offers were rescinded.

On Friday David Anthony said, "I've fallen in love with
Berlin, I'd like to live here."

Five months later we accepted a film offer from Italy.

Mr. Tortini, our Roman agent, picked us up at the airport and drove us to Cinecittà. In the middle of the studio
a young man was standing on a chair screaming a string of
"Silenzios" and "Bastas" at the top of his voice until the
seat broke, leaving him trapped in the frame of the chair
and shrieking for help which no one took the slightest notice of as the uproar that followed his plea for silence was
now approaching a fortissimo furioso. Mr. Tortini introduced him to me as the director. Drawing attention to him-

self with long blasts on a piercing whistle, he was able to find someone prepared to lace me into my costumes. Since he spoke nothing but Italian and no translator had been engaged, his directions consisted of a series of more or less agitated gesticulations, and the tumult of the studio, which remained at full volume even during the takes, drove me to the fringe of desperation within a few days. Sensing my plight, David Anthony said one morning, "My father was Italian."

"I thought he was Greek."

"His father. Mine was Italian and if you ever want to get anywhere with them you'll have to scream—but don't get worked up."

In the middle of a long monologue in which I, as the duchess, had to state my claim to Parma, my gaze fell upon the chattering studio photographer. I took him by his turtle neck and screamed, for several minutes, everything I had picked up during my brief spell of military service. To begin with it made no great effect but gradually a large crowd began to collect and by the time I got to the end it was clear that I had created a new record in vociferousness. The crowd stood in absolute silence, the director kissed me, workers shook my hand, the producer brought a bunch of roses and I was allotted a private dressing room.

When my first salary installments were long overdue and neither Tortini nor anyone from the production had so much as mentioned the fact, David Anthony went to the producer. He looked nonplussed and said "Domani," and did indeed give David Anthony a check the next day, but this was a Saturday and the banks were closed and remained that way until Tuesday—that Monday being a national holiday—turning our weekend into a ticklish affair since we had no money.

The sleepy-looking cashier perked up immediately as David Anthony presented the check on Tuesday morning. He stared at it fascinated, said, "Un momento," disappeared into the back room, and returned after fifteen discomforting minutes with a jocular gentleman who invited David Anthony to his office for a glass of grappa and then asked, "Where did you get this check?"

"From the man who signed it," said David Anthony.

"But he's not authorized to issue checks alone. He has a joint account with three partners and each must sign the checks," the manager said cheerfully.

For three days the producer was nowhere to be found; then, as David Anthony cornered him in his office, he clapped his hands to his head, exclaimed, "How silly of me to forget!" and wrote out a check on another bank. David Anthony drove to the other bank and the cashier went pale as he examined the check, quakingly said "Un momento," and disappeared into the back room, returning after five anxious minutes with an enthusiastic gentleman who introduced himself as the director, invited David Anthony to his office for a glass of grappa and asked, "Where did you get this check?"

"From the man who signed it," said David Anthony.

"But he hasn't had an account with us for over ten years," the director said warmly. "He must have saved an old checkbook," he added appreciatively.

David Anthony's telephone call came just as the director was trying to animate me to play a scene more winsomely by yelling, "Be happy with the teeth!" and I heard David Anthony say, "Stop working right away, go to your dressing room and lock yourself in and don't open it until I get there. The film will be over in four days and all you'll get is a handshake."

At first they tapped, then they hammered, then they tried to break the door down. When David Anthony arrived the corridor resembled an Oriental bazaar, and Tortini, who had been summoned by the producer, threw his arms around David Anthony's knees and swore that the producer was a noble human being, then sank into a corner covering his face with a handkerchief. The production manager came up waving a check.

"Cash," said David Anthony.

"Cash," they all echoed.

"Cash," he continued, "or she doesn't shoot another foot of film," and ended the conversation with a very British "Basta."

The hotel demanded settlement of their bill. One final night was granted. In the morning the third assistant arrived: "They're waiting for you at the studio," he called through the door. A short while later the second assistant, "You'll be sued if you don't come." Then the production manager: "We've notified the police." Then the producer: "We'll make sure that you never work again." Then two hours' peace. Toward midday there was a timid tap. David Anthony had put the chain on the door and opened it two inches. Tortini was standing there shivering. "I've got the money. In cash," he said and cried as David Anthony made him count it out on the floor of the hallway before opening the door. "You've made my agency very unpopular," he sobbed and padded off.

"They'll throw spotlights at us," I said as we entered the studio.

"Here they come," someone yelled.

The whole crew lined up silently as at a state ceremony. Then the director threw himself at us, embraced us, kissed us, the producer joined our hands as though binding us in wedlock, the cameraman thumped his thigh and the chief electrician roared, "Brava, brava." The game was over, we were the victors, and victors must be honored.

"Tonio," I said, "I shall call you Tonio."

"Why that?" asked David Anthony.

"Because of the Italian father."

"As you wish," he said, "but my mother was Scottish."

This was on the way to the airport. You had to fly to London to shoot retakes on a film you'd finished weeks before, and I flew to Berlin. When you telephoned that evening I was in the hospital, the same one in which I had been operated on as a child. I had a temperature of 104.7° and my spine, head, and neck hurt badly and when the woman knocked against the bed with her broom the next morning I screamed and she said, "Don't start carrying on now." I was sent home after eight days. "A virus," they said. My temperature went up again. During the next two months I would leave our house in the morning and not know in the evening where I'd been or how I got back. I couldn't remember names or faces, the date or day of the week. "She's got meningitis," the new doctor said, "it will take a long time before she can work again, you both must have patience." Only one of your friends still wrote, the others weren't awfully pleased at your moving to Germany. "The English think Calais is already jungle," you said.

In the spring of 1960 I was offered a stage engagement. I accepted. I couldn't remember the lines for more than a few hours; every afternoon I went through the play as though I'd never read it before.

People shouted at us in the streets; most of it you couldn't understand because your German was still shaky, which I was thankful for. When a television director came to Berlin and offered me Cocteau's one-woman play *La voix humaine* you said, "You must play it; if you get through that then you'll know you can get well again."

After the live transmission in Munich we drove back to Berlin. At a parking lot the attendant asked you for money and you turned out your pockets and said, "Take it all," for the first time louder than it's your nature to speak. The man turned and fled and we lay under the Snowgoose picking up the money. It was the last we had and the salary I received for the Cocteau was the last we were to see for a long time. We had a few friends and they invited us but couldn't help. It was exactly like Hollywood, 1948. The mail contained nothing but bills and letters from the lawyers handling your divorce and my American tax problems. Fritz Lang wanted to do a film with me but the distributors refused him the money. There were no bridges we might have burned, nothing we might have built up in another town. I tried to get jobs as a poster designer but they laughed when they heard my name. Household Word, Sinner, UFA Star, Broadway Star, Marriage Wrecker.

In September 1960 a theater-tour management had the courage to offer us a contract together. You suggested Kanin's *Born Yesterday* and we played together in Germany for nine months, mostly one-night stands, traveling from town to town and village to village, ending the tour in the summer of '61 at the Kurfürstendamm Theater in Berlin, where we played for several weeks.

One morning—you were repairing the Snowgoose—I went for a walk. Baron Schniebel was standing at the gate. We hadn't seen each other for two years. We walked down the Clayallee and on to Lake Grunewald but it was crowded with people lying on blankets and rubber mattresses playing their transistor radios amid heaps of Coca-Cola bottles, cans, empty cigarette packs, and bags of candy; others were splashing about in the brown water. We climbed up the hill and then I said, "These two years have been sluggish and—I'd be tempted to say degrading, if it weren't such a silly word. You heard about the tour. We've been somewhat better off since the first night in Hamburg, not so much financially, since everything goes on debts, but we've gained a little hope since then. As I came on stage they stood and applauded, as if to say: Enough of the bickering for now, go ahead and act. We have no idea what will happen when the tour's over but, as I say, we're hopeful.

For the past nine months we've been playing in the evening and driving during the day and each night after the performance Tonio sat with the maps trying to find the town we have to be in the next day. Shortly before Easter he was still poring at three in the morning and when I asked him what the trouble was he said, 'According to my list we're supposed to be in Karfreitag tomorrow and I can't find it anywhere.' 'Karfreitag is German for Good Friday,' I broke to him gently. His German's pretty good now but of course there are still a lot of words he just hasn't come across. These are the little japes that brighten our lives, like the fact that we have to invest a good chunk of our salary in hotel rooms—since we're not married we always have to take two. There's still no sign of a divorce. The meningitis pains are weakening and come less often. Pain makes you self-pitying, it isolates you, I can't tell you how I hate the pains and loathe myself for whimpering, they're like a constant artillery barrage, flattening the beauty out of everything. And lapses of memory are only attractive when you've encouraged them, not when they take you unawares.

"Let me prattle on for a little. To give you a clear picture of our position in public life I must tell you the story of the woman at the autobahn checkpoint in the Russian zone. We got to it late one night and the guards searched the Snowgoose and Tonio went off into one of the huts to get our passports stamped. I stayed in the car. A woman came up, tapped on the window, and asked me for a cigarette. She started crying and then told me that she'd gotten out of her car to stretch her legs somewhere in the Russian zone and that her handbag containing all her papers must have slid from the seat as she did so because when she got to the control point it wasn't there any more and they'd kept her standing there for eight hours and wouldn't allow her to go on or go back and look for it and her daughter was waiting for her in West Berlin and would be worried to death and so on and so forth. I handed her all the cigarettes I had and offered to call her daughter the moment I got home. The woman bent down to take the cigarettes and suddenly looked at me and said, 'Aren't you that actress?' I said yes and she threw up her hands and howled, 'Not that too!' I've learned to live from day to day these last years, I imagine everybody has his own tape measure with regard to time. Some divide it off into years, others into months or weeks, we tick off the days. Of necessity to begin with, since we never knew what would happen tomorrow, whether we'd have to move out or whether the electricity or the telephone would be cut off, things like that. When I say we've no idea what's in store I mean it, we don't think about it, we've evolved a new calendar. Only once did we make plans and then only because we knew they were unrealizable. We played a one-night stand in a movie house in Einbeck and the next day we drove out to the village of Sievershausen to visit relatives of my stepfather. The country thereabouts is very beautiful, soft hills and fields and those long uncomfortable country lanes with bumps in the middle like camels' humps and trees planted willy-nilly along the sides, and the air is very raw, 'fresh as a hollyhock' my grandfather would have said. 'One day we'll buy a farm,' we said, one that wasn't automated and we'd live off it—as vegetarians, because how could you possibly slaughter a chicken called Elise or Kunigunde? We sat on the side of a lane and I was happier than I'd ever been. Success doesn't interest Tonio, it does nothing for him. He's less dependent on people than I am. A year ago I made a terrific row at a party because a film producer was going on about someone I knew, an actor who had just directed his first film—brilliantly, it was one of the best films since the war. The producer said, 'Don't let's get too excited until we've seen what he does next.' And off I went: 'It doesn't matter a damn what he does next, he's done this one and that's more than one can say for you,' I spat and swished out of the house. Ages later Tonio came out and said, 'What's up?' 'I had a fight,' I answered him. 'The way you all carry on, I still can't tell the difference between a fight and small talk,' he said. But you see how they all lurk around waiting for failure, the flop that'll wipe out all previous success. They can stand success no more than they can stand beauty, they have to work against it even if the most they can do safely is to query the degree. If they only could realize that their cynicism and belittling springs from their own uncertainty, that these are the tools of a man doomed to failure. In the street where my mother lived when she was evacuated there was a fat lady. She had six or seven children and her husband was a salesman, of schnapps, I think it was, and one day he was called up, which didn't make much difference since he'd hardly ever been home anyway. 'Oh yes, Hermann,' she would always say whenever anyone asked after him, as though she were surprised that she still remembered his name. She would gaze at her many children and say, 'Yes, Hermann is a good person.' Hers was the only house in the street that was never locked and never cleaned. Now and again she would tip a bucket of water over the kitchen floor and then prod the chickens, children, cabbage leaves, and potato peel down the steps with a broom. In the evenings she would stand at the table and say, 'Now just tell your mother what you want to eat and then we'll have a think about how we can get it.' Her children were all bright-blond and rosy-cheeked and the girls were precocious and went smooching with the soldiers from the nearby barracks. They all loved the topsy-turvy house and their fat mother and none of the boys would have dreamed of volunteering before it was necessary. The neighbors said that she was a slut and 'carried on' and when she waddled down the long street they all stood behind their curtains whispering. She looked like a big happy dog that doesn't hear the yapping of the smaller ones tied to their kennels because it's too busy going about the business of living and being happy. What I really wanted to talk to you about was Miller. Next time maybe."

Schniebel and I stood at the gate. It started to rain and my mother came out onto the balcony to shut the windows. "I painted her yesterday," I said. "I tore up the picture before she could see it. She has no colors any more, it's as though her body has thrown away all the reds and greens, as though it needs its strength for something else."

In the autumn of 1962 Schniebel was sitting in the garden of our house in Starnberg. He sat next to the pile of dead leaves I had raked together, looked out over the lake, then at my dirty hands. "You've no need to look at me like that," I said, "I like doing it and the work in the studios is only bearable when I think of the garden and pottering about in it, so why are you looking so snooty?" Tonio came up with a wheelbarrow full of leaves. Schniebel looked at our wedding rings. "I thought you'd be here earlier," I said, "we expected you in June for the wedding."

We then walked along the mill stream, past the nunnery wash-house, went as far as the village of Harkirchen and back. "Your disapproval is all too apparent," I said, "but we like living like this, a garden doesn't have to belong to one in order to plant things in it, you can enjoy it without owning it. Let's see now . . . We've been plodding through a series of second-rate films—one or two weren't even that bad—and the chief editor of a magazine, Heinz Weigt his name is, was obsessed with the idea that I should sing and brought a record producer out to meet us; the record I made became popular and sold very well. What more do you want? We were in the United States in January and I saw Erich Pommer again. He has nothing whatsoever to show for the years he spent in the profession, it took everything, what money he had was lost on a film he made in Germany. Now he lives in his son's apartment, is dependent and sick, lives in a wheel chair. He could cope with anything but he can't cope with not working, it's the greatest dependence there is. I never hated poverty so much as on the day I visited Erich Pommer, a man who is my friend, and whom I can only help with a lot of money. And don't tell me there are worse fates because you know full well that I don't accept that argument since it presupposes failure and attempts to excuse our own incompetence with the whims of fortune, holds ugliness for truth and beauty for coincidence."

And since Tonio gave no sign that he was listening and had lapsed into his hour of silence, I carried on: "Shall I quote Lichtenberg? 'I am admittedly not in a position to swear that it'll be better if it's changed. But of this much I am sure: It will have to be changed if it's ever going to be good.' Or does my uncalled-for aggression tell you that I'm lying? That I'm using gardening as a refuge from the fact that I wasn't strong enough to take the hatred and because, as my friend Else Bongers says, I always have to do everything one thousand percent, even if it's doing nothing? 'You don't just get out, you kick the door after you close it,' she once said."

We sat down on the narrow wooden bridge that spans the stream and followed the flight of a wild duck preparing to land. I said, "Tonio and I are sick to death of the booby-traps we have to set up for each film director so that we can work in comparative freedom and not have to listen to the confusing mumbo jumbo most of them drivel. We work out a much more complicated hodgepodge of scholarly allusions that even the most intellectually potbellied of them could ever dream up and create so much unclarity before the first scene is shot that they don't dare say another word. On *The Three-Penny Opera* we kept a perfectly straight face while telling the director that the part of Jenny was obviously an extension of and a complement to *Richard*

III, and when he launched off on a paralyzing dissertation on Elizabethan drama we raised one eyebrow each and said that we had meant Beowulf, of course, not Shakespeare. The effect effect was stunning. Yes, I know what you're going to say: if we're that bloody clever why don't we do without them and go it alone. But I ask you: How and with what?"

Tonio stood up and moved away, chewing a blade of grass. "Henry Miller was here until yesterday," I said. "The telephone rang one evening about eighteen months ago and a voice said, 'My name's Henry Miller, I'm an American writer.' He'd seen a film of mine, or rather a film I'd played in, in a flea-pit in San Francisco and when he came to Germany he asked his publisher for my number. By the time we met he'd found out everything about us; he knew my horoscope and had even been to Ulm—my birthplace —had got hold of a pile of old newspaper clippings and had them translated. His interest makes a giant of you—it's a gigantic interest, it makes all other interest seem artful and cunning because it's born of an absolute independence and warms to everything and everybody, is never satisfied with half measures. Henry doesn't speak a word of German but his interest kept our tight-lipped Bavarian postman talking to him at the gate for over an hour last week and he's never been the same since—the man was always surly and grumpy and the dogs couldn't stand him but now he's cheerful and positive and asks every day for the friendly gentleman he'd had such an interesting chat with."

Tonio cleared his throat, ran his right hand over his hair from the forehead to the back of his neck, dug his left into the breast pocket of his shirt looking for a cigarette—a sign that he was about to speak. He said, "The Baron's right. Let's do something on our own. We'll find a play and produce, direct, and play it alone. Let's go."

"How?"

"We'll make a start. And if we fall flat on our face at least we'll know why, we'll have no one to blame but ourselves."

We were about to ask Schniebel into the house but he'd gone already.

St. Moritz,
May 1, 1970

I've found a photo: Grandmother and me in Zossen. I'm

wearing my Sunday dress with a woolly cardigan and a crown of daisies on my head. Grandmother's looking down at me, she's angry and I've been crying—the root of my Angst? Who knows. They'd had a fight, Grandfather and Grandmother, she had sat on the bench beside the stove and said, "I'm sick, I can't take care of the child any more and it's not right for her to grow up with an old man. She'd be better off in a home." When the woman from next door came in with a camera I had crawled under the table. They'd pulled me out and straightened the crown of daisies. Then in winter a man came with flowers and chocolates and Grandmother said he wanted to marry Mother. The man looked at me and said, "We'll find a good home for the little one." He never came again but I was afraid that he and Grandmother would find a home.

I call Else:

"Child? What's up?"

"Nothing, We've got snow here."

"Who hasn't?"

"I'm not going to invite you again."

"I'll come as soon as the school holidays start."

"Tonio's rented a house in the south of France for the summer. It's big. You don't have to see me if you don't want to—I mean it's so big we don't have to get on each other's nerves."

"I'll come and visit you and then lock myself in in one of the wings. How's the other child?"

"Among other things she can now say 'Thank you.' I ask myself: Is that good?"

" 'Thank you' has no meaning any more."

"I dipped into a couple of advice-for-parents books last night. They remind me of instructions on guinea-pig culture. There's 'The little chap who won't go bye-bye,' and 'Lillibet, who won't sit on her pottie,' and 'What do mummy and daddy do when they catch their precious one fibbing?' Perhaps one should make the adults bail out over Nepal or New Zealand or wherever it is they still have those wild tribes—Central Australia's still got a few, I believe—and they'd lie there with a broken ankle. How are they going to make themselves understood, what will make those giant heads smile and what not? When will they start hollering and when will they just stomp off? That's how it must have been when we were infants."

"You're foaming."

"No, just fuming. I foamed a couple of weeks ago in the south of France in a restaurant called Tante Marie. There was one of those blodges sitting at the next table and I heard them say 'Boche.' I looked at my Boche child and turned into a fishwife."

"Did you blow your top?"

"I blew my top."

"Only Boches say Boche."

"Christina will be two on the sixteenth."

"Perhaps I'll live to see the day when you'll call me and howl because she's done something you didn't expect. Then I'll be able to say, 'You were exactly the same.' How are you getting rid of all the people?"

"What people?"

"The ones who've spread themselves over your desk in the past year. How do you get them out of the house?"

"I haven't started to try."

"You used to be able to forget. People, films, upsets, catastrophes."

"Possible."

"More than certain."

"You're right."

May 4, 1970

Schniebel was here. I bumped into him next to the newspaper kiosk on platform 1. It was eight in the morning and the Maloja wind was cold. "The lake should have thawed by now," I said, "by the tenth at the very latest, but even so I'd rather have a frozen one than one full of crocodiles. Did you know how fast they are? On the Zambesi a man pulled me back from the bank and said they're the fastest animals alive. In the zoo they always look so numbskulled and nitwitted. . . . The mountains are devouring me, after five months they start to devour you, you long for flatland and breadth, they get to be obstacles, ominous, squash you with their gravity and their protection ceases to be protective and imprisons you like a suit of armor, a moat, a blindfold. With half the snow gone St. Moritz looks like an old man in his underpants, a pensioner in need of a rest. You're going to say that I'm exaggerating, yes, I know. Sometimes I wonder if Hugo's still alive. Hugo was a stag that used to knock on the door with his antlers at six o'clock, on the dot, every evening. We let him in and he would stand in the hall and eat five pounds of carrots and

about the same amount of potatoes. He could eat you out
of house and home. I would take hold of his antlers the
way you steady yourself on a clothes stand in a coffeehouse
and stuff the raw vegetables into his mouth as though I were
stuffing diapers into a washing machine. I had a Czech
housekeeper and she always stood behind the door with an
ax in her hand. She was a very peculiar individual altogether, she always went around with this ax and I still don't
know to this day how she managed to cook with it. This
was in '56, when I came back from New York and lived in
that lonely house near the dairy.

"And then I wonder whether the spook's still spooking—
yes, we had one of those too. He didn't seem to take to me
but the moment Mother went to bed he pulled off her eiderdown, turned the key in the lock, opened the windows
and knocked over chairs. But you haven't come here to
hear about crocodiles and ghosts. Your friend René is rather upset because I apparently misunderstood him. He in-
sists that he was never a boxer professionally, only as a student in Paris. Would you please assure him that I have now
got the message and shall correct the mistake? I have a
friend called Pali and together we once tried to find a word
that rhymes with pugilist; believe me there isn't a proper
one. We wrote each other letters and the rule was that they
must rhyme and be sent off right away, uncorrected, and I
remember one letter stopped at pugilist. I haven't seen him
for a year. Strange, one loses people because one lives too
far away or one's working or God knows what. Pali is still
quite young but even when I first met him he had snow-
white hair. I think it was always white, before it could
plump for any particular color it went white. He grew up
in a concentration camp. His father was Hungarian, his
mother Indonesian. He had a wife at sometime or other,
now he just has a daughter and I always think of her as
being twelve for the simple reason that I never see her, or
very seldom. After the war Pali entered a seminary; it was
his and his guardian's wish that he become a priest. On the
eve of receiving his final orders he went down to the village, from there to the town, and never returned again. He
now works for a record company. Pali has a funny habit:
he stands his cigarettes on a table, balances them on their
filters and lets them go out. It's a wonder that he hasn't
burned down whole cities. 'Who on earth invented the
word happiness?' he says when his *joie de vivre* sinks past

freezing point. He knows hordes of people, wherever you go with him he knows somebody. 'If you're alone you have to know people,' he says then. And once he said, 'When one's not in love one talks about freedom. What would I do with freedom? Give it away, naturally.' We loved going to the movies, we always laughed and cried at the same things, always covered with chocolate we'd bought at the newsstand and wolfed during the newsreel. He made me tell him the story of Frau Zumbrowski at least a hundred times. She was one of the housekeepers in the Wexstrasse in Berlin. Her husband only came home weekends and on Mondays she always had a black eye and told everyone she was getting a divorce. On Fridays she had a hair-do and on Mondays a black eye—sometimes they were both black, when the one from the week before hadn't had time to go down again. It would be nice to go for a walk with Pali, although he doesn't enjoy walking, only in towns.

"And then there's Franz, another friend I haven't seen for ages; he wanted to be a priest and his wish was granted. A Catholic priest. He looks like a skiing instructor in his sweaters—they're not so dressy in Bavaria. We met him about five years ago through a make-up man called Lois who took us to his midnight Mass at Christmas and prodded us when it was time to kneel down or get up again—I don't remember whether we told you but Tonio was never baptized and I'm a Protestant. But to get back to Franz: At first the thought of celibacy made me embarrassed, as though I'd been let in on an awful secret crime. He told us once that he'd suggested a young chaplain for a position in the priesthood that had become vacant but the bishop of Munich turned him down, saying he wasn't intelligent enough. 'But he has great faith,' said Franz. 'Faith wears out, stupidity doesn't,' replied the devout gentleman. Be that as it may, Franz is another friend I haven't seen for a long time and I'd love to go for a walk with him, as I'm walking now with you. And I miss the evenings that sometimes lasted until dawn when we got to haggling about this and that. I miss people here. 'A man should neither be praised nor criticized,' Henry Miller says. I've been praised a great deal and criticized a great deal and sometimes I need to crawl off and hide away from people, making myself empty, forget both praise and criticism. But then I get cocky again, want to take part, itch to cross swords with the rabble. Ambition looms from the cupboard clanking its

bones and grinding its yellow molars, gets plump and fat
and blooms and starts to nag and niggle, tugs at my sleeve
until I shoo it away, slam the door, wait till it comes on its
knees. 'Man's driving force is envy,' some sociologist or
other once said. I prefer Heinrich Mann's: 'If I wish for
another's fortuitous luck, I must wish for his hemorrhoids
too.' In 1967 we spent a holiday in Italy and Chaplin was
staying at the same hotel. He stood on a jetty surrounded
by his children and specks of sunlight bounced up from the
sea across his face, which was unhappy and sour-looking
since he was telling of the bad reviews his latest film had
received. He seemed consumed by this one failure, after a
lifetime of unparalleled fame. For Henry Miller it came too
late, the fame and riches, or exactly at the right time, if you
will. The first time he stayed with us he was wearing a
sweater that had served as a refuge for many generations of
moths; it looked like a wide-meshed sieve, on top of which
he froze in it, so we took him to a shop in the hope of getting him into a new one. 'Seventy marks!' he exclaimed as
he examined the price tag. 'You're rich now,' I said. 'Seventy marks for a sweater is a crime, I lived on less than that
for months at a time in Paris,' he said, and went on freezing. Come on, let's go back to the house.''

We sat in the eternally gloomy living room and I said,
"Work has been good these last years. Soon after we saw
you in Starnberg, Tonio found a play and produced and
directed it with me in the lead and it was a triumph from
Hamburg to Vienna. Right afterwards I tried my hand at
writing song lyrics; we started producing records alone and
very soon they'd boomed to such an extent that we decided
to risk a concert tour, engaged musicians and booked halls
with up to five thousand seats, rehearsed for four weeks
and took the plunge. It worked and, apart from the strain
of holding an audience two hours alone with a band, it was
the most satisfying work I've ever done—yes, probably because it was our own and we were completely independent.
I was awarded golden records and named Best Singer of
the Year and so it went on with concerts and TV shows.
No films; the industry here went down the drain and we
had no time anyway, we still take a lot of time for ourselves, do nothing one thousand percent. 'Why don't you
milk the success?' our friends ask when we cut a tour short
after forty concerts. I shy away from 'milking' as a horse
shies from a mamba. And there's no need to give me that

frosty look, I know it sounds arrogant and it is too. A few years ago we would have done it, would have had to, if there'd been anything to milk."

As Christina came in Schniebel stood up and disappeared before I could say 'Auf Wiedersehen.'"

May 6, 1970

Two years ago today I said to Dr. Surén: "I have a request to make. When I'm lying in your clinic eight weeks from now, will you please introduce me to as many women as possible who'll tell me: 'Even the superintendent said that the birth of my boy was the most complicated he's ever experienced.' " Dr. Surén grinned and said, "I'll do my best."

Ten days later, on May 16, 1968, at 6:15 A.M., the two ambulance men put down my stretcher in the room next to the operating room. Dr. Surén was wearing an ankle-length smock and a surgeon's cap, two young doctors and three nurses stood beside him. "It's seven weeks too soon," I said, "must you operate?" "Yes," he answered.

6:25: I see light-green walls, rings of light from the lamp in the ceiling, a metal stand with cloths in front of my face; I try to catch the doctor's eye, the anesthetist's, feel the needle in my left arm, two flames leap up, thin with yellow points, like raised swords, a shrill tone ripples along them, dies out behind my eyes. "I can't breathe," I want to say.

7:20: Sharp pricking pains in the hands at first, needles with plastic tubes, tubes leading to glass bottles hanging from metal stands. My head is heavy, heavy head pulls heavy body from the table, glides to the radiator, merges with the radiator. Then it starts. Millimeter by millimeter. Starts in the soles of my feet, cuts nerve after nerve, cell after cell, cuts cautiously, instep, ankle, calf, knee-cap, cuts the fresh scar, cuts away the pain, moves to the bottom rib, cuts and snips at my back, cuts away, severs, methodically, assuredly. "I'm dying," I say, hear myself say, know that it's death. "You've got a beautiful healthy daughter," they cry. They're lying. They always lie when you're dying. "I'm dying," I say. No answer. It cuts; clear, cool, collected, millimeter by millimeter. Not painlessly, not swiftly, not insensibly. Exact, correct, to plan. An iron door slams shut, shuts out my head; voices in front of the iron door, behind it a void. Wide-awake clear head in a void. Head minus body behind an iron door, conscious of dying, of its twitching nose, feeling the lids fluttering, growing longer. It cuts, tooth after tooth, palate, tongue, Pedantic death, orderly death. Cell after cell.

Report: Uterine atony, blood uncoagulable, kidney collapse, circulatory failure.

7:20: Administered 1 gram of human fibrinogen. Without effect. Constant transfusions. Road repairs cause a breakdown of all telephones in the area. An intern stops a car on the main road, drives to the police station, the police take him to the Behring Chemical Works in Munich to fetch additional human fibrinogen.

Report: 15 percent hemoglobin.

8:15: Blood congeals after administration of 4 grams of human fibrinogen.

I see Tonio. A sunbeam sweeps his face. "She's very beautiful," he says. I believe him, want to believe him. Don't believe him. "Where is she?" "In another clinic, they had to take her to a special children's clinic. But she's healthy, and beautiful, believe me."

Midday: Report: Gastrointestinal atony, continuous-drop infusion, stomach tubes, Macumar treatment.

May 23, 1968, 5:10 A.M.: The scar bursts. 5:20: Anesthetic needle in the left arm. 3 P.M.: Report: Respiratory depression, Lorfan treatment, acute pain, reverse reaction to sedatives.

Opposite my bed there's a picture, a color photograph of a starlike flower with red leaves. I see worms crawl out of the star, fat brown ones, the star becomes a leer, its leaves a bloody mouth. The bloody mouth swells out over the frame, looking for me, hovering, bobbing toward me—die of laughing to die of fright die of happiness, lonely dying, different death, no one to tell, waiting death, ever-present, hovering waiting. Iron door behind the facade. Iron door despite the search, despite meditation, despite books and belief, despite Joan Grant and Bishop Pike, their walks on the other side, despite Gordon Turner, friend Gordon, clever capable wise Gordon, despite spiritualism and meditation the iron door. I had seen Gordon's face, head inclined, eyes closed. Clearly, as I had seen Manfred George sometimes, when he was in danger. Lesson in dying. Disorderly life, orderly death. To bleed to death's the best way, say those who are still alive. I'm sick to death of this life, say those who are still alive. Who'll prepare us for the crossing, crossing from where to where. Tired to death, they say. Awake to death, say I. We shall die but want to know nothing of dying.

At four A.M. the first pigeon coos, wakes the pigeon colony, they chuckle me to sleep.

One of the nurses comes and changes the bandages on my swollen arms. "I held your daughter in my hands right after the birth," she says, bending over me, "I cut the cord. It's a healthy child, believe me, she'll live, she'll pull through all right. I've been at it for thirty years and I know what I've got in my hands when it comes out of the belly. It's a healthy child and a good one, she's got a good character, we can tell when we hold them in our hands. When they first cry you can tell. You've no idea how often I'd like to say to the parents: This one's no good, it's got a bad character." She sits down on a stool, looks at her hands, massages the knuckles. "It was touch and go with you. You were on the brink for a whole hour, Surén shouted at you not to give up."

"I can't remember, I don't know."

"But we know, he brought you back, you got angry when he shouted, you were furious, and that saved you more than anything." She rubs her eyes, nudges the lids roughly with the backs of her hands like a half-awake child and continues, "We were operating right up till now—two youngsters drove slap into a car on their motorbike, dreadfull mess they were in, one ought to spank their bottoms." She holds her wrist watch under the table lamp and looks at it, gets up. "Three more babies to deliver tonight. There was a woman here in this room before you came, she had a healthy daughter. When we told the father it was a girl he turned around and went out and didn't come back for three days, he was offended, wanted a son and heir." She feels my pulse, tucks her wrist watch back into the pocket of her smock, says, "Try to sleep a little," and goes heavily to the door.

May 24, 1968, 10 P.M. Tonio and Dr. Surén are sitting by my bed. Surén says, "What in heaven's name could still go wrong?" He sips his whiskey, his face is gray.

"Shall I tell you a story?" says Tonio. "We have a doctor friend in Paris called Paul-Emile. He's Russian and has a long sad face. We've been friends for many years and fortunately we'd never had to call on him in a professional capacity until one morning Hilde woke up with a colicky gall bladder. I called Paul-Emile and he came over and said rather pedantically that even though we'd known each other for such a long time he'd have to know Hilde's whole case history before he could attempt a diagnosis or advise treatment. Since she's had, to my knowledge, typhus, yellow fever, infantile paralysis, meningitis, encephalitis, seven jaw operations, two tropical illnesses, peritonitis, a burst appendix, a dislocated spine, a broken shoulder, a torn cartilage, rheumatic fever, five cases of fish poisoning and two of blood poisoning, countless coli infestations, all the children's illnesses including measles which she had twice, fourteen known and umpteen unknown allergies, a broken nose with two subsequent operations, inflammation of the kidneys, dysentery, tonsillectomy, squashed fingernails, cysts and nodules on her vocal cords, I told Paul-Emile that I'd have lunch downstairs and then go to a western that was running on the Champs-Elysees and would expect to find him still there when I got back. He told me not to joke about serious matters like illness so off I went. After the film I bought the English Sunday newspapers and went back to the hotel. Hilde was looking a lot better already and was just getting around to nineteen-fifty nine. Paul-Emile was sitting quite still with his head in his hands. I went into our little salon and read the *Sunday Times* and the *Observer* and sometime later I heard Hilde say, 'And that's about it, I think.' Paul-Emile raised his long ashen face, looked at me and said, 'All these years I have thought Hilde to be the perfect example of the big, healthy, German cow and now I find out she's a museum of horrors.'"

"I keep getting cramps in my calves," I say over the hissing of the oxygen and the menthol spray. Dr. Surén stares at me, gets up and leaves the room without a word. Two nurses come in swiftly, softly, resolutely, pull back the covers. "What's up now?" asks Tonio. "Could be thrombosis," the younger one whispers. Dr. Surén comes back again followed by Dr. Sebald and Dr. Sendtner carrying infusion bottles; they prepare injections, stab them into my thighs, the laboratory technician comes and pricks my finger, smears blood onto small plates of glass. Dr. Surén looks down at me like a peeved father whose son won't stop wetting the bed. I have to laugh, the nurse plants her hands on my belly and whispers, "You mustn't laugh, whatever you do you mustn't laugh."

Christina was five weeks old when I saw her for the first time. I saw her through the glass panes of the premature-birth department and the incubator. "It'll be hard for you, not being able to pick her up," they had said. No, it's not true, nothing is hard. As long as she breathes, as long as you breathe, as long as I breathe. Until the red light on the incubator goes out and I think there's a power cut, knock on the window, the nurse's lips form, "It's all right," until Christina cries, until the doctor says, "It'll take a little time" until Tonio says, "We have to go."

St. Moritz,
May, 16, 1970

The battery-driven funicular railway was the favorite, a whole birthday long; left the magnetic fishing rods, paint-box, big rubber ball and colored plasticine no chance at all, even though the cardboard figures kept falling over and the car slipped from the cable strung up between the chair and the wall lamp and fell to the floor, even though it squeaks and rattles and starts off with a screech and Christina puts her hands to her ears. The steam hammer down by the bridge doesn't disturb her, no more than the whistling jets, or the helicopters. It belongs to her loud life as much as the churning of the dishwasher, chug-chug of the washing machine, rattle of the dryer, is as common as stereo, rock music, airports, elevators, cars. Her noises—mine were the railway, the carpet beaters, bicycle bells, and lathes. The south side of the Bernhardstrasse, or what was left of it, has been turned into a freeway—a freeway instead of "Throw us down a penny," and "Come on up, dinner's ready."

Christina's first disappointment is Evie. Evie, three years old, lives on the Chantarellastrasse; they played together once or twice but Evie has other friends, older ones.

Christina stamps up the hill excitedly, loses her balance, falls down, pulls herself up again, calls out "Evie," and waits. Evie doesn't come out.

Evie, like Sigrid. She had long thin pigtails and a poetry album, all the bigger children were allowed to write in it. Copperplate, buttercups and daisies, blobs of ink, "God bless mummy and daddy"; I was only allowed to look.

Christina doesn't call out any more, not for two days now, When we pass Evie's house she stops and turns around, as she did when Nehru, our Alsatian, ran after a deer. "Bad Nehru," she said and looked after him astonished; then shrugged and walked on.

She learns fast.